E-Journals:
A How-To-Do-It Manual
for Building, Managing,
and Supporting Electronic
Journal Collections

Donnelyn Curtis

With contributions by
Virginia M. Scheschy

facet publishing

 Be sure to visit *www.library.unr.edu/subjects/guides/ ejournals.html*. The companion website to this book offers resources to save you the time and trouble of typing in long URLs. It will also keep these resources updated.

© 2005, Neal-Schuman Publishers, Inc.

Published by
Facet Publishing
7 Ridgmount Street
London WC1E 7AE

Facet Publishing is wholly owned by CILIP: the Chartered Institute of Library and Information Professionals.

First published in the USA by Neal-Schuman Publishers, Inc., 2005.
This UK edition 2005.

British Library Cataloguing in Publication Data
A catalogue record for this book is available from the British Library

ISBN 1-85604-541-2

Printed and bound in the United States of America.

CONTENTS

LIST OF FIGURES

PREFACE

E-Journals: A How-To-Do-It Manual for Building, Managing, and Supporting Electronic Journal Collections is designed to provide a single, high-quality, reliable, and up-to-date source about electronic journal collections for librarians to consult. Within this manual, you will find sound advice and manageable methods for libraries just getting started; tips and shortcuts for institutions struggling to keep their e-journal workload under control; and advanced techniques for those libraries that are ready to give sophisticated users the best possible integrated access to their literature.

The Web has grown from a vast, disorganized, shallow, and intriguing phenomenon to an even vaster, still disorganized, but deeper and richer source of content, turning everyone into an information searcher and shaping their expectations for instant gratification. The libraries that are not willing to provide organized and simplified access to quality Web-based resources risk the loss of their users, their institutional support, and their meaning and relevance in the current and future information and knowledge environment.

NEW PERSPECTIVES

My own work with electronic journals at the University of Nevada, Reno (UNR), was not included in my official job description. However, during my first three-and-a-half years at UNR, perceiving a need and an opportunity, I played a major role in developing and providing access to a large e-journal collection. This job quickly pushed almost everything else onto the back burner. Happily for me, others have now assumed those responsibilities and are doing more than I was able to do, with much better results, and I have turned most of my attention to other challenges.

Stepping away from the day-to-day processing of e-journals has given me a more global perspective and the time to examine public services issues in providing access to them. At conferences I have heard the complex conversation surrounding this subject.

From librarians:

- "My library director doesn't think electronic journals are worth the effort and the cost, so we don't have any yet. Can someone give me a list of the advantages?"
- "Publisher mergers are not friendly to libraries. Journal costs always go up after a merger."
- "We see ourselves as partners with our vendors." Or, the converse "We are not partners with our vendors. We are their customers."
- "The reference librarians don't understand how hard it is to do some of the things they are asking us to do."

From vendors and publishers:

- "Users are hooked on the desktop delivery of content and they want more than most libraries can afford."
- "As for mergers, whether libraries approve or not, we can only buy a company that is for sale."
- "Librarians should use more business sense and do their homework."
- "Sometimes we develop a feature librarians ask for, and it's expensive, and then nobody uses it."

CHANGES IN THE ENVIRONMENT

The universe of electronic journals has changed dramatically since 1999–2000, when I last wrote about the subject. When I began writing this book, I conceived of it as a second edition of that 2000 publication, *Developing and Managing Electronic Journal Collections: A How-To-Do-It Manual for Librarians.* However, since the whole landscape has changed, by default, almost all of the content changed, too. So for this book I've chosen a different, simpler title: *E-Journals.*

The surrounding information environment has also changed a great deal.

- Information overload is even more extreme. There are more than 700 billion pages on the Internet, and scholarly output continues to increase dramatically.
- Access to the Internet has increased with the spread of broadband options, the development of wireless technology, and robust handheld devices.
- More information objects are "born digital." Standards for the presentation of online information are more developed.

Within the education and scholarly publishing environment we have seen other new developments:

- Courseware and the concept of "learning objects"
- More international activity
- New and better technology for the digitization of journal backfiles
- More coordination in the developments of alternative publishing initiatives
- Metadata enhancements—particularly XML and the OpenURL
- Growing international movement to ensure "full and open access to data created with public funding"
- New legal issues—Tasini, Digital Rights Management, etc.
- Embargoes and exclusives in databases
- Inconsistent government policies (e.g., the development and elimination of PubScience)
- Broad-based support for Open Access models

We have also seen some major developments in the library environment:

- Less trust of serials subscription agents after the demise of divine/Faxon
- More outsourcing options with the development of niche services such as Serials Solutions and TDNet, among others
- More complex e-journal management systems developed by both libraries and vendors; back-end systems with user interfaces replacing ILS functions
- E-journal management modules under development by ILS vendors
- New cataloging standards; aggregator-neutral records and major changes in *AACR2*
- "Knowledge management" as a concept

Libraries tend to approach electronic journals the way they have approached other new formats and technological advancements—absorbing them into the current organization, staff functions, and work flow. If a library begins gradually, adding a few at a time, that might work, but in most cases, these journals come in like a tsunami. *E-Journals: A How-To-Do-It Manual for Building, Managing, and Supporting Electronic Journal Collections* is designed to help prepare for the unexpected, or if the tsunami has already hit, to put things back in order, which will likely require developing a new order.

ORGANIZATION OF THE BOOK

Some of the chapters can stand alone as practical guides for specialized library staff involved in a single aspect of acquiring and providing access to electronic journals. However, the first two chapters are recommended reading for everyone. These chapters set the stage, presenting a larger context for understanding the characteristics of e-journals and their users, introducing all the players and their roles in the writer-to-reader process.

Chapters 3 through 9 are incrementally process oriented, from "Shifting Library Resources" (Chapter 3) through "Analyzing Electronic Journal Usage and Evaluating Services" (Chapter 9). In between are chapters on developing the collection (4); licensing and authentication processes (5); ordering and receiving (6); providing and maintaining access (7); and supporting users and promoting the use of e-journals (8). Detailed technical information is presented in the appendices.

Each chapter concludes with a list of references that will provide more information about the topics covered in the chapter. Sprinkled within the pages are URLs for Web sites that will keep your library up-to-date. A companion Web site with links to all the Web sites mentioned in the book is available to readers at www.library.unr.edu/subjects/guides/ejournals.html.

Electronic journals provide significant and ongoing challenges for some of the best minds in publishing and libraries. In successfully meeting the needs of readers, we are all required to be creative, innovative, and fast on our feet. With *E-Journals* I have done my best to provide the tools and advice that will enable libraries to advance gracefully through these turbulent times.

ACKNOWLEDGMENTS

Writing a book when you have a full-time job and a family takes time and energy from those other parts of your life. This book required a long-term reallocation, and my family and co-workers have been extraordinarily accommodating and understanding. I suspect that some of them were not sure I would ever finish it, and there were times I wasn't sure myself. It would not have been possible to complete it without the encouragement of many friends, family members, and co-workers, who stepped in to take care of some of my other responsibilities. My husband and sons have patiently accepted my year-long lack of involvement in household duties and my absence from many family activities. My colleagues at the UNR Libraries have picked up the slack on several occasions when I was unable to put my customary effort into group projects.

My workplace colleagues in the DeLaMare Library—Philip Preston, Susan Handau, and Linda Newman—have demonstrated incredible tolerance and independence during my times of trial. During the last few months, we shared a devastating experience when we lost Juanita Bouldin, a member of our branch family, to death at a young age. It could have been a more serious setback for the book without my colleagues' strength and generosity. Kathryn Etcheverria, my co-director for an NEH-funded Basque Database project, has also willingly shouldered some of the extra burdens that resulted from my overextension in writing this book.

I would like to thank several individuals for their direct contributions: Virginia Scheschy, one of my co-authors for an earlier book on electronic journals, graciously allowed me to incorporate the parts of her chapters on licensing and acquisition that are still current. Lou Amestoy and Araby Greene answered many questions and enhanced my knowledge of e-journal cataloging and the generation of Web pages. Paoshan Yue read some of the chapters and offered excellent suggestions, and also explained complex processes. Paoshan has been an inspiration to me in her role as a dedicated and innovative electronic resources access librarian, and her ideas (and illustrations of her work) are scattered throughout the book.

This book is enriched by the accomplishments of many talented problem solvers in our profession. E-journals are managed in libraries throughout the world by very bright people, who not only create sophisticated, elegant local systems, but also share their methods and the results of their work through publications, presentations, and Web sites. Informal and formal groups have been effective in implementing standards, developing tools and applications, and changing fundamentally the way library research is conducted—within a short time frame. In the spirit of their collaboration, this book encompasses the fruits of many efforts.

I am grateful for the support and patience of my editor at Neal-Schuman, Michael Kelley. His gentle nudges kept me on track, and his repeated willingness to adjust our time frame for the completion of the manuscript has been much appreciated. Finally, I would like to acknowledge my most excellent copyeditor, Eileen Fitzsimons of Chicago, who maintained her tact, good humor, and attention to detail throughout a laborious process, while adhering to a tight deadline, assuming more than her normal share of the task of correcting omissions and bad URLs. The fact that everyone I have worked with on this book is devoted to quality has made my perseverance possible.

1 UNDERSTANDING ELECTRONIC JOURNALS

CHAPTER OVERVIEW

- The Scope and Variations of Electronic Journals
- The (R)evolution of Electronic Journals
- Features and Characteristics of Electronic Journals
- Benefits and Drawbacks of Electronic Journals
- The Scholarly Publication and Access Chain
- Economics and Politics of Electronic Publishing

Chapter 1 provides a framework for understanding the development and characteristics of electronic journals as elements within a total electronic information complex, and not merely as print journals that have moved to the Web. Understanding the issues surrounding the development of e-journals will better enable you to serve your users and plan for the future of your library's electronic journal collection.

E-journals are in the eye of the particular storm that has hit scholarly communication with the growth of the Internet. There are several things going on at the same time as the transition from one format to another. The Web opens up all kinds of possibilities for fundamental changes in the ways that information and research results are shared, and momentum is building for the development of alternatives to traditional journals. At the risk of oversimplification, librarians find themselves operating in parallel universes (with varying degrees of success) in responding to their patrons' current demands while at the same time they position themselves and their libraries for a very different kind of future and, in some cases, acting as change agents to hasten the arrival of that future.

To understand electronic journals means not only to know their features and characteristics, but also the economic and political environment in which they reside and all the participants in the scholarly information chain from author to reader.

THE SCOPE AND VARIATIONS OF ELECTRONIC JOURNALS

In this book, the terms "e-journals" and "electronic journals" are used interchangeably to designate what may also be called

- "online journals,"
- "electronic serials" or "e-serials,"
- "electronic periodicals,"
- "zines" or "e-zines" or "Webzines."

There may be subtle distinctions among some of these other terms, but for the purposes of this book those distinctions are minimized in the spirit of inclusiveness. The focus here is primarily on the management of scholarly electronic journals, but most of what is discussed will apply to all types. In the simplest terms, an electronic journal

- meets the bibliographic definition of a serial;
- is accessible through a computer; and
- has the features of a journal, magazine, or newsletter.

Practically speaking, it is not always easy to determine whether a prospective electronic journal is a serial. What is listed as an electronic journal by one library might be considered a Web site by another library. A Web publication that is called an electronic journal by its creators may not meet anyone else's definition. The Web provides self-publication opportunities for those who may not realize or care that a "journal" should meet certain recognized criteria. Some so-called "electronic journals" illustrate the democratic principle that anyone can be a publisher on the Web.

For the most part, electronic journals will be available through the Internet—usually, but not necessarily, through the Web. This book is concerned with "remote access" electronic journals and not "direct access" electronic journals that are disseminated on physical media such as CDs or DVDs. Online newspapers are a somewhat different beast and in this book they will not be considered electronic journals.

Depending on your library and your purposes and users, you may use a more restrictive definition for electronic journals. Libraries provide electronic access to articles from journals in a variety of ways, some of which stretch or diminish the concept of "journal," and this book explores every access angle. However,

Criteria for Assigning an ISSN

"The criteria for determining if a serial qualifies for an ISSN applies equally to electronic and print publications: an intention to continue publishing indefinitely and being issued in designated parts. In the case of electronic serials—especially those available online, such as on the Internet—the most significant criterion is that the publication is divided into parts or issues which carry unique, numerical designations by which the individual issues may be identified, checked in, etc. Electronic serials that are issued as individual articles also meet this criterion as long as the articles carry a unique designation. Thus, a database issued quarterly on CD-ROM and carrying quarterly date designations would be eligible for an ISSN while the same database as an online service which was being continually and seamlessly updated would not be eligible."

National Serials Data Program, Library of Congress International Standard Serial Number (ISSN)

it is important to maintain a distinction between "electronic journals" and "articles from electronic journals" when it makes a difference to users.

An electronic journal might be available only in electronic format, or it may be an electronic replica of a journal that is available in print. It might have the same title, publisher, editor, and ISSN as a print journal but have some different features from the print journal. It might have less content or more content or the same content in another format.

ISSN STAMP OF APPROVAL

You can generally assume that the successful application for an International Standard Serial Number (ISSN) will guarantee that an electronic journal meets the standards for classification as a serial. But many publishers of electronic-only journals that otherwise fall within the definition of a serial do not apply for ISSNs, so you cannot assume the converse and dismiss a publication because it does not have an ISSN.

According to current rules, an electronic version of a print journal should have a separate ISSN, no matter how identical the content may appear to be. The possession of an e-ISSN assures us that the electronic version meets the definition of a serial according to the agency that assigns the numbers. However, publishers of print journals often do not obtain a unique ISSN for the electronic version and frequently use the same ISSN for both. For more information about the assignment of the ISSN, visit the Web site for the International ISSN Centre at www.issn.org. Separate e-ISSNs have caused at least as many problems as they have solved, so in the future, we may see a change in that practice. Librarians working with electronic journals must often decide for themselves whether an online publication with the same title and ISSN as a print journal is either substantially equivalent to the print version or would meet the definition of a serial on its own.

INCOMPLETE OR DIVERGENT CONTENT

A digitized facsimile of a recognized print journal will be easy to define as an electronic journal. It is more difficult to characterize those that are similar but not identical to a print journal. Libraries have different standards for what is presented to users as full text, standards that can (and do) change as libraries expand or refine their electronic journal offerings.

What some publishers call an electronic journal is often just a promotional Web page with excerpts from or information about a print journal with the same title. These publishers may not have plans to offer the full content of their publications via the Web; rather, they are using the Web exposure to attract subscribers for their print product. Some publishers will offer most of a journal's articles online at no cost to readers, reserving for print only enough feature articles to maintain or expand their print subscriber base. Others will consider their "electronic journal" a supplement or enhancement to the print journal that is intended for their print subscribers.

Incomplete full-text contents or even sample articles or sample issues may include sufficient content to warrant library-provided access to what is not technically an electronic journal. Your library may choose to offer access to incomplete e-journals, but you should let your users know that they are not electronic journals per se. To be too encompassing in your definition will devalue the journals with full electronic content.

AGGREGATION AND DISAGGREGATION

The definition of an electronic journal is further complicated by some of the access options provided by the Web.

Journals in Full-Text Databases

Most of the bibliographic/full-text aggregator databases with which you are familiar—EBSCOhost, FirstSearch, InfoTrac, ProQuest, Lexis-Nexis, and WilsonSelect databases, among others—at first were not designed to deliver intact journals. Their original (and, in most cases, enduring) purpose was to deliver citations and articles in response to a search query, usually to undergraduate students or public library patrons, and they were built and maintained accordingly. For the first few years that they presented full text, they seldom included all the articles from every issue of a journal; and, even when they did, there was rarely cover-to-cover treatment. And some of them lacked some or all of the graphs, charts, and photographs seen in facsimile (often scanned) electronic journals.

As a consequence of new experiences with electronic journals, end users and librarians have demanded, and in most cases have received, more comprehensiveness in full-text aggregator databases:

- More complete coverage, including book reviews and editorials
- Image representation
- Ability to link from a library's online catalog or Web pages to the tables of contents of journals within the database

- Ability to link from bibliographic citations in the databases to the full text of articles outside the database, licensed from other sources
- Ability to link directly to full-text articles in the database from other bibliographic databases

The advent of electronic journals has affected full-text databases in other ways. Now that they have more alternatives for providing access to their journals, including their own Web sites, a few publishers no longer wish to have their articles delivered through an aggregator's database. And some other publishers have instituted an embargo on recent issues in order to prevent the erosion of their library subscriber base (for their print or their own online subscriptions). Librarians accustomed to licensing or purchasing aggregations of articles and abstracts with a search engine expect the content to change as the database vendors' contracts with publishers change—but in times of tight budgets, some libraries have begun to cancel their print subscriptions for journals within aggregator databases, as publishers have long feared they would.

Most of the database vendors have responded to the marketplace in such a way that their aggregations are now considered bona fide electronic journals and you can list them alongside the individual titles to which you subscribe. But be prudent about labeling the contents of certain databases as electronic journals. Unless a database allows the type of searching that will result in a list of results that can be compared to a journal's table of contents, there is no way to be sure that the "full text" for a journal is complete. And there is no guarantee whatsoever for stable access to individual titles in an aggregator database.

Digested E-Journal Content

As some databases have evolved into e-journal delivery systems with sophisticated article-handling enhancements that appeal to librarians and scholars, others remain truer to their original purpose. Several old and new databases provide an easy method for students to find and use reputable journal content, integrated in such a way that retrieval of suitable articles for high school or undergraduate research papers is painless. A new twist on an old practice is for vendors such as Questia to market their term-paper-oriented products directly to students ("75% of subscribers got a better grade due to Questia"). Because of their selectivity, these digests should not be considered collections of electronic journals.

Virtual Journals

In several scientific subdisciplines there are now "multi-journal compilations" of articles from several journals in the field. To the casual browser, the "virtual journal"(VJ) may appear to be an "actual journal." The Web page for *Virtual Journal of Biological Physics Research* (www.vjbio.org/) states:

> This semi-monthly virtual journal contains articles that have appeared in one of the participating source journals [54 journals from 15 cooperating publishers] and that fall within a number of contemporary topical areas [13 are listed] in biological physics research. The articles are primarily those that have been published in the previous month; however, at the discretion of the editors older articles may also appear, particularly review articles. Links to other useful Web resources on biological physics are also provided.

Four other virtual journals are made up of pertinent articles from the same 54 journals:

- *Virtual Journal of Applications of Superconductivity* (www.vjsuper.org/)
- *Virtual Journal of Nanoscale Science & Technology* (www.vjnano.org/)
- *Virtual Journal of Quantum Information* (www.vjquantuminfo. org/)
- *Virtual Journal of Ultrafast Science* (www.vjultrafast.org)

Examples of other virtual journals are

- *Virtual Journal of Geobiology* (earth.elsevier.com/geobiology), relevant articles from 21 Elsevier journals
- *Virtual Journal of Cardiovascular Surgery* (ahavj.ahajournals.org/), five journals published by the American Heart Association

These megajournals should not be considered electronic journals. They do not have an ISSN, and they are more like databases or alerting services. Users can sign up to receive free "contents alerts" in the form of the tables of contents of upcoming VJ issues

Abstracting Journals Online

Closely related to virtual journals, abstracting, or "synoptic," journals, with summaries of articles rather than the articles themselves, can be considered either access tools or actual journals, depending on how they are presented. Elsevier's *Fuel and Energy Ab-*

stracts, first published in 1960, is a typical example of a well-established print abstracting publication that is now available online. A library may include it on a list of online journals, or on a list of indexes, along with similar abstracting journals such as *Communication Abstracts.* Most online synoptic journals that originated as print publications look more like indexes than bibliographic databases, designed more for browsing than for searching.

The Massachusetts Medical Society, publisher of the *New England Journal of Medicine,* has sponsored 11 separate *Journal Watch* "newsletters" (www.jwatch.org) since 1987, each of which "keeps clinicians up to date on the most important research" in their areas and are now available both in print and online. Clinicians may request e-mail delivery of *Journal Watch* contents. Some of the features of the online version of *Journal Watch* take advantage of the potential of the Web, with various subscription options, a prominent search engine, and the ability to customize the service.

Current Cites (http://sunsite.berkeley.edu/CurrentCites/), online since 1990, is an example of a "born digital" abstracting journal that calls itself an electronic journal and has an ISSN. All of these abstracting journals are dependent on other journals for their existence, playing a valuable role in combating "information overload."

E-Prints

Some research communities have shown that they no longer need the structure of the traditional journal in order to share and validate their research results and theories. The high-energy physics community is the best known example of a group that developed an alternative medium. Their e-print (electronic preprint) server ArXiv (developed at Los Alamos National Laboratory, now at Cornell) has been legitimized as the means of "first publication" in the discipline, and research results are made available much sooner than they would be in journals. The success of the physics experiment has spawned other such efforts by scientists. Recently there has been more coordination of efforts to build a new scholarly communication model. E-print initiatives and other alternatives to the traditional journal model fall clearly outside the parameters of electronic journals.

NEW SERIAL FORMS AND EXPERIMENTS

The Internet has changed the nature of scholarly communication. Listservs, e-mail, and Web pages have significantly improved the opportunities for scholars to share their data, information, opinions, and research. The Internet has also helped relax the formality that has long characterized academic discourse.

Somewhere between the formality of published, refereed journals and the informality of listserv discussions, new varieties of electronic-only journals have found a niche. Some are posted on Web pages; others are e-mailed to subscribers. Some of them are simply edited compilations of listserv postings or e-mail messages sent to the editor, which are then redistributed by e-mail or posted on the Web at regular or irregular intervals. Whether these meet the official definition of an electronic journal will depend on how they are edited and distributed. But whether they meet a library's criteria for inclusion on a subject list or in the online catalog will depend on the library's self-defined criteria.

FINALLY—OFFICIAL BIBLIOGRAPHIC CATEGORIES

Official definitions for materials provided by libraries are included in the guidelines, rules, and standards of the profession. In times of rapid change, the old rules don't always apply, so some of them get bent and some get revised. Those who work with serials generally pay serious attention to the interrelated *AACR2*, CONSER, and *LCRI* standards and definitions.

AACR2 Revised

Even before the advent of the Internet, some materials in libraries didn't fit neatly into standard bibliographic categories. But with the rise of Web-based resources, it became quite apparent that the cataloging rulebook, *Anglo-American Cataloging Rules* (*AACR2*), needed serious revision if it was going continue to provide any benefit to libraries. In late 2002, Chapter 12 was updated to reflect new categories, including the main categories of "finite resources" and "continuing resources" with the subcategories "serials" (including "electronic journals") and "continuing integrating resources" (including "continually updated Web pages"). A serial must have "discrete parts" that most people would call issues, preferably numbered. See the comparison chart in Figure 1–1, and for more information on the new *AACR2* categories see http://lcweb.loc.gov/catdir/cpso/aacr2002.html.

CONSER Guidelines

The Cooperative Online Serials cataloging program (CONSER) 2004 *Manual* defines a "remote access electronic serial" as follows:

FIGURE 1–1. December 2002 Revision of *AACR2*	
AACR2, *pre-Dec. 1, 2002*	**AACR2** *categories implemented Dec. 1, 2002*

Publications
I. Monographs
 	
II. Serials (A publication in any medium issued in successive parts bearing numerical or chronological designations and intended to be continued indefinitely.)
	Bibliographic resources (may be tangible or intangible)
	I. Finite resources (issued once or over time with a predetermined conclusion)
	  A. Finite integrating resources
	  B. Monographs (A bibliographic resource that is complete in one part or intended to be completed in a finite number of parts.)
	
	II. **Continuing Resources** (issued over time with no predetermined conclusion)
	  A. Continuing integrating resources
	  B. **Serials** (A continuing resource issued in a succession of discrete parts, usually bearing numbering, that has no predetermined conclusion. Examples of serials include journals, magazines, **electronic journals**, continuing directories, annual reports, newspapers, and monographic series.)*
	
	*• *Discrete* is further clarified to mean "separate parts/issues/articles"
	• *usually* refers to "unnumbered series or first issue not designated"
	• *no predetermined conclusion* means "no obvious finite ness."
	
	Hawkins and Hirons, 2002

A remote access electronic serial is a continuing resource that is accessed "via computer networks." It is issued in a succession of discrete parts usually bearing numbering, and has no predetermined conclusion *(AACR2).* This is in contrast to a direct access electronic resource which is issued on a physical carrier, for example CD-ROMs or floppy disks (CONSER, 2004, p. 11).

Further Clarification from LCRI 1.0

The *Library of Congress Rule Interpretations* (*LCRI*) further clarify when to consider something a remote access serial: "The resource might contain a listing of back volumes, back issues, images of journal covers for sequential issues; only current issue may be available as a separate issue" (*LCRI* 1.0).

THE (R)EVOLUTION OF ELECTRONIC JOURNALS

While the Web is generally celebrated for enabling the free flow of information, the current, expensive scholarly information system still relies on intermediaries—publishers and libraries. The interaction of these two groups has defined many of the developments of electronic journals.

PRE-WEB FORMATS

The first electronic journals, developed in the 1980s, were e-mailed to subscribers or made available through FTP in strictly plain-text format. The community of Internet users was small, and these early specialized journals did not have many readers. As the serials crisis worsened in the early 1990s, anticipation grew for the potential of the Internet to transform the scholarly communication system.

Gopher technology, soon supplanted by the World Wide Web, inspired the imaginations of librarians and scholars who envisioned a place for grass-roots publishing without commercial intermediaries. Some of the early experiments in Gopher-based and Web-based publication were promising and exciting. But the new journals had little impact on scholarship. Not enough users were connected, and for those who were, the Web browsers and modems and desktop computers of the time had many limitations.

Authors were reluctant to publish their papers via a medium that had not yet built up a reputation and had few readers, and readers were reluctant to spend their time with a medium that lacked content. It was painfully clear that an article published in a new electronic journal did not have sufficient standing with promotion and tenure committees. Although technology developed and the Web became popular, the status of electronic-only journals did not improve for several years.

In the meantime, the larger publishers were positioning themselves for taking a chance on electronic dissemination. Elsevier experimented with various graphical formats from 1991 to 1995, working with libraries on various delivery systems in well-publicized experiments, Project TULIP and Project PEAK, which tested both library technology and pricing models for electronically delivered articles.

E-JOURNALS ON THE WEB

The advent of the Web, along with the development of scanning technology and Adobe's portable document format (PDF) protocol, allowed the publishers with some capital to begin offering an electronic version of their journals to libraries. Established journals first began to appear as electronic products on the Web in 1995, with Project Muse from the Johns Hopkins University Press and some journals offered by OCLC's Electronic Collections Online (ECO), then called Electronic Journals Online. JSTOR journals also became publicly available that year. JSTOR (now the actual name) was established in 1993 with a grant from the Andrew W. Mellon Foundation to digitize back issues of core journals in several disciplines. The idea was to allow savings in space (and in capital costs associated with that space) while simultaneously improving access to the content of important journals without affecting current subscriptions.

Most of the major publishers were at least beginning to develop their Web-based publishing strategies in the mid-1990s. All efforts were considered experimental until there were suddenly enough publishers with enough journals available through the Web that some libraries felt they could offer a critical mass to attract the interest of their users.

By 1997, electronic journals from most major publishers were available, and universities had the infrastructure to support them. Pricing structures beneficial to both publishers and libraries were being developed. Publishers that did not have the capability (or an interest in developing the capability) to provide online access to their journals partnered or contracted with intermediaries such as HighWire Press and Ingenta, early players in the journal-hosting arena.

To help satisfy the early need for a critical mass of journals, Academic Press (at the time an independent publisher, now an Elsevier imprint) provided a marketing model that other publishers have since adopted: the consortial package plan. As participants in consortia that acquired electronic access to collectively held subscriptions, many libraries had their first taste of electronic access to journals not previously affordable in print.

Some publishers and aggregators were surprised by the persistent reluctance of the library marketplace to adopt electronic journals. Doubts about stability, concerns over workload issues and high costs, and infrastructure deficiencies held many libraries back.

In the present and near future, publishers, librarians, and users will continue to work primarily with electronic journals that look and act like print journals, with some minor differences, and will continue to face major challenges in providing access to them. As electronic journals mature, they offer new kinds of opportunities and challenges.

Publishers began to realize that they had to provide incentives for early adopters to hasten the major shift to online access. The costs to access journals through platforms such as ECO were adjusted downward more than once. Some publishers offered free access to their packages via long trial periods to libraries, and some important individual journals were made available without charge. Three-year licenses for the "Big Deal" option, in which publishers provided access to all their journals, provided attractive price caps and other inducements for libraries to make a commitment to what was still somewhat of an experiment. New access to hundreds of formerly unaffordable journals attracted many medium-sized and smaller libraries.

Since 1997 libraries have been developing strategies, individually and collectively, to acquire and manage electronic journals during the transitional time in which most librarians believe it is still necessary to maintain subscriptions for the print versions. Publishers as well as libraries are becoming more anxious to move into an electronic-only environment, and some of them have begun to offer pricing options that tempt libraries to let go of print subscriptions in favor of online-only access, even if some of their users may not be quite comfortable with that scenario.

In the present and near future, librarians will continue to work primarily with electronic journals that look and act like print journals, with some minor differences, and will continue to face major challenges in providing access to them. As electronic journals mature, they offer new kinds of opportunities and challenges. There have also been some recent major developments that affect libraries:

- The most significant recent breakthrough has been the new development of protocols for interoperability.
- Other noteworthy developments include the digitization of major publishers' backfiles and advances in the integration of rich, nontext supplemental materials.
- Mergers of large commercial publishers and the lack of relief from rising journal costs have spurred library and academic organizations to provide significant support for alternative scholarly communication models.
- At the same time, commercial publishers now make some of their older content (and in a few cases, their most recent issue) freely available to all readers.
- Established publishers are beginning to experiment with "open access" alternatives to the subscription model as new, online-only open-access publishers have demonstrated instant success.

HOW MANY ELECTRONIC JOURNALS?

Nobody really knows how many electronic journals there are. *Ulrich's Periodicals Directory* reports almost 30,000 online serials. Of the 250,000 active serial listings in *Ulrich's*, fewer than 15,000 are scholarly and refereed. Of those, 80%, or approximately 12,000, are estimated to be available in some kind of electronic form from one or more sources (Boyce, King, Montgomery, and Tenopir, 2004), and the number of titles is increasing rapidly. With some of the constraints removed from publishing and with the ever-accelerating activity of research; the growing number of researchers, disciplines, and subdisciplines; and an increasing amount of interdisciplinary activity, new journals are born every day.

A survey of 149 publishers identified 782 new journals launched in the five years prior to 2003. A new journal has about a 50% chance of making it past the first year. The same survey found that 83% of science, technology, and medicine (STM) titles and 72% of humanities and social sciences titles were available online (Cox and Cox, 2003).

From 1997 to March 2003, the listings of unique electronic journals in EBSCO's title file increased from 1,500 to 11,000 (Henderson, 2003). It is especially difficult to estimate the number of nonscholarly electronic journals. In October 2003, the EBSCOhost Business Source Premier database had 1,044 full-text, refereed journals and 2,538 nonrefereed, full-text journals. A conservative estimate is that there are thousands of popular, trade, and professional journals and newsletters are available on the Web through publisher sites and in full-text databases in addition to the 12,000 or so scholarly e-journals.

FEATURES AND CHARACTERISTICS OF ELECTRONIC JOURNALS

Electronic journals are still in a shakedown period. Each new medium begins by imitating its predecessor, so despite the dramatic differences between the printing press and the Web, the typical electronic journal of the present still looks very much like a print journal transported to a computer screen. The familiar journal-like appearance of most of today's e-journals may represent an essential stage in legitimizing a new medium. However, some publishers, both established and emerging, are beginning to take advantage of options made possible by the Web. Sophisticated features become commonplace as readers are courted with technological bells and whistles by some publishers who never give up on the concept of providing researchers with a home base revolving around their own journals:

> **Brilliant Research Tool** – In addition to the articles themselves, *Blackwell Synergy* offers a range of features designed to improve the quality of research time. These include search functionality helping readers to find relevant articles more quickly, and linking functionality helping readers to make connections between related literatures more easily (Blackwell Synergy, n.d.).

A good idea, as long as "literatures" include journals from other publishers. Publishers sometimes will enhance their services with links to other publishers' articles, but their systems are often designed to feature and increase the use of their own journals. Studies show that users generally do not restrict their interest to the journals of one publisher, so it is up to libraries to integrate e-journal content from many sources and *really* save the time of their users.

ACCESS ISSUES

The thorniest situation the Web has created for both libraries and publishers (on behalf of authors, shareholders, and readers) is the process of restricting the use of e-journals to those who are authorized to use them through license agreements and payment. The Web liberates users from the confines of time and space, and 24/7 remote access is one of the strongest selling points for electronic journals, but there is still a need for the invention and universal adoption of a method to validate users that

- is simple for users to implement,
- does not impede access in any way,
- requires little maintenance by the library or the content provider,
- protects the intellectual assets of the content owner,
- does not breach the security of the content provider, and
- does not violate the privacy of users.

The situation gets worse rather than better as publishers and libraries explore the use of new technologies that promise the seamless integration of journal content from any source. Surfing scholarly literature is still far from simple for most users who have access to some, but not all, electronic journals, since each library provides its users with its own unique mixture of licensed resources. Chapter 5 deals with authentication options and Chapters 7 and 8 suggest ways to optimize users' access to the library's licensed content.

Optimistic librarians believe that the Web will enable the adoption of alternative scholarly communication systems in which all information is freely available and authentication is no longer an issue; recent open access developments have strengthened those hopes. But currently, authorizing access is an enormous issue.

WEB PRESENTATION

Most commercial and society publishers use the portable document format (PDF) to "publish" their journals on the Web. Despite the fact that the pre-publication process for journals is now largely electronic, publishers of some print journals find it more economical to scan the printed pages than to convert from one electronic format (suitable for print production) to another (suitable for the Web). Software enhancements now allow more publishers to convert other electronic formats to PDF, but electronic production is still an add-on to print production in most cases.

Journals with no print ancestor or close print relative, on the other hand, are generally produced in or converted to a Web-oriented format, such as hypertext markup language (HTML), standard general markup language (SGML), or extensible markup language (XML) to better take advantage of the Web environment. Simple HTML is now considered by many to be too limited for serious Web-based publication and is being abandoned for more sophisticated markup languages, but for the sake of this discussion, all versions of Web markup language will be referred to as HTML.

Some publishers offer both PDF and HTML versions of their articles, some use dynamic PDF, and some use HTML supplementation to PDF articles. There are information professionals who are familiar with the innovations of some of the electronic-only journals and who understand the potential of Web-based delivery who have been disappointed by the continued dominance of the PDF approach with its inherent limitations.

Some online journal publishers provide PostScript or other special formats, such as LaTex, to optimize the expression of scientific notation. MathML is an up-and-coming markup language for use with XML. Publishers have strong incentives to move into the XML production environment, including the enhancement of interoperability, the automatic generation of metadata, and more ease of archiving (see Wusteman, 2003).

FIGURE 1–2. Comparison of HTML and PDF	
HTML (SGML, XML) advantages	*PDF advantages*
• more options for linking, searching, and supplementing the text • loads quickly • inexpensive production tools • easy to index and mine • easy to meet ADA accessibility guidelines	• stable, manageable, and cost-effective system for publishers • familiar look for users • standardization for librarians who are building interfaces • easy conversion of "legacy print"
HTML disadvantages	*PDF disadvantages*
• generally more labor intensive to produce • troublesome to print fragmented documents • requires a separate production process from that for a print journal • display may change with different browsers and screen resolutions	• requires readers to have the Adobe Acrobat Reader plug-in (but so do a great many other documents on the Web) • large files, slow to load—an annoyance to those using electronic journals through a low-bandwidth connection • does not make optimal use of the shape of a computer screen

MULTIMEDIA OBJECTS, DATA FILES, AND OTHER SUPPLEMENTARY MATERIALS

The Web provides excellent opportunities to extend an online journal far beyond the limitations of ink on paper. As Internet bandwidth increases and the cost for server space decreases, these opportunities become more attractive and practical.

The cost of using color is restrictive in print but not a problem on the Web. The size limitations of a print journal also determine the length and number of its articles. Links to "supplemental text" or data files are common for journals on the Web. Recent advances in computer-generated scientific visualization offer scientists a chance to demonstrate as well as describe the results of their research through the use of interactive models alongside their articles. For example, through electronic journals,

- engineers can share 3-D models,
- medical researchers can manipulate each other's images and clinical laboratory data,
- computer scientists can share programming code,
- physicists can share animations,

- linguists can share audio files,
- all types of researchers can share all types of data, and
- readers can search a specialized database relating to an article.

Links from articles can transport a reader into a specialized database. Web versions of print rarely take full advantage of Web capabilities at this point, but some publishers do provide some enhancements to their online articles.

One drawback to the use of multimedia in electronic journals is that for all but the most basic image file formats (.gif and .jpg), software plug-ins or clients are required to activate the files, and for some enhancements, applications must be downloaded and installed by users on each PC they use. Even after acquiring the plug-in, readers may not have the author's level of familiarity with its operation, so the viewing or listening experience may not go as planned.

Invoking an article's multimedia portions might be as simple as clicking on an icon or thumbnail image to launch an animation or video clip via a java script or a computer's built-in application; or it might be as complex as manipulating a model after downloading and installing a specialized plug-in and spending 10 minutes learning how to use it. One study of five publishers' journals (Kichuk, 2003) found 52 different file formats requiring 22 different plug-ins. For a list of innovative e-journals, see also Gerry McKiernan's (2001) EJI(sm): A Registry of Innovative E-Journal Features, Functionalities, and Content.

ACCELERATED PUBLICATION

Immediacy is another feature of Web-based publication. The publisher of a print journal must abide by a schedule that is based on selecting, reviewing, editing, and revising sufficient articles for an issue of predetermined size or scope. The printing process requires additional time beyond the camera-ready stage—as does the distribution process.

Some of the preprinting constraints will also affect the online version of a print journal, but a publisher's priorities will determine whether a new journal issue finds its way to the Web as soon as it is ready to be printed (which could be two or three weeks before the print issue arrives in libraries) or whether it is posted at a later date. A publisher's reliance on a secondary Web publisher could also result in a delay for online readers.

A recent enhancement to several publishers' sites is the availability of articles that are ready for publication before an issue is compiled. Here are some examples:

- Springer-Verlag offers an "Online First" feature through *SpringerLink*, making articles available several weeks before the printed issue is complete.
- Synergy's (Blackwell journals) "OnlineEarly–Fully finished, peer-reviewed articles are available online before the print issue is published . . . . "
- Wiley Interscience offers "EarlyView" articles, which are posted "following receipt of the authors' corrected proofs. They include all figures and tables and are fully citeable."
- ScienceDirect has an "Articles in Press" section on the contents pages for many journals. Each unpublished article is prominently labeled either "In Press—Uncorrected Proof" or "In Press—Corrected Proof." Corrected proofs are in final form except for their issue and page numbers.

Producers of electronic-only journals are generally much speedier with the whole publication process. They tend to use a more streamlined, online-only pre-publication process for communicating with authors and reviewing manuscripts. Most online-only journal publishers at this time adhere to the traditional concept of an "issue," but several post papers as they are ready, until they declare an issue closed. *Ecology and Society*, for example, posts an "Issue-in-Progress" (www.ecologyandsociety.org/toc.html). "At semi-annual intervals, the Issue-in-Progress is declared a New Issue."

SEARCHABILITY

"Searchability" is a frequently mentioned advantage of electronic journals over their print counterparts. The effectiveness and value of searching an online journal in its native environment depends quite a bit on the provider's site.

Once an article is on the screen, its text is almost always searchable with one of the following options:

- The browser's "Find" function
- The search function in Acrobat Reader (the binoculars icon)
- A search tool provided by the publisher or the host site (not common)
- A Web search engine if journal articles are freely available at a Web site

Searching for subjects or authors within a journal or group of journals is sometimes made possible by the publisher or the hosting service. Publishers expect readers to browse through the table of contents of a featured current issue. However, a one-journal site usually offers a way to search the table of contents of all issues of a journal by subject or author. A multijournal site will often provide the following search options:

- "This journal"
- All journals on the site
- Journals in a subject cluster

The JSTOR site, for example, offers choices for Boolean searching of specified fields within singular or multiple subject disciplines or within one or a number of journals (www.jstor.org/ search). Highwire allows users to search simultaneously through all 343 Highwire-hosted journals and 4,500 Medline journals with a sophisticated search engine, or a registered and logged-in user can search through "My favorite journals" (www.highwire.org). In mid-2004, the Ingenta database incorporated indexing for 28,672 academic and professional publications; however, only "6,000+" are electronic journals. The user has a choice to search for "online articles" or "fax/ariel articles" (www.ingenta.com). Ingenta provides document delivery as well as electronic journals.

LINKABILITY: TO, FROM, WITHIN, AND BETWEEN ARTICLES

The recent technological developments that allow deep links throughout the online scholarly communication environment are probably the most anticipated and satisfying enhancement of electronic journals. As e-journals become more intertwined through linking, it becomes less important where the user starts a literature review or information quest.

A standard and favored method of searching scientific literature is to follow trails through citations in articles. The Institute for Scientific Information ([ISI], n.d.) has capitalized on this methodology with its citation indexes, "allowing researchers to navigate forward, backward, and through the research literature" which closely resemble natural thought processes.

The Web as we know it—a tangled mesh of related sites and documents—is an ideal milieu for this kind of navigation. Interlinkability, or interoperability, is one of the most compelling features of electronic journals, thanks to the parallel developments of

"Related content is now just a click away: serendipity abounds and almost every bit of data can serve as its own portal through which related information is quickly found."

(Adam Chesler, 2003)

- a cooperative system known as CrossRef that depends on publishers using a persistent "digital object identifier" (DOI) for each article and
- a more generic protocol known as the OpenURL that allows for context-sensitive, on-the-fly links customized by local administrators.

Most information providers are quite willing to facilitate the interconnection of their resources. Journal publishers realize the value of database links for their readers and for themselves. The availability of links to their articles from multiple sources translates into broader name recognition, higher usage statistics, more citations, and a higher impact factor. Likewise, database vendors realize the attraction of products that allow libraries to maximize the use of their e-journals. NFAIS (the official name of the organization), representing major database producers, endorsed these "Guiding Principles" (NFAIS, 2003):

- Linking between electronic resources owned or licensed by a single entity should be strongly encouraged and widely permitted.
- Full-text publishers, information aggregators, and abstracting and information services should pro-actively engage in collaborative efforts to link their resources as long as a secure information environment is in place.
- Information purchasers and users should expect and request broad-based linking capabilities from their information and technology providers in order to maximize the return on their investment in those resources.

Linking practices have come a long way in a very short period of time; however, the more effortless it becomes for users to glide from resource to resource, the more work there is behind the scenes for all the information entities, including libraries.

Links from Databases to External Articles

Library database searchers can now connect to articles in full text e-journals that are external to the native database in three basic ways.

1. Through agreements between most of the major suppliers of bibliographic databases and most of the major publishers of electronic journals, bibliographic records in many databases routinely link to the full text of articles at pub-

lishers' sites (for authorized users) in an environment of interoperability. To reduce the disappointment of "dead-end links," many database providers offer a means for libraries to activate their electronic and print holdings so that users will only see links to their library's resources. See Chapter 6 for more information.

2. Libraries can employ a "link-resolver" system that allows them to define on-the-fly linking options from references in databases to external articles (among other types of links) using the OpenURL protocol. SFX by ExLibris was the first product on the market to take advantage of the capabilities of the OpenURL concept, but several other such products are now available. See Chapter 7 for more information.

3. Some libraries have developed self-contained or semi-self-contained information systems. Individual libraries and library consortia have successfully negotiated with publishers and commercial database providers for the right to mount both electronic journal content and bibliographic databases locally on their own servers. Some have integrated the content from commercial databases and journals into their own searchable databases of article metadata and full text, often including other relevant literature such as internally produced research reports and technical documents.

The U.S. Naval Research Library (NRL) has built such a system, TORPEDO Ultra, with strong search capabilities (King, 2003). Other libraries, for example the Los Alamos National Laboratory (LANL) Library (Luce, 1998), have combined several existing specialized bibliographic databases into one multi-disciplinary database, with links to their locally mounted journal articles. OhioLINK, with a membership of 76 libraries representing 500,000 students, staff, and faculty, provides another home-grown example of a system that links between bibliographic databases and electronic journal articles, about half of them loaded locally. These libraries have ultimate control of their linking mechanisms, usage statistics, user authentication, and the user interface. They can develop their own alerting systems and other targeted services that will meet unique needs of their own users.

However, aggregating databases and journals may not always be the best or most cost-effective practice for a library or library system. By the end of 2002, the California Digital Library had completely reversed its earlier practice of locally loading databases, opting instead to use vendor-based solutions. "The new systems provide better integration and service levels for the abstracting and indexing (A&I) journal and periodical databases, and have resulted in enhanced services for users" (California Digital Library, 2003).

Internal Links

Most e-journal readers have come across articles that provide links from the text of the article to other related parts, such as tables, notes, and the citations listed at the end of the article. For this feature to be useful, the reader must be able to return to the text after linking to a subsidiary part of the article. Most, but not all, internally linked electronic journal articles offer this type of bidirectional linking.

Links from Article to Article

When asked what they want or like in electronic journals, users frequently mention links to related articles from an article's reference list. Researchers (and students) typically follow reference paths during a literature review. Reference-linking initiatives have been underway since electronic journals first appeared on the Web. Most of the early linking was limited in scope, links to articles in other journals by the same publisher, for example; however the development of CrossRef paved the way for electronic journal providers to link from their own articles to articles in journals published by any major publisher. The currency for the CrossRef exchange is a unique digital object identifier (DOI), "an alphanumeric name that identifies digital content," with which the 654 participating publishers and societies (as of publication) encode their content items (over 10 million of which are now registered). For more information see www.crossref.org.

Some primary and secondary e-journal publishers offer a "more like this" or "related articles" feature that provides links from a citation for an article to related articles identified by shared subject headings or descriptors in their records, references in common, or by other means. In PubMed (n.d.), "The similarity between documents is measured by the words they have in common, with some adjustment for document lengths," and with various weights applied. Highwire Press continues to develop methods for the identification of like articles, a value-added service now called "MatchMaker," which is designed to be increasingly interactive. See Figures 1–3 and 1–4.

Readers may or may not understand that the related articles will be identified within a limited information universe, one that is under the control of the site managers. At some sites (Highwire or PubMed, for example) the "related-articles" realm of possibilities is fairly extensive, but at other sites, the potential matches

FIGURE 1–3. Highwire Citation with MatchMaker Option

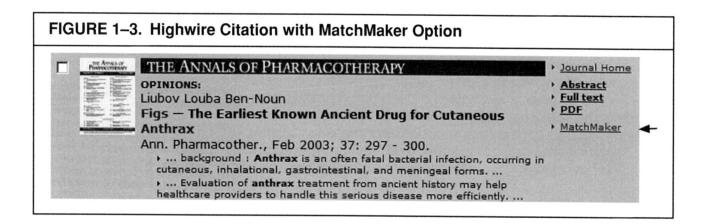

might be limited to articles in journals published by one small publisher.

Links from Articles and Citations to Other Information

One of the more exciting developments in the e-journal linking arena is the value that can be added to journal literature through external links to related resources. Full-text journal databases now interact with scientific databases of chemical structures, genomic data, taxonomies of all types, photographs, library holdings, entries in dictionaries, directories, and just about any information object. Anything with a unique identity can become a link target. The LinkOut feature in PubMed (www.ncbi.nlm.nih.gov/entrez/linkout/) makes good use of the potential of linking to sources of data such as protein sequences and macromolecular structures.

Forward Links

Some e-journal sites and article databases will display lists of "articles that have cited this article." In the Web of Science, which, after all, is based on the relationships between articles, the "citing articles" feature has always been prominent. But any database that includes articles' reference lists can develop this feature. Here again, depending on the site, the universe of citing publications could be small or large.

The "Articles citing this article" tool in the Institute of Physics Publications' (IOPP) Electronic Journals service provides only the citations in other IOP journals or those from the American Physical Society (APS) and the NASA Astrophysics Data System (ADS). They claim that "Forward citing links to other publishers' content will be added to our Electronic Journals service in due course." Some other sites that provide forward links are

Figure 1–4. MatchMaker at Highwire Press

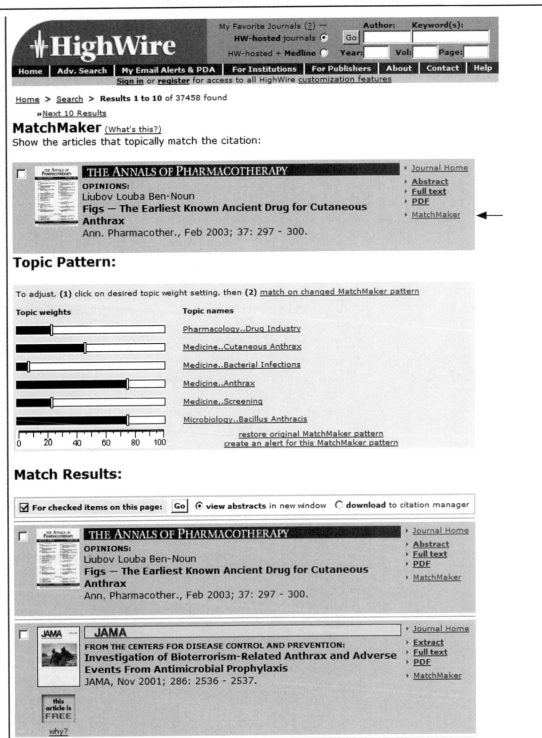

FIGURE 1–5. Forward Linking in IOP Journals

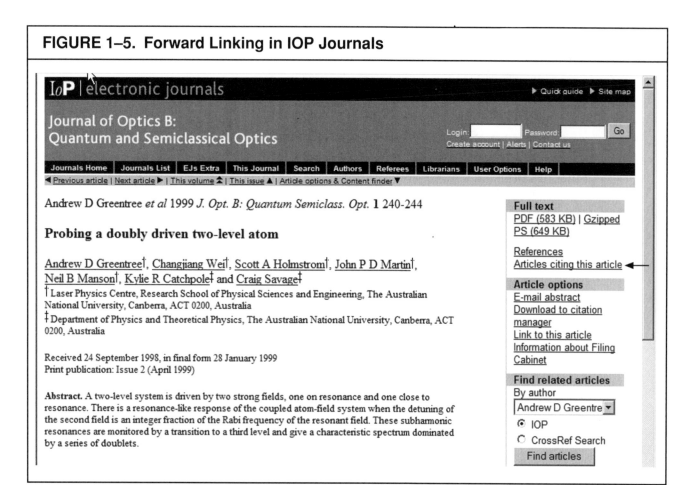

• Synergy
• IEEExplore ("Documents that cite this document" link within the abstract record)

As of late 2003, CrossRef was working on protocols for forward linking using the DOI.

Links from Articles to Databases

A more indirect kind of linking goes from a reference in an article to the abstract of the referenced article in a bibliographic database. If the database has links to the full text of the article, and if the patron's institution has a subscription or license for the journal, then this link into the database will be fruitful. If one or both of those conditions is not met, then at least the abstract might be of interest.

Some databases have a "Related articles" feature, so clicking on the link might eventually lead to the retrieval of previously unknown work, preferably with a full-text link that works. The Entrez PubMed database was one of the pioneers of "bi-directional" linking, encouraging and aiding with incoming links (see www.ncbi.nlm.nih.gov/entrez/query/static/linking.html). "You may generate a query on your Web page and submit it to *PubMed* and the other Entrez databases providing that proper attribution is given to the US National Library of Medicine (NLM) and *PubMed*." Entrez also provides programming tools that allow other sites to retrieve PubMed results outside the regular interface.

INTERACTIVITY AND CUSTOMIZATION

Most of the larger e-journal sites encourage (though thankfully, most of them no longer require) their visitors to become registered users and take advantage of targeted features and the ability to customize interactions. After creating a log in, users can often choose their favorite journals, save search criteria and results, re-execute searches, download citations into bibliographic management systems, and organize saved content in "My Folder" (Highwire), a "Filing Cabinet" (IOP Electronic Journals) or their own "Cubby" (PubMed). In some cases, users can save (and edit) their own notes and annotations to the articles they save at a publisher's site.

Interactivity

Articles in print journals include authors' addresses and, frequently, their e-mail addresses. Electronic journals can allow the reader to initiate an e-mail message with a click. Presumably that will result in more direct contact between readers and authors. Another common feature in electronic journals is a link to an author's Web site.

Print journals have letters to the editor, which may not be printed until months after the original article. Electronic journals often provide a chance to respond immediately, and to respond to responses. It is not uncommon to see a threaded forum on the topic introduced by an e-journal article. Electronic journals have taken several approaches to increase the interactivity between articles and readers.

- A debate that began as responses to an article can last for years, usually morphing into something else. For example, responses to an *American Scientist* article (Walker, 1998) titled "Free Internet Access to Traditional Journals," published in September 1998, became an active e-mail discussion list: "September 1998 American Scientist Forum." As of August 2004, 3,924 messages had been posted to that list (www.ecs.soton.ac.uk/~harnad/Hypermail/Amsci/).

- *BMJ*, the *British Medical Journal*, has a very popular "rapid response" feature (http://bmj.bmjjournals.com/cgi/eletters?lookup=by_date&days=1). Responses are mediated and "may be edited," but all responses "that contribute substantially to the topic," are posted within 24 hours. "All responses are eligible for publication in the paper *BMJ* and its local editions" as well. Rapid Responses to all articles can be viewed together.

- *Ecology and Society* has a peer-review process for responses to articles. Tables of contents use an "R" to indicate that reviewed responses are included and a "C" for comments that are not peer reviewed. Sometimes these reviewed responses are long, formal, and even coauthored. Responses to the responses are also posted.

- The *Chronicle of Higher Education* regularly schedules a "live forum" based on one of its articles, with the authors present, and then posts the transcripts of the chat session. The *Chronicle* also invites readers to "take an online quiz" from time to time, and sponsors "online discussions" about topics that may or may not be associated with a particular article. These discussions have an end date, but they are kept available for readers in an archive.

Alerting Services

Academic and research libraries have long sponsored mediated or unmediated alerting or current awareness services to help their users keep up-to-date with journal literature in their areas of interest. Alerts can work quite well for electronic journals, and in many cases researchers will establish and maintain their own alerts through a publisher's or e-journal provider's site. They might arrive at an e-journal site through various means, but once there, they are invited to maintain a long-term connection with a particular journal by registering for e-mail announcements of new issues. Or, from a publisher's site, a user might select several journals to track. Profile-based alerting services based on keyword or authors are also freely available through many e-journal sites.

Someone who is interested in knowing about the publication of new articles in journals from several publishers may find it too bothersome to register for a multitude of alerts from different sources. For that reason, libraries may still wish to subsidize a subscription-based service that covers most major journals, such as Ingenta or ISI's DiscoveryAgent. Users can establish their own current-awareness profiles with these services, but the e-mailed citations they receive will probably not provide the satisfaction of links to the actual articles—the tools are not yet intelligent enough to be able to discern a user's access rights to various content, and even if the correct links were included in the current-awareness citations, the alerts from commercial services tend to be issued before the publication of the issue.

If commercial alerts are channeled through the library, there is an opportunity to customize links to content the library has licensed and to hold them until the articles are available. This level of service may be excessive for a large library, but feasible for a corporate or specialized research library.

Although free alerting services on publishers' sites are limited to a smaller number of journals, they do offer some advantages to commercial alerting services. A user who has institutional access to a site will have access to the articles linked from targeted current-awareness messages. The publishers will usually not issue an announcement about new content until the content is available in some form.

- The American Chemical Society (ACS) alerting service offers "ASAPAlerts"—daily or weekly e-mail alerts for individual articles as they are made available on the Web, "prior to being assigned to an issue," and "Table of Contents Alerts" for specific issues the day the issue is posted on the Web site.
- The Blackwell (Synergy) table of contents alerts allow users to "click straight through to the abstracts or full-text article from the email link." Like most publishers, Blackwell also offers alerts triggered by author names or keywords.
- Highwire's eTOCs service gives users the option to be notified of an article of interest prior to its publication or after it is available. From an online article, users can also send a request to "Alert me when: New articles cite this article." Another service is "Highwire Remote," which "delivers tables of contents, abstracts, and selected fulltext material from current journal issues to handheld PDAs."
- Wiley's "MobileEdition" also delivers tables of contents and abstracts of articles in medical journals to PDA users.
- Association for Computing Machinery (ACM) journals have a "Peer to Peer" feature—"Readers of this Article have also read: . . ."

STABILITY AND ACCESSIBILITY

In the technical sense, electronic journals are becoming more stable, but in other ways, access and content are not as stable as we would like.

24/7 Availability

One of the strengths of electronic journals is their availability at all hours. However, servers require maintenance and, occasionally, fall victim to unplanned down time. Some publishers and hosting services have at least one mirror site for their journals so if one of the servers crashes or needs to be shut down for maintenance, they can seamlessly re-route users to a functioning server. Other publishers and intermediaries still have their files on just one server, so when it goes down, users get an error message. Maintenance can be scheduled for times of the least traffic to the server, but with an increasingly international user base, there are no times with no traffic.

Fortunately, publishers' systems are now becoming more functional and more reliable, and server problems are usually resolved expediently. Even so, short-term network difficulties can still prevent users from connecting to electronic journals. Approaching hurricanes, large-scale power outages, damaged cables, hackers, and other natural and human-caused disasters can interrupt service.

Shifting URLs

Libraries occasionally find out after the fact that a publisher has moved e-journals to a new server or restructured some directories so that the URLs the library was using to link to the publishers' individual titles no longer work. Behind-the-scenes "seamless" redirection will not always solve the problem if the library's authentication system doesn't recognize the new server address.

Shifting Content

Content goes in and out of full-text databases and e-journal packages quietly. Content loss is quieter than content gain, but it is not unusual for a library to gain access to new journals or a significant amount of new content without knowing about it. You expect new issues to be added at regular intervals, whereas you don't expect 20 years of backfiles to show up suddenly and unannounced, though it would be a happy surprise if they did. Sometimes a publisher will release older issues of a journal or several journals to non-paying readers at large, reserving only the most recent issues for paid subscribers. Sometimes a publisher merger will expand a package at no extra cost to the library during the first year or longer. Aggregator databases frequently gain new content. Generally, new e-journal content is announced or publicized in some way; however, such information may not make it into all the e-journal management nooks and crannies of libraries. Chapter 6 offers suggestions for improving this situation.

Information about diminished e-journal content is much more difficult to find. When content is removed from a full-text database, it is usually at the behest of the publisher, and the database vendor will attempt to replace lost content with new content that is roughly equivalent. These changes are not always announced, though some database providers will send out or post regular reports of changed content. Agreements between vendors and publishers are not permanent, and sometimes a publisher's new "exclusive" arrangement with one vendor will result in the removal of contents from other vendors' products. Updates to source lists on vendors' sites are not always immediate. Librarians attempting to provide accurate links to individual titles in licensed databases need to frequently check the source lists or use a service like Serials Solutions, TDNet, or EBSCO A-Z. Again, see Chapter 6.

Embargoes

A fairly recent practice in aggregator databases is the use by publishers of an embargo period for their journals (generally expensive academic journals), effectively keeping their most current content out of the database. Embargo periods generally range from six months to two years. The publishers' motive is to discourage libraries from canceling their print (or direct online) subscriptions, thus maintaining an important revenue stream. The per-article payments they receive from database providers for each use of current articles does not outweigh the loss of library subscriptions. Database providers that are also subscription agents have their own incentives to adopt practices that will discourage the cancellation of individual subscriptions.

In the major full-text databases the percentage of embargoed titles ranges from less than 5% to over 40% (Chen, 2002). Database users suffer from the proportional reduction in current articles on their topics, and libraries suffer from the additional burden of describing their "holdings," or access rights, to embargoed journals. Chapter 7 provides some suggestions.

Intellectual Property Issues

Content is sometimes removed from a full-text database as a result of a change in a legal interpretation of copyright. The most far-reaching case in recent times is *Tasini et al. vs. The New York Times et al.* The decision in this case clarified that the standard rights obtained by magazine and newspaper publishers from freelance authors, the First North American Serial Rights, which allow only one-time publication rights, also apply to publication in electronic formats. Thus, publishers are not allowed to "republish" freelancers' articles in electronic venues without royalty payments to authors or the purchase of additional rights from authors. Rather than having to deal with the administrative headaches, many publishers have chosen to remove the full text of articles by freelancers from the databases they populate. Publishers have been reluctant to reveal how many articles they have removed from their archives and the aggregator databases they supply. Most reports of Tasini-motivated withdrawals are from newspapers, but we can extrapolate that the archives of at least some weekly news magazines have been similarly decimated. The *New York Times* deleted nearly 100,000 freelance articles, or over 8%, as of February 2001; the publisher of the *Philadelphia Inquirer* and *Philadelphia Daily News* removed one-third of its archive of 2.5 million articles as of March 2001 (Chen, 2002).

Removal of Controversial Content

A less frequent but perhaps more troubling situation in which content is removed from a database or electronic journal issue comes up when an article is challenged for ethical or legal reasons or inaccuracies (especially if the erroneous publication poses a health risk), and an editor or publisher decides to retract it. Sometimes a publisher is required to withdraw content by a court order. For example, the *Economist* removed an article from its online archive by court order of defamation, as reported in its June 7, 2003, issue on page 67 (liblicense-l, 6/16/03). In the print world, such articles remain available in libraries, but in the electronic environment, they are easily erased, as though they never existed. One could argue that these articles that have been withdrawn will have intrinsic historical value in the future.

LONG-TERM ACCESS: ARCHIVING ISSUES

A few short years ago, many librarians were unwilling to invest heavily in electronic journals because the "archiving problem" had not been solved. The lack of a solid plan to guarantee the availability of electronic journals "in perpetuity" was seen as the biggest obstacle to the acceptance of the new format, and it was considered rash to drop print subscriptions in favor of more ephemeral electronic-only access to important journals. The archiving problem is not much closer to a solution, and still causes a great deal of concern, but circumstances have nudged librarians to overlook the severity of this problem in yielding to an inevitable shift to electronic formats:

- The overwhelming majority of users have voted loudly with their keyboards and mice: when electronic access is a possibility, print is no longer acceptable.
- Economic uncertainties can make it difficult for libraries to continue paying a surcharge for content in two formats.
- Major publishers have flipped their pricing models to favor electronic-only subscriptions.
- Libraries are running out of shelf space for current and bound journals.

Despite the enormity of the challenge, many librarians feel hopeful that archiving issues will be solved. The societal stakes now mandate a commitment to finding ways to preserve digital formats—not just electronic journals and the scholarly record, but digital cultural and historical records as well. And advances in technology seem to offer new (though not yet fully explored) possibilities for technical solutions to the archiving problem.

Archiving Challenges Defined

One aspect of the archiving discussion is the problem of continued access to issues of an electronic journal to which the library may no longer subscribe. In the print world, those issues would still be on the shelf after a subscription is canceled. In the electronic world, the publisher's server housing the journal files may refuse access to users from an institution that has not renewed its license. This has become less of a philosophical problem as license agreements routinely grant ownership rights to licensees for content that has been paid for, but it remains a technical and financial challenge for libraries that are not equipped to provide their own means of access to the content, especially if it is delivered without a user interface.

There is another question that has yet to be universally answered: What happens to a library's archival rights to electronic journal content if a journal is acquired by another publisher? Update No. 2 to The International Coalition of Library Consortia (ICOLC) "Statement of Current Perspective and Preferred Practices for Selection and Purchase of Electronic Information"

Will a library user in 2047 be
able to read an article from
an electronic journal that was
published in 1997?

(September 2004) asserts that "the obligation to provide a means of access to issues up to the point of transfer remains with the original publisher." If a publisher is wholly acquired by another publisher, ICOLC "expects" that a condition of sale will be for the acquiring publisher to honor the first publisher's obligations to provide perpetual access to libraries and consortia that have obtained those rights under an earlier license. But in practice, this has not always been the case.

Continued access after the end of a licensing period or a change in journal ownership is not a trivial concern; however, a more significant issue is whether the electronic formats being used today will be readable in the future, even if they are conscientiously preserved. Will a library user in 2047 be able to read an article from an electronic journal that was published in 1997? Information technologies will certainly be different, and our experience tells us that new technologies do not always accommodate superseded formats.

Archiving involves more than providing space on a computer to store files. The files will need to be frequently refreshed and occasionally migrated in order to be compatible with future technology. The archived files will also need to be kept in more than one location because of the vulnerability of electronic formats. As the articles in electronic journals become more intertwined through the interlinking of their references, and more enhanced by multimedia, supplemental data files, and updates, the archiving challenge becomes more complex.

Some Potential Solutions

Solving the archiving problem satisfactorily will require the coordinated efforts of the entire community of electronic journal producers, consumers, and intermediaries. With time, it becomes even more clear that no one group can solve the problem, nor will there be a technological solution that will work without help from a variety of interested parties:

- Individual libraries
- Library consortia
- Publishers
- National libraries
- Large utilities
- Vendors and other intermediaries

Publishers often believe that archiving should be the responsibility of libraries, because preservation of the scholarly record has always been a library mission. Libraries often think it should be the responsibility of publishers, because they produce, house, and already provide access to the journals and coordinate their services with other primary and secondary services. In truth, no one group can manage the challenge alone. The best we can hope for is that most of what is being published electronically today will be preserved by its individual creators, rights holders, and distributors in addition to libraries, institutions, and other organizations through large and small cooperative efforts.

What will become increasingly important is the interoperability and communication between distributed archives. For now, certain efforts, models, and tools offer some hope:

- The OCLC Digital Archive services (www.oclc.org/digitalarchive/) offers some options for storage and retrieval of a library's digital assets (which could include e-journal files acquired by a publisher).
- JSTOR, a self-supporting project based at the University of Michigan, which strives to develop "mechanisms to insure that the important task of archiving makes the transition to the electronic environment." For more information visit www.jstor.org. Participating publishers sign a license agreement that grants JSTOR "perpetual rights" to the electronic files of their journals.
- LOCKSS (Lots of Copies Keeps Stuff Safe) was developed by Stanford (Cal.) University Libraries with help from Sun Microsystems and the National Science Foundation. As they do with their print subscriptions, individual libraries can take responsibility for preserving their users' access to any stable Web content. The system "ensures that hyperlinks to material it is safeguarding continue to resolve and deliver the appropriate content to their readers even if in the Internet at large the links no longer resolve and the content is no longer available." For more information visit the LOCKSS Web site at http://lockss.stanford.edu.
- Project Muse issues a license that promises archival files on CD-ROM and, on request, sends a CD-ROM annually, allowing libraries to load and provide access to the files on their own network. This method provides physical ownership to issues produced during the subscription period. Some other publishers offer the same assurance.
- PubMed Central is the U.S. National Library of Medicine's digital archive of life sciences journal literature. The archives of the hundred or so BioMed Central (BMC) journals are included, along with about a hundred more, from

other publishers. As yet, the archive contains a fraction of the existing biomedical journals.

- The National Library of Australia shares responsibility with the six states and two territories for collecting and preserving electronic documents at a national, state, and local level to build the distributed National Collection of Australian Electronic Publications. There is little commercial publishing in Australia, but electronic journals are included in the archiving plan (Phillips, 1999).

- The U.S. Library of Congress is mandated to play an important archiving role under the National Digital Information Infrastructure and Preservation Program (NDIIPP). Appropriate proposals will be funded through NDIIPP (see www.digitalpreservation.gov).

- Yale University (New Haven, Conn.) and Elsevier are working together under a Mellon Foundation grant to investigate possibilities for a university to become an official archive through a formal commitment to the publisher (www.yale.edu/opa/newsr/01-02-23-02.all.htm). The Andrew W. Mellon Foundation has provided grants to six other universities to explore approaches to the archiving of e-journals.

- Those libraries and consortia that mount electronic journals on their own servers may be able to play an important role in preserving electronic journals. The Highwire statement "There is no local 'collection' for a library to develop and manage" does not apply to OhioLINK, NRL, LANL, the University of Toronto, and a few others. As these libraries and consortia archive the journals for their own users, they may choose to play a larger role in making them available to others.

- XML has promise for making archiving tasks simpler in the future.

- "Open-access self-archiving" is the practice of authors retaining the right to post their own articles on their own Web sites. It is was estimated in late 2003 that 55% of scholarly journals routinely grant authors the right to self-archive their articles. The motive behind the self-archiving movement is to make articles freely available for all to read—preferably in interoperable institutional digital repositories. Institutional repositories will also help ensure the preservation of individual articles.

The major publishers are devoting resources to the archiving issue, and they take it seriously. See, for example, the Elsevier position (www.elsevier.com/inca/publications/misc/ni2164.pdf). It is the journals from the smaller independent and society publishers, and particularly free journals, that may not remain available for future researchers without some help from other groups.

BENEFITS AND DRAWBACKS OF ELECTRONIC JOURNALS

Electronic access to journals brings many benefits to users, libraries, and publishers. During the transition period, the eventual economic benefits cannot yet be known, but we have already seen that early-adopter libraries have more journals at less cost in the electronic environment. As with print journals, there are indirect and hidden costs with electronic journals as well as long-term costs and benefits that are difficult to estimate. And there is more potential for user aggravation as well as user joy. One study found that 75% of the users surveyed swear at their PCs (www.mori.com/polls/1999/rage.shtml). During the transition to electronic publications, some publishers have grown rapidly while others have ceased to exist. Some libraries have managed a graceful integration of electronic resources and services while others have been devastated by problems arising from the transition to electronic formats.

BENEFITS TO USERS
Electronic journals benefit users in that they

- are available to authorized users any time, anywhere;
- interact with other electronic resources;
- save users' time through desktop access;
- provide enhancements, supplements, and searchability unavailable in the print environment;
- are often on the Web weeks before they are available in print format;
- can be read by more than one person at a time;
- are generally suitable for adaptive technologies for visual impairment;
- and do not get lost or stolen or vandalized.

BENEFITS TO LIBRARIES

Electronic journals offer libraries

- superior resource delivery for distance education;
- improved service to homebound users;
- potentially accurate usage statistics to help with collection development decisions;
- some cost savings, or more titles for the same cost;
- reduced shelving and processing costs (long term);
- reduced staffing for claims or replacement of missing issues;
- reduced binding costs;
- public relations opportunities;
- satisfied users; and
- more access by more people to more research information.

DRAWBACKS OF ELECTRONIC FORMATS

Electronic journals do have a downside:

- Coverage is not always as complete as in the print version.
- Authentication issues drain institutional resources and user good will.
- Long-term preservation is not assured.
- Some e-journals are less suitable than print journals for adaptive technologies.
- The library has less control over access to electronic journals than over access to print journals.
- Users' desktop technology does not always keep up with e-journal technology.
- Technical difficulties sometimes render them temporarily unavailable.
- Managing e-journals requires new or reallocated resources.
- The stability of the marketplace has been upset, and sometimes libraries suffer (as in the demise of the vendor Faxon).

Chapter 4 discusses the costs of different options for e-journal content and types of access, and Chapter 9 offers methods for individual libraries and library consortia to determine and weigh the costs and benefits of their electronic resources and affiliated services.

THE SCHOLARLY PUBLICATION AND ACCESS CHAIN

"All of the players in the information chain have been impacted with the shift from print to electronic formats." (Tonkery, 2003, p. 6). And as soon as a journal goes online, a whole new cast of characters appears.

At the research and writing end of the chain, the changes are relatively minor. Publishers may or may not have modified their pre-publishing operations. Some have instituted new electronic procedures for the submission, review, and revision of articles, sometimes with the help of new "manuscript management" software and systems.

At the publisher-to-library-to-reader end, though, nothing is the same. A host of entrepreneurs have found niches as "infomediaries" (Chesler, 2003) and "digital facilitators" (Jacsó, 2003), and established players have developed new roles and services in adapting to the electronic environment. Below is a sketch of participants in the print and electronic journal publication chain.

THE PRINT-PUBLISHING ENVIRONMENT

Four main parties make up the publication chain for an article in a scholarly print journal:

- The author
- The journal publisher
- The academic or research library
- The reader

Others play secondary roles, direct and indirect. For the author to write an article in the first place, some other parties have most likely played a major role:

- A private foundation or government agency may have funded research that resulted in the article.
- An institution with which the writer is affiliated—as an employee or a contractor—may have provided support, along with the other participants in the author's particular incentive system.

The publisher may be accountable to one or more entity:

- A professional association or society
- A larger publishing conglomerate
- Shareholders
- A diversified company

In addition to the in-house staff, a publisher relies on the participation of *editors*, an *editorial board*, and individual *referees*, who might also contribute to the journal as authors. They might or might not be paid.

The library is also accountable to a *parent organization*, which may also be an academic or research institution or firm that employs journal authors, editors, and referees. Libraries often use an intermediary *subscription agency* to facilitate serials transactions.

General and subject-specific *abstracting and indexing services* provide discovery tools for the identification of articles in journals. *Document delivery suppliers* sell articles to libraries and end users when journals are not available locally.

THE ELECTRONIC-PUBLISHING ENVIRONMENT

Electronic publishing includes all the parties that have participated traditionally in print publication (sometimes transformed to play major new roles) plus a host of other affiliated organizations and businesses. Roles of participants in the electronic publishing environment can be indistinct and can change quickly in response to the marketplace.

Journal publishers have several options for making their content available online through libraries or directly to readers. Some publishers want to make their journals available in as many places as possible to increase name recognition and usage, whereas others want to retain control over the presentation of their journals. A few publishers do not provide access themselves, but rely on aggregators or hosting services to do so. Registration and authentication of licensed users is a major new process in the Web environment at the provider end as well as the library end.

E-Journal Publishers

Responses to a 2003 survey by the "major commercial and society journal publishers whose output dominates the acquisitions of most academic libraries" showed that 75% of the journals are available online (83% of STM journals and 72% of humanities and social sciences journals) and "almost all will be in the near future." (Cox and Cox, 2003). The 149 publishers who answered the survey had launched a total of 782 new journals titles during the previous five years. John Cox (2004) reports that when he was the managing director of Blackwell there were 20,000 publisher accounts; most publishers have just one journal.

No publisher of print journals has yet migrated to online-only publication, so most established publishers are maintaining two distribution systems with very little overlap. Mergers promise long-term efficiencies but cause short-term problems. New publishers don't have print baggage, but they also lack experience with the market and may lack the financial support to weather difficulties. The online marketplace is more competitive but also more flexible in terms of pricing models and partnerships with customers.

Subscription Agents

Serials subscription agents have been dramatically affected by the transition to electronic publication. As most of us know, some from painful first-hand experience, one of the largest and oldest subscription agents, RoweCom (formerly Faxon) declared bankruptcy at the expense of many libraries and publishers before being acquired by EBSCO. The business climate is difficult, with reduced operating margins, as a result of decreased publishers' discounts and, in the case of electronic journals, additional costs related to the increased complexity of subscription management (activation, licensing, etc.). With publisher packages and consortial arrangements, subscription agents are often left out of the process altogether. The few agencies that have weathered the changes are providing new services to libraries and publishers, including e-journal hosting. EBSCO, in particular, has always been diversified, selling fishing lures as well as databases.

Publishers as Hosts

Most of the major publishers host their electronic journals on their own Web sites. Their sites have evolved as they have gained experience and technological sophistication, and by 2004, effective tools and "best practices" have emerged. Publishers' electronic journal sites are now, for the most part, reliable and navigable. This reliability comes with a cost to the publishers: in redundant servers and other equipment, and in increases in their IT staffing and outsourced processing and support services.

Most publishers offer the option to search by keyword for articles in the journals on their site—but only the very largest publishers' databases, such as Elsevier's ScienceDirect or those of discipline-specific and discipline-dominant publishers (such as

IEEE or the American Chemical Society), could be recommended as a place to begin a search of the literature.

Publication Hosting, Archiving, and Republication Services

Some intermediaries obtain e-journal files from the publishers and make them available on their own servers; others publish (digitize or reformat) the online version of established print journals. The following intermediaries publish or republish electronic journals:

- SwetsWise, from Swets Information Services, which delivers seamless access to journals published by Swets, those at publishers' sites, and those republished through the Extenza service.
- The EBSCOhost Electronic Journal Service (EJS) database provides access to journals at publishers' sites, those hosted by EBSCO, and those republished by EBSCO through its MetaPress service.
- Highwire Press at Stanford University, provides an e-publishing platform and support services for e-publishers, offering both hosting and portal options.
- Ingenta, like EBSCO, hosts come electronic journals and provides links to others at publishers' sites. Incorporating the former Catchword service, Ingenta provides access to a library's subscriptions at no charge while also providing a fee-based service for articles from non-subscribed titles (paid directly by users or subsidized by the library).
- JSTOR, at the University of Michigan in Ann Arbor, consists of digitized older volumes of key journals in a growing number of disciplines.
- Project Muse, the e-journal publishing arm of Johns Hopkins University (JHU) Press, now provides electronic access to journals published by other university presses as well as to the JHU journals.
- BioOne, a collaborative project of several organizations, provides electronic access to a collection of life sciences journals published by specialized societies.

Aggregators

Aggregators compile databases of e-journals and e-journal articles from different sources. Not all aggregators are the same:

- The e-publishers listed in the above section aggregate content from multiple original (print) publishers, and some of them (Swets, EBSCO, and Ingenta) include integrated access to journals hosted at other sites. For libraries, these are the aggregators that provide long-term, stable access to journals to which the library subscribes (whether through the publisher or the e-provider).

- A few e-journal providers, like SciServer@LANL, simply load e-journal files from publishers and manage searching and browsing interfaces for libraries that subscribe to the journals from those publishers, customizing them to provide access to each library customer's holdings.
- Other aggregators mix full-text journal articles with bibliographic information for non-full-text articles with an emphasis on searching, rather than browsing. See "Journals in Full-Text Databases" in the section "Scope and Variation of Electronic Journals" in this chapter.
- Libraries and library consortia are the ultimate aggregators of electronic journals, providing organized and integrated access to journals from many sources for their users. To aggregate (integrate journals into one collection), a library first needs to dis-aggregate the separate collections it has acquired.

E-Journal Management Services

To help libraries manage their e-journal aggregations, new services have sprung up to provide various levels of support that might include

- customized Web lists, or complete Web pages with holdings information, for all e-journals a library subscribes to through aggregators, publisher packages, or as individual titles;
- MARC records for a library's e-journals;
- a customized database providing journal-title access or article-level access to a library's e-journals.

Prices for these services also vary, with some companies offering something for every budget, some offering simple services, and some offering deluxe services and products. On this list you will see an established company that has developed new niches, new companies, and an entrepreneurial library and library consortium.

- EBSCO Electronic Journals Service A–Z Service: a new niche for a well-known company
- TDNet: a new company "integrating a diversity of access modes to electronic journals, on one unified, coherent site."

- SerialsSolutions: "founded by a librarian" to "deliver tools and services that help librarians and their patrons get the most out of their electronic journals" (now owned by ProQuest)
- Journal Finder: a product of the University of North Carolina, Greensboro
- Gold Rush Electronic Subscription Management: a product of the Colorado Alliance of Research Libraries (CARL)

You will find more information about these companies and their services in Chapters 6 and 7.

Link-Resolver Services

Link resolvers are the most exciting development in the electronic journal environment. See the Linkability section under "Feature's and Characteristics of Electronic Journals." Some libraries build and maintain their own link-resolver system based on the OpenURL and OpenSource software. Most commercially available products have been developed by e-journal management companies or integrated library system (ILS) vendors. Some link resolvers are built into a larger system, but most can also be acquired and used as stand-alone products:

- 1Cate: Openly Informatics (www.openly.com/1cate/)
- ArticleLinker: Serials Solutions (www.serialssolutions.com/articlelinker.asp)
- Gold Rush Linker: CARL (http://grweb.coalliance.org)
- Journal Finder from the University of North Carolina-Greensboro (http://journalfinder.uncg.edu/demo/)
- LinkFinderPlus: Endeavor (www.endinfosys.com/prods/linkfinderplus.htm)
- LinkSource: EBSCO (www.linkresolver.com/)
- OL: Fretwell-Downing (www.fdgroup.com/fdi/pdf/OL2overview.pdf)
- SFX: ExLibris (Aleph) (www.exlibrisgroup.com/sfx.htm)
- Sirsi Resolver: Sirsi (www.sirsi.com/Sirsiproducts/openurl.html)
- WebBridge: Innovative Interfaces (www.iii.com/mill/digital.shtml#webbridge)

Federated Search Products

After the considerable effort of dis-aggregating journals from publisher and aggregator databases in order to include them in browsable lists with URLs of their own, and configuring linking systems to help users arrive at targeted articles, libraries need to gather their packages of electronic journals and full-text databases back together into a searchable whole. Several companies have developed products that will enable libraries to configure their databases to be searched simultaneously. The process of searching multiple databases is sometimes called metasearching, or broadcast searching. The major products and their developers in this arena are:

- AGent – Auto-Graphics
- Chameleon iPortal – VTLS
- MetaLib – ExLibris
- MuseSearch – MuseGlobal – has partnered with the following ILS vendors:
    o EnCompass – Endeavor
    o M3 – Mandarin
    o MAP (Millennium Access Plus) MetaFind – Innovative Interfaces
    o SearchALL – COMPanion
    o SingleSearch – Sirsi
- Polaris PowerPAC – GIS
- WebFeat – has partnered with the following ILS vendors and content providers:
    o Consolidated Searching – Dynix
    o Find-It-All – Follett
    o WebFeat – Web of Knowledge (ISI)
    o YouSeeMore – TLC
- ZonePro – BiblioMondo
- Zportal and Cportal – Fretwell-Downing

Commercial Full-Text Products outside the Library Market

Some companies have developed information products that include e-journal articles intended for high school and college students. In some cases, they are marketed directly to students, and in other cases, to faculty. Libraries are sometimes able to negotiate intermediary roles in purchasing or subscribing on behalf of students. Here are some examples of these products:

- Questia: mostly books but includes 25,000 journal articles. Sold by subscription directly to students.
- XanEdu: marketed to faculty as "on-demand access to copyright-cleared resources from the world's most respected databases." For creating coursepacks; students pay a per-item fee. Includes access to 1,000 full-text journals.
- Jones e-Global Library: resource guides created by librar-

ians, provides access to various "research databases" that include some full-text articles.

ECONOMICS AND POLITICS OF ELECTRONIC PUBLISHING

These are interesting times in the electronic-publishing realm. Librarians, scholars, and publishers are witnessing and participating in a major transition from print-based to electronic-based scholarly communication, and quite possibly there will soon be a noticeable shift from journal-based to article-based services. In the print environment, the most efficient and cost-effective publication model is to periodically gather and process enough articles to comprise an issue at manageable, acceptable intervals, usually four times a year. There is no reason other than tradition to hold articles for cumulation in an electronic journal. Science is not well served by unnecessary and artificial delays in the dissemination of research results.

Some believe that an entirely new kind of Web-based system might render both publishers and librarians obsolete in their role of providing access to journals. Eliminating intermediaries is one possible scenario of this revolution. But what we are seeing up to this point is the appearance of new intermediaries between information and its consumers, and between publishers and libraries.

As librarians strive to satisfy the needs of their current users in today's environment, they simultaneously work to provide alternatives to the status quo and cultivate a new and potentially more favorable electronic-information environment, and to raise awareness among the parties who can influence the changes.

This isn't as schizophrenic as it seems. Libraries have straddled multiple realities before, in the migration of their card catalogs to online catalogs, in changing from print indexes to mediated online searching, then to CD-ROM databases and finally to Web-based databases.

Commercial publishers bring their electronic journals to a somewhat adversarial library market. The situation that has come to be known as the "crisis in scholarly communication" has not put libraries in a good financial position to add new products, and librarians blame excessive publisher profit making for causing the crisis in the first place. Both libraries and publishers stand to gain from a shift to electronic publication, but the transition period, during which it is necessary to provide both print and electronic versions of journals, is difficult for both groups. The length and the success of the transition period will be determined by the amount of cooperation, openness, and mutual experimentation between publishers and libraries in the establishment of a new equilibrium.

CHANGE AGENTS

A number of conditions influence the economic and political milieu of electronic publishing:

- Research and scholarly output continues to explode.
- Scientific organizations are trying to find ways to disseminate research more broadly.
- Commerce and research are becoming more globalized.
- International organizations are advocating for unrestricted access to publications based on government-funded research.
- Government reports in the U.S. and the UK have urged reforms that will make published results of publicly funded research publicly available (UK House of Commons, Parliament Science and Technology Committee [2004]; U.S. House of Representatives Appropriations Committee [2004]).
- Entrepreneurial and idealistic individuals and groups are experimenting with new modes of funding and distributing scholarly literature.
- A growing number of initiatives seek to level the playing field for journal access across institutions for researchers and health care professionals nationwide (the Canadian site license, the Joint Information Systems Committee [JISC] initiative in the UK) and statewide (Utah, Ohio, and others).
- The business climate is dynamic; mergers, buyouts, and bankruptcy frequently affect the publishing industry.
- National and state economics and politics have resulted in tighter library budgets.

The Internet, or course, is a revolutionary change agent on the scale of the printing press and the industrial revolution—changing our individual users and our society in fundamental ways. The entire scholarly communication system is under review, and its functionality is under attack at a time in which technology opens the door for alternatives.

THE SCHOLARLY PUBLICATION CRISIS

Electronic publication has not solved the scholarly publication crisis that has plagued libraries for decades. Some libraries have access to more journals than they had in print through bundled subscriptions, but these deals are hard to maintain without budget increases. The fact remains that both before and after the advent of electronic journals, library budgets haven't been able to keep up with increases in the cost and volume of scholarly publications. Not only have prices increased, but academic libraries get only 3% of university budgets, down from 4% in 1980 (Cox, 2004).

Price Increases and Added Costs

Most of us are familiar with double-digit annual increases in journal subscription prices.

- From 1986–2002 serials prices rose 227% while during that time general inflation in the United States was 64% (see Figure 1–6).
- In the UK, journal prices rose 158% between 1991 and 2001 compared to a 28% increase in inflation.

In general, the larger publishers add a surcharge for online access to print subscriptions, so unless a library opts for online-only access, its budget must absorb the additional cost. Sometimes intermediaries impose access costs for their services. To satisfy the needs of their users, libraries invest heavily in technology, staffing, and outside services to help them dis-aggregate and re-aggregate e-journals to create local searching, browsing, and linking systems. Savings from discontinuing print subscriptions are yet to become significant for most libraries.

Electronic delivery offers the chance for new pricing models to come into play, and they have. One study has identified 61 active models for pricing databases and electronic journals (Rhind-Tutt, 2003). But even though new pricing models may result in additional content for libraries, they rarely result in lower costs for the journals the library requires.

Volume Increases

New research specialties and the increase in interdisciplinary research spawn new journals. Not only that, but the volume of papers has more than doubled in the past 25 years because the number of researchers has doubled. Research output has grown at an average of 3% per year (Cox, 2004). From 1986 to 2002,

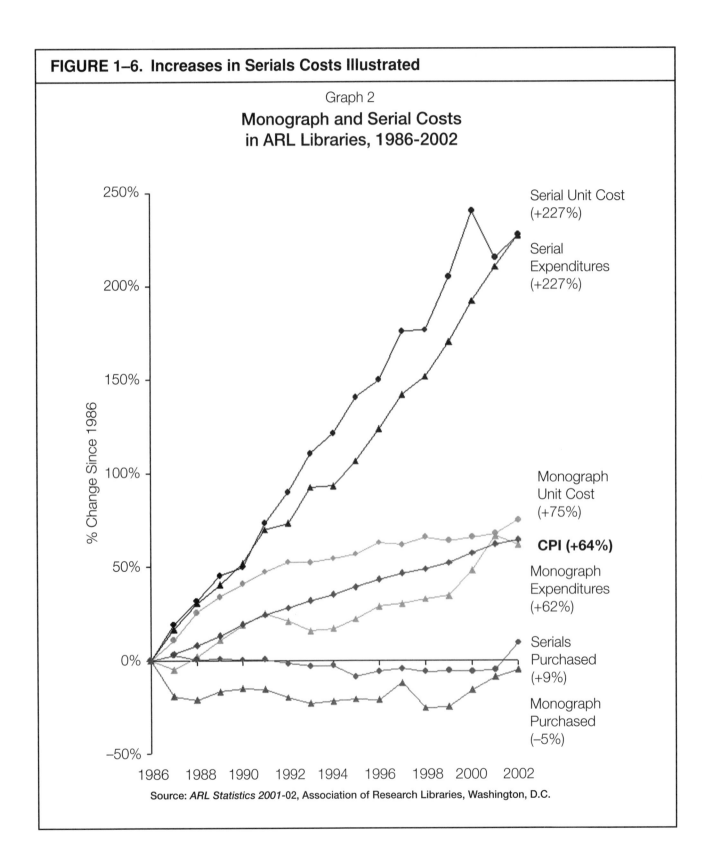

FIGURE 1–6. Increases in Serials Costs Illustrated

Graph 2

**Monograph and Serial Costs
in ARL Libraries, 1986-2002**

Serial Unit Cost (+227%)

Serial Expenditures (+227%)

Monograph Unit Cost (+75%)

CPI (+64%)

Monograph Expenditures (+62%)

Serials Purchased (+9%)

Monograph Purchased (−5%)

% Change Since 1986

Source: *ARL Statistics 2001*-02, Association of Research Libraries, Washington, D.C.

the number of journals published increased by 58%. Some of these new journals were created from splits of existing journals. Electronic publishing makes it easier to start a new journal, so the percentage of new journals will continue to increase.

Mergers and Buyouts

The electronic-publishing environment fosters economies of scale that favor large publishers. We are seeing an unprecedented instability in the publishing world, and the pattern is clear: large publishers are absorbing smaller publishers. Two very large publishing companies now dominate scholarly publishing. With about 1,800 titles, Reed Elsevier has approximately 30% of the STM titles. Candover and Cinven, a UK investment company, bought Kluwer Academic Publishers in late 2002 and a year later acquired Springer. The merged company, now called Springer Science + Business, has 1,350 titles. The "next tier" publishers are also acquiring imprints at a rapid pace. Taylor and Francis, in particular, is growing very fast, having absorbed a dozen or so other publishers over the past several years.

THE OPEN-ACCESS MOVEMENT

For political as well as economic and technological reasons, alternatives to the journal-publishing status quo are gaining momentum. The contrast between a journal subscription costing a library over $12,000 a year and the free flow of other types of information via the Internet is stark. Many (including U.S. congressmen, British M.P.s, and the Organization for Economic Co-operation and Development [OECD]) now see barrier-free access for the public to scientific (especially medical) research results as a necessity, especially if the research is funded with public dollars. A variety of reform initiatives have come to be known collectively as the open-access (OA) movement. In addition to the public appeal of universal access, other attractions are

- possible cost savings for libraries (though the shift from subscription funding to other types can still affect the library, directly or indirectly);
- the end of authentication concerns (and costs) for both publishers and libraries;
- more opportunities to integrate and aggregate journal literature and to deploy effective linking and search and retrieval systems across databases;
- the ability to study and analyze the combined published

"Over the past two decades, increased concentration in the publishing industry has been accompanied by significant escalation in the price of serials publications, eroding libraries' ability to provide users with the publications they need."

—Publisher Mergers: A Consumer Based Approach to Antitrust Analysis Susman, Carter, Ropes, and Gray, 2003

Keeping up-to-date:

**The SPARC Open Access
Newsletter**
www.earlham.edu/~peters/
fos/

**Nature Web Focus: Access
to the Literature**
www.nature.com/nature/focus/
accessdebate/

results of scientific research as "data," for patterns, trends, and connections.

A seminal event for the OA movement was a meeting of the Open Society Institute in Budapest in 2001, resulting in a public statement known as the Budapest Open Access Initiative (BOAI), defining Open Access:

In order for Open Access initiatives to be compatible, metadata standards and harvesting protocols have been developed, along with software and communication networks that facilitate Open Access activities. The BOAI outlines two main strategies for attaining open access: author self-archiving and the development and support of new and existing journals committed to barrier-free access. The Open Access movement faces several interrelated challenges:

- The traditions of the academic peer-review and reward system in relation to high-status branded journals; the "impact factor" system.

- The cost and complexity of maintaining a satisfactory validation and quality control system for disseminating research results and other scholarly work.

- The determination of a resourceful publishing industry to find new ways of adding value to scholarly publication to retain authors and readers.

- Contention among passionate factions within the movement about the best models and methods for pursuing open access.

Author Self-Archiving

Authors are generally allowed to post preprints of their articles (before the peer review) to an institutional site or an e-print archive such as arXiv. An increasing number of journals will allow authors to make the final version of the article available on an individual or institutional Web page. These self-archived articles are then freely available to any users who can find them using a search engine or links from other sites. The use of Open Archives Initiative (OAI) protocols in self-archiving facilitates with the searchability and interoperability of open-access articles.

E-print Repositories

Several discipline-based and institutional repositories are maintained and made available to authors to enable easy self-archiving of their journal articles and other scholarly works. One site lists 182 repositories (http://archives.eprints.org/eprints.php?action=browse).

The dedication, the talent, and the high level of cooperation among the information professionals who manage these repositories indicate that this network of literature could become very valuable to information seekers as well as information scientists. Unfortunately, articles from some major journals are missing because their publishers are unwilling to place them there. Some of the best known and most promising e-print repositories are listed here:

- ArXiv.org: the high energy physics repository developed by Alan Ginsparg at Los Alamos, NM, now housed at Cornell University, Ithaca, NY
- Cogprints: cognitive psychology e-print system organized by Steven Harnad at the University of Southhampton in the UK
- California Digital Library: using proprietary software developed at UC
- DSpace at Massachusetts Institute of Technology (MIT), Cambridge: using Open Source software
- RePEc (Research Papers in Economics): distributed locations, centralized metadata
- The NASA Astrophysics Data System (ADS): four bibliographic databases containing more than four million records
- JISC (Joint Information Systems Committee) Information Environment: currently under development as a "virtual place" for the deposit of research outputs of UK universities

Partial Open Access

Largely to avert a possible threat to their livelihood, many commercial publishers have begun to allow unrestricted access to some of their journals in ways that will further the wide distribution of research results without undermining their profits significantly:

- Some publishers offer free access to at least one new online-only journal, sometimes a digest of articles that appear in their other journals.
- Many publishers participate in initiatives to make e-journals freely available (or at an affordable subscription price) to institutions in developing countries that would otherwise not be able to subscribe to them (see Chapter 4 for more information).
- Some publishers provide unrestricted access to their current issue or most of the articles in the current issue while requiring a subscription to all previous issues.
- Some publishers have established hybrid open-access journals. These allow authors who have the financial support or the conviction to pay the publication charges to ensure that their articles are freely available to readers who do not subscribe to the journal, which is otherwise restricted to subscribers.
- A growing number of publishers open their archives to the world through Highwire Press or PubMed Central or on their own sites while continuing to restrict the access to newer issues to their subscribers. The time period after which the issues are made freely available can vary from six months to two or three years.

This last practice is applauded by many as an important concession by publishers toward open access; however, it has raised some concerns among some librarians. Ann Okerson of Yale University (2001) considers it a somewhat paradoxical model. If the wait for articles to be made freely available is short enough for them to remain useful, then some libraries will view their subscriptions to these journals as prime targets for cancellation when budgets are tight (indeed, there has been little protest over embargo periods in full-text aggregator databases). As has been the case in the past, "prices will rise for the remaining customers," the top research libraries and those that must preserve their positions "in the competitive climate of science."

In a more recent commentary (2004), Okerson argues for moderation and collaboration in "a spirit of hypothesis, experimentation and analysis," cautioning that "to surrender a diverse funding base for a few payers or to ask a small number of research-intensive institutions to support publication for all could actually increase the risk of serious contraction or chaos in the availability of information."

Author Charges and Institutional Memberships

One model for making research literature freely and openly available while still covering the costs of journal production is currently being tested by the Public Library of Science ([PLoS] Manjoo, 2003) and BioMed Central (BMC).

Committed to barrier-free access, these publishers have begun ambitious publishing endeavors with the help of foundations, individual donations, and government grants to establish the impact of their journals as quickly as possible. To sustain their journals without subscriptions, these publishers require authors to pay for the cost of publication. Author page charges are nothing new, but for these new online-only journals, they are high.

Ultimately, the cost of publishing the results of biomedical research in these journals is expected to be borne by the funding agencies as an item in a grant budget, but whether that will be the case is uncertain. University departments and research labs are currently bearing much of the present cost, leading to a new kind of barrier for authors and to disproportionate funding from certain research-intensive institutions. To ameliorate the latter effect, PLoS and BMC have instituted institutional memberships that help offset publication costs and allow authors in member institutions to pay lower fees. The library budget often gets tapped for this membership, leading some to question the difference between an institutional membership fee and a subscription. However, nonmember institutions have totally free access to BMC and PLoS journals.

Some journals offer a hybrid model. Authors can either pay a publication charge to allow the article to be freely available to all readers, or not pay a publication charge, in which case the article will only be available to readers at institutions that subscribe to the journal or who have individual subscriptions.

Volunteer-Subsidized Electronic Journals

Since the dawn of electronic journals (in the 1980s) we have seen the rise (and sometimes the fall) of many freely available e-journals published by individuals, academic departments, or groups that share an academic or political interest. Sometimes a library will play a role in hosting an electronic journal. As institutional repositories become established, e-journals edited or published by members of the institution often gain new institutional support.

The high quality, stability, and acceptance of some of these journals is encouraging to open-access advocates. Successful free e-journals prove to would-be inexperienced publishers that electronic publishing need not be prohibitively expensive. However, an electronic journal doesn't just magically appear. It takes a great deal of someone's time to edit articles, especially if they are peer reviewed, and to make them available to readers on the Web. Journals must be marketed and publicized as well, even if they are free, to attract authors and readers, especially if they aspire to prominence.

An organization with many participants and an infrastructure that provides support for editors is more likely to be successful in the long-term publication of free e-journals. Some organizations use membership fees or financial donations from other organizations to subsidize the cost of producing "free" electronic journals. Examples of organizations dedicated to the online dissemination of scholarship (not only e-journals) through cooperative publishing are

- ELSSS, Electronic Society for Social Scientists (www.elsss.org.uk);
- eScholarship, California Digital Library (http://escholarship.cdlib.org/);
- SciELO, a network of Latin American scientific journals (www.scielo.org); and
- Stoa, a publishing forum for the humanities (www.stoa.org).

Other organizations have a specific social or political agenda that is reflected in the e-journals they publish. Universities continue to subsidize and sometimes reward the editorial work of their faculty. See Chapter 4 for more information about free e-journals and how to find them.

Advocacy and Activist Groups

A movement requires organization and the coordination of efforts. Several library-related groups have organized around the desire to change the scholarly publishing paradigm to better serve researchers, library users, and science. Other established groups have devoted some of their resources and efforts to the cause. These are some of the most active organizations in the OA movement (in addition to the publishing groups already named):

- SPARC (Scholarly Publishing and Academic Resources Coalition) is affiliated with the U.S. Association for Research Libraries (www.arl.org/sparc).
- SPARC Europe (www.sparceurope.org) represents European research libraries, library organizations, and research institutions.
- OSI (Open Society Institute) is "the hub of the Soros Foun-

dation network," a private organization in New York led by George Soros (www.soros.org).

- Ithaka is supported by the Hewlett, Mellon, and Niarchos foundations; it aims to support the innovative use of technology by not-for-profit agencies to benefit higher education (www.ithaka.org).
- INASP (International Network for the Availability of Scientific Publications) is a cooperative based in the UK, aspiring "to enhance the flow of information within and between countries, especially those with less developed systems of publication and dissemination" (www.inasp.info).

A FUTURE FOR COMMERCIAL PUBLISHERS?

In these revolutionary times, some commercial publishers are nervous. The Web has changed users' expectations, and it is increasingly difficult for them to accept a situation in which the results of publicly funded faculty research, reviewed and edited by other faculty volunteers, are sold back to universities at an enormous cost, or else are not available at some universities because the cost is too high.

"Publishers must serve the values of both authors and readers. If they try to enforce an artificial scarcity, charge prices that are too high or otherwise violate the norms of their target community, they will encourage that community to self-organize, or new competitors will emerge who are better attuned to the values of the community."

—Tim O'Reilly

In the print environment, publishers are essential and can set the subscription terms for a journal based on its status and reputation. Users may still demand the "brand-name" journals, but that could change, depending on the success of the alternatives. Publishers are well positioned to carry on with what they do well, continuing to play a key role in authentication and quality control of scholarly and research publications, but new technologies and the probability of new competition are changing the marketplace.

With publishers in control, we should not expect to save money with different delivery and pricing systems. But it is not a big stretch for us to support new, nonprofit systems that will link and deliver individual papers outside the established journal system, and that ultimately may weaken our costly dependence on commercial publishers. A slow corrosion of the status quo may have already begun. In October 2003, financial analysts at BNP Paribas (2003) in London gave an "underperform" rating to Reed Elsevier, expressing "its concern regarding the company's current subscription based access, as compared to the newer and more successful article-fee based open access system."

We can expect some established commercial publishers to experiment with open access models (charging authors rather than readers) in response to the OA movement as it continues to grow.

REFERENCES

Blackwell Synergy. N.d. "Features and Benefits—for Readers and Researchers." Retrieved Sept. 13, 2004, from www.blackwell-synergy.com/info/features_researchers.htm.

BNP Paribas. 2003. "Reed Elsevier Initiated with 'Underperform.'" *BNP Paribas* (October 13). Retrieved Sept. 14, 2004, from www.newratings.com/new2/beta/article.asp?aid=341832.

Boyce, Peter, Donald W. King, Carol Montgomery, and Carol Tenopir. 2004. "How Electronic Journals are Changing Patterns of Use." *The Serials Librarian* 46, no. 1/2: 121–141.

California Digital Library. 2003. "A&I Transition." Inside CDL. Retrieved Sept. 13, 2004, from www.cdlib.org/inside/projects/a-i-trans/index.html.

Chen, Xiaotian. 2002. "Embargo, Tasini, and 'Opted Out': How Many Journal Articles Are Missing from Full-Text Databases." *Internet Reference Services Quarterly* 7, no. 4: 23–34.

Chesler, Adam. 2003. "Beyond Aggregation: Connections in the Information Chain." *Serials Review* 29, no. 2: 100–102.

Cooperative Online Serials (CONSER). 2004. "Module 31. Remote Access Electronic Serials (Online Serials). *CONSER Manual, 2004 Update.* Retrieved Sept. 13, 2004, from www.loc.gov/acq/conser/modlue31.pdf.

Cox, John. 2004. "Where Are the Industry, the Profession and the Art Headed?" *The Charleston Advisor* 5, no. 3 (January): 50–53. Retrieved Sept. 13, 2004, from www.charlestonco.com/features.cfm?id=148&type=ed.

Cox, John, and Laura Cox. 2003. "Executive Summary." *Scholarly Publishing Practice; The ALPSP Report on Academic Journal Publishers' Policies and Practices in Online Publishing.* Rookwood, Braden, Towcester, Northhamptonshire, UK: Association of Learned and Professional Society Publishers. Retrieved Sept. 13, 2004, from www.alpsp.org/news/sppsummary0603.pdf.

Hawkins, Les, and Jean Hirons. 2002. "Transforming *AACR2*: Using the Revised Rules in Chapters 9 and 12." Presented at the North American Serials Interest Group (NASIB). June 22, 2002, Williamsburg, VA. Retrieved Sept. 15, 2004, from www.loc.gov/acq/conser/aacr2002/A2slides.html.

Henderson, Kittie. 2003. "Taming the Greased Pig (pp. 225–226)." In "The Balance Point: Is Check-In Checking Out?" ed. Markel Tumlin. *Serials Review* 29, no. 3 (Autumn): 224–229.

Institute for Scientific Information (ISI). N.d. "Web of Sciences." Retrieved Sept. 13, 2004, from www.isinet.com/products/citation/wos/.

International Coalition of Library Consortia (ICOLC). 2004., "Statement of Current Perspective and Preferred Practices for Selection and Purchase of Electronic Information." To be posted at www.library.yale.edu/consortia/statementanddocuments.html.

Jacsó, Peter. 2003. "Digital Facilitators." *Information Today* 20, no. 6 (June): 17. Retrieved Sept. 13, 2004, from www.infotoday.com/IT/jun03/jacso.shtml.

Kichuk, Diana. 2003. "Electronic Journal Supplementary Content, Browser Plug-ins, and the Transformation of Reading." *Serials Review* 29, no. 2: 103–116.

King, R. James. 2003. "Building the S&T Digital Library at the Naval Research Laboratory: A Report." *Serials Review* 29, no. 2: 76–82.

Library of Congress Rule Interpretations. N.d. Retrieved Sept. 20, 2004, from www.loc.gov/catdir/cpso/lcri1_0.html.

Luce, Richard E. 1998. "Integrating the Digital Library Puzzle: The Library without Walls at Los Alamos." International Summer School on the Digital Library, University of Tilberg (Netherlands), (August 2–14). Retrieved Sept. 13, 2004, from http://lib-www.lanl.gov/lww/articles/tilberg.htm.

Manjoo, Farhad. 2003. "PLoS: The Free Research Movement." *Salon* (July 1). Retrieved Sept. 13, 2004, from www.salon.com/tech/feature/2003/07/01/plos/index_np.html.

McKiernan, Gerry. 2002. "EJI(sm): A Registry of Innovative E-Journal Features, Functionalities, and Content." Iowa State University (August 10). Retrieved Sept. 13, 2004, from www.public.iastate.edu/~CYBERSTACKS/EJI.htm.

NFAIS. 2003. "NFAIS Guiding Principles: Reference Linking." Retrieved Sept. 13, 2004, from www.nfais.org/2003_Guiding_Princ_Ref_Linking.htm.

Okerson, Ann. 2001. "What Price 'Free?'" Nature Online Forum, April 5. Retrieved Sept. 13, 2004, from www.library.yale.edu/~okerson/whatprice.html.

———. 2004. "On Being Scientific about Science Publishing." Nature Online Forum, April 1. Retrieved Sept. 13, 2004, from www.library.yale.edu/~okerson/On-being-scientific.htm.

O'Reilly, Tim. "Information Wants to Be Valuable." Nature Web Debates. Retrieved Sept. 13, 2004, from www.nature.com/nature/debates/e-access/Articles/oreilly.html.

Phillips, Margaret E. 1999. "The National Library of Australia: Ensuring Long-Term Access to Online Publications." *JEP: The Journal of Electronic Publishing* 4, no. 4. Retrieved Sept. 13, 2004, from www.press.umich.edu/jep/04-04/phillips.html.

PubMed. N.d. "PubMed Related Citations Algorithm. Retrieved Sept. 13, 2004, from http://ii.nlm.nih.gov/MTI/related.shtml.

Rhind-Tutt, Stephen. 2003. "Pricing Models for Electronic Products—As Tangled as Ever?" *The Charleston Advisor* 4, no. 4 (April): 52–56. Retrieved Sept. 13, 2004 from www.charlestonco.com/features.cfm?id=128&type=ed.

Susman, Thomas M., David J. Carter, Ropes & Gray, LLP, and the Information Access Alliance. 2003. *Publisher Mergers: A Consumer-Based Approach to Antitrust Analysis*. A White Paper. Washington, D.C.: Information Access Alliance. Retrieved Sept. 13, 2004, from www.informationaccess.org/WhitePaperV2Final.pdf.

Tonkery, Dan. 2003. "A Middleman's View to ICOLC's 'Update No. 1.'" *Serials Review* 29, no. 1: 6–8

Ulrich's International Periodicals Directory. 2002. New York: R. R. Bowker.

UK House of Commons. Science and Technology Committee. 2004. "Scientific Publications, Free for All?" Tenth Report of Session 2003–04 (July 12). Retrieved Sept. 13, 2004, from www.publications.parliament.uk/pa/cm200304/cmselect/cmsctech/399/399.pdf.

U.S. House of Representatives. Appropriations Committee. 2004. Report to Accompany FY 2005 Labor, Health and Human Services, Education, and Related Agencies Appropriations Bill (described by Peter Suber in the *SPARC Open Access Newsletter*, no. 76 (August 2). Retrieved Sept. 13, 2004, from www.earlham.edu/~peters/fos/newsletter/08-02-04.htm#nih).

U.S. ISSN Center. *National Serials Data Program Library of Congress International Standard Serial Number (ISSN)*. Retrieved Sept. 13, 2004, from lcweb.loc.gov/issn/.

Walker, Thomas J. 1998. "Free Internet Access to Traditional Journals." *American Scientist* 86, no. 5 (September/October): 463–471.

Wusteman, Judith. 2003. "XML and E-journals: The State of Play." *Library Hi Tech* 21, no. 1: 21–33.

MORE INFORMATION SOURCES

Albanese, Andrew. 2004. "UK Report Calls for Publicly Available STM Research." *Library Journal* 129, no. 13 (August 15): 16–17. Retrieved Sept. 13, 2004, from www.libraryjournal.com/article/CA443930.

Boyce, Peter. 1997. "Electronic Publishing: Experience Is Telling Us Something." *Serials Review* 23, no. 3: 1–9.

Butler, Declan, ed. 2004. "Access to the Liberature: The Debate Continues." *Nature Web Focus* (March 19–September 13). Retrieved Sept. 13, 2004, from www.nature.com/nature/focus/accessdebate/.

Ho, Le Vu, Siu Cheung Hui, and A. C. M. Fong. 2003. "Monitoring Scientific Publications over the Web." *Electronic Library* 21, no. 2: 110–116.

Houghton, John. 2002. "The Crisis in Scholarly Communication: An Economic Analysis." Presentation at Victorian Association for Library Automation (February 6). Melbourne, Australia. Retrieved Sept. 13, 2004, from www.vala.org.au/vala2002/2002pdf/16Houton.pdf.

Keating, John J. III, and Arthur W. Hafner. 2002. "Perspectives on . . . Supporting Individual Library Patrons with Information Technologies: Emerging One-to-One Library Services on the College or University Campus." *The Journal of Academic Librarianship*, 28, no. 6 (November/December): 426–429.

Luther, Judy. 2003. "Trumping Google? Metasearching's Promise." *Library Journal* 128, no. 6 (October 1): 36–39.

Mayfield, Kendra. 2001. "Post-*Tasini*: Pity the Librarians" (and related articles). *Wired News* (June 29). Retrieved Sept. 13, 2004, from www.wired.com/news/culture/0,1284,44905,00.html.

McDonald, John, and Eric F. Van de Verde. 2004. "The Lure of Linking." *Library Journal* 129, no. 6 (April 1): 32–34.

McKiernan, Gerry. 2002. "E Is for Everything: The Extra-Ordinary, Evolutionary [E-] Journal." *The Serials Librarian* 41, no. 3/4: 293–321.

———. 2003. "Scholar-Based Innovations in Publishing. Part I: Individual and Institutional Initiatives." *Library Hi Tech News* 20, no. 2: 19–26.

———. 2003. "Scholar-Based Innovations in Publishing. Part II: Library and Professional Initiatives." *Library Hi Tech News* 20, no. 3: 19–27.

———. 2003. "Scholar-Based Innovations in Publishing. Part III: Organizational and National Initiatives." *Library Hi Tech News* 20, no. 5: 15–23.

Mikesell, Brian L. 2002. "Fee or Free? New Commercial Services Are Changing the Equation." *Journal of Library Administration* 37, no. 3/4: 465–475.

Obst, Oliver. 1998. "Online First Publications." Message to medibib-l@MEDSUN08.uni-muenster.de, March 19, 1998. Retrieved Sept. 13, 2004, from www.akh-wien.ac.at/agmb/medibib-l/1998.03/msg00020.html.

Prosse, David C. 2003. "From Here to There: A Proposed Mechanism for Transforming Journals from Closed to Open Access." *Learned Publishing* 16, no. 3 (July): 163–166.

Van de Sompel, Herbert, Jeffrey A. Young, and Thomas B. Hickey. 2003. "Using the OAI-PMH . . . Differently." *D-Lib Magazine* 9, no. 7/8 (July/August). Retrieved Sept. 13, 2004, from www.dlib.org/dlib/july03/young/07young/html.

Watson, Paula D. 2003. *E journal Management: Acquisition and Control. Library Technology Reports* 39, no. 2 [Entire issue].

2 UNDERSTANDING USERS OF ONLINE RESOURCES

CHAPTER OVERVIEW

- Characteristics and Information-Seeking Behavior of Web Users
- Academic and Research Library Users
- K-12 Students
- Public Library Users
- Understanding the Users of Your Library's Electronic Resources

As your library reinvents itself to provide more and more resources and services through the Web, you will see less and less of your users. Sometimes it is hard to know if anyone is "out there." Incorrect assumptions about the preferences and behavior of your remote users can undermine the success of your e-journal strategies. To be responsive to user needs and expectations, you will need to use whatever information is available about the characteristics and behavior of online users in general, and about your community of online users in particular.

This chapter summarizes research and theories about the characteristics and behavior of Web users in general and certain sectors of e-journal users in particular, and offers some methods for studying your own users. See Chapter 7 for tips on designing access systems for your users and Chapter 8 for strategies to attract more users, ensure their success in using e-journals, save their time, and earn their enduring appreciation and support. Chapter 9 will help you analyze usage statistics for even more information about your users.

CHARACTERISTICS AND INFORMATION-SEEKING BEHAVIOR OF WEB USERS

It is important to understand prospective users of your e-journals as well as existing users. The Web (as a cultural phenomenon and as a marketplace) has generated quite a bit of research and theory about the online behavior of users. And, according to both its critics and its admirers, the Web has permanently changed our society and all its members.

GENERATIONAL TRAITS

Every generation is shaped by its environment and, in some ways, by its opposition to the previous generation. Most readers of this book will be members of the well-known Boomer Generation or the well-publicized Generation X. All of you have responded or adapted in one way or another to the technology of recent times, but those responses do not define you.

The generation that follows Generation X is commonly identified by the fact that its members are growing up with the Internet. It may or may not stick, but as of 2004 the name most commonly used for this generation is "Millennials"—the oldest among them having graduated from high school at the turn of the century. They are sometimes also called the "Net Generation." Because as a whole, they seem to be more serious, focused, and ambitious than their predecessors, and because it is important to believe that someone will save civilization, this generation embodies hope to some of their elders. This generation will be responsible for transforming libraries for better or worse, according to their needs and expectations.

Millennials

Most freshmen who entered college in the fall of 2004 have used the Web since they were nine years old. Many of them have been using computers since they were four years old, or even younger. They have grown up with game consoles, portable electronic games, and cellular phones, and they are wired (and connected wirelessly). They come to college with PDAs and notebook computers. For the most part, they expect that they will be able to find any information they need on the Web.

Millennials' values and expectations devolve from an "information age mindset" instilled by their use of technology (see Frand, 2000). For example, they do not approach problems in a linear way. In an information search, as with Nintendo, they will try different approaches until something works. They will not read introductory instructions or manuals, but they might consult a contextual online "help" system at the point of need. However, they would be quite likely to abandon a system that is not intuitive. They fish in a well-stocked information ocean. Another information age mindset attribute is "zero tolerance for delays."

My Generation

One analyst christened the first generation of the new millennium the "My Generation." MyGens are accustomed to the personal touch, to customized products, and to e-commerce systems with embedded intelligence that can remember their likes and dislikes and configure themselves for individual customers. MyGens download selected MP3 files for their own players and personalize their PDAs for their own needs (Oliver, 2000). You can expect members of this generation to take advantage of options to personalize their access to e-journals. The name may not have caught on, but these characteristics have been well-documented.

Generational Digital Divide

A 2002 study by the Pew Internet and American Society Project, "The Digital Disconnect: The Widening Gap between Internet-Savvy Students and their Schools (Levin and Arafeh, 2002)," found that middle school and high school students are frustrated and dissatisfied by their Internet experiences at school (see the K-12 section below). Some have referred to this generational difference between what children know about the Internet and computers and what adults know as the "other digital divide" (the first divide being economic).

CULTURAL THEORY: WE CREATE THE WEB AND THE WEB CREATES US

The users of our electronic resources, like all of us, live in a postmodern world, whether we realize it or not. Roughly defined, postmodernism is a cultural state in which there is perceived to be no central authority or single version of reality. The Web is a perfect example of a postmodern artifact: amorphous, subjectively experienced, decentralized, and nonlinear. An interesting article about academic library services (Harley, Dreger, and Knobloch, 2001) describes some of the postmodern elements that characterize undergraduate college students' interactions with information. Their characterization would apply to any users of the Web:

- Consumerism: Information is a commodity. Choosing among competing products, students will often sacrifice quality for convenience and low cost (in terms of time and effort).
- Superficiality: As long as they can make something work, students don't care about the underlying mechanics or structure of a system, the process of doing research, or the organization of resources.

- Knowledge fragmentation: The Web, without critical-thinking skills, can be a misleading place. A Web search can land students on a site without context, and opinion often masquerades as fact.

However, a postmodern librarian will not necessarily impose only "authoritative sources" on users, but rather will understand that information seeking is an art rather than a science. Each user is the center of a unique library search for a set of results that are meaningful for that user and exist in relationship to each other. A postmodern academic library will be inclusive in providing access to electronic journals of all stripes, and not allege that only academic (refereed) discourse has value. At the same time, users who are using nonstandard, nonvalidated sources may need help understanding where their sources fit in relationship to traditional academic values.

MARKET-DRIVEN RESEARCH IN USER BEHAVIOR

Web-based enterprises can fail (as many have) when they don't understand their customers and prospective customers. Market research on characteristics of various segments of Web users is sometimes commissioned and closely guarded by "e-tailers." Other market-research services collect and analyze the behavior of specialized or general Web users and make the information available for a fee to any subscriber. In order to attract customers for their market information, these consulting and research firms will sometimes offer free samples of their findings. Some of these free samples are useful for libraries trying to understand the ways in which their users interact with the Web.

Outsell

Outsell has established itself as a leading analyst of the information-content industry. Most Outsell research on end users of information is conducted for the benefit of content vendors, but library groups and other information intermediaries have also called upon Outsell's consulting and research services. Outsell representatives frequently speak about information users and the information-content industry at library-sponsored meetings and conferences. Outsell carries out an ongoing study of 30,000 users ("knowledge workers") in corporations and universities to track trends in information-content usage. Here is what the most recent results show:

- Of these 30,000 users 75% get their information by self-seeking on the open Web.
- In academia, 78% find what they need on the open Web and are happy with what they find.
- Over half (60%) of the corporate users and 50% of the academic users say they don't need anything they can't find themselves.
- The users will buy content independently as individuals.
- Users trust the library, but the Internet wins for daily information use.
- The institution type, the user's functional role, and the context of the user's information need will drive striking differences in information habits and preferences.
- Print is still the preferred format for using content, but users will find it on the Web and print it out.
- Most of the 30,000 users in the Outsell study prefer to work online and remotely from their offices and homes.

Outsell also publishes regular "Information Briefs" for subscribers. The following excerpts concerning users came from a free sample on their Web site (Curle and Watson Healy, 2002):

> One of the favorite pastimes on the part of traditional content players and information professionals has been user-bashing. Users are sloppy; users don't know what good information looks like; they don't verify sources; in short, they don't approach the information hunt the way an information professional does. The first thing wrong with that approach is that it isn't very productive . . . The second thing wrong with that approach is that it's not accurate . . . our studies, particularly of users in the academic environment . . . show that users are increasingly savvy about how they use information . . . our research shows that when they are using information in mission-critical situations, they do verify it, and do so in perfectly rational and effective ways.

comScore

The company comScore maintains a large database comprised of Internet-usage data from 1.5 million PCs used by volunteers at home, at work, and at universities. The comScore Network calls itself an "Internet audience measurement service." News stories on its site (www.comscore.com) often summarize research findings about Internet users, the sites they visit, and what they do there.

Nielsen//NetRatings

In addition to tracking television-viewing audiences, Nielsen also tracks Internet users on behalf of e-commerce and Web advertisers, paying close attention to the use of broadband connectivity, age demographics, the most popular sites, and how long users spend surfing at those sites. Press releases at www.nielsen-netratings.com/ provide glimpses of the information Nielsen//NetRatings reports to its clients.

ACADEMIC AND RESEARCH LIBRARY USERS

Academic librarians in developed countries can offer electronic journals with the assurance that the vast majority of students in higher education use computers (and most of them own computers) and that they have access to the Internet. Connectivity in residence halls is better in some colleges and universities than in others, and some institutions are further along in providing Web-based or Web-enhanced instruction, but all campuses are moving rapidly into the online world. A Pew Internet and American Life Project study (Jones, 2002) reports that 86% of college students are actively online.

Keeping up-to-date:

Council on Library and Information Resources (CLIR)

www.clir.org

CAROL TENOPIR'S STUDY OF STUDIES

There is no shortage of studies of academic users of electronic journals. To help librarians sift through the bulk, Carol Tenopir (2003) has summarized, analyzed, and integrated the results of 8 major ongoing research projects and 100 smaller-scale studies on users of electronic library resources. This report is highly recommended for an in-depth understanding of academic users. It describes how each type of research methodology results in a certain type of knowledge that needs to be consolidated to provide "a full picture of what users actually do, why they do it, what they would prefer, and what they are likely to do in the future (p. iv)." These are some of Tenopir's synthesized conclusions about users as listed in her executive summary (pp. iv-v):

- Both faculty and students use and like electronic resources and most readily adopt them if the sources are perceived as convenient, relevant, time saving, and fit into their natural workflow.

- Experts in different subject disciplines have different usage patterns and preferences for print or electronic formats.
- Most e-journal users still print out articles that are judged useful—so a printing format such as PDF is popular.
- Subject experts use hyperlinks to view related articles; students' use of hyperlinks is less clear.
- Browsing a small number of core journals is important (in print or electronic forms), especially for subject experts and for current-awareness searching.
- Searching by topic in an article database is important for all other purposes.
- Users will read articles from a wide variety of journal titles and sources if available to them, although most of the readings come from relatively few journals.
- Personal subscriptions to journals continue to decrease, so users rely more on electronic subscriptions subsidized by the library and on the Internet.
- Most journal article readings are of articles within their first year of publication, but a sizeable minority of readings come from materials that are older than one year.
- College and high school students use the Internet more than the library for research, and many believe they are more expert at searching than their teachers.
- Students exercise some quality judgments about materials they retrieve from the Internet, but those quality judgments may not exactly match faculty members' criteria for quality.

SUPERJOURNAL PROJECT

One example of a long-term study of academic electronic journal users praised by Tenopir for its quality is the SuperJournal project in the UK (www.mimas.ac.uk/sj/). Using several methods, the researchers found a great deal of variation in patterns of use depending on subject disciplines and status (faculty, graduate students, or undergraduate students). They found that user preferences were strong and did not change over time. As a group, however, SuperJournal users visited the library less, accomplished tasks more efficiently, and felt more up to date as a result of their experiences with electronic journals. The researchers concluded that in order to accommodate the needs of all its users, an academic library e-journal system should include features that enable

- browsing through tables of contents,

- searching for topics or articles within a designated subject area,
- customizing subsets of journals or articles, and
- searching across all subject areas for articles in as many electronic journals as possible.

DLF/CLIR/OUTSELL STUDY

In 2001, the Digital Library Foundation (DLF) and Council on Library Information Resources (CLIR) commissioned Outsell to "collect data on the relevance of existing and possible future services as well as on student and faculty perceptions of the library's value in the context of the scholarly information environment (Friedlander, 2002)." A total of 3,234 students and faculty members were interviewed. In addition to a summary report (Friedlander), CLIR has made 600 data tables available for further analysis to help libraries answer some of their questions about users of electronic resources (Marcum, 2002), questions such as these:

- Do undergraduate students use only electronic resources for their research?
- Do faculty members consult electronic sources before they consult other sources? To what extent do they rely on paper-based resources?
- Are there differences among disciplines in the use of electronic resources?
- Do students perceive electronic resources to be as authoritative as paper-based resources?
- Do information seekers validate electronic resources before using them? If so, how?
- Are there differences in information use between men and women? Among users of different ages?
- Do information seekers realize that many of the resources they find on the Web are there courtesy of their local university library?
- When do students go to the physical library? How do they use its collections and services?

DISTANCE EDUCATION

The Web has enabled the rapid expansion of distance education as well as radical improvements in the quality of distance learning. Statistics show that enrollment in distance-education courses has almost doubled since 1995. In the 2000–2001 school year, 56% of U.S. degree-granting community colleges and universities offered distance-education courses. Of the institutions offering distance-education courses, 90% used asynchronous Web delivery of instruction, and 43% used synchronous Web delivery (Thomas, 2003).

No longer are distance learners restricted to mailed curriculum materials or uncomfortable videoconference facilities and whatever resources their local libraries have (or interlibrary loan). Electronic journals give distance students immediate access to high-quality materials that are equal to or superior to the library materials their on-campus fellow-students have always had.

Serving students in distance-education courses presents extra challenges to libraries. If a library card is necessary for remote authentication, the distant student may not have one. If librarians do a lot of on-campus instruction on how to access electronic resources from off campus, the distant student won't have attended one of the sessions. A local student can always come into the library to retrieve an article on electronic reserve if there is some kind of access problem at home, but a distant student may not even know how to report a problem, or how to get help. These students have the most to gain from electronic journals, but also the most at stake if something isn't working properly.

Problems may be exacerbated when students in distance programs do not match the profile of on-campus users. Often, remote learners are older than traditional college students and may have been away from school for some time (Starr, 1998). Some of these students may not be as technologically literate or even as well equipped as local students.

Many libraries have a "distance-education librarian" who is introduced to students in distance courses as their contact for information resources, and that librarian may understand those students better than most librarians understand most remote users because of the formalized relationship. The experienced distance-education librarian could serve as a model for all librarians in the e-journal world.

K-12 STUDENTS

Librarians in all types of libraries may want to pay attention to the results of studies of the younger people who are our future college students and public library users. School librarians may want to reconsider the resources they make available to their students. According to a Pew Internet and American Life report (Lenhart, Simon, and Graziano, 2001)

- 94% of students aged 12 to 17 use the Internet for school assignments,
- 78% believe that the Internet helps them with homework,
- 71% of online teens say that they used the Internet as the major source for their most recent school project or report, and
- students are glad to get suggestions about good sources, but most of them believe that they are far more experienced and knowledgeable about the Web than their teachers.

Another Pew study (Levin and Arafeh, 2002) shows that secondary school students

- use the Internet more outside of school than at school,
- often feel that school technology is outdated and that rules and filters at school constrain them,
- believe that the Internet has more current information than their school libraries,
- appreciate the 24/7 convenience of the Web and the ease of cutting and pasting information from the Web into their projects, and
- are more comfortable using the Web from home, and they can use it while babysitting.

Electronic journals could play a larger role for these students. They know that the quality of information on the Web is uneven, and they are sometimes frustrated by what they find and don't find. Students don't expect adults to be able to help them find quality sources, but they will appreciate a school librarian who could arrange for them to have remote access to appropriate e-journals they would otherwise not be able to use.

> Students will appreciate a school librarian who could arrange for them to have remote access to appropriate e-journals they would otherwise not be able to use.

PUBLIC LIBRARY USERS

Most public libraries are not yet active in building electronic journal collections. Full-text databases often provide the only access to electronic journals through a public library Web site. Chapter 4 offers some suggestions for expanding public library e-journal holdings. But before they shift any resources or invest any effort towards acquiring and providing electronic journals, public librarians will want to know if their users would use and value them.

Librarians in academic, research, corporate, and other special libraries know that they are serving connected users. They are accustomed to users asking for access to electronic journals, or access to more electronic journals. Public librarians, on the other hand, may not receive such requests, and may not really know how many of their users are on the Internet and whether they are ready for a heavy dose of online information resources.

WHO IS ONLINE: DEMOGRAPHIC INFORMATION

Targeted demographic information is valuable for understanding the users and potential users of public libraries. As e-commerce and e-government expands, information about who is online and what they are doing online is also growing. Two organizations have been tracking the developments in Internet use and behavior across ethnic, economic, age, geographic, and gender categories for the last few years. One is the Pew Internet and American Life Project (Pew, 2004), which focuses on the United States; the other is the Digital Divide Network (www.digitaldividenetwork.org), a project of the Benton Foundation (www.benton.org), which is more international in scope. The extent of the "digital divide" has been a central concern of both groups. Public librarians can keep a finger on the pulse of American Internet use through their reports, articles, and other resources.

Keeping up-to-date:

The Digital Divide Library of the Benton Foundation

www.benton.org/publibrary/
index.html#thedigitaldivide

Pew Internet & American Life Project

www.pewinternet.org/

NTIA and the Digital Divide

The statistics in the reports of the NTIA portray a steady gain in Americans' access to the Internet, but as we can expect from an executive-branch agency, the interpretation of the statistics seems to have been influenced by the presidential administration in power at the time of the reports. Under the Democratic Clinton administration, the reports of the NTIA were issued under the series title *Americans in the Information Age: Falling through the Net* (U.S. Dept. of Commerce, 1995–2000).

The first NTIA report issued during the Republican Bush administration is titled *A Nation Online: How Americans Are Expanding Their Use of the Internet* (U.S. Dept. of Commerce, 2002). The term "digital divide" is not used anywhere in *A Nation Online*. Despite the optimistic conclusions of the 2002 report, these statistics from the report indicate that a digital divide based on income level still exists:

- 50.5% of all U.S. households had Internet access in September 2001,

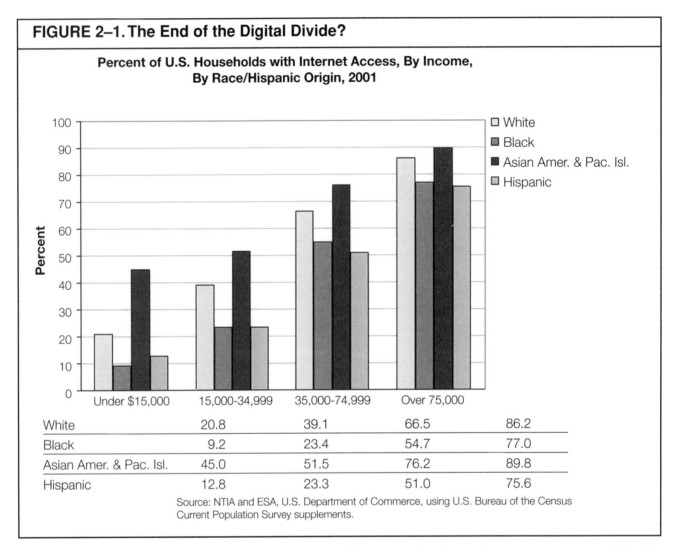

FIGURE 2–1. The End of the Digital Divide?

Percent of U.S. Households with Internet Access, By Income, By Race/Hispanic Origin, 2001

	Under $15,000	15,000-34,999	35,000-74,999	Over 75,000
White	20.8	39.1	66.5	86.2
Black	9.2	23.4	54.7	77.0
Asian Amer. & Pac. Isl.	45.0	51.5	76.2	89.8
Hispanic	12.8	23.3	51.0	75.6

Source: NTIA and ESA, U.S. Department of Commerce, using U.S. Bureau of the Census Current Population Survey supplements.

- 85.4% of U.S. households with an income over $75,000 were online, and
- 14.4% of U.S. households with an income of $5,000–$10,000 were online.

It may be useful to know who was *not* online as of September 2001:

- 49.5% of American households (though some members of some households had Internet access at work or school or another location)
- 62% of disabled Americans
- 3.6 million "Net dropouts"—or 3.3% of Internet users in 2001

- 24% of Americans who have absolutely no direct or indirect online experience

Nevertheless, by 2003 an estimated 55% of American households had Internet access. *A Nation Online* provides details about their online activities. As you would expect, the most popular use of the Internet is e-mail. Shopping, news, banking, games, and chatting are also popular activities. But looking for answers to questions, searching for health-related information, and obtaining information for school assignments or to help children with schoolwork are also major online activities for Americans.

The Pew Internet and American Life Project

In addition to tracking the digital divide, the Pew Internet Project has a mission to "create and fund original, academic-quality reports that explore the impact of the Internet on families, communities, work and home, daily life, education, health care and civic and political life" (Pew, 2004, Mission). Targeted reports and data sets on the Pew Web site can help libraries and other service providers understand trends and patterns in the way their users interact with the Web.

For example, the following reports have recently been issued:

- Faith Online: Two-thirds of Internet users have performed activities online related to their faith experiences or explorations (September 2004).
- How Americans Use Instant Messaging: American adult use of instant messaging continues to grow in intensity, particularly among younger users who appreciate and embrace the tools of expression embedded within IM programs (September 2004).
- Data Memo on Search Engines: The use of search engines is a top online activity and Americans increasingly feel they get the information they want when they perform search queries (August 2004).
- Internet as Unique News Source: Millions go online for news and images not covered in the mainstream. But many are repulsed by what they see (July 2004).
- 28% of American Adults are Wireless Ready: According to a March 2004 survey, 28% of Americans—and fully 41% of Internet users—have within the past month used a laptop that can connect wirelessly to the Internet or a cell phone that lets them send and receive email (May 2004).

To satisfy the browsing function of a current periodical collection and to make it easier for public library users to track down a known article, public librarians can create lists of the journals in full-text databases, with links to issues and tables of contents. Other popular magazines that are not included in databases can be added to e-journal listings for little or no additional cost.

How does this research relate to electronic journals? The Pew studies document the type of information that the public seeks and finds or doesn't find on the Internet. More and more magazines and nonacademic journals are becoming available on the Web, and a growing number of the people who read current magazines in the library, or who are looking for a particular article in an older magazine, would make use of those same magazines via their computers, at home or at work.

Full-text databases are designed to provide information and sources to support a subject-based inquiry. To satisfy the browsing function of a current periodical collection and to make it easier for public library users to track down a known article, public librarians can create lists of the journals in full-text databases with links to issues and tables of contents. Other popular magazines that are not included in databases can be added to e-journal listings for little or no additional cost.

UNAFFILIATED RESEARCHERS AND SCHOLARS AS PUBLIC LIBRARY USERS

As public librarians know, a certain percentage of their users are serious researchers. Not all researchers are affiliated with a university or a workplace with a research library. Retired academics, freelance writers, independent scholars, lifelong learners—many such users of public libraries are not authorized users of electronic journals and databases that are licensed by universities and research libraries. Public libraries need to balance the needs of all their users and purchase materials that will be most heavily used. However, if at all possible, they should not disregard the benefits to some of their users in having access to electronic journals such as *Science*, *Nature*, the *New England Journal of Medicine*, and an increasing number of freely available scholarly journals.

Clifford Lynch has made a case for the college graduates who became accustomed to rich electronic resources provided by their campus libraries. As graduates, some will continue to have access to e-resources relating to their profession, provided by their employers, but electronic content supporting their avocations will be off limits to them.

It is not uncommon—at least historically—for people to graduate from the academy with a lifelong avocation for literature, history, mathematics, or other subjects even though their careers may take them in totally different directions . . . but as content migrates into sophisticated electronic editions and systems, will graduation mean exclusion for these people, as well as for those who never had the opportunity to attend colleges or universities? . . . an informed public can no longer function without extensive access to information resources.

—Clifford Lynch (2003)

UNDERSTANDING THE USERS OF YOUR LIBRARY'S ELECTRONIC RESOURCES

Despite the impressive amount of information that has been generated by libraries' studies of their online users, to really understand the local and unique needs of your own library's users and the potential users of your electronic journals, you will have to do your own user studies. You will need to study your users from several angles, using different approaches, since each type of methodology is best at giving you certain types of information.

Local studies can help answer some of the questions posed by Deanna Marcum (2002) poses about how different groups use the Internet (see the DLF/CLIR/Outsell section under "Academic and Research Library Users" above). Before designing or enhancing access and delivery services for your users, it is helpful to know more about your patrons' wishes and technological expertise:

- What particular e-journals or types of e-journals do they want?
- How will they want to use them?
- What conditions are important for their choice of paper versus electronic journals?
- What features and functionality are most valuable to them in support of their work?
- What services will most enhance their use of electronic journals?
- How do they feel about the convenience and opportunities of personalized access versus privacy and confidentiality issues?
- What kinds of computers (PCs? Macintosh? Unix?); operating systems; Web browsers; and plug-ins do they use?
- What is their level of technical sophistication?
- What are potential barriers in using e-journals?

After your offerings are in place, you may want to know more about how your users are adapting to using e-journals:

- Are they finding their way to the quality e-journals you provide?
- Do they have expectations that are not being met?
- Would they be comfortable with the cancellation of print journals in favor of electronic-only journals?

- Do they prefer HTML or PDF formats for reading, scanning, and printing?

You will also want to know if you can enhance your users' e-journal experiences:

- Do the e-journals and databases match your users' needs?
- Do the navigational and organizational structure make sense to your users?
- Are the instructions and online help effective?

Chapter 9 offers more information on collecting and analyzing data on use for management decision making.

SURVEYS

A common way for libraries to get information about their users is to distribute a questionnaire. The biggest challenges with a survey are (1) wording instructions and questions so that they are clear and unambiguous and (2) getting people to respond. Target users can be randomly selected, or the whole user population can be blanketed with paper questionnaires or requests to participate in an online survey. A survey can be conducted via the Web, e-mail, or postal mail, or a combination of ways (posting flyers or e-mailing a link to a Web survey, e-mailing a paper survey as an attachment).

A survey can be formal or informal, depending on its purpose. It is tempting to take advantage of the opportunity to gather as much information as possible through a questionnaire, but your response rate will be better if the survey is brief. Before going live with a survey, it is recommended that you test it with a few typical users (people who don't work at the library). Generating clear questions using appropriate vocabulary is not easy, so if your library lacks the in-house expertise, you may want to hire a consultant or take advantage of a campus expert if you are in an academic library.

After the results are in, it can be tough to keep the momentum going through the analysis and beyond, to use the results to improve services. Conducting a survey requires a commitment of time and energy.

Types of questions that are good for surveys are those that elicit specific information about users:

- User preferences, beliefs, attitudes, feelings, level of satisfaction

- Reported user behavior ("How many times a week do you . . . ?)
- "Critical incidence" choices ("When you have a citation and you need the article, what do you do?")

You can select any of several forms for survey questions:

- Simple yes or no choice
- Likert scale—a statement followed by numerical choices corresponding to the level of agreement or disagreement
- Multiple choice
- Open ended
- A mixture of the above

Open-ended questions often yield the most interesting and potentially useful responses, but they also require more time and effort to digest. If you don't have the time or the staff resources to interpret and analyze comments, it is best not to solicit them.

Some advantages of surveys are that they

- are generally economical,
- elicit more candid answers than interviews and focus groups,
- identify a baseline and trends, if repeated over time,
- allow respondents to spend as much time as they need,
- can educate or inform participants of services and options they may not know about.

Some disadvantages of surveys are that they

- are time-consuming to prepare, conduct, and interpret,
- generally result in a disappointing response rate—people are oversurveyed,
- do not provide information about contextual factors affecting the use of electronic journals, and
- are, by their nature, somewhat subjective, reflecting the world view of the survey author(s).

When designed and analyzed correctly, surveys can provide information about the general preferences and behavior of specialized groups of users. If you can correlate demographic data with responses to questions, you can draw valid conclusions about different segments of your user population.

Examples of Survey Questions

Stanford University e-journal User Study (eJUSt)
http://ejust.stanford.edu firstsurvey-linked.htm
http://ejust.stanford.edu/ usersurvey2linked.htm
http://ejust.stanford.edu/ followsurvey-linked.htm

DLF/CLIR/Outsell study: Dimensions and use of the scholarly information environment

www.diglib.org/pubs/scholinfo/

(Stanford University and HighWire Press, 2002)

Web-Based Surveys

To collect information about how users interact with your electronic journals, Web-based surveys at the point of use can be very beneficial. For surveys that are open to all comers, a simple pop-up form with one or two questions is often effective. A less intrusive way to provide access to an open Web-based survey is through a prominent button on appropriate pages.

Advantages of a Web-based survey are that you can

- revise it easily, if problems crop up,
- get feedback from users at the time they are using your site,
- collect data in electronic form for electronic analysis, eliminating errors and saving time,
- provide appropriate sets of questions based on type of user,
- allow respondents to skip some questions based on answers to other questions,
- require answers to some or all questions in order to proceed, and
- identify and eliminate duplicate responses.

There are also disadvantages to Web-based surveys:

- The response rate may be low.
- The self-selection of respondents to an open-invitation survey may result in responses that are not representative of typical users.
- They must be completed at one sitting.
- You won't be able to survey non-users.
- They require programming skills if you are going to analyze the results by computer.

E-Mail Surveys

If you have access to the e-mail addresses for representative members of your library's clientele, you can ask them some questions by e-mail about their use or non-use of electronic journals. It is important to let recipients know that their responses will be cumulated with others and their identifying information will be stripped from their messages. You can either target a certain group of users or you can randomize the recipients.

Advantages of e-mail questionnaires:

- They are less expensive than print surveys.
- You can send reminders to non-respondents.
- Personalization may encourage a better response rate.

- Respondents may be more comfortable with e-mail communication than with other types of survey instruments.

Disadvantages of e-mail questionnaires:

- You may not get the candid responses that a more anonymous format will elicit.
- Some users will consider your survey to be spam.
- You will need to preserve the privacy of respondents.
- Compiling the results manually will be time consuming.

Print Surveys

Print survey forms can be handed out personally to library visitors, placed in prominent locations with conspicuous signage, mailed independently, included with other mail from the library or from the parent institution, or sent as attachments to e-mails. Drop-off points need to be clearly identified. If they are to be returned by mail, it is important to include a postage-paid, pre-addressed envelope. To survey users about electronic journals, print forms seem a bit out of place. But there are some good reasons to choose this format over the others.

Advantages of print surveys:

- They do not have to be completed at one sitting; they can therefore be longer than electronic forms.
- Unlike electronic surveys, they serve as their own reminders.
- The library will have fewer constraints in designing the presentation of the form than it has in the online environment.

Disadvantages of print surveys:

- The paper, printing, and postage may be costly.
- They require more time to complete.
- Compiling the results manually will be time consuming.

Telephone Surveys

Telephone surveys are similar to e-mail surveys in that your reach is not limited to those who come into the library or use the library's Web site. You can target users or non-users.

Advantages to phone surveys:

- You can expect a good response rate.

- The interactive nature of a phone call allows you to explain a question or probe for a more in-depth response through follow-up questioning.
- The conductor of the survey has a great deal of control and involvement.

Disadvantages of phone surveys:

- Unsolicited phone calls from a library could be interpreted as nuisance calls and even disallowed in some cases under "do-not-call" regulations.
- Possible surveyor bias might affect responses or the interpretation of responses.
- Recording and compiling results requires a large amount of work.

FOCUS GROUPS

Properly managed focus groups can give your library a broad and deep understanding of user perspectives. The focus-group format works well to ascertain user needs and expectations and to provide some insights on why people do or do not use electronic journals. Focus groups produce the best results when articulate participants are carefully chosen to represent typical users, but are not chosen from a group of well-known "library friends" or those known to have an axe to grind.

The usual format for a focus group session is 7–10 participants discussing 5–10 predetermined, open-ended questions for one or two hours. To avoid the halo effect, use a trained or experienced outside moderator, but make sure the moderator and the participants understand what type of information you expect to gain from the session. Having at least two observers/recorders will help you capture the substance of the group session.

Focus groups are best for the following (Covey, 2002, p. 21):

- Determining questions or appropriate vocabulary for a survey or tasks for protocols (see below)
- Expanding upon or clarifying data gathered through surveys
- Confirming hypotheses about user expectations and needs
- Identifying user problems and preferences
- Identifying user priorities for library materials and services

A good focus group session requires thought, preparation, and attention to detail. Covey (2002) has some advice for organizers:

- Make sure that the participants can easily find the room; put up signs if necessary.
- Ensure that the room will be free from excess noise.
- Arrange for sufficient chairs in the room to comfortably seat the participants, moderator, and observer(s), preferably around a conference table.
- Order food if appropriate (and allow 90 minutes for the session if food is included).
- Photocopy the focus-group questions for the moderator and observer(s).
- Test the audio- or videotape equipment and purchase enough tapes.
- Place a towel or tablet under the recording device to absorb table vibrations.
- Assure participants that their anonymity will be preserved in any discussion or publication of the study.
- Give participants a token of appreciation .
- Have at least two people analyze the data.
- Prepare a written summary of significant findings from each session, with examples and quotations.

Advantages of focus groups:

- Provide results quickly
- Are low cost
- Give you the chance to establish an ongoing relationship with participants
- Provide the opportunity for follow-up questions
- Can be audiotaped or videotaped for later analysis

Disadvantages of focus groups:

- It can be difficult to find neutral participants who are willing to spend the time.
- The results may be inconclusive or "messy"; they can be difficult to classify, compile, and communicate to others.
- A small number of participants may not represent all user groups.
- Managing the group and keeping the participants on track is not easy.
- Some participants may dominate; others may feel shut out.
- Peer pressure or the desire to please the moderator may result in bogus comments.
- Unlike a survey, a focus group session cannot be repeated

in such a way that trends can be identified or progress can be measured.

INTERVIEWS

The use of individual interviews to obtain information about users of online resources is not one of the study methods reported by Covey (2002) in her analysis of the information-gathering practices of 24 leading academic and research libraries. However, a great deal can be learned by talking to individual users about their needs, expectations, experiences, and problems with electronic journals. Your results may not be publishable, but if your sole interest is learning about your users in order to better serve them, you will be rewarded.

Here at the University of Nevada, Reno, several librarians interviewed a total of 53 faculty members who were known to use or presumed to be using electronic journals. We asked five open-ended questions, with follow-up questions when appropriate, and then we listened and took notes:

- Do you browse recent issues of e-journals? (How? How often? Do you use our Alerts Service? Do you use our Web subject pages for e-journals? How? Do you expect them to be exhaustive or selective? Would you be interested in being able to build customized subject pages for yourself?)
- When you have a citation and want to get the article, what do you do?
- When you need to search for relevant articles in your field, what do you do?
- What problems have you had in using e-journals?
- What can we do to improve the way we offer access to e-journals?

Our electronic-resources access librarian compiled and categorized the results of all the interviews. The responses were amazingly diverse and revealed some sharp differences in preferences, as well as some misconceptions. The interviews provided a good opportunity to correct the misconceptions and introduce some undiscovered features. Conducting the interviews helped us feel connected to users in a very direct way, but it also challenged us to meet the range of needs and satisfy the diversity of preferences that were revealed to us.

The interviews reinforced for us that certain users, for certain purposes, used each form of access to e-journals provided by the library: the catalog, subject pages, alphabetical pages, link resolver, the Alerts Service, and our new "search for words in e-journal titles" feature. They liked the journals we were providing, but they wanted more. They appreciated what we had done so far, but they had some problems with e-journals and some suggestions for improvement. Some of them were unknowingly violating our license agreements by posting e-journal articles for their students on course-related, freely accessible Web pages.

One drawback to interviewing individual users is that you can't always believe what they say, according to the one of the world's best-known usability experts, Jakob Nielsen (2001).

Nielsen's "Basic Rules of Usability:"

- Watch what people actually do.
- Do not believe what people *say* they do.
- Definitely don't believe what people predict they *may* do in the future.

For our faculty interviews, therefore, we visited their offices and encouraged them to show us how they used electronic journals while we talked to them. In the spirit of our open-ended questions, we did not give them directions or instructions for their online activities. As appropriate (strictly as an aside, without diverting the attention away from their activities) we took advantage of the opportunity to show some of them some features they were previously unaware of.

Advantages of the interview method:

- The flexible and interactive contact allows the interviewer to clarify questions and probe for more information.
- The informality encourages a forthcoming exchange.
- Lack of structure allows for unanticipated results.

Disadvantages of the interview method:

- Answers may be skewed by a desire to please or a reluctance to appear critical.
- Informality and lack of structure may cause the conversation to stray from the topic.
- Observer bias may influence the line of questioning or the recording/interpretation of the answers to questions.

CONTROLLED OBSERVATION

This method involves close observation of individual users performing designated tasks. They are given an information-retrieval task but not told how to carry it out. You would encourage your subjects to think aloud and to explain their choices. Your role is to observe and record the thought processes and behavior of users as they access, or attempt to access, your electronic journals.

Observing users in a controlled environment is referred to as "user protocols" or "usability testing" for the design or redesign of Web sites. Controlled observation won't give you information about user needs or expectations, or their approaches to conducting their own literature reviews, but it will show you

- whether the library has correctly anticipated user behavior,
- if your routes to electronic journals are intuitive to users,
- if your vocabulary or any other parts of your interface are confusing,
- what should be included in help screens and Frequently Asked Questions (FAQ) pages, and
- whether efforts to improve access to e-journals were successful.

Experienced usability testers (Battleson, Booth, and Weintrop, 2001; Dickstein and Mills, 2000) and representatives of DLF libraries (Covey, 2002) suggest the following general principles for controlled observation of users:

- Videotape the subjects if possible.
- Script your questions carefully.
- Design realistic tasks for the users; avoid recruiting users who are familiar with your system.
- Test the protocols beforehand; practice conducting the study with in-house volunteers.
- Schedule the participants and send a reminder a few days before the session.
- Photocopy the list of tasks.
- Test the audio- or videotape equipment and purchase sufficient tapes.
- Conduct the study in a quiet place.
- Place the tape recorder close enough to the user to pick up comments, but far enough away from the keyboard to avoid capturing each key click.
- Provide incentives or compensation for participation.
- Describe to the users the purpose of the observation; let them know you are not testing them and that difficulties they have will help you identify problems; assure them their anonymity will be preserved.
- Ask the users to verbalize their thoughts; remind them if they forget.

- Do not provide help during the process.
- Conduct a short interview after the tasks are completed to clarify the experience and answer questions.
- Record the results as soon as possible after the test is completed.

Usability experts such as Nielsen believe that if you conduct more than five observation sessions, you will not gain a sufficient amount of additional information to justify the cost (Nielsen, 2003).

Advantages of controlled observation of users:

- There is no better way to understand people than to witness their thought processes.
- Done correctly, this type of study can provide extremely valuable information about how your users interact with your electronic resources and online services.

Disadvantages of controlled observation of users:

- It is a time-consuming process, requiring up to an hour per user.
- It is very hard for librarians not to assist users who are having trouble.
- It is hard to recruit subjects who are comfortable with thinking aloud.
- It may be difficult to interpret and analyze the results of the observation.
- The formality and scrutiny may inhibit users from exhibiting their normal behavior.
- You may not be able to generalize all of the observed behavior of a very few users to a larger user group or other types of users.

TRANSACTION LOGS AND USAGE STATISTICS

Web-transaction logs and vendor-supplied or locally generated usage statistics are covered in depth in Chapter 9. The analysis of aggregated transactions is most frequently conducted as a cost-benefit exercise to aid in administrative decision making. It is difficult, or impossible, to tease out the characteristics of individual users, but usage statistics can show users' overall approaches to electronic journals and average behavior. For example, usage statistics and transaction logs can tell you the average amount of time your users spend with a database, or what percentage of them looked at journal-article abstracts but did not download the articles. Transaction logs and statistics will not represent user preferences or their demographic characteristics. One example of a study that did seek to understand individuals' online behavior by analyzing usage statistics correlated IP addresses (as surrogates for users) with browsing, searching, and downloading choices in using American Chemical Society (ACS) journals (Davis & Solla, 2003).

Some advantages to using logs and usage statistics to understand behavior:

- Empirical data; no subjectivity (from study administrator or subject) to taint the results
- Unobtrusive process; does not require extra time from users
- Plenty of data to analyze

The main challenges in using quantitative data to understand individual users:

- Using IP or log-in information without compromising confidentiality
- Collecting consistent data from numerous sources
- Analyzing, interpreting, and presenting data in a meaningful and useful way

Drawbacks to using institutional logs or statistics for user studies:

- These sources do not count the use of personal subscriptions or access outside the library's system.
- Logs and statistics do not provide information about the motivation, satisfaction, frustration level, or success of your users.

CITATION ANALYSIS

Citation analysis is not mentioned by either Tenopir or Covey as a method for understanding users, and you would not want to use it as your only research tool. However, studying the lists of references in your faculty's publications or your students' papers can show you what they are reading (presumably), and the types of sources most commonly used and valued locally in their disciplines.

FIGURE 2–2. Research Methods for User Studies

Research method	Response rate	Bias factor	Cost	Burden on library	Burden on user	Measures opinions	Measures actions	Teaching opportunity
Web survey (open)	■	■	$			√		√
Web survey (invited)	■■	■■	$			√		√
E-mail survey	■■	■■		■	■	√		√
Print survey	■	■	$ $	■	■	√		√
Phone survey	■■■	■■		■■		√		√
Focus group	■■	■■■	$	■■■	■	√		
Interviews	■■■	■■■		■■	■	√		√
Controlled observation	■■■	■		■■	■■		√	
Transaction logs/ Usage statistics	■■			■■			√	
Citation analysis	■■■			■■■			√	

Advantages to citation studies:

- They rely only on empirical data.
- They are unobtrusive; do not require extra time from users.
- They analyze usage data within a scholarly cultural context.

Disadvantages to citation studies:

- They do not necessarily include all the literature an author has used.
- They do not necessarily reflect the use of library-provided materials.
- It might be difficult to gain access to student papers for analysis.
- It is time consuming to compile and analyze the data.

REFERENCES

Battleson, Brenda, Austin Booth, and Jane Weintrop. 2001. "Usability Testing of an Academic Library Web Site: A Case Study." *The Journal of Academic Librarianship* 27 no. 3 (May): 188–198.

Covey, Denise Troll. 2002. *Usage and Usability: Library Practices and Concerns* (January). Washington, DC: Digital Library Foundation, Council on Library and Information Resources. Retrieved Sept. 20, 2004, from www.clir.org/pubs/reports/pub105/pub105.pdf.

Curle, David, and Leigh Watson Healy. 2002. *Outlook 2003: Issues in the Information Marketplace.* Outsell Briefing 5, no. 58. Burlingame, CA: Outsell.

Davis, Philip M., and Leah R. Solla. 2003. "An IP-Level Analysis of Usage Statistics for Electronic Journals in Chemistry: Making Inferences About User Behavior." *Journal of the American Society for Information Science and Technology* 54, no. 11: 1062–1068.

Dickstein, Ruth, and Vicki Mills. 2000. "Usability Testing at the University of Arizona Library: How to Let the Users in on the Design." *Information Technology and Libraries* 19, no. 3 (September).

Frand, Jason. 2000. "The Information Age Mindset." *Educause Review* 35, no. 3 (September/October): 15–19. Retrieved Sept. 17, 2004, from www.educause.edu/pub/er/em00/articles005/erm0051.pdf.

Friedlander, Amy. 2002. *Dimensions and Use of the Scholarly Information Environment: Introduction to a Data Set Assembled by the Digital Library Federation and Outsell, Inc.* Washington, DC: Digital Library Federation and Council on Library and Information Resources. Retrieved Sept. 14, 2004, from www.clir.org/pubs/reports/pub110/Contents.html.

Harley, Bruce, Megan Dreger, and Patricia Knobloch. 2001. "The Postmodern Condition: Students, the Web, and Academic Library Services." *Reference Services Review* 29, no. 1: 23–32.

Jones, Steve. 2002, September 15. *The Internet Goes to College.* Pew Internet and American Life Project. Retrieved Sept. 14, 2004, from www.pewinternet.org/pdfs/PIP_College_Report.pdf.

Lenhart, Amanda, Maya Simon, and Mike Graziano. 2001. *The Internet and Education: Findings of the Pew Internet and American Life Project.* Retrieved Sept. 14, 2004, from www.pewinternet.org/pdfs/PIP_Schools_Report.pdf.

Levin, Douglas, and Sousan Arafeh. 2002. *The Digital Disconnect: The Widening Gap between Internet-Savvy Students and Their Schools.* Pew Internet and American Life Project. Retrieved Sept. 14, 2004, from www.pewinternet.org/pdfs/PIP_Schools_Internet_Report.pdf.

Lynch, Clifford. 2003. "Life after Graduation Day: Beyond the Academy's Digital Walls." *Educause Review* 38, no. 5 (September/October): 12–13. Retrieved Sept. 14, 2004, www.educause.edu/ir/library/pdf/erm0356.pdf.

Marcum, Deanna B. 2002. "Learning from Library Users." *CLIR Issues* 30 (November/December). Retrieved Sept. 20, 2004, from www.clir.org/pubs/issues/issues30.html#users.

Nielsen, Jakob. 2001. "First Rule of Usability? Don't Listen to Users." *Jakob Nielsen's Alertbox.* (August 5). Retrieved Sept. 20, 2004, from www.useit.com/alertbox/20010805.html.

Nielsen, Jakob. 2003. "Usability 101. *Jakob Nielsen's Alertbox.* (August 25). Retrieved Sept. 20, 2004, from www.useit.com/alertbox/20030825.html.

Oliver, Richard W. 2000. "'My' Generation." *Management Review* 89, no. 1 (January): 12–13.

Stanford University and Highwire Press. 2002. *EJUSt: Electronic Journal User Study.* Retrieved Sept. 20, 2004, from http://ejust.stanford.edu/.

Starr, Leah K. 1998. "Reference Services for Off-Campus Students." *OLA Quarterly* 4, no. 3 (Fall). Retrieved Sept. 20, 2004, from www.olaweb.org/quarterly/quar4-3/starr.shtml.

Tenopir, Carol. 2003. *Use and Users of Electronic Library Resources: An Overview and Analysis of Recent Research Studies.* Washington, DC: Council on Library and Information Resources. Retrieved Sept. 20, 2004, from www.clir.org/pubs/reports/pub120/pub120.pdf.

Thomas, David, 2003. "Distance Education Continues Apace at Postsecondary Institutions" [Press release, July 18]. Washington, DC: U.S. Department of Education. Retrieved Sept. 14, 2004, from www.ed.gov/pressreleases/2003/07/07182003.html.

U.S. Dept. of Commerce. 1995–2000. National Telecommunications and Information Administration. *Americans in the Information Age: Falling through the Net*, 4 reports. Retrieved Sept. 20, 2004, from www.ntia.doc.gov/ntiahome/digitaldivide/.

———. 2002. National Telecommunications and Information Administration and Economics and Statistics Administration. 2002. *A Nation Online: How Americans Are Expanding Their Use of the Internet.* Retrieved Sept. 20, 2004, from www.ntia.doc.gov/ntiahome/dn/index.html.

MORE INFORMATION SOURCES

Abram, Stephen. 2003. "Free Studies on the Web That Are Worth Your Time!" www.acrldvc.org/programs/UsersStudies.pdf.

Crawley, Devin. 2003. "Libraries Need to Reach Tech-Savvy Students, Say U.S. Studies." *University Affairs* (April): 28.

Curtis, Donnelyn 2002. "Getting to Know Remote Users." In *Attracting, Educating, and Serving Remote Users through the Web: A How-To-Do-It Manual for Librarians*, 19–37. New York: Neal-Schuman.

Oblinger, Diana G. 2003. "Boomers, Gen-Xers, & Millennials: Understanding the New Students." *Educause Review* 38, no. 4 (July/August): 37–47.

OCLC. 2003. *2003 OCLC Environmental Scan: Pattern Recognition.* www.oclc.org/reports/2003escan.htm.

Tapscott, Don. 1998. *Growing Up Digital: The Rise of the Net Generation.* New York: McGraw-Hill.

Waits, Tiffany, and Laurie Lewis. 2003, July. "Distance Education at Degree-Granting Postsecondary Institutions: 2000–2001." Washington, DC: U.S. Department of Education. National Center for Education Statistics. Retrieved Sept. 14, 2004, from http://nces.ed.gov/pubs2003/2003017.pdf.

3 SHIFTING LIBRARY RESOURCES

CHAPTER OVERVIEW

- Setting the Stage for a New Show
- Leadership
- Planning
- Work Flow and Organizational Structure
- Shifting Staff Roles and Responsibilities
- Communication
- Financial Shifts

SETTING THE STAGE FOR A NEW SHOW

A library that manages change well will manage electronic journals well (or at least, better than a library that does not manage change well!). Looking ahead to the integration of electronic journals into collections, services, and the workflow of the library, the task seems enormous—and it is. Once the pieces are in place, there is a strong desire to keep them there. But you will find that processes evolve. Procedures that work well when you are providing 200 electronic journals will need to be adjusted when you are providing 2,000 electronic journals. And by the time you have 20,000 electronic journals, your library will have been transformed into a very different kind of organization.

To provide a significant quantity of electronic journals to your users means that even if you can outsource some of the management tasks, a large proportion of your library's staff will still have to take on some new responsibilities, and some positions may need to be completely reconfigured. The Drexel University Library has moved rapidly into an online-only journal environment. According to the dean (Montgomery and Sparks, 2000), "Almost no area of library operations has been left untouched by the migration from print to electronic journals." See Figure 3–1 for Drexel's assessment of the impact of the migration on staffing (Montgomery and King, 2002, 10). Libraries at a beginning stage in the transformation can learn a great deal from the experiences of early adopters of electronic journals.

FIGURE 3–1. Drexel's Transition

The Transiion from Print to Electronic Journals: Changes in Staffing and Other Costs

Department	Activity	Impact
Circulation/access	Reshelving	Reduced staffing
	Stack maintenance	Reduced staffing
	User photocopying	Reduced use & revenue
	Collecting use data	Reduced staffing
Reserve	Article file maintenance	Reduced staffing
	Article checkout	Reduced staffing
	Maintaining e-reserves	Increased staffing
Technical services	Print journal check-in	Reduced staffing
	E-journal acquisitions	Increased staffing
	Claiming	Reduced staffing
	Binding	Reduced staffing
	Binding	Reduced bindery costs
	Cataloging print	Reduced staffing
	Cataloging print	Reduced OCLC charges
	Cataloging e-journals	Increased staffing
	Cataloging e-journals	Increased OCLC staffing
	Catalog/e-journal list maintenance	Increased staffing
	Print subscriptions	Reduced costs
	Electronic subscriptions	Increased costs
Information services	Reference at desk	Increased staffing
	Instruction/promotion	Increased staffing
	Preparing documentation	Increased staffing
	Journal selection	Increased staffing
Document delivery	Faculty copy service	Reduced staffing
	Interlibrary loan—borrowing	Reduced staff costs
	Interlibrary loan—borrowing	Reduced vendor charges
Systems	Infrastucture purchase	Increased equipment costs
	Infrastructure maintenance	Increased staffing
	Infrastructure maintenance	Increased contract costs
	Negotiating contracts	Increased staffing
	Setting up access	Increased staffing
	Developing decision support tools	Increased staffing
	Collecting use data	Increased staffing
	Printing	Increased costs & revenue
Space utilization	Occupying space	Decreased space needs
Administration	Managing the change	Increased staffing
	Attention to decisions	Increased staffing
	Budgeting	Increased staffing

Re-engineering the workflow will require leadership and good communication. To best absorb the impact of e-journals, individual staff and the library as a whole must be as flexible as possible. Long-range plans will still have their place for other purposes, but any detailed plan for managing electronic journals will be obsolete within a year, if not sooner.

Halfway (or further) into a plan that was chosen as the best or the only approach, another method might suddenly make better sense, based on internal or external factors such as a new integrated library system (ILS) module, a new outsourcing option, or new cataloging standards. Abandoning a process can be hard on the morale of those who worked so hard to get halfway to the goal that no longer exists. So each new process should be approached with a provisional spirit.

Written policies and procedures will make everyone's job easier, but they must be adaptable and frequently re-examined. As user expectations change, so will your electronic journal services.

LEADERSHIP

The single most important factor for success in migrating to electronic journals, as with any new initiative in a library, is leadership. However, all of the leadership does not have to come from the top administration. In fact, in some ways, it is better for leaders to emerge from other levels. In a library that is having a hard time getting started with the integration of electronic journals, almost any individual staff member, with the proper encouragement and support, should be able to grab onto an e-journal project and bring it far enough to form the nucleus of a group venture.

The ideal is for the library management to set goals and priorities for a transition to electronic journals that will be strongly supported by the administration of the library, the administration of the parent institution, and the entire library staff. Ideally, sufficient new funds and positions will be transfused into appropriate areas to guarantee a graceful transition.

Very few libraries have attained that ideal (especially the influx of new resources), so most of them must carry out their e-journal initiatives with the resources at hand, and will take advantage of leadership wherever it happens to be. Any of you reading this book could play a leadership role, no matter where you fit into whatever kind of library organization you are part of.

ADMINISTRATIVE LEADERSHIP

The dean or director of a library may provide leadership in developing electronic journal collections and services either (a) *directly,* through establishing priorities that make it very clear to the staff that electronic journals will take precedence over other formats and that managing them will take precedence over other work, or (b) *indirectly*, through

- establishing and promoting a user-focused vision that provides a framework and support for staff members at all levels to adjust priorities and shift their workload in order to provide new resources and services,
- encouraging the development of new approaches, and
- supporting and rewarding initiative and leadership at any level of the library.

Whether the direct or indirect approach is best for your library will depend on its culture, the strengths and weaknesses of the organizational structure, the amount of mutual respect between the administration and the staff, the top administrator's management style, and the staff's propensity for change. Indirect leadership can be more effective because it instills ownership of the project in the people who are carrying it out, but it may not provide enough momentum for such a major shift.

Electronic journals require so much reallocation of staff and financial resources that if there was ever a justification for the use of a top-down mandate, this may be it. Tyranny is not recommended, but if all else fails, the commander in chief may have to assert his or her will, unnatural and unusual as that may feel to those with a more collaborative leadership style. Ongoing building of trust will pay off when a library director needs to ask the staff to make major changes in their job descriptions.

MANAGERIAL LEADERSHIP AND COORDINATION

In a mid-sized or larger library, a middle manager might appropriately take the lead in activating e-journals. Whether "the" leader of an initiative or "a" leader in the chain of command, the middle manager is in a position to provide opportunities to build consensus, to help set library-wide goals, and to communicate up, down, and across the hierarchy. A division director or department head may have a flexible or elastic enough schedule to be able to personally undertake, or at least coordinate, the initial stages of the project, or to initiate a pilot project within a reporting unit.

GRASSROOTS LEADERSHIP

If a library is organized traditionally (that is, in functional divisions or subject-related divisions), there may not be an existing logical grouping of individuals to take the responsibility for acquiring and organizing electronic journals. Whereas cross-functional, team-based libraries may simply be able to define a new team, in most libraries a group of individuals representing different departments or teams might be designated to explore some options, draft a plan, or propose some policies or procedures for electronic journals. This group could be an ad hoc committee, a permanent team, or work group that will carry out the plan or the procedures. From this group a leader may emerge, someone who is interested and enthusiastic and undaunted by the challenges of e-journals. This type of leader could also emerge from the ranks without being part of a designated group.

Should an e-journal enthusiast who works well with others come forth, it would make sense to redefine that individual's position to be a full-time e-journal or e-resource coordinator. If overall coordination is difficult to manage with the existing staff, it would make sense to define and fill a new position (which might mean redefining an unrelated vacant position).

PLANNING

Just because long-range planning for electronic journals is impractical does not mean that a library should forego all planning. E-journals should be part of a library's larger plan that will allocate or transfer the necessary resources.

Your library may be required by its parent entity to produce a formal plan or a component of a master plan. That is your opportunity to articulate your library's vision for enhancing online services for users, saving their time, increasing their productivity, improving their competitive edge—whatever will further the mission of the parent organization.

As you outline the costs and benefits of electronic journals, you should be able to demonstrate that an initial investment in the conversion to electronic formats (extra staff, temporary duplication of content in print and electronic formats, training, software) will result in long-term cost savings for the organization (lower cost-per-use for materials, decrease in space requirements, etc.).

For your own internal purposes, a planning process can focus group thinking and initiate communication. A planning document can serve as a road map, a gauge to measure progress, a target, or even something to laugh at—later. (Of course, that should not be the intention!) A planning document should be no longer and no more elaborate than it needs to be, and the planning process should not divert energy from the "doing" process.

BROAD-BASED PARTICIPATION

Developing a specific plan for developing a collection of electronic journals provides the opportunity to bring people together from all the areas that will be affected by the new collection, giving these individuals a chance to begin working as a group. Involving those whose work will be affected not only distributes the burden of planning and draws upon more brain power, but also broadens the ownership of the plan.

PHASED PLANS

To get from point A (no e-journal offerings) to point B (rich, multi-faceted access to a robust collection of e-journals), or to progress along that trajectory from any point along the way, you might want to aim for a series of short-range targets. For example, your plan might enhance access to electronic journals through the following distinct stages (although keep in mind that this is not absolute):

1. A Web page with links to full-text databases and home pages of licensed e-journal publishers and hosts (keep this phase short!)
2. An alphabetical list—constructed and updated manually—that integrates the individual e-journals in your full-text databases and those from other sources, with links to the journals' tables of contents pages when possible
3. A database of your e-journal titles that can be used to generate and update an alphabetical Web list in a more automated way, perhaps with a search interface for users
4. Web lists of your electronic journals grouped into subject categories in addition to your alphabetical listing
5. Alphabetical and subject lists of journals that include information about the dates for full-text coverage

As staff knowledge and experience increases, each step will build on the preceding steps. Users will have some level of access while the staff is developing the next level. Staff morale and confidence will benefit from a sense of accomplishment in completing each stage.

The above list will not be suitable for every library. A certain amount of extra effort is required to maintain a separate e-journal database, and many libraries will choose instead to use the catalog as the master e-journal database from which Web lists will be generated, or one master database that generates Web pages and catalog records. See Chapter 7 for an in-depth discussion of access options and procedures.

WORK FLOW AND ORGANIZATIONAL STRUCTURE

As you think about the new tasks to be absorbed into the library work flow in acquiring, managing, and providing access to electronic journals (along with other online resources and services), you may realize that your library's organizational structure no longer makes sense.

ABSORBING NEW PROCESSES

A survey on staffing reported in *Serials Review* (Duranceau and Hepfer, 2002) identified 12 acquisition-oriented functions for electronic resource management, many of which bear little or no resemblance to acquisition functions for print resources:

- Acquisition/purchase process
- Licensing
- Setting up access
- Solving invoicing and payment problems
- Cataloging and doing OPAC work
- Managing records and maintaining non-OPAC systems
- Managing proxy-server
- Managing union lists
- Troubleshooting access problems
- Providing systems support
- Monitoring the site
- Setting up and maintaining links to e-journals from I & A databases

The authors of that article acknowledge other processes that are not acquisitions oriented, and, therefore, are not included in their survey:

- Selection
- Marketing
- User instruction
- Collection and analysis of usage statistics

We could list other possible new functions as well:

- Maintenance of link-resolver system(s)
- Configuration of broadcast searching system(s)
- Management of a current awareness service
- Participation in consortial meetings and discussions
- Local configuration of vendor interfaces
- Negotiation with intermediaries and service providers

Most of the libraries that responded to the survey have absorbed the new functions by distributing them among many departments. Several reported the use of a team approach to maintain communication channels in a distributed system. One of the major conclusions of the study was that no library has adequate staffing to cope with e-journals; nevertheless, all of the responding libraries had found some way to forge ahead.

MAJOR REORGANIZATION VERSUS INCREMENTAL REORGANIZATION

If you have the authority to initiate a major reorganization in a mid-sized to large library, you might be tempted to create an electronic resources department in order to consolidate most of the above functions and optimize the workflow. Some libraries have been successful in doing this. But managing e-resources requires a range of expertise, so you will have to reassign staff from acquisitions, cataloging, serials, collection development, reference, Web-development and systems areas; and, as electronic resources and services continue to expand, this new department might ultimately devour a large portion of the library.

Some libraries, recognizing the complexity of e-resource management, have dispersed the responsibilities throughout several departments. Each library has a unique situation, and no one solution will work for every library.

- A survey on the impact of electronic journals on staff in member libraries of the Association of Research Libraries (ARL) (Gardner, 2001) found that "Reorganization did occur, albeit often informally; departments in general became less clearly defined and more dynamic" (p. 28).
- A reorganization at the Massachusetts Institute of Tech-

nology (MIT) Libraries shifted the responsibility for managing electronic resources from one unit to three, and from two part-time positions to parts of six other positions, adding the equivalent of an additional full-time employee (FTE) (Duranceau and Hepfer, 2002).

- The University of Buffalo Libraries created five new e-resource-oriented positions: two that were new, and three that were reassignments (Duranceau and Hepfer, 2002).
- The University of California, Irvine, established a cross-divisional working group of managers who have absorbed the responsibilities of managing e-journals within their units. The library has created a position for an electronic resources acquisitions librarian by redefining a current position (Goldberg and McAdam, 2002).
- In 2002, the University of Wisconsin's subject-based technical services structure was "deconstructed" to functional departments, partly as a result of "the growing impact of electronic resources that crossed subject lines and required complex licenses and greater expertise and control over acquisitions-related work" (Blake, 2002, p. 333).
- The University of Nevada, Reno, Libraries leapt rapidly into the electronic journal world without new positions. In the early days, a group of managers met regularly to strategize and assign tasks to staff. One vacant position was redefined to become the "electronic-resources access librarian" position, and duties were permanently adjusted in several other positions as the collection grew. Figure 3–2 illustrates the shift in staff responsibilities.
- Systems librarians at the University of North Carolina, Greensboro, developed a sophisticated e-journal management database called JournalFinder, which grew into a project that required more staff. Eventually, five positions were devoted to maintaining the database.

It is important to consider whether the benefits of a major reorganization will outweigh the disruption and potential stress for the organization. If the timing is right, a reorganization can energize a library and solve some of its personnel problems. However, a successful reorganization takes time, resources, and broad participation, and most libraries cannot afford it while they are racing to keep up with rapidly changing user expectations. Moreover, a major reorganization in response to technological changes just amplifies the changes and can exacerbate some of the staff's feelings of vulnerability, resulting in unnecessary trauma. Technology keeps changing, so the new organizational structure may

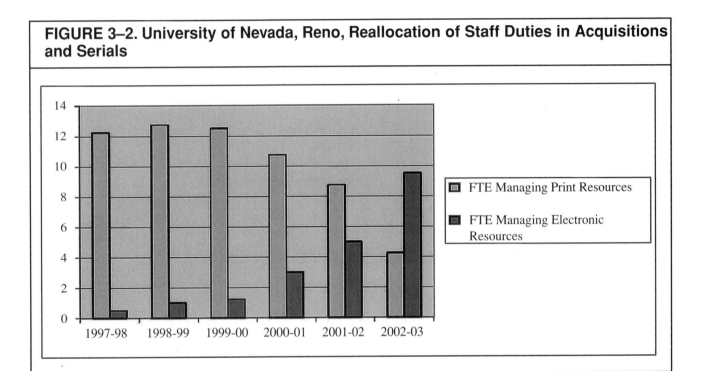

FIGURE 3–2. University of Nevada, Reno, Reallocation of Staff Duties in Acquisitions and Serials

not hold up over time. A more common approach these days is to reorganize incrementally.

Incremental reorganization can have a dramatic effect over time without the risk of traumatizing an organization or taking attention away from the challenges at hand. There are many incremental measures that will effect considerable change:

- Defining and receiving new electronic-resource-oriented positions
- Significantly redefining all vacant positions
- Refocusing departmental and individual goals
- Identifying duties that are no longer necessary
- Adjusting position descriptions
- Reassigning strategic individuals
- Deploying cross-functional committees, work groups, or teams
- Providing incentives and rewards for staff who take on new responsibilities and exhibit leadership and problem-solving behavior

SHIFTING STAFF ROLES AND RESPONSIBILITIES

Whether shifts are sudden and dramatic or gradual and organic, your organizational structure will need to change in order to accommodate electronic journals.

NEW AND REDEFINED POSITIONS

A fortunate library will be successful in advocating for additional positions to manage electronic journals. However, most libraries will be compelled to redefine vacant positions or occupied positions.

Coordinator Role

To pull all of the many pieces of e-journal management together and provide a focus on electronic resources, a number of libraries have created a new position or redefined an existing position to manage the process. An increasing number of job ads are posted for these new positions, for example:

- Electronic resources coordinator
- Electronic services librarian
- Electronic acquisitions librarian
- Electronic products and serials librarian
- Electronic access/serials librarian
- Electronic resources manager
- Science librarian for electronic publishing
- Electronic technical services coordinator

Reporting lines for these positions vary and may be in collection development, acquisitions, cataloging, systems, or almost any library department. The cross-functional nature of electronic resource management contributes to the further blurring of lines between units.

A "coordinator" position has a great deal of appeal to individuals who want to make a difference or to lead a new initiative without having to be burdened with managerial tasks such as supervision and evaluation of staff, especially if the compensation is also attractive. Coordinating without supervising has its pitfalls, so the person in this position should have exceptional communication skills, tact, and the ability and institutional support to be a leader and a decision maker.

Taking Advantage of Staff Talent

Some public institutions are constrained by a system of rigid position descriptions that cannot be adjusted on the basis of the skills of the occupant of the position, though most systems allow positions to be redefined in terms of changes in institutional priorities. Redefining or upgrading a position based on the incumbent's talents and interests can be risky—should the person in the customized position leave the library, you may have a hard time finding someone else who is a good match for the job. However, not making adjustments that will allow a talented and interested person on your staff to contribute to your e-journal initiative would be wasteful, and might even result in that person leaving the library for other opportunities.

During a major adjustment of your priorities, you cannot afford not to match the abilities of your existing staff to your needs, and to compensate staff adequately for assuming a higher level of responsibility. Be creative, and use all possible legal workarounds to overcome bureaucratic personnel restrictions without violating the intent of the restrictions (fairness, diversity, nondiscrimination).

ADDITION AND SUBTRACTION

A crucial element of assigning the tasks and duties of processing e-journal subscriptions to existing positions is deciding what tasks and duties will be reduced or eliminated or handled differently. This is where strong and wise leadership makes a difference. A step-by-step approach is sometimes best. An incremental redefinition of individual positions reduces disorientation and stress for staff. Changes in job duties can also be introduced on a trial basis.

Trials for New Procedures

The University of Nevada, Reno, has become somewhat infamous in serials circles for the decision to stop checking in issues of print journals in order to better concentrate on providing faster processing of and better access to e-journals. Administrators felt that an inordinate amount of time was being spent on a decreasingly important part of the collection.

Abandoning check-in seemed just as wrong to some of the staff as it does to most serials people who hear about it for the first time; in fact, some staff were passionately opposed to the idea. In response to staff concerns, the new system was introduced as a pilot project. Staff were reassured that if the results were as dire as they predicted, they would resume checking in the issues as soon as the mistake became obvious.

The pilot project was considered a success, the results were not dire, and some of the strongest opponents now agree that there has been little negative impact on users. In fact, access to current print journals has even improved because issues reach the shelves earlier. Some problems that would be identified during the check-in process get overlooked, but the problems that affect access are usually brought to the attention of the staff and corrected at that point. And much more staff time is now available for e-journal tasks, as predicted.

Had staff concerns been brushed aside in a mandate, chances are good that those staff members would have remained negative about the discontinued process. If staff consensus had been required before initiating the new plan, it never would have been initiated.

Fine Tuning

New procedures are rarely implemented exactly according to the plan. Even the best planning process cannot anticipate all of the consequences of adjusting responsibilities, so everyone needs to understand in advance that alterations to the plan will not mean the plan has failed. This is not as simple as it sounds—because some of the staff may secretly hope that a new plan will fail.

TEAMWORK

An ad hoc committee, work group, or team operating within or alongside an existing structure will allow your library to experiment with different configurations and affiliations without your having to re-do personnel documents or disrupt reporting structures.

A designated team can

- draw upon cross-functional expertise,
- act as a communication conduit throughout the library,
- share the workload,
- generate synergy,
- build consensus from within,
- minimize internal conflict.

Overlaying a team structure upon an existing hierarchical structure will be more successful if policies clearly identify (1) the proportion of time that will be spent by members on team activities and (2) the method by which the team's work will be evaluated.

Careful selection of a team leader is also important, and may require some training or mentoring if the designated leader lacks experience as a manager.

STAFF TRAINING

Almost everyone in the library will benefit from some kind of training in the management or support of electronic journals. Trickle-down training is the most efficient. An electronic-resources coordinator will come to know something about all aspects of the process, and one of the major responsibilities for this position should be to determine training needs for the rest of the library's participants and to conduct some of the in-house training. Someone who is reassigned or appointed to a coordinator position will generally have a strong interest in electronic journals and some experience in at least one aspect of their management, and filling in the knowledge gaps should be the highest priority.

In a library that doesn't have an e-journal coordinator, managers will need to develop a training plan for the staff who are assuming new roles and responsibilities. There is a variety of ways to learn about e-journal management and user support:

- Reading the professional literature (including how-to books!)
- Using Web-based tutorials (free or fee based)
- Exploring other libraries' Web sites
- Attending conferences, teleconferences, and pre-conference workshops
- Subscribing to discussion lists, browsing list archives
- Visiting libraries that are farther along with e-journal management
- Accepting vendors' offers for on-site or remote demos and training
- Utilizing the traveling workshops sponsored by OCLC regional affiliated networks

Discussion Lists for Continuing Education

E-mail discussion lists can be an important tool for keeping up-to-date with developments in the e-journal world. Most library discussion lists keep archives that are searchable, though in some cases (identified with *), only listserv subscribers can view them:

- **ERIL** * (Electronic Resources in Libraries): www.arches.uga.edu/~jconger/ERIL/ (includes links to resources)

- **ARL-EJOURNAL** (E-Journals in Libraries): www.cni.org/ Hforums/arl-ejournal/
- **Liblicense-l** (Electronic Content Licensing for Academic and Research Libraries): www.library.yale.edu/~llicense/ index.shtml (includes links to resources)
- **SERIALST** (Serials in Libraries Discussion Forum): www.uvm.edu/~bmaclenn/serialst.html
- **AUTOCAT** * (cataloging and authority control in libraries): http://ublib.buffalo.edu/libraries/units/cts/autocat/
- **ACQNET** (acquisitions and collection development; includes links to resources): www.infomotions.com/serials/ acqnet
- **Web4Lib**: http://sunsite.berkeley.edu/Web4Lib/

In addition to these lists, vendors have mailing lists designed around their products, to answer questions from customers, to inform customers of new enhancements and underused features, and to help users network. ILS user group lists are especially useful for continuing education. These are some of the major ILS discussion lists:

- **Innopac List**: www.innopacusers.org/list/
- VTLS Users Group (**VUG List**): www.vtls.com/Support/ listservs.shtml
- **ALEPH-NA** (Aleph users of North America): www.naaug.org/contact/lists.html#alephna
- **Voyager-L**: http://voyager.ship.edu/voyagerl/

Some functions of electronic journal management require special training, especially licensing and cataloging.

Licensing Training
- The Liblicense Web site (www.library.yale.edu/~llicense/ index.shtml) provides many good resources for independent learners who want to learn about licensing.
- ARL's Online Lyceum sponsors a formal online course: "Licensing Review and Negotiation" (www.arl.org/training/licensing.html). ARL also sponsors advanced workshops for librarians. You will find them listed at www.arl.org/scomm/licensing/index.html.
- ALA's Office for Information Technology Policy sponsors online tutorials. See www.ala.org/ala/washoff/oitp/ oitpofficeinformation.htm#tutor.

Electronic Serials Cataloging Training

The Cooperative Online Serials organization (CONSER), a division of the Library of Congress, sponsors a Serials Cataloging Cooperative Training Program (SCCTP) consisting of five courses, including "Electronic Serials Cataloging." (See http://lcweb.loc.gov/acq/conser/scctp/home.html.) Trainers are located all over the U.S. and Canada and in Mexico. Libraries volunteer to sponsor the training sessions and make the necessary arrangements. The e-serials class covers the following topics:

- Definition of an electronic serial and how it is different from a print serial and from other electronic resources
- E-serials cataloging
- Providing access to e-serial aggregations/packages
- CONSER single-record approach
- Title, location, format changes
- Complex cataloging situations

Other Training Needs

In a report of a recent survey (ALCTS Continuing Education Task Force, 2003), catalogers identified the nontechnical skills or qualities needed to deal with digital projects:

- Work flow analysis (78.7%)
- Team building (74.3%)
- Project leadership (72.7%)
- Time management (71.1%)
- Negotiation skills (60.4%)
- Presentation skills (56.7%)
- Statistical analysis (40.1%)
- Other skills (grant writing, written communication, budgeting, etc.) (13.9%)

Cross Training

You won't want your e-journal processing to grind to a halt because one person is sick, on vacation, or no longer works for the library. Staff should be trained to provide backup for each other in the case of an emergency. Written documentation of all processes will help in the training of co-workers, and will provide valuable help to the person who will be doing an unfamiliar task on an irregular basis.

REWARDS AND INCENTIVES

Depending on the library's institutional context, you may or may not be able to modify your evaluation and reward system to reflect your library's changing values. If your system of evaluation is based on measures of output and productivity, you will have a hard time convincing staff to spend time designing new procedures and developing policies, especially if some of the new work is not as quantifiable as the old work.

However, in a time of change, you don't want staff to be afraid of the consequences of making mistakes. In most systems of evaluation you will be able to identify, acknowledge, document, and reward activities that show initiative, leadership, and problem-solving abilities. Risk taking is more difficult to define. A positive spirit and the willingness to try new approaches should definitely be rewarded if you can do so within your system. If you can't use monetary rewards, you can always let the innovators know they are valued and that they are doing something that will make a difference in users' lives.

COMMUNICATION

It is highly unlikely that every person who works in your library will agree with all the decisions and new priorities regarding electronic journals or the resulting changes in their job responsibilities. Participatory planning ensures a certain amount of staff buy-in, but you can't afford to wait for everyone's blessing, especially since it is likely that you will never persuade some of the staff members that you're not making a big mistake in shifting resources to electronic formats.

However, some of your skeptics and critics will eventually be convinced by frequent exposure to the logic behind the changes that affect them. Justifications are generally not internalized by those who don't believe them, but a combination of seeing positive or well-received results and hearing again the reasons for changing can convert a nonbeliever.

Just as new services need to be republicized frequently in order to catch users at a receptive moment, internal explanations of new goals and priorities should be reiterated at regular intervals. The persistent question in the back of some people's minds will be **Why?** To maintain or rebuild staff morale, leaders should feel comfortable discussing certain issues and should be prepared to address typical unspoken concerns, as well as chanting the vision mantra as often as necessary.

FREQUENTLY UNASKED QUESTIONS ABOUT NEW PRIORITIES, WITH SUGGESTED ANSWERS

Q: *What if electronic journals are just a fad?*
A: They are definitely not a fad; they are here to stay and users will value them and use them heavily as long as they are easy to find and use. The Web will replace the library unless the library can find a meaningful role in relation to the Web.

Q: *What if this experiment doesn't work?*
A: Making e-journals available to our users may seem experimental in the beginning, and some of our plans may need adjusting after they are in place, but any kind of access is better than no access. Procedures can be refined (or more likely totally revamped) later to improve access. Nothing will be lost as processes are improved.

Q: *By prioritizing electronic journals, aren't we favoring some disciplines over other disciplines that don't make heavy use of e-journals?*
A: Some academic disciplines embraced electronic journals earlier than other disciplines, but most journals in all disciplines will be online very soon. Some predict that in five years, all journals will be available in electronic format.

Q: *Why provide access to free electronic journals when we have a backlog of uncataloged books and other materials we have paid for?*
A: Some e-journals that are freely available or free with print subscriptions will be in higher demand than some of the purchased materials that are in the queue for cataloging. Furthermore, if you want to build a critical mass of e-journals to satisfy users, high-quality free e-journals will make a difference.

Q: *Why should we drop everything to fix an access problem for an electronic journal when other mistakes in the catalog are not always fixed immediately?*
A: Solving access problems with e-journals should be a high priority because

- problems are generally detected and reported by someone who wants to use the journal;
- a problem with one e-journal may signal a problem with

many other e-journals from the same source; and
- when new services are rolled out, we want them to work. Frustrated users may not give us a second chance.

Q: *If we devote our time to making electronic resources available, won't we have a bigger backlog of books and other materials that need cataloging?*
A: Decisions about e-journal processing should be made with the full recognition that some of the library's other materials may not be accessible. As the remote use of library collections and services increases, user contact with library staff and browsing of the physical collection will decrease, so it becomes even more important to provide online intellectual access to physical items, despite the demands of e-journal access.

- Rush processing should always be an option for any materials that are in demand or time sensitive.
- Switching to core-level and collection-level cataloging for other backlogs can keep those materials moving through the pipeline.
- Outside-the-catalog listings or Web-based accession databases might provide acceptable temporary or permanent access to backlogged materials.
- Strategic links from the catalog to existing finding aids or accession databases can provide inexpensive and satisfactory granular access to uncataloged materials.

If it appears that the library is turning its back on tangible items that have already been purchased in favor of intangible, unstable resources that are licensed (or free), it is only natural for some staff to question the new priorities. Certainly in the first rush to incorporate electronic journals into the library's catalog or Web pages, it will appear (and it will be true to a certain extent) that the library is abandoning some of its quality-control functions. For example, catalog records for journals in an aggregator database that have been downloaded from the vendor's site or acquired from a secondary service and uploaded into the catalog may not list holdings in a standard format. Or a record may not include earlier titles for the journal. A library database of e-journal titles imported from vendors' sites for the purpose of creating e-journal Web pages may include some titles that are commonly used but not officially correct.

Concerns about lower standards and abandoned processes may be the most difficult in terms of morale. Library staff identify with their work and take pride in what they have accomplished.

A sudden shift away from previous priorities can leave them feeling disoriented, demoralized, and uncertain about the worth of their past and future contributions.

The quality of cataloging and indexing in most libraries is something staff can be proud of. Careful work, attention to detail, and rule-based behavior have traditionally been valued qualities in library employees. It can be difficult to accept that the work you have been doing eight hours a day for years is suddenly considered irrelevant or too costly for the library to maintain. Difficult though it may be to accept, some library staff may need to be retrained to favor speed and efficiency over perfection, and to use common sense in the absence of rules. The following are questions staff are likely to ask followed by answers administrators might give.

Q: *If I will be working with electronic journals, how will my other work get done?*
A: We can no longer afford to continue doing some of the traditional library work, and it is no longer as important to users. In order to stay relevant to them, and in order to survive in a changing information environment, we need to devote our efforts to new priorities.

Q: *If the library has decided to stop doing a process that was my entire job, does that mean my previous work is worthless and I have wasted years of my time?*
A: Adopting new priorities does not mean that previous priorities were inappropriate at the time. The richness and accuracy of the catalog will still be valued, and classification skills will still be useful in providing access to electronic resources.

Q: *Having been valued for my attention to detail and trained to be meticulous, how can I in good conscience carry out batch processes that will result in errors we may not catch?*
A: Processing electronic journals requires careful work, too, though it may not be carried out on an item-by-item basis. There will be new ways to catch or search for errors, and the relative simplicity of e-journal records and listings makes them less error-prone. Mass production has its own rewards. It may not be something we want to celebrate, but we can't ignore the fact that users have been conditioned by the Web to accept a certain measure of error, and for the vast majority of users, it is much more valuable for new e-journals to be made available quickly than for records to be reviewed for minor inaccuracies before they are released. Records can be fixed when access problems are identified.

Q: *If we outsource some of the maintenance of our e-journal holdings, will we lose all control over the quality of our catalog?*
A: We will lose some control of the quality of a catalog that is populated by records we do not create ourselves. However, our business partners also value quality, and any errors we help them correct will also benefit users of other libraries. Likewise, other libraries using the same services will catch errors that will be corrected on our behalf as well as theirs.

Q: *Why are we using new cataloging standards that are clearly inferior to the old standards for providing information to users?*
A: Full cataloging is not necessarily superior to abbreviated cataloging for electronic full-text items. Catalog records that are surrogates for books and other materials in the physical library are generally most useful when they supply as much information as possible to help users know what to expect, especially in describing the content. Seeing a book's assigned subject headings, its length, and whether it has illustrations could help someone decide whether to make a trip to the library for the book. Having the table of contents or a synopsis of the book helps even more. But a catalog record for a full-text journal is the gateway to the journal, and too much information in the record can be an impediment. It is easy for the user to get more information by clicking into the resource itself.

Q: *What's in it for me?*
A: Well . . . the satisfaction of helping the library move forward, and maybe saving it from extinction. The knowledge that you will be making library users very happy. And a chance to polish your problem-solving skills.

INTERNAL COMMUNICATION

There is no getting around the need for meetings among the key participants in managing e-journals. At the University of Nevada, Reno, our new electronic resources access librarian called a series of meetings for all the players in the e-journal process soon after her arrival. The meetings brought together people from two distinct departments (with distinct mind-sets), acquisitions/serials and cataloging.

Beginning at the beginning of the processing cycle (ordering the different types of e-journals), the people involved in each step explained their duties in detail to the others. The participants asked each other questions, and as the meetings progressed, everyone gained a much deeper understanding of the big picture and the details, and some processes were improved through group thinking. The group identified and solved several problems. Systems and reference people were invited to some of the meetings to provide input and for their own edification.

Detailed notes from each meeting were sent to all participants and to their supervisors and other interested parties in the library. After the final meeting, a flow chart for the current processes and for the planned next phase were shared with administrators and public services librarians in a larger and more general meeting, and procedural documents were posted on the intranet for future reference. One advantage of a series of meetings like these is that they come to an end. Subsequent communication can be more targeted and informal because everyone knows exactly who is responsible for what, and a shared vocabulary has been developed.

FINANCIAL SHIFTS

It is important for several reasons to continue to try to predict and to document the cost of shifting from print journals to electronic journals. The main reasons are budgeting and accountability. It is also very difficult both to predict and to document the comparative expenses for the two formats.

COMPARISONS OF PRINT AND ELECTRONIC COSTS

Most libraries can document a shift from print indexes to electronic databases over the past several years. However, accounting systems can go haywire when electronic journal packages enter the picture. Libraries that have been tracking database and journal subscriptions with subject or departmental codes find that this system doesn't accommodate multisubject packages of electronic journals.

Consider the library's accounting nightmare when a publisher changes a pricing model from a subscription fee for print journals with add-on charges for electronic access to the "flip model," wherein a content fee is paid for electronic subscriptions with add-on charges (or "deep discounts") for print issues. If payments for electronic resources and print resources are coded differently, then reports of financial activity in these categories could be wildly skewed from one year to the next for the same product. Other factors make it difficult to compare costs for print and electronic journals as well:

- Electronic subscriptions often include several years of backfiles.
- Backfiles for e-journals may be sold separately, as a one-time purchase.
- A one-time purchase of electronic journal backfiles might also require an annual "maintenance fee."
- Access fees might be paid to a hosting site that are separate from the subscription fees paid to publishers.
- Consortial purchases may include a "buy-in" fee or a coordinator's fee.
- Federated-searching or link-resolver software might generate new expenses related to electronic journals.
- MARC records or customized reports of your library's e-journals might be purchased from a vendor or intermediary.
- Binding costs should be included as a print journal expense.
- Space considerations represent real costs that can be saved by discarding print in favor of electronic journals.

It is not impossible to untangle and track the expenses related to print journals and e-journals, but doing so will be yet another staff responsibility that did not exist in the print-only world. Chapter 6 discusses tools and methods for tracking some of the costs.

OTHER COST SHIFTS

A recent *D-Lib Magazine* article (Montgomery and King, 2002) reports on a careful study of the comparative costs of purchasing and maintaining print and electronic journal collections. The per-title cost is based on five figures:

- space costs (shelves and rental of equivalent space, over 25 years)
- systems costs (hardware and software)
- supplies and services (including binding)
- staff, and
- subscriptions

The overall **per-title cost** for Drexel averaged

- $62 for electronic journals;
- $100 per print journal.

Divided by actual usage statistics, the **cost-per-use** average was

- $2.00 for electronic journals;
- $17.50 for print journals.

The exact costs would differ from lilbrary to library, but the model for determining the costs could be used by any library. Analyzing the impacts of the shift from print journals to electronic journals is another new task for someone in your library. Cost-benefit results such as Drexel's (which are presented in conjunction with the positive results of a readership survey) will convince both staff and administrators that new efforts are worth the short-term costs and difficulties. A Council on Library and Information Resources (CLIR) analysis of the relative costs of processing and managing electronic and print in several libraries concluded that long-term cost savings for e-journals would be significant enough to allow libraries to bear the major costs of archiving electronic journals (Schonfeld, King, Okerson, and Fenton, 2004). See Chapter 9 for more information on evaluating your own e-journal collection and services.

REFERENCES

ALCTS Continuing Education Task Force. 2003, August 8. "Cataloging for the 21st Century: A Proposal for Continuing Education for Cataloging Professionals." Submitted to the ALCTS Advisory Task Force on the LC Action Plan for Bibliographic Control of Web Resources, August 8, 2003. Retrieved Sept. 20, 2004, from http://darkwing.uoregon.edu/~chixson/cetf/CETFpublic.html.

Blake, Julie C. 2002. "The 2002 Acquisitions Institute at Timberline Lodge: Session 8." *Serials Review* 28, no. 4: 333

Duranceau, Ellen F., and Cindy Hepfer. 2002. "Staffing for Electronic Resource Management: The Results of a Survey." *Serials Review* 28, no. 4: 316–320.

Gardner, Susan. 2001. "The Impact of Electronic Journals on Library Staff at ARL Member Institutions: A Survey and Critique of the Survey Methodology." *Serials Review* 27, nos. 3/4: 17–32.

Goldberg, Sylvia M., and Timothy McAdam. 2002. "A Collaborative Approach for Processing Electronic Resources at the University of California, Irvine." *Technical Services Quarterly* 20, no. 2: 21–32.

Montgomery, Carol H., and Donald W. King. 2002. "Comparing Library and User Related Costs of Print and Electronic Journal Collections: A First Step towards a Comprehensive Analysis." *D-Lib Magazine* 8, no. 10 (October). Retrieved Sept. 20, 2004, from www.dlib.org/dlib/october02/montgomery/10montgomery.html.

Montgomery, Carol H., and JoAnne L. Sparks. 2000. "The Transition to an Electronic Journal Collection: Managing the Organizational Changes." *Serials Review* 26, no. 3: 4–18.

Schonfeld, Roger C., Donald W. King, Ann Okerson, and Eileen Gifford Fenton. 2004. *The Nonsubscription Side of Periodicals: Changes in Library Operations and Costs between Print and Electronic Formats.* Washington, DC: Digital Library Foundation, Council on Library and Information Resources. Retrieved Sept. 20, 2004, from www.clir.org/pubs/reports/pub127/pub127.pdf.

MORE INFORMATION SERVICES

Alan, Robert, and Nan Butkovich. 2003. "Libraries in Transition: Impact of Print and Electronic Journal Access." *Against the Grain* 15, no. 2: 32, 34.

Anderson, Rick, and Steven D. Zink. 2003. "Implementing the Unthinkable: The Demise of Periodical Check-In at the University of Nevada." *Library Collections, Acquisitions, and Technical Services* 27, no. 1: 61–71.

Jordan, Mark, and Dave Kisly. 2002. "How Does Your Library Handle Electronic Serials? A General Survey." *Serials* 15 (March): 41–46.

Lugg, Rick, and Ruth Fischer. 2003. *Agents in Place: Intermediaries in E-Journal Management.* An R2 White Paper (October), written with support from Otto Harrassowitz KG, Wiesbaden, Germany. Retrieved Sept. 20, 2004, from www.ebookmap.net/pdfs/AgentsInPlace.pdf.

Montgomery, Carol H. 2000. "Measuring the Impact of an Electronic Journal Collection on Library Costs." *D-Lib Magazine* 6, no. 10 (October). Retrieved Sept. 20, 2004, from www.dlib.org/dlib/october00/montgomery/10montgomery.html.

Tumlin, Markel. 2003. "Is Check-In Checking Out?" *Serials Review* 29, no. 3: 224–229.

4 DEVELOPING A COLLECTION OF ELECTRONIC JOURNALS

CHAPTER OVERVIEW

- A Framework
- Collection Policies and Guidelines
- Building the Collection
- Individual Titles
- Aggregations and Bundles
- Access Options

Selecting electronic journals is the fun part of building a collection. But it is not easy! The marketplace is complex, the choices are confusing, and we worry about the long-term consequences of some of our decisions. The stakes are high in the migration to electronic formats. Having a plan that reflects your users' needs and your library's circumstances and values, and translating that plan into a collection policy for electronic journals will make the selection process much smoother and more consistent. No library's collection will include every e-journal, and no two libraries will have identical e-journal collections.

Chapter 4 suggests some approaches to collecting e-journals and introduces the elements of an e-journal collection and how to build one. The pricing of electronic journals is one of the major factors in building a collection, and also the most confusing. This chapter covers pricing in a basic way. You will find more detail on pricing models and negotiating your price in Chapter 6, along with approaches to renewal decisions for print and electronic journals. The terms of license agreements, the subject of Chapter 5, will also affect your selection decisions. Chapters 4, 5, and 6 together will give you a complete knowledge base for developing a collection of electronic journals.

A FRAMEWORK

Every library has its own set of circumstances that will shape its approach to acquiring electronic journals. Figure 4–1 categorizes some of the factors that will determine the character of the online collection. Some aspects of your environment will remain static, but changes in other conditions may well change your framework over time. Each library's combination of factors will be unique.

YOUR PRINT COLLECTION

Your type of library and the type(s) of users you serve will naturally influence the type and the scope of electronic journals you will collect. The subject coverage, the target audience, and some of the titles in your e-journal collection will be the same as what is in your print collection. The *size* of your existing print collection and other local collections will be a factor in your decision making for these reasons:

- Publishers often use the library's existing print subscriptions as the basis for pricing a collection of e-journals. Libraries with large print collections generally pay a large price for their electronic journal packages.
- A large print collection means that users already have access to journal literature whether your library moves quickly or slowly into the electronic journal environment.
- Package deals and other aggregations are attractive to libraries with a small print collection because access to journals will be greatly increased.
- If your library is in close proximity to a research library that has a mission to preserve a large print collection, you may feel more secure in disposing of print.
- If your library has a very small print collection, you may have to pay a "buy-in" fee to participate in a consortial deal.
- Your space situation—whether you have run out of stacks or storage space, will run out soon, or you have plenty of space—will also influence policies about electronic journals.

TIMING, SPEED, AND USER PREFERENCES

The desirability and the timing of a major e-journal deployment will depend in part on the readiness and the eagerness of your users. Their readiness will depend partially on the computer equip-

FIGURE 4–1. E-Journal Collection Policy Factors

Library type	Print collection	Users	Timing	Library values	Budget	Consortium
Research	Large	Ready	Electronic only	Big deal = evil	Ample funds	One
College	Small	Not ready	Gradual change	Preservation mission	Modest funds	Many
Public	Large nearby	Clamoring	Critical mass	Risk taking attitude	Static	Subsidizing
Specialized		Apathetic		Comprehensive	Shrinking	None
K-12		Equipped		Selective		
		Not equipped		No compromise on terms		

ment at their disposal and their willingness and ability to overcome technical obstacles. Their eagerness will most likely depend on what they would gain in the way of content. The library can employ different methods to influence both their readiness and their eagerness:

- Public relations initiatives
- Promotion of e-journal trials
- Communication with IT managers in the academic or corporate workplace concerning the infrastructure and support requirements for e-journals
- Training and demonstrations

... the library may be required to lead its users into new territory. They may not ask you to make the journey, but you can be assured that they won't ask you to turn back.

The studies reported in Chapter 2 demonstrate that academic users have not had major problems in making the adjustment to a new way of accessing journal literature. However, their appreciation for the convenience of desktop access generally comes after they have had some experience with e-journals, so your likelihood of gaining their support in advance will hinge on the access you can provide to new content.

If your users have been clamoring for electronic journals, or more electronic journals, you are in a better position to drop print subscriptions in favor of online access to more journals. If your users seem content with print journals and you rarely get a request for e-journals, it would be wise to let them get accustomed to the new format before removing the old format. Do not let your users' apathy or reluctance deter you from moving ahead with electronic journals. The tide has turned, the days are numbered for the print format; this is one of those times when the library may be required to lead its users into new territory. They may not ask you to make the journey, but you can be assured that they won't ask you to turn back.

LIBRARY VALUES

Before you can develop a policy for selecting and collecting e-journals, you may need to articulate some of your library's core values. Vegetarians will be able to prepare a tasty meal without meat, but it is more difficult for meat-eaters to cook for vegetarians. Philosophical discussions can be divisive, but ultimately, in order to proceed, the library needs a consistent position on the following issues:

- "Big Deal" transactions
- Support for alternative publishing
- Archiving versus access

Positions can shift over time as factors and participants change, but institutional values must be reflected in policies.

Bundling: What's the Big Deal?

One of the ways that libraries have managed to provide their users with electronic access to a significant number of additional scholarly journals is through arrangements with large publishers willing to provide all of their journals as a package, or bundle, at a price the library can afford (more information below and in Chapter 6). This model, which has come to be known as the "Big Deal," or "portfolio pricing," has sparked controversy in the library world, especially after the publication of a highly critical article by Ken Frazier of the University of Wisconsin in *D-Lib Magazine* (Frazier, 2001) highlighting the "dark side" of this model, especially in terms of the impact on attempts to change the scholarly communication paradigm. Before jumping into Big-Deal license agreements, you may want to consider the following arguments:

- Big-Deal licenses are generally three-year or even five-year commitments. On the plus side, the price for a large amount of additional content might be quite attractive, and price increases are capped at an agreed-upon percentage for the duration of the contract. The down side is that your library will have committed an increasing amount of its budget to that publisher for several years. To balance your budget, you may end up having to cancel a disproportionate number of journals from smaller, independent, and nonprofit publishers in order to pay for the Big Deals.
- The Big-Deal approach to collection development takes selection out of the hands of librarians and requires the library to pay for journals that are unneeded or unwanted. This argument presupposes that the library (1) has always had the means to select the journals that are needed and wanted and (2) knows exactly which journals are needed and wanted. Large research libraries subscribe to a large number of journals in print and may very well not gain access to many desirable new journals through a publisher's bundled offer, whereas smaller libraries stand to gain many new journals that are needed and wanted.
- Through bundling, lower-quality journals are able to maintain a subscription base that allows them to survive undeservedly. On the other hand, very specialized new journals that support emerging fields might not be able

to establish a sufficient subscription base in difficult economic times without the Big Deal. The enhanced exposure they receive through these deals helps feed emerging areas of research.

- If your library becomes unable to bear the cost of the bundled product, unbundling it will be painful for users as they lose access to many of the journals because of the much higher cost for individual titles.
- The Big-Deal model "obscures journal prices and reduces competition among individual titles from different publishers, contributing to the monopolistic trend of the market." (Van Orsdel and Born, 2003, p. 53). The bigger the publishers get through mergers, the bigger the bundle gets.
- Short-term benefits for your university through Big Deals may feed the long-term "serials crisis," jeopardizing (or delaying) the success of alternative models that might solve it.

Few libraries and library consortia have made the decision to boycott the Big Deal for the common good, though some have rejected it for their own economic reasons. Each library must weigh the potential benefits (which extend beyond price considerations to efficiencies in processing and other economies of scale, better searchability, and popularity with users) against moral arguments such as Frazier's. Some libraries would jeopardize their own future by withholding something their users want for philosophical reasons.

Support for Alternative Electronic Publishing

Though your library may join many others in participating in big deals for the advantages it gives your users, at the same time your policies could support the development of alternative cost-saving forms of scholarly publishing. Libraries that support scientific research have had little choice but to pay the steeply rising costs of journal subscriptions, at the expense of other materials and services. New journals that challenge overpriced core journals have met with early success, but to break the publishers' stranglehold will require larger efforts, including the transformation of the academic-reward system, which will take time, if it is even possible. If you want your library to help build the subscription base of some of the struggling start-ups, you may need to ensure that your policies do not interfere with long-range-investment collecting.

If the print version of an e-journal is the only version still available in 50 years, will it matter if the physical volumes are in your library or another library?

Archiving versus Access

Shifting library resources from print to electronic format makes preservationists nervous, and for good reasons. Considering the inefficiencies and economics of processing and paying for materials in two formats, we want to believe that the electronic version will be usable into the indefinite future, but difficult issues have not yet been resolved.

Despite the challenges that lie ahead in archiving electronic journals in such a way that the content will be preserved and will remain accessible to those who will use future technologies, some libraries are choosing electronic-only access to journal literature. Other libraries believe it is necessary to acquire and retain a paper backup for their electronic journals until the archiving challenges are met. Chances are good that e-journals from major publishers will remain accessible "in perpetuity," but chances are not so good that similar attention and expense will be devoted to the preservation of specialized, obscure, and independently published e-journals.

If your library is not a major research library, then you may already rely heavily on other libraries to loan and supply materials you lack. If the print version of an e-journal is the only version still available in 50 years, will it matter if the physical volumes are in your library or another library? Are there any e-journals that may not survive if your library does not take the responsibility for their preservation? These are important questions to think about before you develop an e-journal collection policy.

BUDGETARY FACTORS

The condition of your budget will influence your e-journal collection policy. An expanding budget gives you the freedom to experiment with new formats, but a shrinking budget also gives you an opportunity to justify uncomfortable changes based on cost-effectiveness (i.e., to implement "emergency measures"), and sometimes your budget woes will allow you to negotiate for a lower price from a vendor that wants your library's business. Replacing print journals with electronic journals can save your library money, and in a budget crisis, your users (and your staff) should be able to understand the need to make a quick transition.

An important consideration is whether your budget can absorb a shift of priorities. Most libraries need a few years of overlap between their print and electronic collections as they solve access problems and acclimatize users. During those years, extra funds are very helpful, whether they have been reserved for the occasion or reallocated from other parts of the collection budget, the library budget, or the institutional budget. Without an infusion of funds for e-journal collection development, you will have to (a) develop your collection more slowly or (b) prepare your users for a very fast transition.

The Frugal Collector

You can build a decent collection without spending additional money (especially if your print subscriptions are numerous). However, you will build a bigger and better collection faster if you can pay for subscriptions, either individually or in packages. See the "Individual Titles" section below for sources of free electronic journals and ways to find them.

The Speedy Transition

If you hope to drop print subscriptions in favor of online access in the very near future, you may want to avoid long-term licenses that require you to maintain a print subscription in order to have online access. Negotiate for the "flip model" (see Chapter 6) that treats the electronic copy as the subscription, with add-on pricing for a print subscription. This model is becoming increasingly common as tight library budgets encourage libraries to take a chance on providing electronic-only access to journals.

Most academic libraries will face some resistance from faculty during a sudden switch from print journals to electronic journals, so if you don't have years to prepare them, plan for a robust public relations initiative, and line up support from your university administrators.

One-Time Funds

Do you have end-of-the-year or other one-time funds? If you are a risk taker you can spend them to build an electronic collection with the assumption that electronic access will become so popular you will be able to cancel print materials to support the cost in the near future. You can gamble on the possibility that publishers will alter their current pricing structures. Or, you can use one-time funds for something like JSTOR, which has a large one-time "development fee" and a much lower "annual-maintenance fee." One-time funds can also be used to acquire electronic journal backfiles.

CONSORTIAL ARRANGEMENTS

Participating in consortial deals will enhance your library's ability to acquire e-journals, and it will also disrupt your orderly ap-

---

FIGURE 4–2. Example of an E-Journal Collection Framework

Digital Library Collection Development Framework, University of Texas, Austin

Electronic Journals:

Goals: To license access to a critical mass of high-quality electronic journals throughout all subject areas.

Observations: Because the acquisition of any particular electronic journal is staff-intensive and involves the work of many people over a period of months—initial collecting efforts will focus on acquiring a solid core of proven e-journals from respected publishers.

Qualifications: E-journal publishers vary greatly in their familiarity with electronic publishing issues, and in their familiarity with needs of the scholarly and library community. In some cases e-journal publishers have unrealistic expectations as to the prices libraries can afford, and in the technical and format barriers they expect libraries to scale in order to access their journals. The library has limited funds and staff time that can be devoted to problematic publishers. In those cases where the content is desirable, but the price and practical barriers are too formidable, we will not pursue the electronic versions of the journal, but will provide access through other formats or delivery mechanisms.

(www.lib.utexas.edu/admin/cird/policies/subjects/framework.html)

proach to the selection of electronic journals. If you are lucky enough to belong to a statewide or national consortium with central funds for statewide licenses, you may be the beneficiary of electronic journals and databases your library would not have otherwise chosen. You may want to seek the opportunity (which can also be a burden) to participate in the selection process.

Some publishers and vendors will allow you to form a consortium for the sole purpose of obtaining a discount. Others will require a formal membership in an established, legally defined consortium. If your university is part of a larger system of higher education (governed by a chancellor or one board of regents), you will want to take advantage of any opportunity to cooperate with your sibling institutions to negotiate one license for all interested campuses at a much lower cost per library.

If a consortial discount or statewide subsidy gives you an opportunity to subscribe to a package of e-journals that is otherwise beyond the reach of your budget, then you will need to decide if you want it and if it fits within your collection policies. You should also decide how much you are willing to pay for it, because the original offer is often based on full participation of the members of the consortium, and some of them may decide they do not have the desire or the funds for this purchase. With fewer members, the quantity discount decreases, and there are not as many parties to share the cost. You might go through a few rounds of discussion before the final participants are identified and the consortium knows whether the deal will go through. Many of them don't. Chapter 6 details some of the complexities in ordering through a consortium.

Despite the bother, working with a consortium is often the only way you will be able to have access to desirable electronic journals. Your library might want to experiment with different groups to find one with a selection process and philosophy that is compatible with yours. Your consortium mates will be your selection partners, so it is worth some effort to build a good relationship with them.

COLLECTION POLICIES AND GUIDELINES

Building a collection of electronic journals for a library is like making soup. The flavor you end up with will depend on the ingredients at hand, local tastes and preferences, cultural influences, and the skill of the chefs or librarians. Using a recipe or a collection plan will improve your chances for success.

Policies and procedures will change as electronic journals and libraries change, but it is important at the outset to have a consensus on a clear set of selection criteria that fits into an overall plan. A written collection policy for electronic journals is the best way to establish consistency and avoid conflicts, and it is useful for communicating with others, responding to requests, and educating users.

Some libraries adapt their regular collection policies to include electronic resources; others develop separate selection criteria for electronic journals. These policies can be brief.

ESTABLISHING CRITERIA

A collection policy should help a library decide whether or not to offer electronic journals based on standard criteria:

- Cost and value
- Publisher/Indexing/Reputation

- Accessibility
- Content
- Longevity/Currency/Comprehensiveness
- License restrictions and Consortial considerations

Cost and Value

As with any kind of collection development, the cost in relation to the value of electronic journals will be an important selection criterion. It is always difficult to measure value, but for electronic journals, it is sometimes difficult to determine the cost. Pricing models for electronic journals are complex, inconsistent, and at times idiosyncratic. Pricing may be per database; by title; or for each article that is viewed, printed, or downloaded. It may vary depending on the number of simultaneous users allowed to access a publisher's collection of journals. The price might be tied to the cost of the library's print subscriptions in an intricate way, or tied to the print holdings of all the libraries in a consortium. At least some of the cost of print subscriptions must be factored into the cost of a package of e-journals if your license prevents you from canceling some subscription that you would otherwise not want to maintain.

With experience, you can recognize good value for the price. But it is hard to describe those attributes in a policy.

Publisher/Indexing/Reputation

Libraries usually consider the reputation of a publisher and the reputation of the journal itself before making a decision to add a journal, whatever the format may be. With e-journals, new groups have entered the publishing arena. You may want to keep your policy flexible enough to allow you to support experimental and unproven efforts.

Indexing may or may not be a consideration. It takes time for a journal to build a track record in order to be included in an indexing database, and online-only publications are sometimes excluded as a class from abstracting and indexing databases. However, as linking initiatives grow (see Chapter 1), you probably will want to activate subscriptions (within your budget) to journals that are linked from certain databases. The selection process could include checking and pricing the lists of the journals that are linked from your databases.

Accessibility

A traditional library collection policy will not apply to the access considerations in acquiring electronic journals. The criteria for the modes of access you are willing to accept and support is one of the most important sections of an electronic journal collection policy. Your library needs to develop a stance on the following:

- Authentication requirements (passwords, IP addresses)
- Geographical limitations (library only, campus only, unrestricted)
- User definition (authorized users, walk-in users)
- Browser, reader, plug-in, or client requirements
- Simultaneous use
- Usage statistics
- Interoperability with other products
- Catalog records

When there are choices of access providers, your policy should be able to help you make a decision. This part of the policy will need to be updated frequently to accommodate changes in technology and products. You may want to have "required" and "preferred" sections for access criteria.

Content

In general, content selection will be much less of an issue with traditional journals in electronic format (free or fee-based) than with electronic-only free journals. Each library will have its own standards of quality for the content of electronic journals. If they are free, you might be more willing to relax some of your standards if you believe that it doesn't hurt to offer them just in case someone, sometime might be interested. On the other hand, if you will be promoting your service to skeptical users as a scholarly resource, you might want to use the same standards for all electronic journals, or use the criteria you normally use for your print subscriptions.

If you will use criteria for your free journals that are different from those for your paid subscriptions, consider having two policies. See Appendix A for a sample "Free Access Electronic Journal Collection Policy."

Longevity/Currency/Comprehensiveness

When developing criteria for content selection, there is more than the relevance to the information needs of your community. You should also consider the currency and comprehensiveness of full text.

Some journals have only the current issue on the Web. Some libraries include these journals in their collections, some do not.

FIGURE 4–3. Academic Library Electronic Resources Collection Policies

Examples of Academic Library Electronic Resources Collection Policies

Boston University Law Library
   Electronic Resources Collection Policy
   www.bu.edu/lawlibrary/tech/colldevpolicy/eresources.htm
Boston College
   Electronic Journal Collection Policy
   www.bc.edu/libraries/resources/collections/s-journalpolicy/
Dartmouth College Library
   Collection Development Policy: Information in Electronic Format
   www.dartmouth.edu/~cmdc/cdp/electronic.html
University of Oregon Libraries
   Collection Development Policy for Electronic Journals
   http://darkwing.uoregon.edu/~chadwelf/ejoupoli.htm
California State University
   Principles for CSU Acquisition of Electronic Information Resources
   www.calstate.edu/SEIR/principles.shtml
MIT
   Selection criteria for digital resources purchases
   http://macfadden.mit.edu:9500/colserv/digital/nerd/criteria.html

---

Sometimes the issue on the Web is the only issue that was ever published, and that was two years ago. You may want to provide guidelines for when to include incomplete content.

Sometimes free trials last for months, or even years. Your library may or may not want to make the trial journals available to your users; you may want to have some criteria for trial access.

License Restrictions and Consortial Considerations

If some conditions in license agreements that would be unacceptable to the library, list them in the policy statement. For example, you may not want to offer electronic journals that cannot be used in course packs or electronic reserves.

If your library is active in a consortium, you may want to specify how that might affect your selection of electronic journals. For example, you may want to state that you will not independently acquire any journals or packages of journals that are on your consortium's agenda for future consideration.

CUSTOMIZING AND UPDATING YOUR POLICY

See Appendix A for hypothetical examples of collection policies for electronic journals. Some libraries post their policies on their Web pages; see Figure 4–3 for examples. Each policy shows what is important to the library that developed it. Your library will have its own philosophy, types of users, resources, and technical issues, and your policy must reflect that. Revisit it often, because everything in this territory changes quickly: the technology, the products, the users, and your library.

APPLYING SELECTION CRITERIA

A collection policy for electronic journals represents the library's position when faced with requests or opportunities. However, the process of applying the variables in a policy can be confusing. The library may want to use a decision tree such as one shown in Figure 4–4. Each library would have its own key questions on its decision tree depending on its policy. Assumptions in this example are that a separate policy exists for journals that are freely accessible and that a good package deal would override some other considerations. Another library might not have separate criteria for free or fee-based journals or might spurn package deals for budgetary or political reasons.

Selection Decisions

The process of building a collection of electronic journals in a mid-sized to large library bears little resemblance to the process of adding print journals. In the print environment, subject bibliographers or liaisons to departments (or special constituencies) are generally given some autonomy to manage a distributed budget according to a collection policy and the needs and wishes of the users they serve. Increases in journal costs may trigger periodic cancellation projects, or the library may have a policy that requires cancellations to offset the addition of new titles. New interdisciplinary journals sometimes elicit creative internal-funding strategies.

In the electronic environment, the bundling of journals that serve many subject areas can upset the subject-manager approach. A multiyear deal that forbids the cancellation of existing subscriptions can also restrict the freedom of the subject specialist to manage subscriptions. Your library may have to impose unaccustomed limits on the acquisition of individual new subscriptions in order to afford a new package that will add a considerable number of new journals in all subject areas, but that new package may not quite fulfill the wishes of all your specialized users. A group's high-

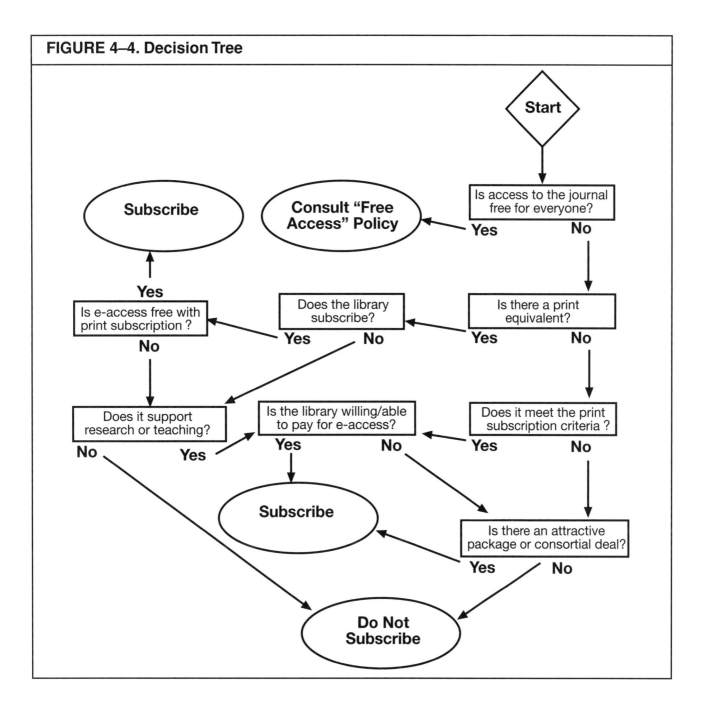

FIGURE 4–4. Decision Tree

est priority journal might be available electronically only in a pro-hibitively expensive package or with terms that are unacceptable to the library. The complexity of the electronic marketplace can be frustrating for library staff as well as users.

The management of the collections budget might become more centralized during the development of a new or expanded e-journal collection. Administrators throughout the library organization may want to be involved in decisions that involve hundreds of thousands of dollars and major upheavals in staffing and workflow.

Some libraries use a form to guide selectors through a series of questions reflecting the library's policy or preferences. See the NIH Online Journal Evaluation Form in Appendix A (Publicker and Stoklosa, 1999).

BUILDING THE COLLECTION

Once you have a policy for selecting electronic journals, you will need to find them. Some e-journals will find you—through lists from your subscription agent, advertisements or direct offers from publishers, or by way of proposals through a consortium. They could come from a variety of sources:

- Individually selected subscriptions
- Electronic access to your print subscriptions
- Electronic access to a group of journals collectively held by a consortium
- Packages offered by publishers (the entire list or subject bundles)
- Aggregated subscriptions from multiple publishers
- Full-text aggregator databases

Sometimes, a user will request a subscription for a particular electronic journal. More frequently, librarians will seek out sources of e-journals that will fit the criteria of the collection policy.

USER RECOMMENDATIONS
Library users sometimes ask for specific journals that they know are available in electronic format or that they are hoping will be available in electronic format. If information does not accompany a request, you will first need to identify the publisher and the options for access, and then you will need to determine whether the journal meets your criteria. If it does, you will initiate the order process. If it doesn't, you will need to explain the reasons to the patron, who may not understand the concept of cost (for something that is on the Internet) or the fact that not all journals are available electronically. The most difficult explanations are the technical ones. If a publisher requires the use of pass-

words or if special client software is required, these conditions might be acceptable to the individual who requested the journal, but they might complicate things too much for the library to make an exception to its policies for a single user.

Subscription Information for Requested Journals

Chapters 5 and 6 cover the licensing and ordering processes, during which you will have a great deal of contact with e-journal providers. At the selection stage, for decision-making purposes you will need to know roughly the subscription costs or options and basic information about access (is a site license available, is remote use allowed, etc.). Using Google or another general search engine to search for the title (with quotation marks) is generally the quickest way to find the publisher of a journal and information about subscribing. (See Figure 4–5 for information on how to obtain subscription information.)

"portal: Libraries and the academy"

Believe it or not, publisher Web sites are not always the most reliable sources of information about subscription prices and terms. Also, a search engine such as Google will sometimes take you to a superseded page that is still around. Furthermore, library tools such as *Ulrich's International Periodicals Directory* also have incomplete and outdated information (even the frequently updated online version), especially inaccurate URLs. You may need to consult several sources before you get the information you need.

After gathering all the information you can gather from the Web, you may need to contact the publisher or vendor for more information before you can make a selection decision. In some libraries, all phone calls and e-mail inquiries are conducted by the acquisitions department in order to keep communication simple and to have one point of contact in case the inquiry results in an order. In other libraries, subject specialists or product advocates play an active role in the information-gathering stage. The MIT Libraries post a guide "Investigating New Digital Prod-

---

FIGURE 4–5. Tracking Down Subscription Information for Individual Electronic Journals

---

- Google
  www.google.com
  tip: use quotation marks around the title

- *Ulrich's International Periodicals Directory* (requires a subscription)

- *Standard Periodical Directory* (requires a subscription)

- *Fulltext Sources Online*, published by *Information Today* as an online database updated weekly, and twice a year in paper. It contains information about the full-text content of aggregator databases and free journals. See www.fso-online.com for more information.

- AcqWeb Publisher listings
  http://acqweb.library.vanderbilt.edu/pubr.html

- Your serials subscription agent

---

ucts (Helpful Hints for Product Sponsors)" at http://macfadden.mit.edu:9500/colserv/digital/nerd/newproducts.html; and "Roles of Product Sponsor and Digital Resources Acquisitions Librarian" (reprinted as Figure 6–3) to help reduce confusion during the selection and ordering process.

INDIVIDUAL TITLES

Selecting individual titles is the traditional way to build a journal collection, and lets you choose what will be best for your user population. But it is time-consuming and labor-intensive, and at this point, some journals are only available as part of a package. If the portfolio pricing model becomes unsustainable, many of us will be doing a lot more work with individual titles.

Sometimes you might want to select journals from lists of what is available. Other times, usually in response to a request, you will want to know whether a particular journal is available electronically, and from whom, and under what terms, and for how much. It might be accessible through various gateways.

SERIALS SUBSCRIPTION AGENTS

One of the services provided by agents is customized electronic files or printed lists of available electronic journals with their prices and access information. The information is usually structured in such a way that it will lead you to another of their services, ordering the journals. See chapter 6 for a discussion of the pros and cons of using serials agents for ordering electronic journals.

One of the reasons to acquire electronic journals from a subscription agent is to gain free access to the vendor's gateway service. These services provide a uniform interface to many journals at one stable location, usage statistics, and other advantages similar to those of fee-based services such as Electronic Collections Online (ECO) and Ovid Full Text. EBSCO provides free access to e-journals through the Electronic Journals Service (EJS) Basic Service, and Swets also provides a database that can be configured to provide free access to some of your library's electronic journals.

ONLINE ACCESS TO PRINT SUBSCRIPTIONS

Many publishers offer both print and online access to their journals. Pricing models vary. Sometimes online access is free to print subscribers; other times there is an additional "access fee" for both print and online subscriptions. There are still other times when an electronic subscription might cost as much as a print subscription—or somewhat less—regardless of whether your library already subscribes.

A publisher's pricing model may be designed to encourage migration to online-only subscriptions or to safeguard print subscriptions, or it may be format-neutral. Some publishers provide access at their sites, whereas others require you to work out an arrangement with another e-journal hosting service.

With some publishers, your agent can arrange the activation of your online access to journals you subscribe to. For other publishers, it will be up to you to send information that will enable them to activate your access. Some publishers may ask you to give them a code from the label of a print issue.

Free Online Access to Print Subscriptions

When free online access to your print subscriptions is an option, there is no reason not to activate it. This can be a good way to begin your e-journal collection. The main challenge is to determine which subscriptions those are, and sometimes there are additional challenges in the activation process.

Your subscription agent should be able to provide you with a list of your subscriptions that include free online access. If you don't use a serials vendor, a quick way to find many of them is through the ECO site, which lists about 2,400 journals. You needn't be an ECO customer to look at the list of publishers that belong to the "print subscriber program," which provides free online access to print subscribers. The publisher list at the OCLC site links to Web pages of publishers so you can see for yourself if you can sign up for access to the publisher's site. The ECO information site also provides a list of individual titles from the print subscriber program publishers. Print out the journal lists and check your library's holdings. You can then contact the publisher to activate your online subscription or arrange access through ECO or another provider. A few of the publishers do not provide their own electronic access to their journals, and ECO access is the only access. See www2.oclc.org/oclc/fseco/printsubs.asp for information on ECO and which publishers generally provide online with print.

Most of the major publishers currently offer tiered services—limited free online access to print subscriptions and more robust access for a fee. For example:

- ScienceDirect Web Editions offers free online access to the most recent 12 months of your Elsevier print subscriptions on a rolling basis. Elsevier now provides at least 1,800 titles, including several recently added through the acquisition of other major publishers. For an additional access fee, you can arrange to provide online access to the most recent four years of your subscribed content (selectively or complete), which builds for the duration of your license. Electronic-only access for your print titles at a discounted subscription price is another option. See www.sciencedirect.com/web-editions.

- Customers who hold print subscriptions to Wiley journals are entitled to activate, free of cost, a limited form of online access for their authorized users under a "Basic Access License (BAL)." Only one person at a time can use an article, and there are restrictions on remote access. For an additional 10% of the library's subscription costs, the "Enhanced Access License (EAL)" gives the library access to journal backfiles, and caps price increases. Online-only access for subscriptions is the same as the price for the print subscription under the BAL; for the EAL, contact Wiley. See www3.interscience.wiley.com/aboutus/institutionalCustomers.html.

- The Blackwell Publishing "Standard Subscription" allows

libraries to provide online access through Synergy or another site to the current volume and the previous year of journals for which they have print subscriptions. For an additional 10% fee, "Premium Subscription" allows access to all available online content, the use of articles in course packs and for interlibrary loan, and access to "Online Early" articles before they are published. Premium subscribers can also choose online-only access to subscribed journals for 95% of the standard subscription price. See www.blackwellpublishing.com/cservices/journal_online.asp.

FREE ELECTRONIC JOURNALS

There are hundreds, if not thousands of reputable, Web-based, free journals that you could add to your collection if they meet your criteria. These free e-journals are of many types:

- Archives
- Popular magazines with print counterparts, such as computer magazines, often supported by online advertising
- Company-produced newsletters or technical publications
- Association newsletters or magazines
- New, born-digital journals; often subsidized by universities or special-interest groups, often experimental or multimedia, sometimes peer reviewed
- Government periodicals
- Long-lasting free trials

Many of these free journals are scholarly and peer reviewed. Some have innovative features that take much better advantage of electronic possibilities than do page images of familiar print journals. But you have to find them. Their publishers generally do not have marketing teams or sales representatives (unless they have another revenue model, such as payments by the author for publication).

Often, a free e-journal will be the only one published by an individual or group. It may be a labor of love or a medium for a message. It may be stable and long-lasting, or a short-term experiment that is worth preserving. Count on spending some time looking for them. Fortunately, many of these journals have already been collected in Web directories.

Archives

A growing movement to "free the scientific literature" conflicts with publishers' need for revenue and desire for profitability. However, a number of publishers have begun to free their e-journal archives, making them available, while preserving subscriptions to current issues. Some commercial and society publishers provide one or more of their journals without charge. Here are some examples of significant collections of archived and complimentary e-journals:

- Highwire Press (www.highwire.org) offers "637,171 free full-text articles as of 11/25/03" from 21 free journals, 147 subscription journals with free back issues, and several journals with very long trial periods. To receive announcements of new journals, contact notify@highwire.stanford.edu.
- The NASA Astrophysics Data System (ADS) (http://adswww.harvard.edu/) provides access to over 300,000 articles (mostly historical) scanned from 35 prominent journals.
- The Electronic Library of Mathematics (www.emis.ams.org/journals/index.html), maintained by the Electronic Publishing Committee of the European Mathematical Society (EPC-EMS), includes approximately 60 international journals. Some have current issues, some are archival.
- ScienceDirect (www.sciencedirect.com/science/journals) provides access to about 40 "complimentary" journals. These journals are indicated with a yellow icon on the complete journal list.

Scholarly Open-Access Journals

An impressive number of freely available, high-quality scholarly journals have recently become available as the result of a favorable conjunction of several efforts:

- Organized activism in the library community (and other scientific and academic communities) against the conditions that have caused the "crisis in scholarly communication"
- An international movement organized by scientists and governments to use the capabilities of the Internet to make the results of scientific research (especially the research funded by governments) more immediately, freely, and openly available to other scientists
- New revenue models for sustaining "born-digital" journals
- The development of standards and technologies for publishing on the Web

- Independent efforts of individuals and institutions to create high-quality niche outlets for the dissemination of scholarly work, particularly in new fields of inquiry
- Organized responses to an overabundance of Web-based scholarly information; new metajournals that synthesize, review, or filter information from other sources in order to save researchers' time

This movement is growing rapidly, so you will want to continually monitor the sources listed below. You can select individual titles or provide access to all the titles from the following organizations:

- Biomed Central (BMC) provides a number of peer-reviewed free journals (currently 100). "Article processing charges" are paid by submitting authors or by authors' institutions through an annual institutional membership fee. Research articles in other journals are free at the BMC site, but a subscription is required to view other content. See www.biomedcentral.com.
- PubMedCentral (PMC) is a repository for life sciences journals sponsored by the National Center for Biotechnology Information (NCBI) at the U.S. National Library of Medicine. The role of PMC is to preserve and provide searchable, open access to electronic journals. About 140 journals are freely accessible through PMC, and deep backfiles for many of these journals are being digitized, a decade at a time. See www.pubmedcentral.org/.
- Highwire Press offers 21 freely accessible journals in mostly biomedical disciplines. There is some overlap with PMC. See www.highwire.org.
- FreeMedicalJournals.com lists 1,380 journals as of publication (some with embargoes). There is overlap with Highwire and other sites, but this is a very comprehensive collection. The site, sponsored by the AMEDEO group, lists high-impact journals on the opening page. See http://freemedicaljournals.com/.
- SciELO, the Scientific Electronic Library Online, is a collection of over 200 scholarly electronic journals from Spain and Latin America. See www.scielo.org.
- The Public Library of Science (PLoS) began as a group of scientists signing a petition pledging to boycott journals with unreasonable subscription prices. In 2003, PLoS began publishing *PLoS Biology*, with *PLoS Medicine* to follow in 2004. PLoS imposes a "modest charge" on authors

or those sponsoring research for articles that are published. See www.publiclibraryofscience.org/.

- EEVL: the Internet Guide to Engineering, Mathematics, and Computing is a "hub" created and managed by a team of information specialists from several universities and institutions in the UK, led by Heriot Watt University. EEVL provides free, full-text access to hundreds of trade and society journals in these fields, and an e-journal search engine. The main site is at www.eevl.ac.uk/. Engineering journals (150) are listed at www.eevl.ac.uk/engineering/resource-results.htm?sect=eng&res=JOUR01. Math journals (80) are listed at www.eevl.ac.uk/mathematics/math-journalsft.htm, and 120 computer science journals are listed at www.eevl.ac.uk/computing/resource-results.htm?sect=comp&res=JOUR01 (see Harrison and MacLeod, 2003, for more detail).

Other free scholarly journals are only available at individual sites, but libraries and the participants in the open access movement compile up-to-date lists. Use the following sources to track them down:

- DOAJ: Directory of Open Access Journals (www.doaj.org), sponsored by Lund (Sweden) University and organized by subject areas, lists a growing number of "free, full text, quality controlled scientific and scholarly journals" in all languages. This is one of the most organized and up-to-date listings at the time of this writing.
- Scholarly Journals Distributed via the World Wide Web, University of Houston (Tex.) Library. "This directory provides links to established Web-based scholarly journals that offer access to English language article files without requiring user registration or fees." http://info.lib.uh.edu/wj/webjour.html
- The Max Planck Society Electronic Journals Library (http://rzblx1.uni-regensburg.de/ezeit/) database allows you to retrieve lists of international journals "with freely available full-text content" organized by subject. Click on the British flag for the English-language interface.
- NewJour archive (gort.ucsd.edu/newjour/). The NewJour listserv, managed primarily at Georgetown University, is designed for the announcement of newly available electronic journals, many of which are free. Archives are kept up-to-date. You can receive daily announcements by subscribing to the list at listproc@ccat.sas.upenn.edu.
- The Scholarly Publishing and Academic Resources Coali-

tion (SPARC) "Publisher Partners" page (www.arl.org/sparc/core/index.asp?page=c0) lists Open Access journals.

- The Internet Public Library presents annotated lists of "magazines, journals, E-zines, and more." Organized by subject categories (www.ipl.org/div/serials/)
- The E-Journal Miner (ejournal.coalliance.org) database, compiled by the Colorado Alliance of Research Libraries, allows you to limit your search for e-journals to those that are free or to limit your quest to peer-reviewed journals.
- Other libraries' Web sites often distinguish the free journals from those that are licensed for their users.
  Google → "free electronic journals" site:edu
- Professional journals and newsletters, both online and in print, review and refer to e-journals and articles in e-journals. For example, the daily online *Chronicle of Higher Education* (http://chronicle.com) has a section "Magazine & Journal Reader," which introduces articles of interest to an academic audience; the review often concludes, "The article is online at . . ." with a link to the article, which is often in a free e-journal you may not have known about. Ask your staff to be on the lookout for such pointers to electronic journals that are not on your list.

George Porter from the California Institute of Technology, Pasadena (Caltech), is an active monitor of free scholarly journals. Caltech provides access to a text file that is exported from their online journal database daily, for "anyone wishing to benefit from the efforts of the Caltech Library System." This pipe-delimited file includes both free and subscription journals. If you import it into Excel and sort it by status, you will have a list of hundreds of free electronic journals with their URLs and ISSNs. Find it at http://ojdb.library.caltech.edu/ojdb/gnu_export.txt.

Some librarians are skeptical about the longevity of free electronic journals and don't want to bother with them. It is true that volunteer efforts sometimes lose momentum when volunteers move on, so it is surprising that a study of 86 free, refereed, scholarly e-journals that were published in 1995 found that 49 (57%) were still published in 2001 (Crawford, 2002). Since half of new journals don't make it past their second year, these are doing as well as any print journals published by major publishers.

Long-Lasting Trials

Some publishers make their new electronic journals freely available for the first few months to give you an opportunity to become familiar with the journals and the publisher's approach to electronic publishing. If you are not sure you will be subscribing when a subscription cost is instated, you may or may not want to make free-trial journals available to your users. A trial can allow you and your users to make an informed choice about whether to substitute an electronic subscription for a print one.

If you are considering a subscription to an expensive electronic journal or to a package of journals, you might request a trial to be sure you are satisfied with the product. Instead of bothering with requests for trials, most publishers will offer free issues from some of their journals or another type of limited access at their Web sites.

Government Serials Online

The United States government now publishes most of its serials online. Government serials do not necessarily meet the standard definitions for electronic journals, though many do, for example:

- *Journal of Research of the National Institute of Standards and Technology*
- *FDA Consumer*
- *FBI Law Enforcement Bulletin*
- *Emerging Infectious Diseases*

The Tennessee State University Library (www.tnstate.edu/library/gov_doc/GovDocPonline.htm) maintains a good list of dozens of current online government periodicals with Persistent URL (PURL) links.

The *LexisNexis Government Periodicals Index* covers around 170 U.S. government periodicals, most of which are freely available online on government agency Web sites. You can find a list of the indexed periodicals at www.lexisnexis.com/academic/1univ/govper/content.asp, and then track down their location through a search engine such as Google Uncle Sam (www.google.com/unclesam). Note that many of the titles in the *Government Periodicals Index* are superseded or defunct titles, but current titles are on the list also. In providing access to government periodicals, you should use the PURL that has been assigned to the periodical by the Government Printing Office (GPO). To find it, add the word "purl" to your title search in Google. Using the PURL in your access system rather than the sponsoring-agency URL will get your users to the periodical even if its actual URL is changed by the agency host.

It is important to note that although government periodicals are published by government agencies and funded by the federal budget, some of them are available only through subscriptions or commercial databases. To keep up with new online serials (as well as other online documents), consult GPO's New Electronic Titles (NET) at www.access.gpo.gov/su_docs/locators/net/index.html.

FEE-BASED "DECLARATIONS OF INDEPENDENCE" JOURNALS

Editors and editorial boards from some high-priced journals have resigned in order to establish competing journals that have much lower license fees, more editorial freedom, or both, but they are not free. New journals always have some difficulty building a subscription base, especially when economic conditions and commitments to bundled e-journals are prompting cancellations in many libraries. Examples of these journals are

- *Journal of Vegetation Science,* an alternative to *Plant Ecology* (previous title: *Vegetatio*),
- *IEEE Sensors Journal,* an alternative to *Sensors and Actuators, A and B,*
- *Organic Letters,* an alternative to *Tetrahedron Letters*, and
- *Portal: Libraries and the Academy*, an alternative to the *Journal of Academic Librarianship*.

If your library wants to support new journals such as these, you can periodically check two good sources that list them:

- The SPARC Publisher Partner pages, at www.arl.org/sparc/core/index.asp?page=c0
- Peter Suber's "Lists Related to the Open Access Movement" at http://www.earlham.edu/~peters/fos/lists.htm#declarations

AGGREGATIONS AND BUNDLES

The quickest and easiest way to build an e-journal collection is to buy journals in bulk. Individual publishers, journal hosting and gateway services, and full-text databases offer bundled collections for every budget and type of library.

PUBLISHER PACKAGES

Both commercial publisher and society publishers have seized upon the bundling model as a way to get more of their journals into more libraries without losing their profit margin. Bundled journals and library consortial buying clubs developed symbiotically.

In the early days of e-journals, publishers often touted the searchability of their full-text journal databases as a selling point. User studies have proved what public services librarians already knew: most users do not remember journals by their publishers, and if their only mode of access is through a publisher's database, they are not well served.

Publishers now realize that libraries want to integrate their journals with the other electronic resources, providing federated searching across journal databases, links from bibliographic databases to full text, and browsable access to individual titles. Chapter 7 will help you create these other access modes. The main reason that libraries are interested in bundled packages is to gain access to additional content at an affordable price.

Commercial Publishers

The unprecedented number of buyouts and mergers among scholarly publishers in recent months is likely to continue, so any list of publishers with portfolio pricing is bound to be inaccurate as soon as it is published. Nevertheless, these major publishers will undoubtedly remain in business, perhaps as even larger publishers with bigger packages:

- ScienceDirect, Elsevier's e-journal distribution service, contains the full text of more than 1,800 journals. Individual institutions or consortia can license the entire collection of Elsevier journals. "Pricing is on a custom basis," according to the ScienceDirect Licensing Options page. "Subject collections" of Elsevier journals are also available. Elsevier recently absorbed Academic Press and Harcourt publishers.
- The publishers Springer (700 journals) and Kluwer (650 journals) were both purchased by a third company in 2003. In 2004, the merged publishing operations, which took the Springer name, will be the second largest journal publisher. Since both publishers have offered bundled licenses in the past, and since the appointed CEO was a former Elsevier CEO, it is likely that consortia (and perhaps individual libraries that can afford it) will have the

option to license the new Springer titles as a package.
- Taylor and Francis is now in third place with 800+ journals after acquiring Dekker, Swets and Zeitlinger Publishers, Frank Cass and Co., and CRC Press in 2003.
- Blackwell Publishing offers a package of 650 journals to consortia. "We have developed a range of online-only offers for libraries in purchasing consortia, giving you a choice of purchasing access to our complete list, selected subject area(s), or a selection of individual titles at a discount."
- Wiley's InterScience offers the Enhanced Access License for Consortia, which allows individual consortium members to access the subscribed journals of all participating consortium members at no additional cost beyond the license fee they pay for access to the journals in their individual collections. Although information is not available on the Interscience Web site, Wiley does offer its complete package of 400+ journals to consortia.

Scholarly Associations

Societies and professional associations have long published journals to advance the communication of knowledge in their respective disciplines. Some society journals have always been published by commercial publishers, but many control their own publishing, and new Web-based technology has allowed some societies to take on their own journal publication.

A study at the University of Wisconsin (Soete and Salaba, 1999) indicates that overall, journals published by nonprofit enterprises, such as societies and associations, cost substantially less than journals issued by commercial publishers. Some of these organizations see an opportunity in providing their publications in electronic form to keep their prices low. To encourage subscribers to access their online resources, subscription costs for print may include the electronic version of a title for a small additional fee or without any added cost.

Libraries should look at their print subscriptions to association journals and check to see if an online version is available. This is a way to provide access to a number of highly regarded publications at minimal cost. Also, some of these organizations seem to be more sensitive to the need for archiving, and several have committed themselves to doing so. Listed below are some scholarly associations that offer packages of electronic journals. This list is by no means complete. These associations, among others, offer packages of electronic journals:

- American Astronomical Society (AAS), www.aas.org/
- American Chemical Society (ACS), www.acs.org/
- American Institute of Physics (AIP), www.aip.org/
- American Mathematical Society (AMS), www.ams.org/
- American Psychological Association (APA), PsycARTICLES, www.apa.org/
- Association for Computing Machinery (ACM), www.acm.org/
- American Society of Civil Engineers (ASCE), www.asce.org/
- International Electrical and Electronic Engineers (IEEE), www.ieee.org/
- Institute of Physics (IOP), www.iop.org/
- Royal Society of Chemistry (RSC), www.rsc.org/
- Society for Industrial and Applied Mathematics (SIAM), www.siam.org/

Multipublisher Packages

Occasionally, publishers and societies will contract with a third party to make their journals available to libraries. Small societies may find that banding together with other societies to create a package of journals is the only way to protect themselves in the marketplace. Below are some examples of major third-party publishing initiatives:

- BioOne is a partnership between the Greater Western Library Alliance, SPARC, the University of Kansas, Allen Press, and the American Institute of Biological Sciences to provide a package of biological, ecological, and environmental sciences journals that otherwise would be unavailable in electronic format. See www.bioone.org.
- JSTOR is a growing package of older issues of about 360 major journals by commercial publishers and societies made available by a nonprofit organization at the University of Michigan. Journal issues are digitized back to volume 1. Subject collections are available, and libraries pay, according to their size, a one-time (capitalization) fee and smaller annual maintenance fee. In order to preserve publishers' subscription revenues, there is a "moving wall" between current issues and the most recent JSTOR issues, a time period determined by the publisher, from two to five years. One of the main reasons for JSTOR's existence is to provide a reliable alternative to older print journals, allowing libraries to save space by removing them from active collections. See www.jstor.org.

- Project Muse, which began as a package of the 46 journals published by Johns Hopkins University Press, now includes more than 250 journals from 37 other publishers, mostly university presses. Consortia with more than five members are eligible for a generous discount for the entire package of Muse journals. More information about Project Muse is available at muse.jhu.edu.
- Highwire Press hosts (and helps with online publication for) 346 journals from several publishers of high-impact journals in science, technology, and medicine (STM) fields. You can activate institutional subscriptions to these journals through the Highwire site, but Highwire acts only as an intermediary. According to the Highwire site, "Academic Consortia and Institutions with multiple sites [at least 6] are welcome to contact the Highwire Outreach Team for assistance with negotiating special pricing to many of the online journals we host here at Highwire Press. See www.highwire.org/.
- The ALPSP Learned Journals Collection aggregates 247 journals from 25 nonprofit publisher members of the Association of Learned and Professional Society Publishers (ALPSP). Libraries or consortia can subscribe to the full collection or any of three discipline-specific packages. The online publisher and host is Extenza, a division of Swets. See www.alpsp-collection.org/.

Publisher Packages: Advantages and Disadvantages

There are several advantages to the package approach:

- The price per title will usually be considerably less than if purchased individually.
- The library will most certainly be providing access to titles that were not previously represented in its print collection.
- Users are presented with a single search interface to multiple titles.
- Serials staff deal with only one order, one license agreement, and only one contact for all titles that are included.
- This is a quick way to build the critical mass necessary to attract users.
- Usage statistics are easily collected for bundled journals.

Librarians like to think that they know what their users want. Academic librarians have been building their collections of print journals around the curricular and research areas in their universities, responding to requests when they can. Theoretically, interlibrary loan and document delivery statistics make known which of the journals to which the library does not subscribe are of interest to the users. So you would expect that if you provided a publisher's package that includes a large number of journals that were not previously available to the users, many of them would not be used. It is a great experiment, if you can manage it.

Studies of the use of bundled e-journals in research libraries, such as those belonging to the Northeast Research Libraries (NERL) consortium, show that there is much higher use of the journals that the libraries already had in print (Davis, 2002). However, in libraries that did not previously subscribe to journals in the bundle, such as those in OhioLINK, use patterns are much different (Sanville, 1999). There is much higher use of newly available journals by users of libraries that have small print collections to begin with. At the University of Nevada, Reno, we have observed unexpectedly high use of certain e-journals acquired through Big Deals, some of them journals that we did not subscribe to in print because they were never requested; nor were articles from those journals heavily requested through interlibrary loan (Yue and Syring, 2004).

There are, however, some philosophical issues (see the "Framework/Library Values" section above) and some challenges for the library that purchases electronic journals in this way:

- Even though the per-title cost might be very attractive in a publisher's package, the total cost will probably be higher than what the library was paying for selected print titles from the publisher.
- Buying and selling and merging of journals and publishers can suddenly change the terms of access to journals in a package. An agreement that was negotiated with a publisher that no longer exists may or may not be honored by the new owner of the journals.
- Depending upon the requirements of the publisher, you may be prevented from canceling the print version of any of your subscriptions from that publisher.
- The specific titles in the database may change, thus requiring a way to identify those changes, along with the need to edit and update the library's Web page, online catalog, and any other paths to access.
- If the library is canceling esteemed print subscriptions to support electronic journals or for any other reason, it may be difficult to explain why you are adding or retaining

FIGURE 4–6. Full-Text Database Contents, a Snapshot in Late 2003

Database	Vendor	Subject	Peer reviewed	Full-text journals	TOC access
Academic Search Premier	EBSCO	Multi	3123	4406	yes
Academic Search Elite	EBSCO	Multi	1298	2037	yes
MasterFile Premier	EBSCO	Multi	N/A	1959	yes
MasterFile Elite	EBSCO	Multi	N/A	1156	yes
Business Source Premier	EBSCO	Business	480	1122	yes
Business Source Elite	EBSCO	Business	1061	3606	yes
ABI/Inform	ProQuest	Business	720	1193	yes
ProQuest 5000	ProQuest	Multi	2172	4234	yes
Wilson OmniFile	HWWilson	Multi	636	1750	no
Health Reference Center	Gale	Health	210	734	yes
Expanded Academic ASAP	Gale	Multi	940	2052	yes
Business & Co. Resource Center	Gale	Business	254	2823	yes
LexisNexis Academic Universe	CIS	Multi			no

some of the lower-quality titles in the package.
- If the library can no longer afford to maintain the package, users won't be happy with losing access to a large number of journals

In some cases, the package plan may be the only way to obtain access to some of the electronic journals that are important to your users. It is up to each library to determine whether the value of the resource to its users is worth the purchase price. Your budget, or lack of budget, for electronic journals may be a determining factor. It doesn't hurt to ask for a price quote. You might be surprised to find you can afford a package deal, despite the size of your library and the size of your budget. Pricing models for electronic journals are much more elastic than for print journals. Adding more online customers does not have the impact on their costs that having more print subscribers does, and complex models allow publishers to make adjustments for individual circumstances (see Chapter 6).

FULL-TEXT DATABASES

Last, but certainly not least, many libraries have ready access to a large number of electronic journals through at least one full-text database from a vendor such as EBSCO, ProQuest, or Gale. Some libraries have come to think of the full-text content of these databases as their electronic journal collection, and even sometimes adjust their print collection accordingly. But to users, a full-text, aggregated database appears to be an article collection.

For a journal in a full-text database to be recognized as a journal by your users, it needs to be presented as something resembling a print journal, with separate volumes and issues, each having a table of contents with links to articles. Only if you can connect users to individual journals in a database without requiring them to use the database interface can you consider it to be an e-journal collection. Chapter 7 will help you transform the contents of your database(s) into a collection of e-journals. But you must keep in mind that an electronic journal collection derived from full-text aggregator databases is intrinsically unstable.

Full-text databases, such as those in Figure 4–6, have evolved from abstracting and indexing services such as *Reader's Guide to Periodical Literature*. Once periodical indexes became electronic, first on CD-ROM and then on the Web, full-text was added as an enhancement, usually as ASCII text without graphics, or with graphics as separate files. Neither indexing nor full text was provided on a cover-to-cover basis. Users searching the databases naturally preferred retrieving articles (even incomplete articles) to retrieving citations to articles, and database vendors continued to compete with each other on the number of full-text journals in their databases, especially scholarly, refereed, full-text journals.

When publishers began offering browsable access to online images of articles in their journals, aggregator database vendors responded by adopting some of the features of these new products: facsimile article images (generally PDF format) with more comprehensive coverage of journals and a volume/issue, tables-of-contents structure with durable links so that libraries could provide direct access to the individual journals from outside the database, providing access through the library catalog or Web listings.

No Substitute for Subscriptions

There is still one major deficiency in terms of building a collection using aggregator content: there is no guarantee of perpetual access to the journals in the databases. Though they may be intact, it would be risky to cancel their print counterparts on the basis of duplication. You are subscribing to the database, not to individual titles. As libraries cancel subscriptions to journals that they are getting through full-text databases, the publishers' response is to remove their journals from the databases or, at the very least, to impose an embargo so that recent issues (six months to two years) are not available to your users through the databases. Another option would be for publishers to demand higher royalties from database vendors, driving up the price of the databases.

When budgets are tight, libraries will take risks and accept tradeoffs. Depending on your situation, your only choice might be to cancel print subscriptions or cancel full-text databases. If so, you should be comfortable with the possibility that some of those journals may disappear from the databases altogether. If you must resubscribe to any of the journals you cancel, you may end up with no local access to a few volumes. Some libraries feel safer canceling a print journal that is represented in at least two databases; but chances are good that if a publisher removes journals from one database, they will be removed from all databases. A recent example is the decision by Sage to gather its journals into discrete, subject-specific groups, removing the full text of individual journals from the general databases produced by EBSCO, ProQuest, and other vendors.

At least half of the articles indexed by most of the databases listed in Figure 4–6 are not available as full text through the databases. Recent advances in linking standards and technologies enhance the value of non-full-text bibliographic records by enabling users to move easily from the record in the database to the full text from another source.

Evaluating and Comparing Content

In the turmoil of today's electronic marketplace, change is so rapid that any specifications for databases will not be accurate for long. The information in Figure 4–6 is a snapshot from November 2003, and is no longer accurate. You will need to conduct your own evaluations and comparisons of the current products when making a decision to add or drop a full-text database. You should consider your users' needs as well as your library's total electronic environment. These questions will help you evaluate content and usability:

- Is full text from every article of every issue of every journal included? If not, what are the criteria for inclusion? What is missing?
- Are articles delivered in plain-text format? If it is a discipline-specific database, is text alone sufficient for the needs of the users?

- If separate graphics are included, is every graphic available for each article? Is the display/print quality adequate?
- Do you like the search interface? Is it simple and intuitive for users? Are there advanced options for expert searchers?
- If articles are presented as image files, such as PDF, do they load, display, and print adequately?
- Can volume/issue content lists be retrieved and displayed? Can the library link to specific journal content lists within the database?
- How many of the full-text journals are refereed?
- How deep are the full-text backfiles?
- Can you get catalog records from the publisher? Do they meet your library's standards?
- Can you link from non-full-text records to the full-text you license from other sources? Are the linking protocols compatible with your systems?
- How often is the database updated?
- How current are the articles? How many titles have embargoes?
- How many full-text journals are included? Are the titles suitable for the scope of the database?

The last question requires some follow-up. Competing database providers will try to impress you with the number of full-text journals in their databases, but you will need to ask another question: What kinds of journals? Some source lists for databases will include special issues and supplements as titles; some might include pamphlets and monographs. Small town newspapers and local magazines may also be included in the count.

Be aware that comparing lists of journals in competing databases for overlapping titles, unique titles, depth of coverage, and other characteristics is an exercise in frustration. The ISSN is the best point of comparison for titles, but a large percentage of titles on any vendor's list will lack ISSNs. Title listings are often inaccurate. Standardization is lacking, and terminology is sometimes confusing. Dates of coverage are expressed differently by each vendor, so to compare them you will need to massage the data. Lists on vendors' sites are often out of date, and sometimes you can find title lists in two areas of a publisher's site that don't agree. Gaps in content will not always be listed. Words like "halted" and "ceased," in reference to full text, have specific meanings that aren't always clear. On some vendors' lists, new titles and former titles are listed separately. On other vendors' lists, they are lumped together.

Companies can provide database title lists in a format that is easier to compare. See information in Chapter 6 about TDNet, Serials Solutions, and JournalWebCite. Paula Watson's article in *Library Technology Report* (2003), "E-Journal Management: Acquisition and Control," offers an excellent overview of aggregated full-text databases as sources for e-journals.

Full-text aggregations are a cost-effective means of providing high-quality journal articles to users' desktops. However, as Dorn and Klemperer (2002) point out, "They will probably never provide a complete electronic content service. To fulfill all their users' needs, libraries must complement their aggregations with individual journal subscriptions, abstracting and indexing services, local reference-linking systems, and title-listing services."

ACCESS OPTIONS

There is one more aspect of selecting electronic journals. You need to decide how you will provide access to the journals. In some cases, there is only one choice, which could be the publisher's or aggregator's site. If you are getting access to journals through a consortial license, then your only access choice might be the consortial server, if there is one. But in many other cases, you can choose from a variety of gateway services that aggregate journals from several publishers and provide a search engine and sometimes other services, such as transactional article delivery (pay per view), links to other full-text sources, links from abstracting and indexing databases, and current awareness services. In some cases you will need to pay a fee in addition to subscription fees.

Some vendors mount the journal contents on their own servers; others provide a gateway through their databases to the articles on the publisher's server. You can usually link from your Web pages and online catalog to the tables of contents of individual journals at the publisher's or vendor's site.

The main advantage in using an intermediary service for access to electronic journals is that one (usually pretty good) search engine will search the contents of journals from several publishers and many disciplines, providing a uniform interface for users. Another advantage is that the vendor will sometimes arrange for licensed access to the journals, so you need not work through all the access issues with multiple publishers.

The main disadvantage to an intermediary service is the fees that you must usually pay in addition to subscription prices. Each service is a little different, so it is difficult to make generalizations. And they change, so it would prove useless to provide too many details. You will need to evaluate your own library's needs and the benefits each vendor can provide. These are some issues to consider:

- In most cases, your library will not subscribe to all the journals that are available in the database, so when your users search the database they will get a mixture of articles and abstracts. Some vendors provide an option that allows users to search only for articles that are available in full text.
- Some electronic journal databases have citations and abstracts for articles from journals that are not available to anyone in full text. The service includes delivery of articles on demand, transactionally. This may be something you want, or not.
- All vendors provide usage statistics of some kind, but they vary in format, frequency, and depth. If usage statistics are important to you, investigate the details.
- Some vendors promise to archive the electronic journals and provide perpetual access to your users for the issues published during the period of your subscription. Others do not.
- The depth of backfiles will vary by product. If you are thinking of providing access through a gateway service rather than a publisher's site, you should compare the dates of coverage first.
- Some of the aggregator services provide links from the database to your library's online catalog, giving users the chance to find articles in print journals in your library, and to your link resolver, if you have one, so that your users can link to full text that you provide from other sources. Other services enable links from external databases to the journals they host.

These are some gateway and hosting services for e-journals:

- EBSCOhost Electronic Journals Service (EJS) has a basic version, providing free access to journals acquired through EBSCO, and a fee-based enhanced version, with more features, of course. EJS hosts some journals on-site and acts as a gateway for others. Other EBSCOhost databases link to the library's EJS journals. See www.ebsco.com/home/ejournals/.
- Ingenta offers 6,000+ full-text, online journals from 260+

academic and professional publishers. Libraries can set up a free account that allows users to access content through the Ingenta service. Ingenta provides a bibliographic database that also includes citations for 22,000 journals that are not available in full text, which feeds its document delivery service. Searching is free. You will still have to subscribe to your Ingenta journals through regular channels. A free alerts service also helps its documentary-delivery business.

- SwetsWise, from the serials agent Swets, also provides a gateway to e-journals, in addition to an ordering and set-up service. See www.swetsblackwell.com.
- Journals@Ovid is a collection of approximately 900 biomedical journals. Ovid has a much smaller collection than ECO with narrower subject coverage, but offers similar searching, browsing, and linking options from the Ovid databases and to other journals through references. Individual journals or collections of journals can be ordered and accessed through Ovid. See www.ovid.com.
- OCLC's Electronic Collections Online (ECO), a FirstSearch database, now includes about 4,600 electronic journals from about 70 publishers that have agreed to let OCLC archive their issues and provide perpetual access to subscribers, through OCLC. The cost is determined by the number of journals the library accesses through ECO, ranging from $10–$18 per title. More information is at www.oclc.org/electroniccollections/. OCLC encourages libraries to work with subscription agencies to obtain access to e-journals through ECO.
- ScienceServer @ LANL (Los Alamos National Laboratories) hosts journals from major science and technology publishers, including Elsevier, Kluwer, Springer, Wiley, IEE, IEEE, Institute of Physics, and ACS, using ScienceServer software. External customers are welcome on an annual-fee basis. See http://lib-www.lanl.gov/libinfo/libproducts.htm for more information.

REFERENCES

Brooks, Sam. 2001. "Integration of Information Resources and Collection Development Strategy." *Journal of Academic Librarianship* 39, no. 2: 316–319.

Crawford, Walt. 2002. "Free Electronic Refereed Journals: Getting Past the Arc of Enthusiasm." *Learned Publishing* 15, no. 2 (April): 117–123.

Davis, Philip. 2002. "Patterns in Electronic Journal Usage: Challenging the Composition of Geographic Consortia." *College and Research Libraries News* 63, no. 6: 484–497.

Dorn, Knut, and Katharina Klemperer. 2002. "E-Journal Aggregation Systems: Only Part of the Big Picture." *Library Collections, Acquisitions, & Technical Services* 26, no. 3: 307–310.

Frazier, Ken. 2001. "The Librarians" Dilemma: Contemplating the Costs of the 'Big Deal.'" *D-Lib Magazine* 7, no. 3 (March). Retrieved Sept. 20, 2004, from www.dlib.org/dlib/march01/frazier/03frazier.html.

Harrison, Nicola, and Roddy MacLeod. 2003. "Free Full-Text E-journals and EEVL's Engineering E-Journal Search Engine." *Ariadne*, no. 35 (April). Retrieved Sept. 20, 2004, from www.ariadne.ac.uk/issue35/eevl/.

Publicker, Stephanie, and Kristin Stoklosa. 1999. "How the National Institutes of Health Library Selects and Provides E-Journals via the World Wide Web." *Serials Review* 25, no. 3: 13–23.

Sanville, Tom. 1999. "Use Levels and New Models for Consortial Purchasing of Electronic Journals." *Library Consortium Management: An International Journal* 1, no. 3/4: 47–58.

Soete, George, and Athena Salaba. 1999. "Measuring Journal Cost-Effectiveness: Ten Years after Barschall." Madison: University Libraries, University of Wisconsin. Retrieved Sept. 20, 2004, from www.library.wisc.edu/projects/glsdo/cost.html.

"To the Editor" [response to Frazier, Ken. "The Librarian's Dilemm." 2001. *D-Lib Magazine* 7, no. 4 (April). Retrieved Sept. 20, 2004, from www.dlib.org/dlib/april01/04letters.html.

Ulrich's International Periodicals Directory. 2002. New York: R. R. Bowker.

Van Orsdel, Lee, and Kathleen Born. 2003. "Big Chill on the Big Deal?" *Library Journal* 128, No. 7 (April 15): 51–56.

Watson, Paula. 2003. "E-Journal Management: Acquisition and Control." *Library Technology Reports* 39, no. 2 (March-April): 6–18.

Yue, Paoshan W., and Millie L. Syring. 2004. "Usage of Electronic Journals and Their Effect on Interlibrary Loan: A Case Study at the University of Nevada, Reno." *Library Collections, Acquisitions, and Technical Services*, 28, no. 4 (in press).

MORE INFORMATION SOURCES

Cummings, Joel. 2003. "Full-Text Aggregation: An Examination of Metadata Accuracy and Implications for Resource Sharing." *Serials Review* 29, no. 1: 11–15.

Jewell, Timothy D. 2001. *Selection and Presentation of Commercially Available Electronic Resources: Issues and Practice.* Washington, DC: Digital Library Federation and Council on Library and Information Resources. Retrieved Sept. 20, 2004, from www.clir.org/pubs/reports/pub99/contents.html.

5 TRAFFICKING IN INTELLECTUAL PROPERTY: LICENSING AND USER AUTHENTICATION

CHAPTER OVERVIEW

- Copyright, Fair Use, Contract Law, and Digital Rights Management
- Model Licenses and Licensing Guidelines
- Reviewing the License
- Terms of the License
- Negotiating Changes
- Signing and Managing the License
- Access Management and Authentication
- Prevention and Management of License Violations and Security Breaches

To subscribe to most electronic journals and other electronic resources, you or someone at your institution will be required to sign a license. This is a legally binding contract, often written in obscure legalese, potentially with many terms and provisions.

Licenses or contracts are not new to the digital world. Every time you open a new piece of software, you are agreeing to abide by the restrictions contained in the shrink-wrap license. This is a contract, although it is unilateral with all of the terms imposed by one side. It is not unusual for Web sites to present you with a list of terms to which you must agree before you can access their resources. This is referred to as a click-wrap or Web-wrap license. This type of license has become so commonplace that it is little regarded by many users, who do not even take the time to read the text of the license before they agree to its terms.

When we sign a written contract, however, we feel a sense of personal as well as a legal obligation to ensure that the requirements to which we have agreed are met. Therefore, the first time you review a license it can be intimidating as well as a little confusing. What liabilities might your library be incurring? Are you giving away your fair use rights? The first part of this chapter will summarize the reasons for licensing, the key points to look for during license review, and the negotiation of contract changes. Licenses for electronic journals generally restrict their use to authorized library users. The second part of the chapter discusses the ways to limit access to authenticated users.

The cost to the library for accessing licensed e-journals is also subject to negotiation, generally as part of the license agreement, and the final result of pricing discussions may put a stop to any further discussion, since selection and prioritization of new products (Chapter 4) is often dependent on the price. So, unless other license terms seem more problematic than the price, you may want to deal with that aspect first. Pricing issues are covered in Chapter 6.

COPYRIGHT, FAIR USE, CONTRACT LAW, AND DIGITAL RIGHTS MANAGEMENT

A license for an electronic product is a legal agreement that overrides copyright law if both parties sign it. The Association of Research Libraries (ARL) has established a "Statement of Principles" (Association of Research Libraries et al., 1997) for licensing agreements, asserting that licenses "should not be allowed to abrogate the fair use and library provisions authorized in the copyright statute." It is up to those who negotiate on behalf of a library or a consortium of libraries to uphold that principle.

COPYRIGHT

You must know the rights to which you are entitled in order to protect them during the license negotiation process. Article I, Section 8, Clause 8 of the U.S. Constitution provides the authority for copyright in this country. Copyright was intended by our founding fathers ". . . To promote the Progress of Science and useful Arts, by securing for limited Times to Authors and Inventors the exclusive Right to their respective Writings and Discoveries." Copyright protects intellectual property and the rights of people who make their living from the creative process, whether it is writing, composing, or performing. Copyright also promotes the public good through furthering and advancing knowledge by providing authors with an economic incentive to write and publish.

Laws have been passed over the years to expand on and clarify the copyright clause in Section 8 of the Constitution. During the past few years, the development of the Web has spurred several legislative initiatives to further define the rights of owners and users of electronic content. To understand some of the issues involved in licensing, it is useful to look at the rights defined in Public Law 94-553, better known as the Copyright Act of 1976. Although passed on October 19, 1976, the law did not take effect until January 1, 1978. It is contained in Title 17 of the U.S. Code.

- Section 102 to 105 defines works protected by copyright.
- Section 106 defines exclusive rights of the copyright owner to reproduce, adapt, distribute, perform or display the copyrighted work.
- Section 107 provides the basis for fair use.
- Section 108 authorizes certain types of library copying.

Fair Use

Section 107: The Copyright Act of 1976, Section 107, permits the use and reproduction of copyrighted works for educational purposes. This is defined as teaching (including multiple copies for classroom use), scholarship, and research. This limited personal use is allowed (whether the format is print or electronic) with the intent that it will not interfere with the rights of authors to benefit and profit from their work.

Section 108: This section provides specific guidelines for reproduction or copying by libraries. The library may make three copies of a work for preservation, security, or deposit for research in another library. Assuming the library has made a reasonable effort to obtain a replacement copy at a fair price, a new copy may be made to replace a work that is lost, stolen, damaged, or deteriorating. Reproducing or copying a work may be done under the following conditions:

- There is no commercial advantage to the library.
- The library is open to the public and/or researchers.
- The reproduction includes a notice of copyright.

Copyright Term Extension Act

The Sonny Bono Copyright Term Extension Act, Public Law 105-298, was passed in October 1998 and lengthened the term of copyright from life plus 50 years to life plus 70 years. A facsimile or digital copy may be made for preservation, scholarship, or research if an original copy cannot be obtained at a reasonable price. During the last 20 years of protection, the Act permits libraries and educational institutions to treat a copyrighted work as if it were in the public domain.

TECHNOLOGY AND FAIR USE

The digital environment makes it very easy to copy files and distribute or transmit copyrighted text. It is also possible to easily reformat and manipulate the data in copyrighted works when they are available in electronic form. This is a major concern for copyright holders, but with a license the publisher or resource provider can legally control use of an electronic journal or database. Contract law has replaced copyright as a way to protect the rights of authors to profit from their work and to protect the publisher's investment, including current and future sales.

The 2001 update to the "Preferred Practices" statement by the International Coalition of Library Consortia (ICOLC) states:

> Licenses drafted by publishers have not been consistent in their approach to copying and have deterred research and studies by users. The principle and applicability of fair use should be affirmed, and limitations through licensing terms should be substantially reduced, if not eliminated (www.library.yale.edu/consortia/2001current practices.htm)

A library's mission is to support educational and other uses of information. Be aware that provisions in the licenses you are expected to sign to gain access to resources may limit or restrict the rights granted by fair use. It is the librarian's responsibility to negotiate licenses to balance the rights of copyright owners (whether authors or publishers) with the needs of users for information and the free exchange of ideas.

Digital Millennium Copyright Act

Public Law 105-304, also known as the Digital Millennium Copyright Act (DMCA), was signed on October 28, 1998. It brings the United States into compliance with international treaties of the World Intellectual Property Organization (WIPO) and attempts to update copyright law as it relates to the digital environment. Impact on libraries is in these areas:

- Permission for preservation and storage of works in a digital format and a mechanism for handling preservation of works in formats that are now outmoded

- Copyright management information, including a prohibition against altering information imbedded in digital works by copyright owners
- Limitation of liability for online service providers
- Prohibition against circumventing technological measures used to protect copyrighted works
- Commitment to study the issues associated with distance education and the use of digital networks

The DMCA guarantees protection to copyright holders for their electronic creations, whether by password, encryption, or other means. However, limited fair use is allowed for digital preservation, electronic interlibrary loan, and distance education.

TEACH Act

In 2002, the Technology, Education, and Copyright Harmonization (TEACH) Act was signed into law (PL 107-273), affirming the rights of academic institutions to make fair use of electronic copyrighted materials in digital-education programs and defining their responsibilities in making sure that these materials are protected. For example, the TEACH Act restricts the provision of electronic reserves to the duration of the course. According to John Schuler (2003), "The law resolves some of the more difficult aspects of fair use in an academic digital environment, but it increases the burden of ambiguity on libraries in how they will now relate to this form of electronic teaching." In his analysis of the ways in which the TEACH Act affects libraries, Kenneth Crews (2003) encourages librarians to take a role in "securing permission from the copyright owners for the use of materials beyond the limits of the law."

CONTRACT LAW

Electronic information is licensed rather than sold. With a license, the copyright owner gives permission to the licensee to use a copyrighted work during a specific period of time for a limited purpose. The owner is prescribing who can use a resource and how it may be used. Remember, the library/licensee does not *own* the information; your library is just paying to use it.

By agreeing to the terms in a license, you and the vendor are replacing copyright law with contract law—and contract law is easier to enforce in the court system. The terms of the license, which is a legally binding contract, override any privileges to which you are entitled based upon copyright and fair use.

On a Web site that does not require a license, the provisions of copyright do apply. However, once a license has been signed, the terms of the license or contract govern use of the online resource.

Digital Rights Management

Digital Rights Management, or DRM, refers both to the technologies that control how digital content is used and to the policies governing the use of digital content that are drafted by organizations such as the Motion Picture Association of America (MPAA) and the Recording Industry of America (RIAA). DRM policies are becoming established through federal legislation and regulations, standards organizations, and the courts. The concept has been developed in terms of e-commerce and Internet piracy.

Library and educational groups are concerned because some aspects of DRM legislation threaten fair use under existing copyright law. Librarians are challenging restrictive DRM policies and are becoming involved in developing principles for the use of DRM in such a way that it does not jeopardize "the unimpeded flow of information" that "is fundamental to the mission and activities of both higher education and libraries" (American Library Association, 2003). DRM tracking technology can also threaten users' privacy and confidentiality.

Just as licenses can restrict activities that are allowed under the fair-use component of copyright law, they can bypass DRM policies and regulations. Nevertheless, boilerplate DRM language finds its way into license agreements, and DRM technology finds its way into electronic products licensed by libraries. "While for now it may seem removed from the day-to-day reality of managing and sourcing research data, DRM could shape the nature of future information provision, regardless of the form or sector in which that information resides" (Spedding, 2003). Furthermore, DRM technology that is embedded in files, through systems designed to thwart copying, printing, and downloading by unauthorized end users, could seriously interfere with fair-use activities now being carried out by authorized users through library licenses.

Some believe that DRM could improve upon current authentication options and help with the retrieval of usage statistics. DRM could affect the delivery of electronic content in a number of positive and negative ways, so librarians need to be aware and involved in the developments.

UCITA

Because in the United States, contracts are governed by state law and not federal law, content owners have proposed the Uniform Computer Information Transaction Act, or UCITA, to state legislatures to standardize their rights to control the use of their content. So far, very few states have adopted UCITA, which is regarded by most library organizations as overly restrictive and very detrimental to the rights of users of electronic content, but it has not been declared dead, so we may see it adopted in more states. See Anna May Wyatt's (2002) article in the *Journal of Library Administration* for a summary of the impact UCITA could have on licensing electronic products.

MODEL LICENSES AND LICENSING GUIDELINES

The license of one publisher or vendor can differ significantly from that of another. But over time, as publishers and librarians become more experienced in license negotiation, licenses have become more standardized. Several organizations, including the International Coalition of Library Consortia (ICOLC) and the Association of Research Libraries (ARL), have suggested models or standards to be used by those who develop licenses, and it is clear that vendors have begun to adopt the models.

Model licenses are generally developed by groups that include representatives of both the publishing industry and the library market, and they are designed to be used as well as consulted, so they are made freely available on the Web in rich text (.rtf) or Word (.doc) formats that can be downloaded and modified using common word processors. Guidelines are generally written by and for the librarians and consortial representatives who will be negotiating license agreements. Some examples are listed below.

MODEL LICENSES

A representative group of subscription agents, publishers, and librarians hired an international publishing consultant, John Cox Associates, to draft model licensing agreements for different types of libraries. The starting point was a model developed by the Publishers Association in the UK and the Joint Information Systems Committee (JISC) of the Higher Education Funding Councils. Four different model licenses were developed:

- Academic libraries
- Academic library consortia
- Public libraries
- Corporate and special libraries

The licenses are comprehensive, but also flexible in that different clauses can be selected to meet the needs of various libraries and database providers. The models are also intended to be international in their application. Commentary is provided on various clauses as well as guidance for using them. The model licenses, which are in the public domain, are available on a Web site (www.licensingmodels.com).

The "Liblicense Standard Licensing Agreement" was developed by the Council on Library and Information Resources (CLIR), the Digital Library Federation (DLF) and Yale University. This model had significant input from publishers, librarians, lawyers, and university officials (www.library.yale.edu/~llicense/modlic.shtml).

The California Digital Library's "Standard License Agreement" is posted at www.cdlib.org/vendors/CDLModelLicense.rtf.

LICENSING GUIDELINES

The licensing guidelines listed below depart from model licenses in that they strongly represent the library perspective. Since licenses originate with publishers, most of the clauses and language are naturally designed to protect publishers' interests and address publishers' concerns about the use of the product. Most publishers do not object to inserting clauses that protect the library's interests, but you will need to request these additions, and understand that adding clauses to a publisher's license might slow the licensing process considerably, especially if your library is the first to request a particular modification (see Figure 5–1). Frequently requested modifications will eventually find their way into the publisher's standard license. Some licensing guidelines are available on the Web:

- *Licensing Electronic Resources: Strategic and Practical Considerations for Signing Electronic Information Delivery Agreements,* sponsored by **ARL** (http://arl.cni.org/scomm/licensing/licbooklet.html).
- "Principles for Licensing Electronic Resources," developed by **ALA, ARL**, and four other library associations in 1997 (See References.) (www.arl.org/scomm/licensing/principles.html)
- **The California Digital Library's** "Checklist of Points to be Addressed in a CDL License Agreement" (www.cdlib.org/vendors/checklist.html)
- Northeast Research Libraries (**NERL**) "Principles for Electronic Journal Licenses." (www.library.yale.edu/NERLpublic/EJrnlPrinciples.html)

FIGURE 5–1. Five Elements to Aim for When Licensing Digital Products
• Ease of access to the works being sought • "One stop" transactions where no additional permission, payments, or clearances are required once the library has chosen and paid for the works requested • Clear definitions of what uses are permitted and what uses are not permitted, by whom and where • Access beyond the termination of the license agreement • Liability clear regarding the use of licensed content by public Harris, 2002. *Licensing Digital Content*, p. 6.

- "International Licensing Principles," drafted by the International Federation of Library Associations and Institutions (**IFLA**) (www.ifla.org/V/ebpb/copy.htm)
- Chapter 7 of Lesley Ellen Harris's *Licensing Digital Content*, "Questions and Answers on Licensing," (made available by **ALA**, the publisher, at www.ala.org/ala/ourassociation/publishing/alaeditions/samplers/harris_licdigcon.pdf).

PUBLISHERS' LICENSES AND OTHER RESOURCES

It is very useful to look at various actual license agreements and compare the terms. This will help you to determine current licensing standards in the publishing industry. It will also give you a feel for what publishers and database providers may be willing to negotiate. If a license you are reviewing prohibits interlibrary loan, and you notice that most licenses permit the lending of at least print copies, you are in a stronger position to negotiate a change in that clause.

Hundreds of standard publishers' licenses are available through the EBSCO E-Resources Access and Management site at http://ejournals.ebsco.com/ejournals/license.asp. The Liblicense site provides links to dozens of publishers' licenses at www.library.yale.edu/~llicense/. The Liblicense resource pages provide a wealth of information for those involved with licensing electronic resources.

FIGURE 5–2. Liblicense Resources

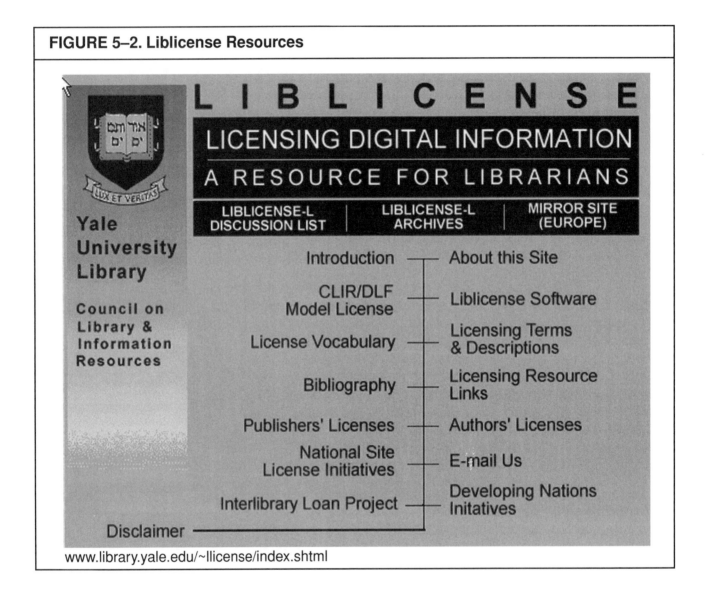

www.library.yale.edu/~llicense/index.shtml

REVIEWING THE LICENSE

In the past, licenses may not have been carefully reviewed or thoroughly understood. You may have signed a license with the assumption that it was a standard document that other institutions had already agreed to sign—so certainly there would be no problem with your signing, too. It is no longer safe to make that assumption. You must do more than quickly scan the licenses you sign. Each license should be carefully read, along with any attachments. You must understand the terms of the license and ask questions about anything that is not clear.

FIGURE 5–3. Goals of License Review

Clearly Define the Goals of License Review:

- What elements are objectionable?
- What needs to be removed/changed/altered?
- What needs to be added?
- Does the license cover fair use of the material?
- Are the definitions of uses and users acceptable?
- Can you live up to all of the obligations/restrictions in the license?

(From Brennen, *Licensing Electronic Resources: Strategic and Practical Considerations for Signing Electronic Information Delivery Agreements*, 1994)

Another reason to review licenses carefully is the differences you will find from one vendor or publisher license to the next. There is not yet a standard format for licenses, so they cannot just be "rubber-stamped." Each time you review and negotiate a license it is a learning experience, not only for you but for the publisher, who may be learning what libraries want and what they will refuse to accept in a license agreement. A renewal license might not be at all like the original license you signed.

REVIEW PROCESS

Be consistent in your approach to reviewing licenses. Use a checklist (see Figure 5–4), and highlight information in the license that appears on your checklist for easy reference later. Determine if any language in the license needs to be edited or deleted, or if anything needs to be added. Check to make sure that you have every attachment that is mentioned in the license, then carefully read all of the attachments. Confirm that you and your institution can comply with all the requirements and restrictions presented in the license. The ARL Guidelines make the following excellent recommendation: **"Focus on your users and their needs."**

THIRD-PARTY REVIEW
Subscription Agents

In trying to find ways to streamline e-journal acquisitions, some libraries delegate the review of licenses to a subscription agent, since most agents now offer this service. Unless your representative has a very deep and thorough understanding of your library's needs and preferences, you should probably review licenses yourself. In order to manage licensed resources, you must be familiar with the terms to which you have agreed. You and your staff will be responsible for complying with those terms, and it is your signature, not that of the subscription agent, that will appear on the license.

Consortium Partners

If your library is part of a consortial buying group, you should not assume that someone else is reviewing licenses with attention to your specific concerns. In the rush to close a prolonged negotiation process, the consortial representative may send an addendum to each library to sign without sending the actual license. Since you will still be responsible for meeting the terms that were approved on your library's behalf, you should ask to read a copy of the agreement before you sign anything. You will need the final agreement for your files. And if you ask for modifications before you will sign, chances are you will be doing the other libraries a favor, despite the inevitable delays.

Legal Council

It would be time consuming and expensive to have an attorney review every contract that the library signs. However, if you have questions about any of the provisions, the language of the contract, or the ability of your institution to comply with any of the terms, consult legal counsel at your institution.

License review may initially seem somewhat daunting. However, with experience you will become familiar with contract language, and you will note that certain provisions are common to most licenses. Experience will also give you confidence in your ability to recognize what is standard and identify where you need to question terms and negotiate changes.

TERMS OF THE LICENSE

There is as yet no standard for the provisions you will find in licenses. However, certain terms or clauses are typically present in the majority of licenses. You may be further guided by policies of your institution regarding provisions that are required or prohibited, or there may be a requirement for specific language that must be a part of the contract. Expect to see the name of the resource being licensed, the names of the parties to the license, definition of selected terms used in the license, and the time period covered by the license.

Listed below are many of the license provisions you will encounter as you do your review. Comments are included on what you should watch for, and what you might want to negotiate out of the license. The many provisions you may encounter can be organized into five categories:

- Users
- Uses
- Content
- Access
- Contractual Obligations

The price you have agreed to pay is also part of the license; however, that part is covered in Chapter 6.

USERS
Authorized Users

If you are in an academic library, you will want to make sure that authorized users include all faculty, staff, and students. Do not forget to include visiting faculty or scholars as well as emeritus faculty. Make sure that walk-in users who are not affiliated with the institution can also access electronic resources while in your library. A fairly typical definition of authorized users is in the license for the American Society of Civil Engineers, available online (www.pubs.asce.org/journals/institut.pdf):

> For purposes of this Agreement, "Authorized Users" means only the employees, faculty, staff, students officially affiliated with the Subscriber, and persons with legal access to the library's collections and facilities on-site, using an IP address within the range identified in the Appendix.

Most vendors will accept a university's definition of faculty and staff; however, you should have a reasonable definition on hand in case you are asked to be specific. "Adjunct faculty" who provide an occasional service to the university or subcontractors funded by research grants should not necessarily be allowed to have access to a university library's licensed resources. If your definition of faculty and staff includes marginally affiliated professionals in your community who would otherwise subscribe to the electronic product individually, a vendor might consider you to be in breach of contract if this part of your definition is not specified in your license agreement. Be prepared to provide an official description of your community of users, and use it consistently.

Privacy and Confidentiality

The user's privacy should always be protected and respected. This may be an issue in the collection of usage statistics, which should not compromise the privacy (identity) and the confidentiality (usage of information) of individual users. The library may wish to have a clause included in the license that will guarantee user privacy and confidentiality. The model license agreement for academic libraries created by Cox Associates contains such a clause, and is available (www.licensingmodels.com):

> Such usage data shall be compiled in a manner consistent with applicable privacy [and data protection] laws [and as may be agreed between the parties from time to time], and the anonymity of individual users and the confidentiality of their searches shall be fully protected.

User Agreement

Once the library has signed a license with the database provider, the library user should not be required to agree to the terms of a click-wrap license as well in order to access the resource. The California Digital Library has specified this in a checklist they have available on their Web site (www.cdlib.org/libstaff/sharedcoll/docs/checklist.pdf):

> The publisher/vendor should not cause authorized users to enter into a potentially binding agreement with the publisher (e.g., a "click-through" license) independent of the institutional agreement with the University as a condition of use of its product.

USES
Authorized Uses

There should be a specific, detailed statement in the license that defines how the electronic journal may be used. You will often see a statement that permits use of the data for educational and other noncommercial purposes consistent with fair use. Make sure that text from the electronic journal or database can be quoted, and that there are no unreasonable restrictions on use. A clause in the license of the American Meteorological Association (www.ametsoc.org/pubs/jnl/elicense.pdf) gives permission to the users:

> . . . to use, with appropriate credit, figures, tables, and brief excerpts from the journals in scientific and educational works or similar work product of the Authorized User, except those portions thereof that are so noted as in the public domain or are U.S. government works, for which no permission to copy is required.

Fair Use

When negotiating a license for an electronic journal, package, or database, do not give up the rights that are granted to you by Sections 107 and 108 of the Copyright Act. Publishers are understandably uncomfortable with the ease with which files can be copied and transmitted to others. As a result, some have imposed restrictions that may limit access and use even by authorized users. Know what the law will permit you to have, and do not settle for less. In a videoconference on "De-mystifying the Licensing of Electronic Resources," Molly Sherden (1999) suggested that licenses be amended to add the following clause if there is no reference to fair use:

> Notwithstanding anything to the contrary in this Agreement, no term or provision of this contract shall he interpreted to limit or restrict the "fair use" rights of the Library provided by statute in 17 U.S.C. §§ 107 and 504.

Limit of Liability

The library should incur no liability for the actions of individual users who misuse the resource, as long as every effort is made to inform users of restrictions and prevent misuse. If misuse does occur, the library is almost always required to take some kind of corrective action. Sherden (1999) suggests that the following clause be added to licenses:

> Library will exercise reasonable, good faith efforts to inform Authorized Users of the restrictions on use of the licensed material and to enforce such restrictions; however, Library shall not be liable for the actions of individual users who act without the knowledge or consent of the library.

Printing and Downloading

Authorized users should be able to freely print and download articles from the electronic journals to which the library subscribes.

Some licenses prohibit the downloading of entire volumes or issues. This is not an unreasonable restriction and provides some protection for the publisher. Such a clause is present in Kluwer's license for Kluwer Online, and is available at the publisher's Web site (www.kluweronline.com/common/kap/gw-kolicense.htm):

> Permitted access by authorized users includes the retrieving, displaying, searching, downloading, printing and storing of individual articles for scholarly research, educational and personal use. Copying and storing is limited to single copies of a reasonable number of individual articles. Copying and storing of entire issues is not permitted.

Interlibrary Loan

Interlibrary loan is a right given to libraries by Section 108 of the Copyright Law of 1976. Ideally, the license should permit you to provide print or electronic copies of an article to fill interlibrary loan requests. However, you may find that you are limited to print copies only. Make sure you communicate any restrictions the license imposes on ILL activity to the appropriate staff. An example of a restriction on electronic ILL is contained in the license of the American Association for the Advancement of Science (AAAS) for Science Online available at their Web site (www.sciencemag.org/subscriptions/terms-unlim.shtml):

> Because of the easily reproducible nature of electronic publications, AAAS explicitly prohibits Inter Library Loan of articles or components of Science Online including Science and ScienceNOW in any electronic or digital form. It will, however, be permissible for your institution to print out occasional articles for Inter Library Loan under CONTU guidelines, provided the printing is done at your location and at your expense, and that only a limited number of copies of such articles will be made and distributed in this way.

The Interlibrary Loan Project on Yale University's Liblicense Web site (http://www.library.yale.edu/~llicense/ILLproject.html) was developed by "a working group formed to document publishers and aggregators/vendors license provisions for fulfillment of electronic ILL for the academic library community." Vendors are invited to provide information about their provisions for ILL in their licenses—so far a few vendors have done so.

Course Packs and Electronic Reserve

It should be possible for you to provide print copies of an article from an electronic journal for course packs to be used for instructional purposes by your authorized users. The license should also permit a print copy of an article to be placed on reserve. If URLs are available for individual articles, it should also be permissible to provide a link to an article that is placed on electronic reserve. When the course is completed, the print copy of the article should be discarded and the link to the electronic copy should be deleted. Some licenses prohibit the use of articles in course packs or reserves without permission. For example, the standard Taylor and Francis license (www.tandf.co.uk/journals/terms.pdf) states:

> For the avoidance of doubt, the Licensee may not incorporate all or any part of the Licensed Materials in Course Packs and Electronic Reserve collections without the prior written permission of the Publisher or the Publisher's Representative, which may set out further terms and conditions for such usage.

Usage Statistics

Usage data should be provided to you on a regular and continuing basis. This is not something that all publishers are able to provide. Let them know the importance of this to your library by adding it to the contract. For example, usage data will help you in making decisions on renewing specific titles or databases, and will let you know if you should be promoting some resources more aggressively. For these and other reasons, accurate and timely usage statistics are essential to managing electronic journals efficiently. The model licensing agreement from Cox Associates (www.licensingmodels.com) suggests the following clause:

> The Publisher shall provide to the Licensee or facilitate the collection and provision to the Licensee and the Publisher by the Licensee or the Agent of such usage data on the number [of titles] [of abstracts and] of articles downloaded, by journal title, on [a monthly] [a quarterly][an annual] basis for the Publisher's and the Licensee's private internal use only.

To guarantee that you will receive usage statistics that are usable and compatible with other statistics you track, you can specify that the vendor comply with COUNTER code of practice. An increasing number of publishers and database vendors use these guidelines, formulated with the help of librarians, to design their usage reports (www.counterproject.org).

CONTENT
Contents of Database

A description of what you are purchasing or leasing should be included in the license. This will ensure that there is no misunderstanding on the part of the library regarding the content of the database. Often the content will be listed in an appendix, as in the BioOne Subscriber License (www.bioone.org/images/sub-license.pdf):

> Licensed Material: The electronic material listed in Appendix B, or in new Appendices to this License that may be agreed to by the parties from time to time.

If no provisions are included for the removal of content, you may wish to insert a clause in the license that will require the vendor or publisher to notify the library of changes in content, especially if the change is substantial or if there is a reduction in content. The standard BioOne subscriber license deals with reduction in content as follows:

> BioOne reserves the right at any time to withdraw from the Licensed Material any item or part of an item for which it no longer retains the right to publish, or which it has reasonable grounds to believe infringes copyright or is unlawful. BioOne shall give notice to the Licensee of such withdrawal. In the event that the total amount of material removed constitutes more than ten percent (10%) of the total content of the Licensed Material, BioOne will refund ten percent (10%) of the then current Subscription Fee (www.bioone.org/images/sub-license.pdf, p. 4, sec. 5.3.).

The Greater Western Library Alliance (GWLA) "Guidelines for Licensing Electronic Information Resources" suggest the following preferred clause:

> In the case of withdrawal of content, Licensor shall give sufficient prior written notice, by letter or electronic mail, at least sixty (60) calendar days in advance of the withdrawal. The Licensor shall provide a reimbursement proportional to the value of the discontinued titles, pro-rated

for the balance of the contract term, which may be in the form of a credit memo applied to the subsequent year renewal, additional content proportional to that removed, or a cash refund. The form of reimbursement is to be negotiated between Licensor and Licensee (www.gwla.org).

Another option is to require that the license be renegotiated when a significant amount (which needs to be specified in the license) of content is withdrawn.

Archiving and Ownership

Determine if access to data is in perpetuity or only for a specific period of time. What do you own or have access to when your subscription expires? If the information provider does not assume responsibility for permanently archiving content, you will want to obtain an archival copy of the data. Project Muse, a nonprofit publisher, offers generous ownership terms in its standard license (http://muse.jhu.edu/proj_descrip/terms.html).

A subscribing library may download and archive materials at its own site and place contents on its own file server, including electronic reserves, providing that access to the file server is restricted to the campus/institutional community. Approximately 90 days after the expiration of an annual subscription term, Project Muse will provide, upon request, an archival (non-searchable) file on CD-ROM or other appropriate media as determined by Muse, containing the content of all issues published online during the 12-month subscription term.

Taylor and Francis provides continuing online access to licensed content (www.tandf.co.uk/journals/terms.pdf):

On termination of this License, the Publisher shall provide continuing access for Authorised Users to that part of the Licensed Materials which was published and paid for within the Subscription Period except where such termination is due to a breach of the License by the Licensee which the Licensee has failed to remedy as provided in 10.1.1 and 10.1.3 of this License.

The Society for Industrial and Applied Mathematics (SIAM), on the other hand, offers no such ownership rights in its license (www.siam.org/eaccess/ojsa98.pdf):

Access to material is for the length of the Agreement period only. There is no access to material after the Agreement is terminated.

Warranty

Warranty clauses generally are written in capital letters or appear in boldface. The content provider is telling you that they are not responsible for the accuracy, completeness, or currency of the information that they provide. Database aggregators, for example, are simply passing on to you and your users the content that they obtained from publishers. Even when publishers provide the data, they use the warranty to avoid litigation that could result from incorrect or incomplete data caused by technical problems or human error. An example of a warranty is on the Oxford University Press Web site (http://www3.oup.co.uk/access/InstSiteLicence.pdf):

> 6.2 Save as provided above, licensor gives no warranty, express or implied, and makes no representation that (I) the licensed work(s) will be of satisfactory quality, suitable for any particular purpose or for any particular use under specified conditions, notwithstanding that such purpose, use, or conditions may be known to licensor; or (II) that the licensed work(s) will operate error free or without interruption or that any errors will be corrected; or (III) that the material published in the licensed work(s) is either complete or accurate.

ACCESS
Authorization

Some method (either use of a password or of IP addresses) is likely to be defined to limit access to authorized users. If your library is not prepared to deal with passwords, make sure that the license permits access to users via IP address. A typical statement to this effect is in the license for the American Institute of Physics, which is available on their Web site (ftp://ftp.aip.org/aipdocs/forms/subinst.pdf):

> Authorized Users will be recognized and authorized by their Internet address. IP addresses and/or address ranges for the Subscribing Institution are indicated in the Appendix.

Be careful that any restrictions on access do not provide a barrier to use by your patrons, such as the requirements for one electronic journal:

- Only one simultaneous user is permitted.
- A ten-minute waiting period is mandatory between users.
- A password is required and will be changed frequently.

See more discussion about authentication issues later in this chapter.

Site

If an authorized user wishes to access an electronic journal, this should be possible regardless of the user's location. Watch for licenses that limit access only to the library, or to the campus. This will disenfranchise all of your distance-education students, plus any authorized user who is off-site. Some licenses require that the entire campus be physically contiguous, which would eliminate access to users who are in a building or department that is not on the main campus. A clause such as the one below from the Association of Asian Studies provides a broad definition of campus; the full license is available on their Web site (http://www.aasianst.org/bas-sub.htm):

> If the Subscriber has one or more remote sites or campuses which do not have their own central administrative staff, but are instead administered by the subscriber's site or campus, persons affiliated with those remote sites or campus will also be considered Authorized Users.

Publisher/Vendor Responsibility

There may be a clause in your license in which the publisher or vendor will describe the kind of performance you can expect and the technical support they are willing to provide. This is sometimes phrased in terms of "reasonable effort," so it may be difficult to enforce. A typical clause to this effect is in the license of the American Mathematical Society on their Web site (www.ams.org/customers/jour-license.html):

> The AMS will not be liable for any delay, down time, or other failure of performance, but will use reasonable efforts to correct any performance problem brought to its attention.

You may wish to include language in your license that will extend the contract by the number of day(s) you are without access to the resource as a result of problems the database provider is having. The Committee on Institutional Cooperation (CIC) suggests the following standardized language to its members who are negotiating licenses:

> If, due to causes within its reasonable control, Licensor is unable to provide Licensee with access to the Product for a period exceeding twenty-four (24) consecutive hours, Licensor agrees to extend the license period for corresponding twenty-four (24) hour increments at no additional cost to Licensee (www.cic.uiuc.edu/programs/ CLIConsortialAgreementProgram/archive/ResourceList/ contracts/standardized_agreement_language.htm).

Force Majeure

This term literally means major force, and when included in a license, absolves the licensor from liability in the case of a natural disaster, war, or other event over which the licensor has no control. An example may be found in the license for the American Institute of Physics ([AIP] ftp.aip.org/aipdocs/forms/ subinst.pdf):

> AIP, however, will not be liable for any delay, downtime, transmission error, software or equipment incompatibilities, force majeure or other failure of performance.

CONTRACTUAL OBLIGATION
Controlling or Governing Law

State, not federal law, governs contracts. Many licenses prescribe the governing law to be that of the state in which the publisher or aggregator has its headquarters. If you work for a state institution, it is possible that you will be forbidden to enter into a contract with this requirement. Ideally, governing law should be the jurisdiction of your institution. In the event of problems with the contract, that is the law with which your attorneys will be most familiar. However, the choice of governing law should be workable for both parties to the contract. Another option is to simply delete the clause prescribing governing law from the license. The CIC recommends the following clause in contracts negotiated by its membership:

This Agreement will be construed under and pursuant to the laws of the forum in which any controversy hereunder is adjudicated. Any suit and/or proceeding in connection herewith will be brought and prosecuted only in the home state of the party against whom that suit and/or proceeding is instituted (www.cic.uiuc.edu/programs/ CLIConsortialAgreementProgram/archive/ResourceList/ contracts/standardized_agreement_language.htm).

Indemnifying the Publisher

Some contracts require the library to indemnify or hold the publisher harmless against all claims of third parties arising out of their use of the product. For example, data in an electronic journal article referenced by a researcher may be inaccurate, causing damage to his professional reputation. The library should not have to protect the publisher. Do not accept financial responsibility for damages that the publisher or information provider may suffer. Delete clauses such as this from your contract:

> The subscriber assumes the sole responsibility for all use of all electronic journals and agrees to indemnify and hold the Licensor harmless from any liability or claim of any person arising from such use.

Renewal/Cancellation

Some licenses specify an automatic renewal unless you contact the licensor within a designated period of time to cancel. Presumably you will be invoiced, but if the invoice arrives after the cancellation deadline, you are committed to the resource for another year. You may wish to maintain a calendar or spreadsheet, or code the order records in your serials system to alert you to these deadlines. A typical example of a renewal clause is in the license for the American Mathematical Society (www.ams.org/customers/jour-license.html):

> This Agreement is signed and will remain in effect thereafter for successive calendar years so long as annual subscription fees are paid. Either party may terminate this Agreement, effective on the next renewal date, by at least 30 days written notice to the other party.

License Termination

Most licenses may be terminated before the end of the subscription period if there is a breach of contract. Should such a breach occur, you must be given adequate notice and a chance to correct the situation during a defined remedy period. Also, termination rights should be mutual. If the publisher or aggregator fails to deliver as promised, the library should be able to cancel the contract and receive a pro-rated refund. Wiley's Basic Access License for its InterScience product includes a termination clause in the sample license (http://www3.interscience.wiley.com/spreadsheet_documents/sample_ballicense.pdf):

> Either party may terminate this License if the other party materially breaches its obligations under this License and fails to cure such material breach, provided that the non-breaching party shall give written notice of its intention to terminate and shall allow the breaching party 60 days after receipt of such notice to remedy the breach.

As universities and municipalities face budget uncertainties, multiyear licenses are a mixed blessing. Significant cost-savings can be realized through caps on price increases for the duration of the license; however, libraries are understandably nervous about committing to a large ongoing expense, and some state laws prohibit signing such a license without some kind of escape clause. Publishers are reluctant to agree to an escape clause that will render the multiyear terms meaningless, so it must be carefully crafted. Watson (2003) proposes the following language:

> Licensor acknowledges that the ability of X library to participate in the agreement is subject to and contingent upon the availability of funds appropriated by the state legislature or institutional budget processes. The Library shall make a good faith effort to obtain the funding to meet the obligations as set forth in this Agreement. The Library may terminate participation in this Agreement only at the start of a subscription calendar year (January 1) by giving the Licensor notification within (90) days prior to the start of that subscription calendar year. The Library agrees to pay to Licensor a termination fee of 2% of the portion of the then annual Database Fee.

Assignment

You will likely find a clause in most contracts you review that prohibits the library from assigning or transferring its access rights to a third party. An example of a unilateral contract clause is present in the license for SIAM, available on the Web (www.siam.org/eaccess/Ojsa.pdf):

> The Subscribing Institution may not assign or transfer its rights under this Agreement.

However, you are less apt to find a clause that prohibits the vendor or publisher from transferring its contract with you to another company. You may wish to add such a clause to protect the library in the event the company is sold or merges with another. The likelihood of buyouts and mergers has increased over the past few years. If the contract is being transferred, you should have the right to renegotiate or cancel your existing contract. Or you can try to include a clause such as the one required in the GWLA "Guidelines for Licensing Electronic Information Resources" (www.gwla.org):

> In the event the Licensor is sold to a new owner, the terms and conditions, and rights and privileges, will be honored throughout the Term of this Agreement.

The Northeast Research Libraries (NERL) consortium pushes for even further protection in its Principles for Electronic Journal Licenses:

> Any grant of perpetual rights included in a contract must be guaranteed to be permanent without regard to contingencies such as mergers and acquisitions, insolvency, or transfers of ownership to another publisher (www.library.yale.edu/NERLpublic/EJrn/Principles.pdf).

Entire Agreement

There is generally a clause in the license stating that the document you are signing and any attachments to the document constitute the entire agreement between the parties. This means that any verbal agreements you have made with the publisher or vendor are not legally binding. Make sure you get all verbal agreements in writing and that they are included in the license or in an attachment to the license. The clause below is from the license for Taylor and Francis journals, which can be found on their Web site (www.tandf.co.uk/journals/terms.pdf):

> This agreement constitutes the entire agreement between the parties and supersedes all prior communications,

understandings, and agreements relating to the subject matter of this License, whether oral or written.

Nondisclosure

Some licenses may ask that you not disclose contract terms to a third party, and keep the information confidential. Nondisclosure may not be appropriate, or even possible, for a public institution that is spending taxpayers' dollars on electronic resources. Also, you may wish to share the terms of your license with other libraries as everyone attempts to learn from each other about best practices in this area.

CHECKLIST

The checklist that follows will assist you in determining if the licenses you review contain the terms needed to define and preserve the library's rights. Not every license will contain all of the information on the checklist below. Some licenses may have additional terms or provisions. It is up to you, and in some cases your institution's legal counsel, to determine if the presence or absence of specific terms means you are unable to sign a given license.

ATTACHMENTS

Some information specific to your institution may appear as one or more separate attachments to the license. All attachments are an integral part of the contract that you sign, and there will be language in the license to that effect. The following is some of the information that may appear in an attachment:

- License period, when the subscription starts and when it ends
- A clear and unambiguous statement of price, including any additional charges that may be involved beyond the annual subscription fee
- Payment options, if the library is not going to be invoiced for the full amount immediately
- Other terms related to the cost (e.g., price cap on annual renewals with a long-term contract; any restrictions on canceling print; discounted price when subscribing to print and online)

FIGURE 5–4. Electronic Journals License Checklist

Preliminaries

_____ Name of resource to be licensed
_____ Parties to the license
_____ Grant clause describing what licensor is providing to the library
_____ Length of contract
_____ Fees included in license or in attachment to license
_____ Definition of terms

Users

_____ Defines authorized users (students, faculty, staff, affiliated users, walk-ins)
_____ Does not compromise privacy or confidentiality of users

Use

_____ Defines authorized uses, without unduly restricting user needs
_____ Does not limit rights provided by fair use
_____ Does not make the library liable for actions of individual users
_____ Permits printing and downloading
_____ Allows articles to be sent to other libraries through interlibrary loan
_____ Allows electronic interlibrary loan
_____ Permits use for course packs and electronic reserves
_____ Provides usage statistics

Content

_____ Describes the data to be leased or purchased
_____ Provides some option for access if subscription is cancelled
_____ Provides compensation for removal of content
_____ Provides for archiving of content if publication or service ceases

Access

_____ Provides for authentication by IP address
_____ Permits access by authorized users who are off-site
_____ Describes technical support provided
_____ Promises reasonable efforts to provide continuous access
_____ Defines hardware, browser, and networking requirements

Contractual Obligations

_____ Does not mandate controlling or governing law in another state or country
_____ Does not require the library to indemnify publisher against third-party claims
_____ Provides an option for cancellation by either party, with written notice
_____ Includes right to terminate for breach of contract, with a remedy period allowed
_____ Specifies a reasonable period of time to remedy a breach of contract
_____ Protects the library's interests in the event of a change of ownership or insolvency
_____ Does not include a nondisclosure agreement

FIGURE 5–5. Required Features in an Acceptable License .

Required Features (a.k.a. Deal Breakers)
University of Washington Libraries

- Clear, complete statement of terms and conditions
- Confidentiality for users
- Fair use of all information for non-commercial, educational, instructional, and research purposes by authorized users, including downloading portions of the electronic information for personal use and unlimited viewing
- License must not hold UW Libraries responsible for unauthorized use as long as reasonable and appropriate methods are implemented to notify user community of restrictions
- Termination rights appropriate to both parties
- Warranty of systems functionality and service

(Soete and Davis, 1999, p. 59)

NEGOTIATING CHANGES

Do not be passive when licenses do not suit your needs, but actively seek to negotiate a license agreement with terms favorable to you and your users and consistent with fair use guidelines. If you are negotiating on behalf of a consortium, you will have even more influence. While consortial purchasing is usually done to get a better price, do not overlook the fact that it will give you added leverage in negotiating a favorable contract.

If you do not understand a particular clause in the license you are reviewing, ask that it be rewritten in laymen's terms. You may want to delete clauses that do not apply to your institution. Make sure that any verbal agreement made with a marketing representative of the company is included in the license, since the verbal agreement is not legally binding. If you have negotiated several changes, you will want to have the contract rewritten, but if changes are very minor, they can be made on the original copy of the license and initialed.

In some cases a resource may be sufficiently unique or in high enough demand to warrant compromising on some of the terms of the license. What is a "deal-breaker" for one resource may not be for another. If you are forced to compromise, seek to renegotiate the terms of the license for the resource when it is renewed.

Also, check to see if any other vendors or aggregators have started to provide access to the resource. Often it comes down to a matter of supply and demand; with limited supply or high demand you may not have as much flexibility to negotiate a favorable contract for the library.

License terms are not carved in stone. You have the power to change the terms of a license to benefit the library and its users. Keep in mind that the publisher or aggregator will usually be happy to work with you to resolve problems, clarify language, and make it possible for you to sign the license. Your purchase of the resource they are selling depends upon it. They expect to have to make some changes in the license to accommodate your library's interests. After all, the license was written by their attorneys to protect their interests; without your input, it remains one-sided.

SIGNING AND MANAGING THE LICENSE

The person authorized to sign licenses will vary from one institution to the next. It could be your serials or acquisitions librarian, the head of collection development, or someone in purchasing. You may have a position dedicated to the management of electronic resources, which includes handling all the details of negotiating and signing licenses. The dean or director of your library may be the only person with the authority to enter into a legal contract of any kind on behalf of the library. In some cases it may even be necessary to have the institution's legal counsel review and sign a license, although that is a rather expensive option.

If the person who signs the license is not the one who reviews it, the reviewer should provide a summary of the terms and make a note of anything that is considered questionable. A checklist could be useful for this purpose. The license should be signed by both the library and the vendor or publisher, and a signed copy should be kept on file in the library.

MANAGING LICENSES

ARL SPEC Kit 248 is *Managing the Licensing of Electronic Products*. It reports the results of a survey of 44 ARL libraries on their license management policies and procedures and a small collection of representative documents. The documents include position descriptions, information on training, forms and checklists, and examples of standard contract language. The editors recommend that the license management process include the following tasks:

- Prepare and maintain policies on licensing.
- Prepare and maintain a generic agreement with standard language concerning the rights and privileges that are important to the library.
- Provide guidance to collection development staff on licensing issues related to evaluating electronic products for purchase.
- Negotiate licenses with vendors.
- Maintain files of signed license agreements.
- Interpret license agreements to library staff and users, and educate them in their rights and responsibilities.

AUTOMATED LICENSE MANAGEMENT SYSTEMS

Libraries that are party to a large number of license agreements have developed various methods to keep them organized and to provide ways for staff to find answers easily to questions about terms, such as the number of simultaneous users, ILL provisions, and renewal parameters.

Homegrown Systems

Homegrown e-resource management databases, such as VERA at MIT and ERLIC² at Penn State (see Chapter 6) frequently include license-tracking components. Some libraries scan the text of license agreements to make them available through an intranet to distributed staff. Intranet pages can also be used to provide license negotiators with easy access to institutional information, such as IP ranges and the user census. *A Web Hub for Developing Administrative Metadata for Electronic Resource Management* (at www.library.cornell.edu/cts/elicensestudy/) reports on locally developed solutions for managing administrative information contained in license agreements.

Commercial Products

The library automation industry has begun to recognize a market in libraries for sophisticated software that will help manage metadata for licenses and other administrative information about libraries' electronic resources. Innovative Interfaces, Inc., (III) is the first ILS vendor to develop an electronic resource management (ERM) module that includes enhanced order records for electronic databases and e-journal packages, enabling library staff to "manage licensing and purchasing details in a single interface"

FIGURE 5-6. Simple Explanation of User Rights and Responsibilities

University of Nevada, Reno Libraries   Search | Site Map | HELP

Catalog | Subjects | Databases | Reserves | Journals | eBooks | Reference

Terms of Use for Licensed Online Resources

Use of the online databases and ejournals provided by the University of Nevada is governed by license agreements. These agreements require the University to give access only to its students, faculty, and staff (though, in most cases, they also allow use by unaffiliated visitors who are physically present on campus). They also place certain obligations on the individual user.

Among these are the following:

- To use the information contained in these products for personal, noncommercial purposes only;
- To refrain from systematically downloading significant portions of the online content;
- To refrain from redistributing the content to others outside the University community;
- To refrain from copying or tampering with the software by which the information is organized and displayed.

As you use these resources, please keep the above obligations in mind. If you fail to adhere to them, you may lose your network privileges and face other disciplinary action. Severe breaches of the license terms can result in the entire University losing access to important online resources.

For more details about your obligations when using University computing and network resources, see the Campus Computing Policies page

---

and "define relationships between electronic resources." Other ILS vendors with e-journal management systems in place or under development are Endeavor (Meridian), ExLibris (Verde), and VTLS (VERIFY). EBSCO and Swets have also been developing products to manage administrative metadata. See Chapter 6 for more information.

INFORMING AND EDUCATING USERS ABOUT LICENSE TERMS

Some licenses explicitly require the library to inform users of restrictions; others are less direct but still hold the library responsible for preventing inappropriate uses of their journals. Libraries can only be required to make "reasonable efforts" to educate users about their rights and responsibilities. Most users won't spend the time to read about the license terms governing the use of library-provided electronic resources. But a library is usually protected from liability in a breach by a user if the terms of use are made available in some way. Some libraries use a "click through" page that summarizes allowable uses of licensed resources; others provide links on their e-journal menu pages to a page designed to educate users about their rights and responsibilities according to individual licenses.

ACCESS MANAGEMENT AND AUTHENTICATION

"... There does not seem to be any simple, inexpensive, ready-to-deploy comprehensive solution for authentication and access management; while there are many promising components available, management complexity, user training and acceptance, system integration, and cost are still major issues."

—Clifford Lynch, 1998
(still true in 2004)

One of the most troubling and troublesome aspects of electronic journals for both providers and libraries is the matter of managing access to licensed resources. Licenses designate who is or is not an authorized user, and libraries agree to restrict access to licensed users only. There are several ways to do this; unfortunately, however, there is no simple way. Evolving technology offers new options, but we are still waiting for a breakthrough.

Every library must weigh its own technical resources and users' needs in choosing an access-management option. Consider how a system's features fit your situation, for example:

- Scalability
- Security
- Ease of deployment
- Flexibility
- Privacy and accountability
- Community acceptance
- Affordability

(Parkhurst, 2002, pp. 208–210).

AUTHENTICATION AND AUTHORIZATION

Authentication and authorization are not synonymous, and a library needs to do both. Authentication validates a user's credentials as part of a user group, and then authorization determines, based on the parameters of the license agreement, whether the institution can permit the authenticated user to have remote access to a particular resource.

Authentication takes place locally; it is based on attributes or status such as being a currently enrolled student or currently employed staff member of an institution, or (for public libraries) living in the area served by the library and registering with the library for access to online resources. The library's authentication process should

- be efficient,
- be unobtrusive,
- require the presentation of credentials only once during a session, however that is defined,

- protect patrons' privacy, and
- be trustworthy from a vendor's point of view.

Most content providers won't care how your library controls access, as long as you can differentiate between eligible and ineligible users and keep ineligible users out. No system is perfect, nor can you be expected to foil every attempt to circumvent it. But your system must assure reasonable security.

Most academic libraries, and many public libraries, already have some experience in authenticating remote users of their licensed databases, but providing access to a large number of additional electronic journals to off-site users will dramatically increase your remote traffic and may call for new approaches. Many libraries have started with one authentication system but changed to another (perhaps more than once) to make remote access easier or more secure, or to enable access to a greater number of resources. If your library has provided remote access to only one major database or to databases from only one vendor, you may have been able to use a proprietary authentication system maintained by the vendor that will not work for resources from other vendors. As a result of viruses and other kinds of attacks on computers and networks using the Internet, new security precautions by parent institutions and Internet service providers sometimes interfere with a library's authentication process.

Security and ease of access are both critical factors in determining how best to authenticate users, although you may be limited by the methods your resource providers can support. The security issues have become more complex, and ease of use becomes increasingly crucial as users become increasingly impatient with obstacles on the Web. It has been documented that use of a resource will decrease as barriers to access increase. The library needs a system that will examine and approve or reject credentials through a database of legitimate users, a log-in process, or by location (e.g., on campus or in designated buildings), or a combination of methods. There are several common methods of authentication:

- Local password verification
- IP address permission
- Referring URL validation
- Cookies
- URL-embedded user-id/password
- Vendor-provided script

Password verification and IP addresses are the most common

methods used to provide user authentication, often in combination. In the future, there may be other methods of authentication that are based on technological developments in fingerprinting, voice recognition, and retinal scans.

USER NAME AND PASSWORD AUTHENTICATION

There are two types of password access to licensed resources:

- One username/password combination that gets all authorized users into a particular resource
- A unique username/password combination that allows a particular user to access many or all of the library's licensed resources

With either method, users are typically prompted for a user ID and password in order to access an online resource. Password authentication is difficult for most libraries since it usually involves distributing a single password to hundreds, or even thousands, of users, or managing the distribution and upkeep of unique usernames and passwords. The library must then trust that users will keep a password confidential and not e-mail it to their friends, post it to a listserv, or add it to their personal Web pages. If the confidentiality of the password is compromised, the library must have a secure and efficient way to distribute a new password to all authorized users. An integrated system of linking or searching across resources exacerbates the difficulties in using passwords for database and e-journal access.

It is not uncommon for academic and other libraries to refuse to purchase access to a resource that offers only password authentication. Vendors will, and have, responded to this kind of customer feedback by offering IP authentication.

However, for some situations password access is the best option. An example would be a corporation with many regional or even international offices, each with separate staff handling network concerns, addressing, firewalls, and so forth. Rather than distributing passwords, some corporate libraries have developed a more user-friendly option and embedded the user ID and password into the URL for the journal-title link. However, to meet licensing requirements, this would only work if the company has a very secure network or intranet that excludes access from anyone outside the corporation. Some special libraries provide lists of passwords for databases and e-journals on a protected intranet page.

Recently, some very large library systems have chosen to use password access to solve problems inherent in other methods of authentication. INSPIRE, or Indiana Virtual Library, which provides access to licensed full-text databases for all citizens of Indiana, authenticates by IP filtering whenever possible, with a backup password system. From the INSPIRE FAQ:

> We have gathered IP addresses from local Internet service providers, colleges, libraries, K-12 schools and businesses so we can authenticate users who connect to the Internet within the state of Indiana. If you use any Internet Service Provider (ISP) that serves areas outside Indiana (such as AOL, CompuServe and Prodigy), you will need to apply for an INSPIRE Password (www.inspire.net/faq.html).

INSPIRE passwords are only mailed to Indiana addresses, and are good for a year. To deal with caching server problems, the current date is displayed on the INSPIRE entry page, with a note: "If the date showing is incorrect, please refresh or reload your browser."

The entire UK academic community has united to implement the Athens system, under which each user can choose a unique username and password that allows access to all resources licensed by that user's institution (www.eduserve.org.uk/athens).

If your authentication system uses passwords, you should follow these guidelines:

- Do not post the password(s) on Web pages that are publicly accessible.
- Do not e-mail password(s) to users.
- Change passwords frequently (at least once a semester for academic libraries).

IP RECOGNITION

Every computer on a network has an assigned numeric IP address that is unique. An example of a unique IP address is 134.197.29.16, with 134.197 identifying the network domain; 29 representing a subdomain, such as a building; and 16 representing the node for a computer on that subdomain. A server hosting licensed resources is able to recognize an incoming IP address for a computer that is attempting to connect to those resources, allowing or disallowing access based on whether the IP address falls within a range of authorized IP addresses provided by the subscriber. Internet service providers offering dial-up connections might assign "dynamic" IP addresses during each dial-up session from a pool of available IP addresses.

On-Site Users

The institutional home of the library, whether it is a university, a hospital, school system, research laboratory or complex, government agency, or corporate office will generally have a computer network of some kind. Computers that are part of the institutional network (usually represented by a range of IP addresses) are considered to be "on site" in most licenses, though some licenses are more literal in defining a site geographically. Simple IP recognition on the part of the publisher should allow all computers on the network to access that publisher's electronic resources without their users having to do anything.

However, if you share a network with other institutions, you will need to compile a more refined list of the IP addresses for the computers that are part of your institution only. Some licenses restrict on-site usage to members of the institution, in which case you may need to authenticate users of your public-access computers by some means (usually a log-in procedure). An institution-wide log-in procedure for accessing the network will make it easier to identify violators of the license agreement (see "Prevention and Management of License Violations and Security Breaches," below), but your larger institution will need to be involved in implementing a network-wide authentication process.

Remote Users

IP recognition for off-site users is much more problematic, since in most cases they will access the Web (including online library resources) through an Internet service provider (ISP). If your institution acts as an ISP for your employees or students (and does not provide this service for anyone who is unaffiliated), the server through which they access the Internet will be on your network with an IP address that will allow your remote users to be identified as authorized users.

If your users are required to use a third-party ISP, or even if some of them do so voluntarily even though you provide ISP services, their IP addresses will be affiliated with the network used by the unaffiliated ISPs. Those IPs may be static or dynamic, depending on the type of connection the ISP provides. Most license agreements would not allow the registration of IP addresses that are outside your library's domain, and you would not want to keep track of those external IP addresses unless you have fewer than 10 users. The use of a proxy server is the most common way to authenticate remote users, either through a mechanical process or an application-level process, but neither method is simple.

PROXIES

Proxy systems enable a library to control authentication at the local level. Proxies can be mechanical (Web proxy server) or application level (gateway).

Proxy Server

A mechanical proxy method uses the hypertext transfer protocol (HTTP) to authenticate your users locally through a computer on your authorized network, thereafter making it appear that authenticated users are coming from the IP address of the proxy server. This method requires the user's browser to be configured to direct all outgoing traffic through the proxy server, so that each request for a URL will be checked against a table (maintained by library staff) of URLs for all licensed resources. When users request URLs that are in the table, they will be prompted for usernames and passwords, usually their library-card numbers or a campus-ID number. The log-in information will be checked against the library's patron database for circulation or another locally maintained database of authorized users.

Here is an example of how the proxy-server process might work. The assumption is made that the user's browser has been properly configured (see "Proxy-Server Browser Configuration" below):

- The IP address of your library's proxy server is given to a database provider, for example, Elsevier.
- The user tries to access Elsevier's ScienceDirect from home using AOL or a local ISP.
- The IP address of the ISP does not correspond to any that you have registered with Elsevier as being within the valid range for authorized users.
- The user is now automatically prompted for name and library bar-code number.
- The data entered by the user are verified against the patron database in your library's online circulation system.
- The data match an entry in the library's database, so the user is authenticated and the request for access is passed on to Elsevier.
- Elsevier sees the address of the proxy server from which the request is made, and verifies that the address is included within the valid range of authorized IP addresses you have submitted.
- The user's request is filled, and the browser is now able to display the needed journal article.

It should be noted that some libraries pass all users through a proxy server, so even those who are accessing licensed electronic resources from within the library must provide the information to the proxy server needed for authentication. If the vendor or publisher's definition of authorized user excludes walk-ins, this method will allow you to limit access even from within the library.

Proxy-Server Browser Configuration

A challenge for library staff and users alike is the complexity of configuring browsers to use the proxy server. Generally speaking, the user is embedding the URL of the proxy server into the browser software, and each browser needs to be configured only once, unless other proxy servers are used for other purposes. However, the method of doing so is different for each type of browser, and even for different versions of the same browser. Browser configurations will not be the same for computers that use a dial-up connection and those that are on a broadband or local area network.

Library staff should be very familiar with the procedure and capable of talking frustrated users through the process, as well as assisting with troubleshooting. Instructions must be presented clearly and logically, and should be available in print and on the Web. Be sure to let users know what to expect when they log on to the proxy server. Will they be prompted for their names, their social security numbers, their student-identification numbers, a patron bar-code number, or a library-assigned PIN?

Despite the best efforts of library staff to provide clear and concise instructions, there will still be problems, some of which you can probably anticipate:

- Some versions of some browsers (e.g., Netscape 6.0) do not handle proxying very well.
- If users have an existing proxy on their browser, such as a proxy for their ISP or a company firewall, they will not be able to access the licensed library databases.
- For security reasons, some ISPs do not allow their customers to use proxy servers, and some have disabled the use of certain ports, which may interfere with users' access to your proxy server.
- Many services will not work properly with AOL's own browser. You may need to have your library users with AOL service download Internet Explorer or Netscape in order to use the library's remote databases.

- Proxy servers are mission-critical systems that need to be constantly available.

The proxy-server method of authentication is expensive and both labor and resource intensive for libraries. The process requires staff with the skill to manage and administer the technology. But the users and content providers must also take action in order for the proxy server to function.

- *The library* must install and maintain proxy software, maintain and support the server, and provide support to proxy-server users; the process must be reliable to ensure access and scalable to accommodate growth.
- *The user* must configure his or her Web browser with the proxy server's IP address; it will be problematic if the user is already required to configure the browser for their ISP's proxy server.
- *The resource provider* has little overhead with this method, other than being able to identify the IP address from which users are coming.

Administration of a proxy server is complex and requires considerable technical expertise and support, and details on how to manage a proxy server are outside the scope of this book. However, one thing that is very important for librarians to know, especially if they are using a proxy server that is administered by someone outside the library, is that proxy servers must be kept secure. Open proxies invite abuse, allowing unaffiliated users to access your databases without being challenged for credentials. JSTOR experienced several thefts—systematic unauthorized downloading of a significant amount of content—by people who were able to search for and detect unsecured proxy servers (see Cain, 2003).

Proxy Rewrite

Another authentication option is growing in popularity because it does not require users to make changes in their browsers. The proxy-rewrite method is application based, using software from an ILS vendor (integrated with the patron database of the circulation module), from a third party, or home grown in the library. URLs for licensed resources that are configured according to the protocols are rewritten on the fly to invoke a script that asks users for log-in credentials. A cookie is passed to the user's computer so that the authentication process does not have to be repeated for subsequent use of other licensed resources during that session (as long as the browser is not closed).

Using a proxy-rewrite system requires some ongoing configuration work on the part of the library, but the benefits of simplifying the process for users and providing a method for users who have obstacles preventing them from using a mechanical-proxy process outweigh the drawbacks for many libraries. Currently EZproxy (www.ezproxy.com/), an inexpensive third-party authentication software, is gaining in popularity.

Some libraries have run into some technical problems with the proxy-rewrite method requiring troubleshooting that could conceivably involve

- the configuration of the software,
- the configuration of the local network,
- parameters of communication with the patron database,
- methods for creating local files (e-reserves scanning, for example), and
- technical issues with resource providers.

The biggest implementation challenge is in educating users. Unlike proxy servers, through which a user's Web request is channeled regardless of how it originates (as long as the browser is configured correctly), the proxy-rewrite method will not work unless the licensed resources are accessed through specially scripted URLs. In other words, library-licensed resources must be accessed through library Web pages. Users who have bookmarked the native URL for a favorite journal, search engine, or database will not be taken to the authentication page and thus will be denied access to that resource. Power users can learn the formula for changing a native URL to the scripted URL themselves, but most users will simply assume that access to the full text is not available.

Other Application-Level Proxy Systems

Less commonly used authentication options using application-level proxy protocols are

- pass-through proxies,
- reverse proxies, and
- relay proxies.

See Parkhurst (2002) for a technical discussion of proxy methods.

VIRTUAL PRIVATE NETWORK (VPN)

In terms of authenticating users of electronic library resources, the use of a virtual private network, or VPN, can solve some of the problems associated with proxy servers. It is similar to a proxy server in that it channels authorized users from remote computers through a server that has an institution-based IP address, but remote users of a VPN will be able to configure their computers so that they will be perceived as being on-site by using an assigned IP address. This involves registering with the VPN service configuring their computers one time, and thereafter gaining access to the VPN network through an institutional log-in name and password. Wireless access at universities is frequently handled through a VPN.

Using a virtual private network will require a close working relationship with the networking professionals in your larger organization, and does not solve some of the problems associated with proxy servers that are caused by firewalls and other incompatibilities with users' Internet service providers. But for most academic users it will provide a more seamless and integrated online campus experience. See Covey (2003) for more information.

OTHER AUTHENTICATION OPTIONS

This section discusses some of the possible authentication methods. Several are being used in libraries and by groups of libraries. Other methods that are in the trial stage or the development stage promise better options for the future.

Digital Certificates and Public Key Infrastructure

Secret key cryptography methods are very secure and allow barrier-free authentication of users once they are in place. Public key infrastructure (PKI) is a system for managing digital certificates, which are software-based encrypted identifiers that confirm a user's identity. Certificates are usually issued by independent third-party vendors, like Verisign or Cybertrust, which keep track of registered users.

Libraries can set up their own "attributes servers" to accept users with a qualifying certificate. Encrypted certificates can contain a user's name, e-mail address, and a variety of other types of information. They must be installed on the user's computer(s). The advantage to users is that they eliminate the need for any kind of log-in process. The ISO standard for digital certificates is X.509. A related protocol that extends the capability of digital-certificate technology is the Lightweight Directory Applications Protocol (LDAP). See Gettes (2002) for instructions on operating an LDAP system. These systems work well for users once they are in place, but they are complicated to install and do not work well for users of multiple computers. For libraries they require an ongoing investment of time and technical expertise.

MIT has developed Kerberos to authenticate Web-page access across an insecure network connection. Kerberos software is freely available for use by other university libraries. Information is available at the MIT Web site (web.mit.edu/kerberos/www).

Cookies

Cookies are also an unobtrusive authentication method that allow a computer to be recognized as having already been authenticated after the first successful visit (that will require credentials or some kind of log-in). This method is less secure than encryption, and it will not work for users who don't allow cookies or who frequently delete them.

Smart Cards

Smart cards utilize a small chip embedded in the card that stores information that can then be used to authenticate users as well as for other purposes, like conducting e-business or buying food or services on campus. These cards require hardware that can read the "smart" part of the card (the credentials of the user), which would resemble a card reader for a photocopy machine or print station. They still require some kind of PIN or password.

Shibboleth

Shibboleth software represents the Holy Grail for academic library systems administrators who understand very well the appeal of coordinating the library's authentication process with the process used for other campus log-ins (such as registration functions, online courses, or the use of computer labs).

Designed for interinstitutional sharing of Web-based resources, Shibboleth has the potential to simplify the management of consortial licenses, as well. A preliminary version of Shibboleth software has been developed by the Internet2 Consortium and is ready to deploy, but unfortunately, most campuses and vendors do not yet have the infrastructure to support it.

On campus, Shibboleth requires a single sign-on protocol and a directory of authorized users. Vendor systems need to be able to accept Shibboleth credentials. Major vendors such as EBSCO, Elsevier, Proquest, and OCLC have enabled their services to work with Shibboleth, but until all of its content providers are compliant, a library will not be able to use Shibboleth for authentication.

PREVENTION AND MANAGEMENT OF LICENSE VIOLATIONS AND SECURITY BREACHES

Despite your best efforts to abide by the terms of your license agreements and restrict your licensed resources to appropriate usage by authorized and authenticated users, it is probable that eventually you will be faced with an incident involving your users or your site. Anticipating the types of infractions you may encounter and having policies and procedures in place to quickly resolve them can help you avoid a situation in which all of your users would be denied access for a long period of time. These are typical incidents that require an immediate response from the library:

- Systematic downloading of all articles from several issues of one journal or several journals from your site
- Unusually heavy use of one or several resources from a particular computer at your site
- Atypical heavy use of your resources from a known or unknown remote location
- An extreme spike in the usage of a particular resource

Any of these situations could indicate illegal harvesting of e-journal content or access by unauthorized users, or both. One of your users might be zealously and innocently building a personal database of thousands of articles from some of your licensed electronic journals, or an outsider in another country might be orchestrating the robotic downloading of articles from electronic journals through a security hole in your system in order to package and sell a pirated product. In either case, your library has the responsibility to stop the act as soon as possible and to cooperate with the content owner to apprehend a perpetrator of piracy.

Some vendors have the capability to detect possible violations as they happen. Other vendors will become aware of infractions only when compiling reports of usage statistics. If your library or your larger institution is able to monitor unusual traffic patterns on your local network, you may be able to identify and correct a situation in its early stages without the vendor becoming involved.

PREVENTING MISUSE AND INFRACTIONS

No library will be able to prevent every possible type of intrusion or violation of license terms. But you can minimize your chances of being hacked or compromised if you

- authenticate all users, even those using on-site computers;
- monitor local network traffic for unusual patterns of use;
- post appropriate use guidelines (see example, Figure 5–6). Some licenses require that you inform users of terms, so you will be protecting yourself somewhat in the case of an infraction; and
- regularly check for "open proxy servers" in your internal institutional environment.

In late 2002, JSTOR reported a widespread orchestrated attack on its archive through unprotected servers of unwitting licensees. The attacker(s) had identified several Web servers at several institutions that were incorrectly set up; they lacked the proper security to prevent them from being hijacked for the purpose of harvesting articles. JSTOR reported that approximately 51,000 articles from 11 journals were downloaded through open proxy servers (see www.jstor.org/about/openproxies.html). A library in a university that does not impose reasonable precautionary measures could be in violation of all of its license agreements. A reasonable amount of vigilance on the part of a university will help prevent more serious breaches of security.

RESPONDING TO MISUSE AND INFRACTIONS

Publishers will try at all costs to avoid suing for breach of contract. However, they may shut down your institution's access to their journals until a problem is solved. You will be expected to cooperate in tracking down perpetrators of misconduct. A case of misuse might be no more sinister than an over-enthusiastic graduate student attempting to create a database on a local server with an experimental interface; nevertheless, such an action would violate your license agreement and, if allowed to continue, could jeopardize access for your entire institution.

Paula Watson (2003, p. 37) reports that the American Institute of Physics (AIP) has contacted the University of Illinois a number of times to report "large chunks of a journal poured into a campus workstation." AIP will shut off access from the computer with the offending IP address until "sanctions are applied." The library is expected to take some kind of action and report on the outcome.

A good license will not hold the library responsible for actions of an individual user unless the library is aware of an incident without taking corrective action. But you must

- respond quickly to a report of a possible infraction,
- document your efforts to solve the problem,
- update your vendor frequently during the course of investigating the problem,
- communicate with the vendor by phone as well as by e-mail,
- inform your administrators that a problem has occurred and keep them informed of your actions, and
- be prepared to play a role in disciplinary action for repeat offenders or users who knowingly and deliberately violate your license agreement.

There are some steps you can take to make it easier to respond quickly:

- Designate one person (with backup) to be responsible (and known to be responsible) for the complete resolution of incidents.
- Arrange in advance for someone at the library to have access to information to server logs and authentication records.
- Retain copies of authentication records and server logs for at least two months.
- Develop good relationships with your local network administrators and ensure that they understand intellectual-property issues and the consequences of license violations.

REFERENCES

American Library Association. 2003. "DRM: Statement of Library and Higher Education Concerns." (April). Retrieved Sept. 20, 2004, from www.ala.org/ala/washoff/WOissues/copyrightb/digitalrights/digitalrightsmanagement.htm#lbry.

Association of Research Libraries, American Association of Law Libraries, American Library Association, Association of Academic Health, Sciences Libraries, Medical Library Association and Special Library Association. 1997. "Principles for Licensing Electronic Resources." Retrieved Sept. 20, 2004, from www.arl.org/scomm/licensing/principles.html.

Brennen, Patricia. *Licensing Electronic Resources: Strategic and Practical Considerations for Signing Electronic Information Delivery Agreements.* Washington, DC: Association of Research Libraries, 1997.

Cain, Mark. 2003. "Cybertheft, Network Security, and the Library without Walls." *The Journal of Academic Librarianship* 29, no. 4: 245–248.

Covey, Denise Troll. 2003. "The Need to Improve Remote Access to Online Library Resources: Filling the Gap between Commercial Vendor and Academic User Practice." *Portal: Libraries and the Academy* 3, no. 4: 577–599.

Crews, Kenneth D. 2003. "New Copyright Law for Distance Education: The Meaning and Importance of the TEACH Act" rev. ed. Indianapolis: Copyright Management Center, Indiana University—Purdue University, Indianapolis. Retrieved Sept. 20, 2004, from www.copyright.iupui.edu/teach_summary.htm.

Gettes, Michael R. 2002. "A Recipe for Configuring and Operating LDAP Directories." Retrieved Sept. 20, 2004, from www.duke.edu/~gettes/giia/ldap-recipe/.

Harris, Lesley Ellen. 2002. *Licensing Digital Content: A Practical Guide for Librarians.* Chicago: American Library Association.

———. "Questions and Answers on Licensing." In Licensing Digital Content: *A Practical Guide for Librarians,* 99–110. Chicago: American Library Association. This chapter (Chapter 7) also available at www.ala.org/Ala/ourassociation/publishing/alaeditions/samplers/harris_licdigcon.pdf.vb. Retrieved Sept. 19, 2004.

Liblicense. N.d. Licensing Digital Information: A Resource for Librarians. Retrieved Sept. 20, 2004, from www.library.yale.edu/~llicense.

Lynch, Clifford. 1998. "Access Management for Networked Information Resources." *Educause Review* 21, no. 4: 4–9. Retrieved Sept. 19, 2004, from www.educause.edu/LibraryDetailPage/666&ID=CEM9842.

Parkhurst, Carol. 2002. "Supporting the Remote User of Licensed Resources." In *Attracting, Educating, and Serving Remote Users through the Web,* ed. Donnelyn Curtis, 197–225. New York: Neal-Schuman Publishers.

Schuler, John A. 2003. "Distance Education, Copyrights Rights, and the New TEACH Act." *The Journal of Academic Librarianship* 29, No. 1 (January/February): 49–51.

Sherden, Molly, Pamela Clark, and Trisha L. Davis. 1999. "De-mystifying the Licensing of Electronic Resources: Participant Materials." [A Distance-Learning Videoconference presented by the Special Libraries Association and Association of Research Libraries on March 4, 1999.]

Spedding, Vanessa. 2003. "Digital Rights Management. Research Information: Business Saviour or Content Enslaver?" *Research Information* (Summer). Retrieved Sept. 20, 2004, from www.researchinformation.info/risum03digitalrightsmanagement.html.

Watson, Paula D. 2003. "E journal Management: Acquisition and Control." *Library Technology Reports* 39, no. 2.

Wyatt, Anna M. 2002. "UCITA's Impact on Library Services." *Journal of Library Administration* 36, no. 4: 83–94.

MORE INFORMATION SOURCES

Agnew, Grace. 2003. "An Introduction to DRM: Part I." Guest Perspective, OCLC Community Forum. Retrieved Sept. 20, 2004, from www.oclc.org/community/topics/rights/perspectives/archives/agnew1.htm.

———. 2003. "An Introduction to DRM: Part II." Guest Perspective, OCLC Community Forum. Retrieved Sept. 20, 2004, from www.oclc.org/community/topics/rights/perspectives/default.htm.

Brennan, Patricia, Karen Hersey, and Georgia Harper. 1997. "Licensing Electronic Resources: Strategic and Practical Considerations for Signing Electronic Information Delivery Agreements." Retrieved Sept. 20, 2004, from www.arl.org/scomm/licensing/licbooklet.html.

Davis, Trisha L., and John J. Reilly. 1998. "Understanding License Agreements for Electronic Products." *Serials Librarian* 34, no. 1/1: 247–260.

Felten, Edward W. 2003. "A Skeptical View of DRM and Fair Use." *Communications of the ACM* 46, no. 4: 57–59.

NINCH (National Initiative for a Networked Cultural Heritage). "Copyright, Fair Use, and Licensing in a Digital World." Retrieved Sept. 20, 2004, from www.ninch.org/ISSUES/COPYRIGHT.html.

Schottlaender, Brian E. C. 1998. "The Development of National Principles to Guide Librarians in Licensing Electronic Resources." *Library Acquisitions: Practice and Theory* 22, no. 1: 49–54.

Soete, George J., and Trisha Davis, comp. 1999. *Managing the Licensing of Electronic Products.* ARL SPEC Kit 248. Washington, DC: Association of Research Libraries.

Stanford University Libraries. "Copyright and Fair Use." Retrieved Sept. 20, 2004, from http://fairuse.stanford.edu.

TEACH. 2001 (signed into law 2002). P.L. 107-273 (11/2/01). Text retrieved Sept. 29, 2004, from http://frwebgate.access.gpo.gov/cgi-bin/getdoc.cgi?dbname=107_cong_bills&docid=f:h2215eas.txt.pdf.

———. "The TEACH Act and Some Frequently Asked Questions." Retrieved Sept. 19, 2004, from www.ala.org/ala/washoff/WOissues/copyrightb/distanceed/teachfaq.htm.

Tyson, Jeff. "How Virtual Private Networks Work." HowStuffWorks. Retrieved Sept. 20, 2004, from http://computer.howstuffworks.com/vpn.htm.

6 ORDERING AND RECEIVING ELECTRONIC JOURNALS

CHAPTER OVERVIEW

- A New Routine
- Processing Requests
- Working with Consortia
- Ordering and Receiving Electronic Journals
- Managing Administrative Information: Tools and Processes
- Processing Renewals
- Canceling Print
- Opportunities for Countries in Transition

A NEW ROUTINE

Your established work flow for acquiring new print journals will not apply to the nonlinear process for selecting, licensing, and ordering electronic journals. There are more decisions to make at every step, involving more people, who are sometimes engaged in parallel processes.

Librarians, publishers, and subscription agents are experimenting with new ways of doing things—while trying to maximize efficiency, serve library users, cover expenses, and make a profit. New kinds of e-journal management services have found a lucrative niche. While change is a constant, there are nonetheless some guidelines that can help ensure that all factors are considered and all steps followed in the acquisitions process. The library with an acquisitions or serials department will find that most of the tasks described in this chapter are a logical extension of work already done by staff in those areas.

The Electronic Resource Management Task Force Initiative of the Digital Library Federation (DLF ERMI) has developed a complex set of diagrams illustrating the details of a typical work flow for acquiring electronic journals. Figure 6–1 shows samples of

FIGURE 6–1. Flowchart for DLF ERMI Electronic Resource Management Work Flow

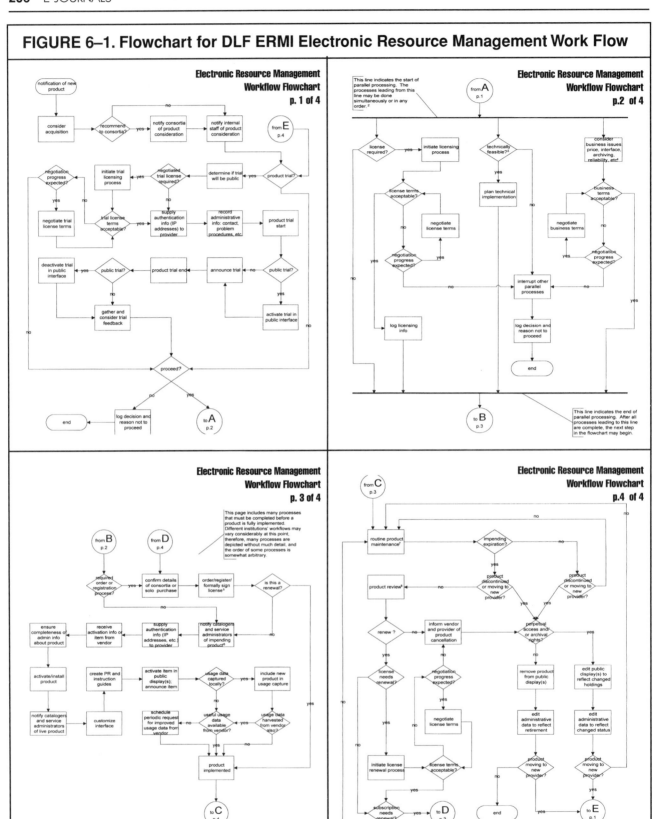

See this flowchart in a readable size at www.library.cornell.edu/cts/elicensestudy/dlfdeliverables/fallforum2003/Workflow_final.doc.

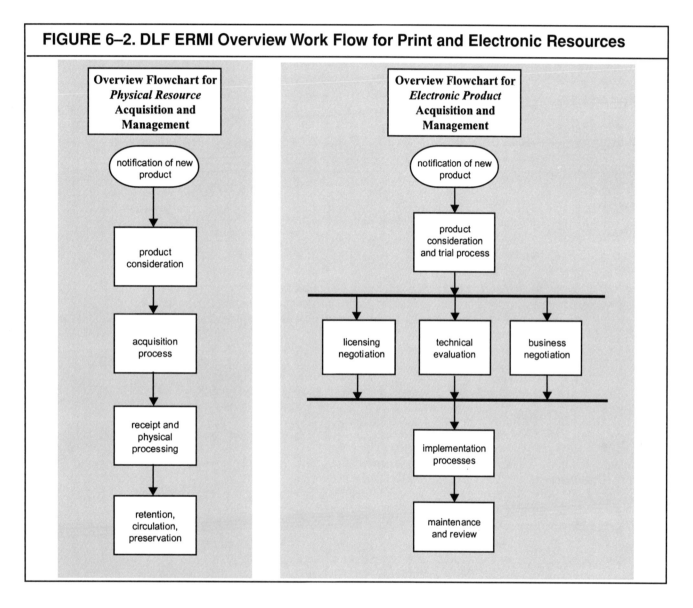

FIGURE 6–2. DLF ERMI Overview Work Flow for Print and Electronic Resources

these diagrams. Figure 6–2 shows the DLF ERMI overview comparison of the work flows for print journals and electronic journals.

PROCESSING REQUESTS

The biggest challenges in processing orders for electronic products are

FIGURE 6–3. Role Clarification at MIT Libraries

MIT LIBRARIES

NERD Resources

Roles of product sponsor and Digital Resources Acquisitions Librarian

The roles of the two individuals will vary somewhat from product to product and will be worked out between the two individuals within the following guidelines.

Product Sponsor

- Coordinates with other key librarians in related subject areas
- Maintains awareness of user needs and communicates with academic departments
- Compares and tests existing product options and product interfaces and consults with digital acquisitions librarian regarding vendor issues and options
- Gathers information from providers re: pricing, content, functionality
- Manages trials for products of local interest and/or contacts digital resources acquisitions librarian to request a centralized trial for products with broad interest
- Prepares product purchase proposal for review by NERD, if NERD funding is being sought
- Manages the in-library and user aspects of implementation, e.g. training, documentation, publicity
- Sustains in-depth knowledge of product & use of product; queries vendor re: functionality issues (other than access problems)
- Maintains awareness of new or alternative data offerings, product formats, interfaces, pricing options
- Participates actively in renewal decision-making

Digital Resources Acquisitions Librarian

- Maintains general awareness of development of products by vendors
- Provides context of other negotiations with vendors
- In conjunction with Systems, as needed, defines access options available and equipment requirements
- Works with Systems/IS as needed to assess viability of products
- Arranges and publicizes trials and demos for library staff for products being considered for purchase with central funds
- Acts as the liaison with the vendor during process of considering and purchasing a product, relaying questions, determining pricing options, and bringing relevant information back to the library staff
- Reviews license, manages license negotiation, obtains Director's signature
- Acts as liaison to serials acquisitions for issues related to acquisition procedures: order, encumbrance of funds, and invoice approval
- Manages license compliance awareness and record-keeping

Ellen Duranceau, August 15, 2002

http://macfadden.mit.edu:9500/colserv/digital/nerd/partnership.html

Both publishers and libraries have short-term and long-term strategies to help with the transition to electronic journals, and a pricing model that works for both parties during one stage may not work at another stage of the transition.

- uncertainty about when a request becomes final, especially if the selection depends on the price and the negotiations are protracted;
- potential misunderstandings over who is responsible for doing what; and
- determining the price.

Forms, checklists, and written procedures detailing responsibilities can help minimize confusion and keep the process on track and efficient. Negotiating an acceptable price requires business sense, doing your homework, understanding the market issues, practice, and a certain amount of assertiveness.

PRICING CONSIDERATIONS

The person who negotiates the prices the library will pay for electronic journals and databases is frequently the same person who negotiates the terms of license agreements on behalf of the library. In fact, pricing details and terms are often included in the license agreement, in the body or as an appendix.

The results of pricing discussions may well influence selection decisions. In most cases, e-journal pricing is much less straightforward than the pricing of print subscriptions. Most publishers distribute a price list that applies to electronic journals, but you will find that these prices aren't necessarily firm. Journals can be sold in bundles or in pieces (with current years and back issues sold separately, or with payment required for individual articles). The definition of "site" for a site license, the number of concurrent users, or the size of your university or city or company might affect your cost. Multiyear agreements might guarantee a cap on price increases, and consortial discounts can result in significant savings for individual libraries.

Library considerations, in addition to budgetary constraints, include the cost of access, which might be paid separately from content fees, to a third party. A library that is ready for online-only access can factor shelf-space savings into the overall savings, as well as savings for binding. Both publishers and libraries have short-term and long-term strategies to help with the transition to electronic journals, and a pricing model that works for both parties during one stage may not work at another stage of the transition.

As in any kind of negotiation, the determination of prices for electronic journals will be most successful if the needs of both parties can be met, which usually involves compromise and an understanding of the other party. Publishers have flexibility in the electronic world to work with libraries' individual situations,

The anticipated savings to publishers resulting from the elimination of print will not materialize until all customers are willing to accept online-only access. In the meantime, the publishers that have opted to provide both print and electronic access to their content have developed strategies to contain their costs and keep the revenue stream flowing.

so you should be prepared to share information about your short-term and long-term plans for electronic journals in your library, as well as your constraints. And libraries should attempt to understand publishers' and vendors' situations as well. Sometimes you will need to do your homework in order to differentiate between profit motives and survival strategies of e-journal publishers.

PUBLISHER STRATEGIES

Publishers have the same "first-copy" expenses for an online journal as for print, including peer review, editing, marketing, and other overhead. They are able to eliminate some expenses by not having to print or mail paper copies, but most publishers continue to offer both print and online. Also, they need to recoup costs incurred in developing new methods of access and providing the servers and technical staff to support that access. Even university publishers and organizations that already have a Web infrastructure will have added expenses. At the present time, some libraries, for their own reasons, are subscribing to online-only access whenever possible. But the majority of libraries (and individual subscribers) continue to want both formats.

The anticipated savings to publishers resulting from the elimination of print will not materialize until all customers are willing to accept online-only access. In the meantime, the publishers that have opted to provide both print and electronic access to their content have developed strategies to contain their costs and keep the revenue stream flowing. Over time, publishers' pricing options have become more complex, and libraries have more options, partly in response to the variety of library preferences and requests.

Mergers and Buyouts

Electronic publication benefits from economies of scale. Therefore, smaller publishers have a harder time keeping their costs down and are susceptible to purchase offers from other publishers. When one publisher absorbs another publisher and operations are combined, jobs are eliminated during the consolidation, and other efficiencies will be realized, though some customer service may inadvertently be lost as well during the transition (and beyond, in some cases). The instability of access and the maintenance work for wandering titles are hidden costs for the library, but overall publishing costs will ultimately decrease after a merger. Those cost savings may or may not be passed along to library customers. But the point here is that acquisitive publishers have a financial cushion that individual small publishers do not have in the transition from print to electronic publication.

Some professional associations and scholarly societies have contracted with commercial publishers for the first time in their publishing history rather than dealing with the licensing and access challenges of providing their journals online. Other groups are taking back the publication of their own journals because the Web makes it possible for them to do so.

Publishing Cooperatives

Publishers that choose to maintain their independence or associations that want to retain control of their journals will sometimes band together to realize some of the benefits of consolidation, such as shared marketing, bundled subscription offers, and distributed online publishing costs. Examples are the journals published by the Association of Learned and Professional Society Publishers (ALPSP) and BioOne.

Bundled Subscriptions/Portfolio Pricing

Some publishers have always offered discounts for a package of subscriptions to related titles. Electronic publishing has allowed publishers to maximize the opportunity to offer libraries a large amount of additional online content and price caps on future subscription prices in exchange for multiyear commitments from libraries to maintain most of their "print spend," that is, what they have been spending on print (even if the library decides to migrate from print subscriptions to an electronic license).

The costs and benefits of package deals to libraries are discussed elsewhere in the book. The main benefit to publishers is stable (and sufficient) revenue from libraries during the transition from print to online publishing. Another benefit is more exposure for their journals, which can increase citations to articles, raise their impact factor, and ultimately increase their value and marketability. Nonprofit organizations offer packages consisting of all their journals more frequently than commercial publishers (Cox and Cox, 2003).

As publishers merge and libraries pull away from unsustainable commitments to increasingly large package deals, this strategy has begun to be replaced by more flexible and sophisticated deals that will continue to benefit both publishers and libraries. This is discussed more fully later in the chapter.

Customized Pricing and Tiering

Print subscriptions are generally the same price, no matter who subscribes. Electronic subscriptions are often priced in anticipation of their value to the institution and what the institution can afford. "Tiered" or "banded" pricing gives publishers a chance to recoup their costs by expanding their markets—by basing the price on the usefulness of their journals for each market segment. Some indicators of the library's interest in or ability to pay for new electronic journals are the

- number and character of current or recent print subscriptions,
- library's materials budget,
- number of potential users (university FTE or a discipline-based subset, population-base for a public library, number of researchers or employees served by a research or corporate library),
- type of library (sometimes based on the Carnegie Classifications of Higher Education (2000) or the types of degrees offered), and
- e-journal(s)' actual usage statistics (for renewals).

A "sliding scale" can bring electronic journals into libraries that never had any hope of subscribing to those same journals in print format. Tiered pricing is relatively simple for both parties, but sometimes the price increase can be dramatic if a library moves up into the next tier through an increase in its user population or ranking.

Deadline-Based Discounts

Some publishers offer appealing price discounts for orders placed by a certain deadline in hopes of attracting new customers for their individual or bundled electronic journals. Libraries can benefit from these special offers, but you should not be enticed into subscribing to something just because the discounted price seems too good to pass up. The subscription price will be more normal in subsequent years. If you are interested in the product anyway, you will probably want to take advantage of the discount, but don't let the deadline prevent you from reviewing the license carefully. Most publishers will extend a deadline beyond the announced date if you need more time rather than lose the possibility of gaining your business.

More Customers More Easily through Library Consortia

Electronic journals have been responsible for the formation and expansion of numerous library consortia. Consortial deals benefit publishers through savings in marketing expenses and the time it takes to negotiate a license with each individual library. One sales representative can represent hundreds of titles to one representative of a consortium consisting of dozens of libraries, on behalf of tens of thousands of users. Large consortial contracts also give vendors a way to dominate a regional market in some cases, as in a statewide contract for full-text databases (Carlson, 2003).

A consortial deal usually gives libraries electronic access to journals held in other participant libraries, and often gives all the libraries access to all of the publisher's journals. These deals sometimes fall apart during negotiations and during renewals. Large libraries that may have been willing to subsidize smaller libraries in the consortium may not be able to be as generous when their economic situations change. Some publishers see the Big Deal with big consortia as an interim strategy—overdependence on this model puts them in a vulnerable position. See the "Working with Consortia" section below for a look at the details of a typical consortial deal.

Print/Electronic Interplay

As described in Chapter 4, many publishers offer free online access to their library subscribers. This practice doesn't generate additional revenue to cover the costs of electronic publishing, but it does introduce their e-journals to library users and paves the way for libraries to migrate to online-only access or a package deal for more of the publisher's content. Sometimes free online with print access is limited to recent years, and then for an additional fee libraries can access back issues, usage statistics, and other features.

Not incidentally, free online access with print discourages libraries from canceling their print subscriptions, helping to preserve the publisher's revenue stream. Some publishers will offer online-only access for a discounted fee in order to entice libraries to move more rapidly into an environment that will allow publishers to discontinue print publication.

For publishers that charge fees for online access to print subscriptions, "flip-model" pricing can be attractive to libraries that are ready to let go of print subscriptions. In this model, the list price is for the electronic journal with an add-on cost for the print counterpart (usually an additional 10–25%). This model is especially attractive when the online subscription costs less than the preflip print subscription.

Adding Value

Some publishers hope to attract more revenue for the electronic publication of their journals and encourage online-only subscriptions by offering features that are unavailable in the print version, for example, providing the text of "forthcoming articles," multimedia, supplementary data sets, and links from and to articles in their journals. In particular, involvement with linking initiatives will give their journals more exposure, potentially increasing their value and desirability.

Other Online Outlets

Some publishers will take advantage of every opportunity to leverage their electronic content. Aggregator databases offer one such opportunity for publishers to be paid for the use of articles from their journals, but library subscriptions are the best paying, most stable source of revenue. Selling individual articles on demand through intermediaries or their own services also brings in additional proceeds.

LIBRARY STRATEGIES

Most publishers have developed a variety of pricing models to attract the largest possible customer base. Your library plan should help you decide what is affordable and what kinds of pricing models are best for each stage of your e-journal implementation. If you don't have such a plan, see Chapter 3. Some publishers' survival strategies also benefit libraries, at least in the short term, so you should take advantage of those whenever possible.

Taking Advantage of the Sales Curve

You can benefit from understanding the cycle of the marketplace. When an electronic product is new, pricing is uncertain, and publishers will experiment. They may offer very attractive discounts to the early-adopter libraries that are willing to take a chance on something new. These publishers may then publicize their contracts with early customers in order to attract other libraries.

When sales become easier, prices may rise and stabilize for awhile. Then, after the target market is saturated, a publisher will sometimes try other pricing strategies to gain customers who ordinarily would not subscribe to their journals at all. Finding an advantageous place for your library on the sales curve can help you save money.

Are E-Journals Cost-Effective?

Some librarians believe that electronic journals will not save libraries any money, and, in fact, will eat up an ever larger portion of the budget. However, if you compare the size and cost of the e-journal collections of some of the early adopters to the size and cost of their present or former print journal collections, you can see that the cost per title is much lower for electronic journals, and these pioneer libraries' users have access to a great deal more

The Electronic Journals Collection "has more than quadrupled the buying power of Ohio higher education."

—OhioLINK Snapshot

"There are other purchasing models which could give both parties the advantages of the 'Big Deal' without the disadvantages."

—Fred Friend (2003, p. 154)

content than they had in pre-e-journal days. Libraries may not be paying less for journals in the electronic environment, but most of them are getting much more for their money.

Being part of a consortium is the most cost effective way to gain access to electronic journals, though the degree of gain can vary a great deal among consortia and among members in a consortium. Users from several smaller academic institutions in Ohio take advantage of new access to thousands of journals through OhioLINK deals. The value of those deals is demonstrated by the fact that the use of articles from newly accessible e-journals is about the same per title as the use of articles from the journals that had been received in print by the group. For OhioLINK, "the incremental cost of expanding title access is very, very low on most of our licenses." (Sanville, 2003, p.7). Other examples are just as successful. See "Working with Consortia," below.

Developing Alternatives to the "Big Deal"

The major disadvantage to the bundled deal, other than its high cost for libraries with static or declining budgets, is the even higher cost that a library or a consortium could face when a publisher acquires a significant number of new titles. "Neither publisher nor consortium may wish an offer to be enlarged in this way, or if they do, the pricing may be a major issue complicating the existing relationship . . ." (Friend, 2003, p. 154).

When a publisher's package of subscriptions is up for renewal, you can consult usage statistics to determine whether the additional journals to which library users had access through the package were actually used or not. Based on usage data, libraries are in a good position to negotiate for limited packages, or for a much lower per-title price for the unused segment of the package.

One analysis of the use of an Academic Press package (Davis, 2003) showed that users from the Northeast Research Libraries (NERL) consortium (large research institutions, medical schools, and private liberal arts colleges) used 10 times more articles from e-journals to which they already subscribed in print than from those titles they had not subscribed to. So the new journals this consortium gained may not have justified the additional cost; they already had the journals that were in most demand, and online access to subscribed titles might be good enough.

Update No. 2 to the International Coalition of Library Consortia (ICOLC) "Statement of Current Perspective and Preferred Practices for Selection and Purchase of Electronic Information" (September, 2004) suggests some ways for publishers to implement "orderly attrition" when it is necessary for a library to reduce spending when renewing a package deal:

- Shave off unused titles and provide a credit for them.
- Shave off titles that libraries choose to do without (or buy articles "by the drink") and provide credit for those.
- Provide cancellation allowances for each year (p. 5).

"Specific changes in business models currently being sought by library consortia" in the 2001 and 2004 updates of the ICOLC Statement suggest that the publisher:

- move from a "print plus" to an "electronic plus" purchase model;
- offer a selective purchase model, including "all-you-can-eat" for selected groups of titles with "pay-by-the-drink" blocks of articles for titles not selected;
- eliminate no-cancellation clauses;
- stop repackaging content; and
- change—but do not eliminate—the roles of intermediaries.

Usage-Based Pricing, Pay-Per-View / Document Delivery

To pay on the basis of actual usage rather than predicted usage may or may not benefit the library—but if usage statistics will help determine pricing, it becomes essential to understand what the publisher means by "use," and how it is measured. Some libraries resist a model that would penalize them for promoting electronic resources and increasing their use.

A cost-effective way to provide access to peripheral or noncore journals is to subsidize users' orders for individual articles from titles not subscribed to, either directly or indirectly. A large number of publishers provide a means to download individual articles from their sites, for a price. An early experiment with e-journals, Project PEAK (Mackie-Mason and Jankovich, 1997), sold access to a set number of articles from the full range of Elsevier e-journals. With this model, articles that were used remained available at no additional charge to the community of users. Though the experiment was considered a success, the library purchase and subsequent ownership of "blocks" of articles has not become a widely accepted model. Accounting and access challenges are significant, and it is difficult to budget for unpredictable use.

Wiley offers an option to use "tokens" for articles from non-subscribed journals as part of the subscription-based Expanded Access License. Wiley's ArticleSelect service guarantees that whenever tokens have been spent on a particular title equaling 115% of its subscription price, the library is "auto-subscribed" for the

> . . . a library could theoretically save money by subscribing to heavily used or core e-journals and subsidizing pay-per-view or document delivery for those journals in less demand.

year, so it will not be necessary to use additional tokens for articles from that journal.

Most publishers now offer some kind of "pay-per-view" option, but these are generally designed for individual users without library intermediation. Users of SpringerLINK, for example, are expected to register individually and set up accounts for purchasing articles, which will then be perpetually available for view anytime through those accounts. One feature of the EBSCOhost Electronic Journals Service (EJS) Enhanced is a pay-per-view function that can be enabled or disabled. The organizational pay-per-view function allows the library to set up an account for the purchase of articles by users.

Based on some libraries' experiences with saving substantial amounts of money by substituting patron-initiated article delivery for a large number of canceled subscriptions, librarians have speculated about using a pay-per-view model instead of licensing e-journals individually or through packages. The technology is available, along with tables of contents and the best discovery tools ever. However, judging from published reports of the numbers of downloaded articles by academic library users, some libraries would pay a great deal more for article downloads than they do for a large number of subscriptions to electronic journals. For example, assuming an average of $20 an article (which might be low):

- Drexel University users downloaded about 250,000 articles a year, which would cost a total of $5 million.
- OhioLINK would have paid $40.6 million instead of $19 million for articles from electronic journals if the 5.7 million downloaded articles had been purchased separately.
- The University of Nevada, Reno, Libraries would have had to pay $1.2 million last year for the 60,000 articles downloaded from Elsevier journals.

Even after factoring in the additional access costs and staff time to process and provide access to electronic journals, in cases like these it is much more cost effective to subscribe to the journals than to buy the articles for users. However, a library could theoretically save more money by subscribing to heavily used or core e-journals and subsidizing pay-per-view or document delivery for those journals in less demand. Tom Sanville points out that even for OhioLINK, "We see in our usage data that use is made of all titles but is concentrated in a very few " (Sanville, 2003, p. 7).

WORKING WITH CONSORTIA

As has been demonstrated, library consortia can help publishers expand their markets for electronic journals and at the same time make it possible for libraries to have hundreds or thousands more journals than they could otherwise afford. If your library belongs to a consortium, you have probably been approached to participate in consortial agreements. If the consortium has an organized, discriminating, and participatory approach to collection development, there is a good chance you will be interested in at least some of their proposals. Those who are responsible for electronic journal selection will establish the library's level of interest in a proposal, but things can quickly become complicated for the prospective participants, especially if some of them are undecided.

Some library consortia have centralized funding from a national, state, or provincial legislature, or government or private grants. They may also have professional staff who will handle the substantial amount of work it takes to complete a successful consortial agreement. A given library may have little choice or minimal involvement in a statewide license for a full-text database. The less a library's own funds will be used, the smaller its role will be in the negotiation process. The opposite is just as true.

Commonly, a library that has decided to order a package of electronic journals or a full-text database discovers that there is an attractive consortial discount and seeks out potential consortial partners that might also be interested in the same product. If the consortium does not have an administrative infrastructure, the participating libraries will be on their own to negotiate a license agreement. Even in some formal consortia, a "sponsor" library with the strongest interest might take the lead in brokering a deal.

Various pricing models have evolved to increase the market share for publishers and lower the price for consortia. When a license agreement clearly benefits both the publisher and the consortium, its elements tend to be adopted by other publishers, so agreements are becoming somewhat more standardized.

Advantages of the Consortium Approach

A consortial license provides a stable market for the publisher. As it builds an electronic-delivery infrastructure, the publisher reaps certain benefits:

- Guaranteed retention of subscriptions that might otherwise be canceled
- Potential buy-in income from new customers

- Additional surcharge income without much additional expense to the publisher
- One point of contact; one license negotiation; one payment
- Increased use of journals that are otherwise not accessible to some of the users (resulting in more citations that lead to more demand and more use)

TYPICAL PRICING AGREEMENT FOR CONSORTIAL ACCESS TO JOURNALS

This simplified hypothetical license agreement between Publisher Z and Consortium X includes many conditions that are typical to consortial agreements, though details will vary:

1. Publisher Z produces 50 journals in both print and electronic format.
2. Each print or electronic subscription is $500 (for one format).
3. There is a 15% surcharge to receive both the print and electronic versions.
4. A consortium can pool its subscriptions and all participants will gain electronic access to the titles held by any of the participants.
5. Subscription costs are based on the price of the previous year's subscriptions ("base-year titles").
6. The three-year license requires each participating library to maintain its current subscriptions in electronic format (though they can cancel their print subscriptions and avoid paying the additional 15% per year).
7. There will be a 6.5% cap on price increases for subscriptions during the three years of the agreement.
8. Nonparticipating members can be added at the beginning of each subscription year for the remainder of the license period, but their surcharge will be based on their subscriptions during the base year.
9. One invoice will be issued to the consortium; one list of IP addresses will be submitted.
10. A library must have $3,000 worth of journals in order to participate without paying a "buy-in fee," which is $3,000, or the difference between $3,000 and the library's base subscription costs.
11. The publisher offers the consortium electronic access to the remainder of its journals for 20% of the list price.
12. If some of the libraries are willing to give up print subscriptions to duplicated titles, electronic access to journals of equal value can be substituted for the consortium.

13. Three-year journal backfiles are available for a one-time cost of $200 per title per institution; if acquired at the beginning of the agreement, the price is $150 per title.

Item 3 could be negotiated, especially if the consortium is large. Items 5 and 8 are intended to stop a library from embarking on a cancellation spree to lower its costs in anticipation of the deal. However, a library that can convince the publisher that a cancellation project was well underway or completed before the proposal appeared on its horizon might be able to compromise on this condition, especially if it is a deal breaker. Some publishers will relent on item 9 if the consortial infrastructure seems dangerously shaky. It won't hurt to try to negotiate item 10 on behalf of a very small library that could not possibly get much use from the journals. Item 13 might present another topic for negotiation.

There are several advantages in a deal like this for the libraries:

- Electronic access to their own subscriptions at a reasonable cost
- Free access to additional titles
- Very low-cost access to titles of lesser interest
- Guaranteed control over price increases
- The option to choose electronic access without penalty for dropping print subscriptions
- Joint access to a pool of resources that can be used to develop value-added services
- The chance to offer a "level playing field" to all researchers in a state, province, or country, regardless of their institutional affiliations

Considerations for libraries:

- You will be locked into a commitment for three years.
- There is no discount for electronic-only subscriptions.
- You will be getting more than you had, but you will probably be paying more.
- You may not really need or want access to most of the additional journals.
- You may have to compromise with other libraries over the terms of the license agreement.
- Peer-pressure participation may not be in the library's best interest.

FIGURE 6–4. Consortium X Costs for Publisher Z Journals

Lib	Subs	Unique	Gains	Price	Surcharge	Buy-in	Backfiles	8 add'l	Total p+e	Cost/title	Cost/new title
A	5	1	45	$2,500	$375	$500		$100	$3,475	$70	$13
C	15	5	35	$7,500				$250	$7,750	$155	$7
C	25	15	25	$12,500	$1,875		$5,000	$450	$19,825	$397 (4 yrs e)	$218 (4 yrs e)
D	0		50			~~$3,000~~				$60	$60
E	0		50			$3,000			$3,000	$60	$60
Total	45	21		$22,500	$2,250	$3,500	$5,000	$800	**$34,050**		

In our simplified scenario, the five libraries in consortium X collectively subscribe to 32 titles. There is overlap in the subscriptions, but 21 of the titles are held by only one of the libraries. Libraries C and D are community college libraries. The publisher or someone in the consortium has compiled the following chart (Figure 6–4) to help the members decide whether to participate.

- Four libraries decide to participate in this deal, and together to pay an additional 20% for the titles that none of them subscribe to. They will split that cost proportionately according to their print subscriptions.
- Library A will gain electronic access to 50 journals for $975 more than they were spending for print access to five titles.
- Library B wants to participate, but does not want to pay for the backfiles or dual-access surcharge. This library is willing to accept electronic-only access to their subscriptions. Electronic access to all 50 journals will cost the library only $250 more than they were paying for 16 print journals. Since this library decided not to have print subscriptions anyway, they can substitute 10 new titles for those that are duplicated in libraries A and C. So together, the three libraries then will subscribe to 42 of the journals.
- Library C will participate, gaining access to 25 new titles. The electronic access to their own subscriptions alone is worth the cost, and their budget can handle it. They want the backfiles, and are very interested in the additional titles to which they currently do not subscribe.
- Library D has no interest in the journals, and cannot afford the $3,000.
- Library E feels it is worth it to gain online access to 50 titles for the amount that it would have had to spend for six print subscriptions; a $25,000 value for $3,000. It is a growing college with a growing budget, but cannot afford the backfiles.

The license is signed, and the publisher's invoice for $11,550 is sent to Library C, the coordinating library, which sends invoices for reimbursement to the other participants for the charted amounts. (In the example of Consortium X, payment for the print subscriptions, which total $22,500, is handled by a subscription agent).

The expenses are calculated and invoices are sent by Library C:

- Library A: $975 (surcharge, $375; buy-in fee, $500; additional titles, $100)

- Library B: $250 for additional titles to which no library in the consortium subscribed; no surcharge
- Library C: $7,325 (surcharge, $1,875; one-time backfiles, $5,000; additional titles, $450)
- Library D: not participating
- Library E: $3,000 (buy-in fee)

Two lists of IP ranges are sent to Publisher Z: those for libraries A, B, C, and E for access to the current file of all 50 journals, and one for Library C for access to the backfiles. Library B notifies its subscription agent that it will be receiving electronic access rather than print issues of the journals, and adjusts its title list to reflect the substitutions. They pay no publisher surcharge since they have elected to receive the titles in a single format.

Consortial arrangements almost never go this smoothly. If one of the three libraries with subscriptions opts out, the others will need to decide whether they will still participate. In this case, their cost will remain the same no matter who participates, but they would have access to fewer journals.

Lump-Sum Fee

In other kinds of consortial agreements there is a lump-sum fee for a package, no matter who participates, so if some of the members opt out the others have to pay more, which then might cause some of them to drop out. A new price scheme has to be calculated each time a library decides to be in on or out of the deal. Thus, an attractive proposal might become less so. Some publishers will demand a certain level of participation (sometimes 100%) or they will not negotiate. With fading participation they might change the terms, for example, increasing the percentage for the surcharge.

Fee Based on Print

A pricing structure that is based on the participants' previous subscriptions tends to be fair. The smaller libraries get the best deal, but they wouldn't be able to participate otherwise, and they can be expected to generate much less use than the larger institutions.

Fee Distribution

In some kinds of agreements the individual libraries' prices are not determined by the vendor, so the libraries must negotiate among themselves for a fair distribution of "lump-sum" fees. Library B feels it should pay less than the others because it has contributed five unique titles to the total number available to the consortium. Library C thinks it should get a discount for coordinating the whole deal and handling invoicing. This hypothetical agreement between Publisher Z and Consortium X is a fairly straightforward scenario, with only five potential participants. With more members, more options for customization, and more individual choices available, consortial deals can be complex puzzles. Consortia can help libraries save money, but they certainly won't save you time or headaches if you are the one who is negotiating on behalf of your library or your consortium.

OTHER PRICING MODELS

Publishers and vendors use various models to price their products for consortia. Publisher Z's model is commonly used with libraries that already subscribe to some of the publisher's journals in print, but it won't work for other kinds of situations. You may want to consider some of the other models that have been developed for consortial pricing:

- Concurrent user: Users at participating institutions will share a designated number of access ports (works best for specialized databases).
- Per user with volume discounts: Lexis-Nexis took this to a multiconsortial extreme for *Academic Universe* (5.5 million FTEs from 1,047 institutions as of 9/1999).
- Added-institution discounts: The initial site pays the base price, discounts are given to subsequent sites.
- Wholesale: Relatively low-priced raw data goes to the consortium, which is responsible for delivering it and recovering delivery costs.
- Size of institutions: Pricing is based on categories using Carnegie classification (2000), degree programs, or enrollment figures in Peterson's (often inaccurate).

COST DISTRIBUTION

Distributing costs can be one of the thorniest matters in consortial spending. Establishing a mutually acceptable formula can save time, shorten the negotiation period, and help maintain good relations among consortial members. But even the best formula won't work for every consortium every time, and sometimes representatives just need to sit down together and massage the numbers. The starting point for distribution of costs will usually be resource based or user based. The Consortium Purchasing Electronic Resources: A National Approach (PER:NA) of New Zealand uses the following pricing principle (www.epic.org.nz/nl/about.html#costallocationmodel):

- Pricing should be fair.
- Pricing should aim to be affordable for all libraries.
- Pricing should aim to be attractive to small libraries in every sector.
- There should be clear benefits to membership in the PER:NA consortium.
- Pricing structure should be simple to understand.
- Pricing model should include a contribution towards PER:NA administrative costs.

Criteria for Cost Redistribution

One advantage to receiving one invoice for the consortium is that even if the publisher has used a pricing formula that is based on characteristics of individual participating institutions, the consortium can redistribute the costs based on other criteria. "Good neighbor" policies can come into play if there is a disparity in funding, or one library's desire to obtain a consortial deal may provide the motivation to pay a larger share in order to ensure others' involvement.

Redistribution Based on Resources

There are resource-based options for sharing lump-sum costs or rearranging predetermined costs:

- Divide the cost equally (this will work best with equivalent institutions).
- Use a sliding scale based on materials budgets (calculate them uniformly).
- Divide the cost proportionally based on related print subscription costs.
- Use the e-bay model—ask each member what it will pay to be part of the deal and then decide if it is enough.
- Calculate the cost of what each member would pay as an individual institution, subtract equivalent amounts.
- Use the (U.S.) National Public Radio model, in which the libraries that are willing and able to pay will subsidize the participation of the libraries that are unwilling or unable to pay.

Redistribution Based on Users

User-based approaches for sharing lump-sum costs or rearranging predetermined costs will often use census numbers rather than library-card holders for public libraries and full-time equivalent (FTE) data rather than the number of enrolled students for universities. FTE calculations can be done many ways, so it is important to standardize the counting process. Since researchers are expected to make more use of electronic journals than vocational school students, some consortia have developed a weighted FTE formula. Some consortia use pricing bands to distribute costs based on the size and type of library.

Usage

Usage patterns can be determined after a service has been in place. It might seem logical to apply the first-year's usage statistics heavily in distributing the second-year costs, but some consortia shy away from creating any kind of disincentive for using electronic journals.

The Combination Approach

Other consortia use a combination of factors to distribute costs. For example, they use a flat fee + a weighted fee (this can be hard on small libraries) or a flat fee + usage patterns + FTE.

OTHER CONSORTIAL CONSIDERATIONS

Libraries that obtain electronic journals through consortia pay lower prices, and sometimes this is the only way to get access to a publisher's journals. If your library does not belong to a consortium, investigate the possibilities in your geographical area. Each member of the International Coalition of Library Consortia (ICOLC) has a listing on the ICOLC Web page with basic information about the consortium that includes

- legal structure,
- primary functions,
- number and type of member libraries,
- significant electronic-content licenses or resources,
- funding,
- principle databases,
- contact information.

If the consortium has a Web page, there will be a link from the ICOLC page at www.library.yale.edu/consortia/. ICOLC documents such as the "Statement of Current Perspective and Preferred Practices for the Selection and Purchase of Electronic Information" (along with the updates) may also prove useful.

Keeping up-to-date:

International Coalition of Library Consortia

www.library.yale.edu/consortia

Form a New Consortium

If there is no appropriate consortium in your area, you might consider forming one; there may be other orphan libraries nearby.

Forming a consortium is beyond the scope of this chapter, but in general, you don't need to be elaborate. Your library director will need to meet with other library directors who will agree to the idea of collaborating on electronic licensing. An informal agreement and a consortial name will satisfy some vendors. Others will require that you be a legal entity. Within a state or a metropolitan area, there may be an organization of libraries or universities that will offer you its legal umbrella for your purposes. If you want bylaws and a collection development policy, you will find some models through the ICOLC Web page. If your library is in a developing country, eIFL can assist you in forming a national or multinational consortium (see "Developing Countries" section, below).

A new consortium without an established infrastructure requires a commitment of time from some people on behalf of others, as the above example illustrates. Negotiating license agreements, determining and implementing the cost-sharing plan, and especially communicating with the participants can take an immense amount of time.

Outsourcing Consortium Work

As serials subscription agents reinvent themselves in response to a new business climate in which consortia deal directly with publishers (in 2002 25–58% of the library business of medium and large publishers was with consortia), the surviving large agencies have developed services for consortia. Agents' gain would be service fees for new content obtained by individual libraries. EBSCO has "regional consortia specialists" offering the following services to consortia and publishers to facilitate deals:

- Information gathering for the publisher
- Communicating the goals of the consortium
- Conducting the inventory of titles in each library, including those not acquired through EBSCO
- Collecting demographic information
- Communicating publishers' terms and policies to the consortium
- Handling invoicing and payments

Swets offers Consortia and Multisite Management, a "modular range of services" (http://informationservices.swets.com/web/show/id=40034):

- Planning and consultancy: Facilitating consortial and organizational objectives, requirements, and reporting needs

- Brokering: Providing quotes, negotiating with publishers, and resolving licensing issues
- Administration: Ordering and renewing, ensuring electronic access, payment, central split-invoicing (i.e., vendor invoices each member separately), and budget allocation
- Access: Special single-route, multisite access for end users of SwetsWise Online Content
- Training and support: Ensuring maximum benefits from your consortia deal

Additional Consortium Facts

Here are a few final considerations for dealing with consortia:

- Your library may belong to more than one consortium, which will allow you to shop for the best deal on a product.
- The larger your group, the more latitude you will have in negotiating.
- The larger your group, the more difficult it will be to work together; if a consortial deal does not favor large groups, you may want to work with a smaller group.
- Vendors have more flexibility if they are primary vendors than if they are secondary vendors.
- If you want to get a better price on your renewal of a package or database, look for partners who would be new subscribers.
- Vendors often impose an unrealistic time frame for a decision on a consortial agreement; for example, a certain discount may only be good until a certain date. If the consortium is moving at a reasonable pace towards a decision, ask for an extension; you will usually get it. Don't succumb to pressure to make a premature decision.

ORDERING AND RECEIVING ELECTRONIC JOURNALS

"Ordering" means different things for different kinds of e-journals. Freely available e-journals may or may not pass through the hands of acquisitions staff, depending on your particular processes and work flow. Licensing and payment processes will not apply, but for the chosen free journals to be included in the library's catalog or Web lists, you will need to process them along with fee-based products at some stage. The rest of this section refers to purchased and licensed products (including the activation of access for free-online-with-print subscriptions).

SUBSCRIPTION AGENTS

Keeping up-to-date:

Association of Subscription Agents and Intermediaries

www.subscription-agents.org/

Serials subscription agents will gladly handle your orders (and your renewals) for individual electronic journals—and for packages if the publisher allows that option. You should be able to find information and initiate the order using the same procedures you use for new print subscriptions. The role of the vendor or subscription agent is becoming more defined when dealing with electronic journals. However, some libraries still find it easier to deal directly with the publisher when negotiating pricing and licenses, as well as clarifying the technical aspects of online journal access. For print subscriptions, one of the areas in which the subscription agent's service is of most benefit to the library is the claiming of missing issues, but claiming as we know it in the print environment does not have an online counterpart. Even so, there are a number of services that the vendor or agent can provide:

- One point of contact for subscriptions
- A single invoice and renewal list
- Notification of online access available with your print subscriptions
- Assistance in explaining and interpreting licenses
- Assistance with registering IP addresses
- Free access to an aggregated database of journals from many publishers
- Assistance in negotiating license agreements and processing the required subscription forms
- Avoidance of penalties or interrupted access for late renewal payments

The number of subscription agencies has been getting smaller. These are some of the subscription agents with electronic journal services:

- DA Information Services (for libraries in Australia and New Zealand): http://www.dadirect.com/serials/serials.asp
- EBSCO Information Services (has special division for e-journal management, including subscriptions): www.ebsco.com/home/ejournals/default.asp
- Harrassowitz: www.harrassowitz.com/periodicals_e-journals.html

- Kinokuniya Company Ltd. (for libraries in Japan): www. kinokuniya.co.jp/
- Swets Information Service: www.swets.com
- W. T. Cox Subscriptions: www.wtcox.com/services.html

DEALING DIRECTLY WITH PUBLISHERS

Subscription agents help to consolidate services, but libraries may find it easier to deal with publishers directly. Unless you have a very close relationship with your agent, someone in the library should always assume the responsibility for license review and negotiation, since it is up to the library to assure compliance with the terms of the license. In the end, it is up to you to determine if the services offered by a vendor or agent for electronic journals are worth the price. If you want to order directly from the publisher (you will usually end up communicating with them anyway, if you want a site license), you can generally find contact information on their Web sites.

OPTIONS FOR PLACING SUBSCRIPTIONS

Depending on the options available, you may order by phone, fax, e-mail, or postal mail. Some publishers and vendors will permit or even require you to order via a form on their Web sites. Publisher's Web forms often ask for the subscriber number for your print subscription. If you used a vendor for the order, then the vendor can send you the number. It may also appear on the mailing label, but if the issue was received in a wrapper of some kind, that will have been discarded upon receipt. Regardless of how the order is submitted, it should be represented in your local library acquisitions system, complete with appropriate vendor and fund information.

GETTING WHAT YOU'RE PAYING FOR

Some libraries may want ongoing assurance that they are getting value for the dollars spent on electronic journals, and will consider a check-in process of some sort. Checking and recording that each individual issue for every title is "received" is not practical for most libraries; nevertheless, some follow-up is necessary after the order is placed. A publisher can sometimes confuse the IP addresses or the titles to which you have access with those of another institution. Unless you check that your institution has access to every new title, or at least carry out random spot checks, you may not be getting what you paid for. If this is impractical, be sure that you have a prominent means for users to report problems (see Chapter 8).

Confirming Access

When a library subscribes to an electronic journal title or journal package, they are often not notified when access is available. Your library needs to confirm that it is getting what it has paid for. Someone needs to be responsible for checking periodically to determine when the resource becomes available to your local users. When that occurs, depending on your policies and workflow, both a cataloger and library Webmaster should be informed so the title can be cataloged and the necessary links added to your home page. A possible drawback of eliminating regular check-in is the difficulty in identifying title changes. However, if your publisher or vendor has an alerting service, this is likely to solve that problem.

Checking Links

An online equivalent to claiming might be a process to ensure that the link to the remote server is active. For journal packages this does not confirm if something has been added to the site or if a title has been dropped. As indicated above, these kinds of checks should be made when the package comes up for renewal. If the site is stable, you may wish to depend upon user feedback to alert you to problems. You should also run some link-checking software at regular intervals.

Responsibilities for Setting Up Access

A work-flow chart for your library can help you determine who is responsible for what at the access end of the acquisition process (as well as at the selection end). It will be different for each library. See Figure 6–5 for a sample work-flow chart.

FIGURE 6–5. The Relative Roles of Acquisitions Staff

Selection	Acquisition	Access
E-journal collection continuum →		

Library A:

Selectors	Acquisitions staff	Webmaster

Library B:

Selectors	Acquisitions staff	Serials Dept.	Cataloging

MANAGING ADMINISTRATIVE INFORMATION: TOOLS AND PROCESSES

Keeping up-to-date:

A Web Hub for Developing Administrative Metadata for Electronic Resource Management

www.library.cornell.edu/cts/elicensestudyhome.html

Placing an order and receiving access to new electronic journals is just the beginning of a long and complex relationship. As anyone working in acquisitions knows, thorough record keeping for easy retrieval of information about every library purchase is an essential part of the acquisitions process. There are more kinds of information to keep track of for e-journals. Libraries have had to find their own ways to automate the management of their electronic resources, since existing acquisitions modules in integrated library systems are not equipped to contain and report the type of information that is crucial for electronic journal acquisitions, though ILS vendors are working on new modules.

Libraries have taken a variety of approaches to managing subscription information: developing their own in-house databases, using features of their integrated library systems, or using a vendor-maintained database. Some libraries use simple spreadsheets to track their e-journal subscriptions. Others have developed simple or complex databases to manage administrative metadata. A carefully maintained and detailed subscription management database can also provide a search interface for users, generate Web pages for electronic journals, or even catalog records (see Chapter 7). "A Web Hub for Developing Administrative Metadata for Electronic Resource Management" at www.library.cornell.edu/cts/elicensestudy/home.html is the Digital Library Federation E-Resource Management Initiative (DLF ERMI) clearinghouse for information to help libraries manage their electronic journals and databases.

COMMERCIAL PRODUCTS

As of the time of publication, very few products are available for managing electronic resources in libraries. However, a hungry market exists, and several vendors are developing products. The DLF ERMI steering group has identified functionality requirements and guidelines for the development of administrative e-resource metadata products based on the experiences of libraries that have developed their own systems to meet their own needs. Detailed requirements have been compiled based on these guiding principles:

- Integrated environment for management and access
- Interoperation and exchange of data with existing services:

OPACs, Web portals, library management systems, link-resolution services, etc.

- A single point of maintenance for each data element

According to the DLF group, an e-resource management system should be able to

- represent relationships among individual e-resources, packages, licenses, and online interfaces;
- associate characteristics of a license, interface, or package with the resources to which it applies; and
- provide robust reporting and data export capabilities

The DLF ERMI Web Hub maintains a list of commercially available products. These e-journal management databases and their future competitors include user interface features as well as e-journal administration features for staff. You can expect most of them to be elaborate and expensive. To further evaluate the functionality of a commercial e-resource metadata management systems, consult the DLF ERMI report Functional Requirements for Electronic Resource Management. DLF ERMI-determined core requirements are outlined in Figure 6–6.

Electronic Resource Management from Innovative Interfaces

Electronic Resource Management (ERM) is available from Innovative Interfaces Incorporated (III) as an integrated module for the III Millennium system or as a stand-alone product. ERM:

enables libraries to keep track of their e-journal licensing and purchasing details using a single system, streamlining workflows, and eliminating the need to maintain separate databases. ERM enables libraries to

- manage licensing and purchasing details in a single interface;
- provide additional fields for storage of relevant data. For staff, this may include URL, username/password, IP addresses, contact information, etc. For patrons, this may include printing permissions, interlibrary loan availability, etc.;
- display information about electronic resources in the Web OPAC for public services staff and patrons;
- define relationships between aggregators or publishers and the resources they provide; and

---

FIGURE 6–6. Working Document of the Digital Library Federation

Core Functional Requirements for E-Resource Metadata Management Systems

Record license permissions and agreement metadata
- Authorized users
- Permissions and restrictions
- Obligations of the parties
- Link to redacted license

Support selection and acquisition work flows through customizable routing and notification tools

Support integrated bibliographic access and management
- Provide relevant license information to the end user
- Share and/or exchange bibliographic data with other local systems and data exchange partners

Store access-related information: URLs, IDs, passwords, IP addresses

Store administrative information
- Administrative URLs, IDs, passwords
- Configuration information metadata (Z39.50, MARC records, OpenURL resolvers)
- Usage statistics

Support the troubleshooting of access and performance-related problems
- Incident log/call tracking
- Ability to flag resources as unavailable
- Incident history reports to monitor vendor performance

Provide contact information for vendors

Make complex business information available to staff
- Pricing models
- Cancellation restrictions
- Cost-sharing and consortial arrangements
- Archival Rights

Facilitate renewal and termination actions and decisions

(Digital Library Federation
Electronic Resource Management Initiative, 2003)

- manage payments and other financial and subscription details.
  (www.iii.com/mill/digital.shtml)

EBSCO Electronic Journal Service

EBSCOhost Electronic Journals Service (EJS)

> handles electronic journal access and management needs. EJS Enhanced offers extensive features that help with e-journal management tasks such as: tracking the registration status of e-journals, authentication assistance to facilitate both on-campus and remote access to e-journal content, automatic management of e-journal URLs and much more (www.ebsco.com/home/ejournals/default.asp).

The EJS Enhanced fee covers these services for subscriptions acquired through EBSCO subscription services; to include other journals there are "Expanded Access Fees." EJS also offers a pay-per-view option for articles in journals not included in library subscriptions. Libraries can pay for users' articles through EJS or pass the cost along to users.

Colorado Alliance Gold Rush

Gold Rush, "A Discovery and Management Tool for Electronic Resources" is a "suite of web-based tools to help librarians better manage subscriptions to electronic resources. The Gold Rush tool set encompasses the full process of electronic resource management—from purchasing to user access to statistics and renewals." The "Gold Rush Basic" product has a staff interface that

> includes an electronic resource subscriptions management tool, which allows library staff to track terms of use, access URLs, admin URLs, usage statistics information, costs, and contacts for each subscription in which the library participates (http://grweb.coalliance.org/).

Gold Rush is moderately priced, and the Colorado Alliance, a library consortium, offers discounts to other consortia.

VERIFY from VTLS

VTLS has recently developed an electronic resource management system called VERIFY (VTLS Electronic Resource Information and Funding utilitY) as a Virtua (ILS) module and a standalone product. Check www.vtls.com for more information as this product is brought to market.

Verde from Exlibris

Verde, under development by ExLibris, "builds on the power of the SFX link server" and is advertised as "a stand-alone product that can be integrated with existing environments, including SFX, OPACs, and applications that handle acquisitions, A-Z lists, and more." See www.exlibrisgroup.com/verde.htm.

Meridian from Endeavor

Endeavor is developing Meridian with the help of Elsevier's user interface design team. "Whenever possible, Meridian incorporates data available from the library's integrated library system, Voyager or another ILS, eliminating time-consuming data entry and maintenance" (www.endinfosys.com/prods/meridian.htm).

HOMEGROWN E-JOURNAL MANAGEMENT SYSTEMS

The Web Hub for Developing Administrative Metadata for Electronic Resource Management provides a wealth of information about several local e-resource management systems (www.library.cornell.edu/cts/elicensestudy/home.html). Some of these systems are simple, and others are very sophisticated. Most are databases.

Forms and Checklists

If your library does not have an intranet or file-sharing network, you may need to use paper forms and checklists to keep track of electronic journals during the order process. A form gives you a tangible way to represent an order in process, and something to hand off to the next person in the work flow. Another use for paper forms is for prototyping of a database. Using a form for a few orders will give you a sense of how much work it is to record various bits of information, and what information is actually needed as the form is passed along. The elements that you settle on for the form or checklist would become the fields in a database or columns in a spreadsheet. Each library has its own administrative processes, so the same form wouldn't work for every library. Here are some suggested elements to keep track of:

- Title
- Purchase order number
- Library fund charged
- Consortium (if any)
- Usage statistics information
- Administrative site, username, password, technical contact
- Date order request received

- Publisher
- Vendor, if not ordered direct
- Print subscriber number, if applicable
- Annual cost
- Renewal date
- URL in library
- Dates of coverage
- Authorized users
- License restrictions

- Date license reviewed
- Date license signed by library representative
- Date license signed by publisher representative
- Date copy of signed license received
- Date title ordered
- Date serials cataloger notified of availability
- Date Webmaster notified of availability

A Simple Spreadsheet

A spreadsheet for keeping track of information about electronic journal orders and subscriptions is a big step up from paper forms. The information in a spreadsheet can be shared electronically, easily viewed, and used by anyone in the library. A spreadsheet can be sorted and cross-sorted to help compile summary reports.

With a fairly basic understanding of Excel, you can reorganize columns and set a print area to produce a simplified list. Information from an Excel spreadsheet can be easily copied or saved into a Word document. With a more advanced knowledge of Excel, you can de-dupe a spreadsheet or turn it into a list of journals on a Web page or even a series of catalog records by adding columns with HTML or MARC coding.

Spreadsheets do have their limitations for tracking e-journal administrative data. You will probably want your spreadsheet to perform functions of a database, and although you can do quite a bit of data manipulation with Excel, it was designed for other purposes. It isn't easy to find help with using Excel to perform nonstandard functions. And relational database software has much more functionality for producing reports and providing access to users. Nevertheless, if Excel is the tool at hand, you can use it with good results.

Homegrown Databases

Many libraries have created their own inventory databases to manage their electronic journal administrative data. Often these databases also drive the system or systems that provide access to users (Web lists, the library catalog, a Web-based search engine).

This chapter addresses the back-end features intended for staff-only access. Libraries use the database technology they are most comfortable with, frequently Microsoft Access or FileMaker Pro. Some libraries migrate their database to a more robust platform as its functionality becomes more complex, or use more powerful tools from the start. Software and platforms that libraries have used for their homegrown databases are SQL, Cold Fusion, and Oracle. The DLF ERMI steering group is conducting tests with XML and developing XML schema as yet another tool.

Before developing your own database, you will want to develop specifications. The DLF ERMI Web Hub has links to helpful information from libraries that have developed e-resource management databases, including their data elements or fields, table structures, and specifications. A good example of database specifications was developed by the University of Minnesota, Twin Cities Campus (http://staff.lib.umn.edu/cdm/erse/inv-db/specs.html).

One of the earliest examples of a robust electronic resources database was Penn State's Electronic Resources Licensing and Information Center (ERLIC) system (now enhanced as ERLIC^2), built originally to track resource acquisitions. It was later expanded to include information regarding authentication, supplier- and gateway-usage statistics, license restrictions, supplier-contact information, document-delivery privileges, and system-performance information, with links to scanned licenses, invoices, and order documentation. The system generates renewal alerts and incorporates announcements from vendors. The original Microsoft Access ERLIC template is available as shareware (without support) from www.libraries.psu.edu/tas/fiscal_data/ERLIC_SHARE/Publish/index.html. As Penn State's database got larger (13,000+ e-journal records), it was moved to a Cold Fusion/Oracle platform as ERLIC^2. See Figure 6–7 for more examples of homegrown systems.

Other Approaches

The University of California at Santa Cruz (UCSC) uses a Web-based tracking system for internal communication and solving problems with e-resources. Request Tracker (RT) is an open-source software program used primarily by IT and computing units to report and follow up on "incidents." USCS uses the RT system to enhance communications, generate management statistics for evaluation purposes, and track access problems (McCaslin, 2003).

PACKAGE AND FULL-TEXT DATABASE CONTENT

Chapter 7 is all about connecting users with your electronic journals, and there is much discussion about managing access to individual titles within packages and databases. Acquisitions staff, in acquiring the packages, are generally concerned with tracking

---

FIGURE 6–7. Examples of Homegrown Systems

- Electronic Resources Tracking System (ERTS)—The Tri-College Consortium
  www.haverford.edu/library/erts/
  FileMaker Pro

- Virtual Electronic Resource Access (VERA)—MIT
  www.hennigweb.com/publications/vera.html
  FileMaker Pro

- Hopkins Electronic Resources ManagEment System (Hermes) Johns Hopkins University
  http://hermes.mse.jhu.edu:8008/hermesdocs/
  Open-source software

---

information about the package or database as a whole. However, they will sometimes play a role in the internal management of the content. You might be asked to do an analysis of the overlapping content in two databases prior to a renewal or purchase decision. You can do it yourself using Excel; or Serials Solutions, TDNet, and Gold Rush will provide comparison reports.

PROCESSING RENEWALS

One of the important roles in e-journal collection management is to deselect journals that no longer meet users' needs. As you may know from experience, sometimes journal subscriptions have to be canceled in order to balance the serials budget. In times when budgets are tight and accountability is required, your parent institution may expect every renewal to be justified, whether it is a print journal, a database, or an electronic journal.

CRITERIA FOR RENEWAL
Content

Check to see if there are any changes in content. This is especially important if you are subscribing to a package rather than to an individual title. Consider the following questions:

- Has the vendor or aggregator added resources, or conversely, removed some titles to which you previously had access?
- If you subscribe to multiple full-text databases, is there increasing duplication in the titles offered by aggregators?
- How many unique titles are in each package or database to which you subscribe?

Check to see how current the electronic journal is vis à vis the print version of the title. Does it come out prior to the print, which is certainly an advantage to your users, or is there a time lag before the electronic version is available? If there is a substantial delay, one of the most compelling advantages of the electronic journal—currency—is lost to users.

Pricing

Many electronic journals are available from several vendors or aggregators. Renewal time is a good time to check the options from other providers. New packages may be available at more competitive prices, or with a title mix that is more compatible with your collection. A particular vendor interface may be more intuitive and easier to navigate for your users.

Usage

Usage statistics are now available from most e-journal publishers, although the depth, timeliness, and ease of use varies a great deal. Do not be satisfied with a "default" report that lists only titles most frequently accessed, excluding titles that are seldom or never used. Look for the following information in the statistics that are provided to you:

- What is the number of sessions or log ons?
- What is the number of queries or searches done?
- What are your times of peak usage—by day, by hour?
- Are users being turned away? Do you need to purchase additional or unlimited simultaneous users?
- What is the cost per use for the title or database? A general interest resource should be relatively low in cost,

whereas a more focused and specific resource with a small potential user population may be more expensive.

Aggregated data can be used to prove the popularity of your electronic journals, to help with funding and other support, or to do a cost-benefit analysis of a publisher's package. But title-level numbers are necessary for decisions to renew individual electronic subscriptions or to cancel print subscriptions. Chapter 9 provides more information about usage statistics.

CANCELING PRINT

Sooner or later the time will come to cancel print subscriptions for the journals you receive online. But like everything else about electronic journals, it is not as easy as you might think.

For some libraries, the only way to acquire a significant number of electronic journals is to choose the "online-only" pricing option whenever it is available. However, if you can manage it financially, it is much more desirable to have a period of overlapping coverage between print and online journals while the library works out authentication and access kinks and users become accustomed to new ways of finding and using journals.

The length of the transition period will vary, but eventually the dual access will become burdensome to the library in terms of direct costs—the additional fees for subscriptions in both formats and indirect costs of handling and managing both formats, shelf space for print journals that are barely used, and staff time to process them. Sooner or later the time will come to cancel print subscriptions for the journals you receive online. But, like everything else about electronic journals, it is not as easy as you might think.

STABLE, ENDURING ACCESS

You will want some level of assurance that there will be stable, enduring access to the electronic version of a journal once your print backup is no longer available. Your level of assurance will depend on your source for the electronic version.

E-Journals in Aggregator Databases

For most libraries, the source for the largest number of electronic journals is one or more full-text databases from vendors such as EBSCO or ProQuest. As explained in earlier chapters, these economical e-journals offer all the features and advantages of e-journals obtained at a much higher cost through individual or packaged subscriptions—except one. The biggest drawback of an aggregator database as a source for e-journals is the lack of long-term stability of access (and in some cases, recent-issue access) to individual titles. You will be gambling if you cancel a print journal based on the probability of its continued availability in one of these databases. See Chapter 4 for a more complete discussion of this issue.

Free Online Access with Print Subscriptions

Obviously, if your access to an e-journal is made possible by your print subscription, you will lose that access if you cancel the print version. Or so it seems. But if you let the publisher know that you prefer the online version, you may be able to arrange for online-only access for the price of your print subscription, or less if they are ready to experiment with new pricing models. A publisher that does not have a system for managing online-only subscriptions may agree to discontinue sending print issues although you are a subscriber. If not, you can choose not to process or shelve the print issues. Your online access will be as secure as your print subscription has been.

E-Journal Subscriptions

Subscription-based (as opposed to aggregator-based) access generally provides a high degree of assurance that you will not lose access to the online journals you select and license from publishers. Even if the journal or the publisher changes ownership, you should be able to continue to subscribe—from the new publisher. You might not like the new publisher's price, but the situation is no different from having a new publisher for your print journals. Usually, when electronic journals change hands, the new publisher will honor the license agreement you have signed with the former publisher for its duration.

Access after Canceling Electronic Journals

You will probably feel more comfortable canceling a print journal if your license for the electronic version guarantees that if you cancel entirely, your users will continue to have online access to the issues published during the time your library subscribed to the online journal. A study sponsored by the Association of Learned and Professional Society Publishers (ALPSP) found that 72% of commercial publishers and 54% of nonprofit publishers provide such continuing access (Cox and Cox, 2003). Check your license agreements for this clause.

TRUSTWORTHY PRINT AND ELECTRONIC ARCHIVES

A common concern is the long-term preservation of electronic journals. We know how long paper lasts and how to extend the life of printed materials. We have control over the availability of our print journals for users far into the future, but we can't be sure that the electronic journals we subscribe to this year will be available to our users in 50 years. The 2003 ALPSP study indicated that 52% of commercial and 45% of nonprofit publishers had made formal commitments for long-term preservation, either on their own, or through OCLC, Highwire's LOCKSS, or JSTOR (Cox and Cox, 2003). Large publishers are investing in archiving partnerships with libraries, such as those Elsevier has arranged with Yale (www.diglib.org/preserve/yalefinal.html) and the National Library of the Netherlands (www.infotoday.com/newsbreaks/nb020903-2.htm).

The Trust Factor

One of the reasons for JSTOR's existence was the belief that digitizing the older volumes of core journals would allow libraries to dispose of their print runs, saving them a large amount of space. JSTOR's commitment to perpetual archiving has been one of the main features of the project. Surprisingly, after several years, little change has occurred in libraries' holdings of the print titles. There still appears to be a lack of trust among libraries in the long-term viability of JSTOR journals. In fact, the Center for Research Libraries (CRL) has developed a "dark archive" for print copies of JSTOR journals for added security (Blake, 2003). Other libraries and groups of libraries have made commitments to store print copies of their online journals, often in off-site locations, to satisfy concerns about the long-term viability of electronic formats.

A First Step: Remote Storage for Duplicated Print

To deal with space issues and/or to test users' attachment to print resources that are also available online as a first step towards cancellation of print subscriptions, several libraries and groups of libraries have sent some of their print journals to remote storage facilities. For a year (October 2001 through September 2002), the University of California experimented with removing print issues of 300 journals that were available online from one library (Library A) while keeping them on the shelves in another library within the system to measure the usage of both the print and electronic versions in both libraries. They found that there were very few requests for the print journals in remote storage and very moderate use of print journals that were in the "control library," Library B:

Library A (print journals in remote storage)
  Usage of electronic journals – 160,180 (99.87%)
  Requests for print issues in storage – 201 (.13%)

Library B (print journals shelved in library)
  Usage of electronic journals – 97,473 (94.16%)
  Usage of print issues – 6,044 (5.84%)

(www.slp.ucop.edu/consultation/slasiac/042903/
CMI_SurveyResultsForSLASIAC04-29-03.doc)

The University of Alberta has explained their print-cancellation policy nicely at www.library.ualberta.ca/aboutus/collection/ejdirections/index.cfm.

OTHER CONSIDERATIONS

Despite the duplication of content in print and electronic formats, there are situations in which you will not want to cancel the print version. Each library will have its own considerations, based on its users' needs and its mission, so you will want to develop your own policy. Your exceptions might include some of the following:

- The journal regularly contains articles that are too long to print.
- The print version contains large-sized supplementary materials that cannot be viewed, or cannot be viewed easily, online.
- Accreditation of a program requires the print subscription.
- Access to the online journal is provided through unstable channels.
- Issues are monographic and cataloged under separate titles for better access.
- Collection-sharing agreements with other institutions preclude cancellation.
- The electronic version requires special software or equipment.
- The electronic version is not equivalent to the print version.
- The print version continues to receive heavy use, despite the availability of the e-version.

OPPORTUNITIES FOR COUNTRIES IN TRANSITION

Libraries in developing countries now have several opportunities to subscribe to electronic journals at dramatically reduced prices through special arrangements with publishers and the efforts of organizations dedicated to international equity in access to scholarly communication and research. Most of these publishers and coordinators have predetermined lists of eligible countries, based on a country's gross domestic product (GDP) or other criteria. The largest initiatives to date are Electronic Information for Libraries (eIFL) and the Health InterNetwork Access to Research Initiative (HINARI).

eIFL

An independent foundation, eIFL was first established as part of the Open Society Institute (OSI) and sponsored by the financier and philanthropist George Soros and EBSCO Publishing to bring commercial databases and electronic journals to libraries that could not afford them. Now its core purpose is "negotiating affordable subscriptions on a multi-country consortial basis, while supporting the enhancement of emerging national library consortia in member countries." The foundation "strives to lead, negotiate, support and advocate for the wide availability of electronic resources by library users in transition and developing countries." In addition to helping consortia form and negotiate with vendors, eIFL provides grant funding to help cover the costs of consortial licenses. See www.eIFL.org.

HINARI

HINARI, part of the United Nations Health InterNetwork Initiative, provides free or low-cost access to over 2,000 journals from major publishers to public institutions in 113 eligible developing countries. Led by the World Health Organization (WHO), the Health InterNetwork was designed to "bridge the digital divide in health" in order to strengthen public health services through access to high-quality, relevant, and timely health information. At least 35 publishers participate in this initiative. See www.healthinternetwork.org/.

Keeping up-to-date:

Developing Nations Initiatives
www.library.yale.edu/
~llicense/develop.shtml

eIFL.net—Other Initiatives
http://www.eifl.net/others/
others.html

ALPSP Hot Topics:
Developing Country Initiatives
http://www.alpsp.org/
htp_dev.htm

OTHER INITIATIVES

The "Developing Nations Initiatives" section of the Liblicense site (www.library.yale.edu/~llicense/develop.shtml) links to several programs and publishers that have made commitments to enable libraries throughout the world to subscribe to their journals at a discounted price.

REFERENCES

Blake, Julie. 2003. "The 2002 Acquisitions Institute at Timberline Lodge." *Serials Review* 28, no. 4: 328–334.

Carlson, Scott. 2003. "Libraries Consortium Conundrum." *Chronicle of Higher Education* 50, no. 7 (October 10). Retrieved Sept. 20, 2004, from http://chronicle.com/free/v50/i07/07a03001.htm.

Carnegie Foundation for the Advancement of Teaching. 2000. "Carnegie Classification of Institutions of Higher Education." Retrieved Sept. 21, 2004, from www.carnegiefoundation.org/Classification/.

Cox, John, and Laura Cox. 2003. "Scholarly Publishing Practice: The ALPSP Report on Academic Journal Publishers' Policies and Practices in Online Publishing." Rookwood, UK: John Cox Associates for the Association of Learned and Professional Society Publishers. Retrieved Sept. 20, 2004, from www.alpsp.org/news/sppsummary0603.pdf (Executive summary).

Davis, Philip M. 2003. "Patterns in Electronic Journal Usage: Challenging the Composition of Geographic Consortia." *College and Research Libraries* 63, no. 6 (November): 484–497.

Digital Library Federation. "Report of the DLF Electronic Resource Management Initiative." 2003. Appendix A: *Functional Requirements for Electronic Resource Management*. Retrieved Sept. 20, 2004, from www.library.cornell.edu/Cts/elicensestudy/dlfdeliverables/fallforum2003/FunctionalSpec20031114.doc.

Friend, Fred. 2003. "Big Deal—Good Deal. Or Is There a Better Deal?" *Learned Publishing* 16, no. 2 (April): 153–155.

Mackie-Mason, Jeffrey K., and L. L. Jankovich. 1997. "PEAK: Pricing Electronic Access to Knowledge." *Library Acquisitions, Practice and Theory* 21, no. 3: 281–295.

McCaslin, Sharon [recorder]. 2003. "Web-Based Tracking Systems for Electronic Resources Management." Workshop report, North American Serials Interest Group, 2002. *The Serials Librarian* 44, no. 3/4: 293–297.

Sanville, Tom. 2003. "Reassessing Aggregate Licensing." *Reassessment of Bundled Subscriptions to Electronic Journals*, 5–7. Vantage Point [series]. Birmingham, AL: EBSCO Subscription Services.

MORE INFORMATION SOURCES

Anglada, Lluis, and Nuria Comellas. 2002. "What's Fair? Pricing Models in the Electronic Era." *Library Management* 23, nos. 4/5: 227–233.

Boss, Richard W. 2004. "Automated Library System Vendors and Electronic Resource Management." *Tech Notes*. Public Library Association. Retrieved Sept. 20, 2004, from www.ala.org/ala/pla/plapubs/technotes/ermgmt.htm.

Chan, Winnie. 2002. "Creative Applications of a Web-Based E-Resource Registry." *Science and Technology Libraries* 20, no. 2/3: 45–56.

Cyzyk, Mark, and Nathan D. M. Robertson. 2003. "HERMES: The Hopkins Electronic Resource Management System." *Information Technology and Libraries* 22, no. 1: 12–18. Retrieved from www.ala.org/ala/lita/litapublications/ital/2201cyzyk.htm.

Duranceau, Ellen Finnie. 2002. "E-journal Package-Content Tracking Services," *Serials Review* 28, no. 1 (Spring): 49–52.

Forsythe, Kathleen, and Steve Shadle. 2002. "University of Washington Libraries Digital Registry." *Journal of Internet Cataloging* 5, no. 4: 51–65.

Ginn, Claire. 2002. "Calculating Pricing Models Choices: Rising to the Challenge." *Learned Publishing* 15 (July): 199–203.

Goodman, David. 2002. "A Year without Print at Princeton, and What We Plan Next." *Learned Publishing* 15 (January): 43–50.

Hennig, Nicole. 2002. "Improving Access to E-journals and Databases at the MIT Libraries: Building a Database-Backed Web Site Called 'Vera.'" *The Serials Librarian* 41, no. 3/4: 227–254.

Hoyle, Mary Sue. "Managing Electronic Journals from a Vendor's Perspective." *The Serials Librarian* 45, no. 2: 135–144.

Jewell, Timothy D. 2001. "Selection and Presentation of Commercially Available Electronic Resources: Issues and Practices." Digital Library Federation and the Council on Library and Information Resources. Retrieved Sept. 20, 2004, from www.clir.org/pubs/reports/pub99/contents.html.

Medeiros, Norm, Linda Bills, Jeremy Blatchley, Christee Pascale, and Barbara Weir. 2003. "Managing Administrative Metadata." *Library Resources & Technical Services* 47, no. 1: 28–35.

Mitchell, Anne. 2002. "Tracking Aggregator Coverage with Spreadsheets." *The Serials Librarian* 43, no. 1: 19–23.

Rupp-Serrano, Karen, Sarah Robbins, and Danielle Cain. 2002. "Canceling Print Serials in Favor of Electronic: Criteria for Decision Making." *Library Collections, Acquisitions, and Technical Services* 26, no. 4: 369–378.

Schulz, Norman. 2002. "E-journal Databases: A Long-Term Solution?" *Library Collections, Acquisitions, and Technical Services* 25, no. 4: 449–459.

Scigliano, Marisa. 2002. "Consortium Purchases: Case Study for a Cost-Benefit Analysis." *Journal of Academic Librarianship* 28, no. 6: 393–399.

Stern, David. 2002. "Pricing Models and Payment Schemes for Library Collections." *ONLINE* 26 (September/October): 54–59.

Turner, Rollo. 2003. "E-Journal Administration—Fragmentation or Integration?" *The Serials Librarian* 45, no. 1: 75–84.

Watson, Paula. 2003. "Acquisition of E-Journals." *Library Technology Reports* 39, no. 2 (March-April): 28–44.

7 DELIVERING ELECTRONIC JOURNALS AND MAINTAINING ACCESS CHANNELS

CHAPTER OVERVIEW

- Designing, Building, and Maintaining Delivery Systems
- User-Centered Access
- Web Access
- Catalog Access
- Electronic Reserves
- Integrating Articles with Courseware
- Context-Sensitive Linking
- Serials Cataloging and Acronyms and Initialisms

"I'm realizing just what an unstable and difficult bibliographic world we are trying to control!"

—Jean Hirons (2003)

This chapter explores the ways that libraries provide access to electronic journals through listings on Web pages, their catalogs, and online course-delivery systems; and how they keep these pathways operable, accurate, up to date, and simple for users to negotiate.

The chapter is not intended to be a complete course in electronic serials cataloging, but rather it gives readers a solid grounding in the fundamentals of providing access to electronic journals through multiple channels. Cataloging standards, tools, procedures, and issues will be discussed in a context that assumes the reader has a background in cataloging or access to training resources. Likewise, the section on providing Web access does not cover the essentials of Web-page authoring or design, and it assumes that the reader's library already has a Web site.

DESIGNING, BUILDING, AND MAINTAINING DELIVERY SYSTEMS

Even libraries that already have an e-journal delivery system in place continue to struggle with decisions about how best to serve their users and encourage more use of their electronic journals. A delivery strategy that was carefully chosen six months ago may no longer be the best option. New tools and technologies provide new choices. Users' expectations change. Their preferences must always be at the center of any discussion about access options, but it is important to understand that simplicity for users is inversely proportional to the amount of work required for the library to achieve those results.

No two libraries are identical in their resources, their technological infrastructure, the abilities of their staff, and the types of users they serve. So there is no one "best way" to provide access to your electronic journals. In designing your system, you should involve everyone who will be responsible for creating and maintaining the system, and build in as much flexibility as you can. User preferences evolve as the Web evolves, and to make the most of your library's investments, your access system must evolve as well.

THE CATALOG *AND* THE HOME PAGE (AND MORE)

When electronic journals were new, librarians debated whether they should provide access to them through the library's catalog or Web pages. Through experience, we have learned that the correct answer is "both." Different kinds of users will look in different places, and each source has its advantages and disadvantages.

Libraries have found that many users prefer to use Web lists in order to "get a feel" for the library's e-journal collection, but for those who are tracking down a particular article in a particular journal, the catalog can provide thorough and accurate information about the journal in all its formats and locations. The biggest challenge for most libraries is to provide a system for both kinds of access without double the work.

In addition to providing searching and browsing access through your catalog and your Web site, you will also want to ensure that your users can connect with articles in your electronic journals through links from your non-full-text databases, their course syllabi and assignment Web pages, and your library's course reserves system. It's a tall order.

SYSTEM MAINTENANCE ISSUES

The ideal situation is to maintain one master database that populates both the library's catalog and e-journal Web pages and gives users the opportunity to search as well as browse titles. Many libraries have successfully built a system that allows them to maintain only one database that controls all access options. But this is not as easy as it seems.

The Catalog as Master Database

One attractive option is to use the catalog itself as the central database (since in essence a catalog *is* a database) to generate Web lists as well as search options within the catalog, and OPAC displays of information about e-journals. Some libraries have been successful with this approach, for example:

- Los Alamos National Laboratories (see Knudsen, 1997)
- University of Washington (see Parks, 2002)
- University of Michigan (see Rothman, 2002)
- University of Victoria (see Paul, Romaniuk, and Cheng, 2004)
- University of Sydney (see Online Catalog Group (OCG), 2002).

The main problem with using the catalog as a master database is timeliness. Cataloging is time and labor intensive, and most libraries that acquire electronic journals want to provide access to them as soon as possible and are unwilling to wait for them to make it through the cataloging process.

Populating Two Databases

Until their backlog of e-journals is cataloged, libraries often initiate a short-term process that may last a long time—producing Web lists from a separate database or spreadsheet. This usually means obtaining e-journal metadata from publishers' or vendors' sites or purchasing custom lists from a third party, such as Serials Solutions. Most outside e-journal management services will supply libraries with frequently-updated Web-ready lists of the titles in their collections of licensed journals, with links to individual journals within each package or full-text database.

These same lists can be used to semi-automate the creation of brief e-journal records for the catalog, but not every library will accept a batch method of populating its catalog. Any such "quick-and-dirty" process can undermine the quality and integrity of the catalog, so some libraries will opt instead to catalog each title

Outsourcing Title Maintenance

Serials Solutions
www.serialssolutions.com/home.asp

TDNet
www.tdnet.com/

GoldRush
http://grweb.coalliance.org/

EBSCO A-Z Service
http://www.ebsco.com/atoz/default.asp

individually. In these libraries, Web pages can generally be updated more quickly than the catalog.

Master Database

Libraries commonly maintain a permanent database separate from the catalog and use it simultaneously to maintain the catalog and produce Web lists. The master database can be updated manually or through feeds from a third-party service. The University of Tennessee Libraries in Knoxville harvests information from a database of aggregator titles to create brief records for the catalog until full cataloging can be done (see Johnson, Manoff, and Sheffield, 2003). In addition to its role(s) in providing access to the library's e-journals, the master database is often the library's management tool for acquisitions and collection development, containing information about renewals, pricing, usage, and license agreements. Journal Finder, developed by the University of North Carolina, Greensborough, is perhaps the best known. Chapter 6 elaborates on the back-end features of elaborate e-journal management databases.

GENERAL DISPLAY ISSUES

After you have determined how to manage the information your users will see, you will have to make some decisions about how much and what kind of information they will see. Policies can save staff time and provide consistency for users, but they will need to change over time. Whatever access channels you maintain for your users, you will need to make some decisions:

- Whether to link to (a) the journal's home page (which may consist primarily of information about the journal with links to content), (b) the most current issue with information links to archives and information about the journal, or (c) an archives page, which usually provides links to tables of contents of all issues including the current issue.
- How much (if any) information to provide about source/vendor(s) of the journal.
- Whether you want to provide different kinds of access depending on the type of source (for example, you might handle titles in aggregator databases differently from the way you handle more stable e-journals).
- If you want to link to the database interface for journals that do not have persistent, individual URLs, or if you will even list titles from databases that require users to do a search to find a specific journal.

- Whether you will want to list all sources for the journal or just the preferred ones.
- How you will prioritize the presentation of journals from multiple sources.
- Whether (and how) to provide subject access.
- What kind of holdings information to provide—how specific? How will you explain about embargoes? Will you want to include frequency statements?

It is natural to make decisions about process and display based on philosophy, convenience, past practices, a desire for consistency, and the comfort level of the staff, but, wherever possible, you should make decisions based on what is best for the users of your library, even if it means adjusting your work flow or reallocating priorities (see Chapter 3).

USER-CENTERED ACCESS

Users' information and research needs remain fundamentally unchanged by new developments in online delivery systems, although their expectations and behavior in satisfying those needs may have changed radically. In every discipline, the development of a body of research or theory is documented through sanctioned means, usually articles in peer-reviewed journals, and current e-journals simply deliver those articles in a different format. These needs remain unchanged:

- Faculty and other researchers who submit manuscripts to journals that will legitimize and disseminate the results of their work still need to conduct and describe a literature review that demonstrates their knowledge of prior related research.
- Funding agencies still require that proposals include a bibliography.
- High school and undergraduate college students still need facts and quotations from authoritative sources and other kinds of substantiation for their own opinions and assertions. Even if they are assigned to develop a PowerPoint presentation, multimedia project, or Web site rather than writing a "term paper," they are nonetheless still required to gather and synthesize information from other sources.

- Graduate students still do exhaustive literature searches for their theses and dissertations.
- Physicians, attorneys, accountants, dieticians, and other professional practitioners still need access to the latest theories and practices in their fields.
- Consumers still need accurate and timely information about products.

Libraries still have an enormous role to play in connecting people with the information resources they require. What has changed is the way users expect to find and obtain information. Expectations of the amount of time and effort it should take to do an information search or a literature review and to obtain the article(s) are much different from what they were only a few years ago as a result of other experiences with the Web. Users basically expect immediate gratification.

The library no longer has a monopoly on scholarly, quality, authoritative information resources. We may have large, pure, and comprehensive online collections, and we may be able to provide our users with free online access to commercially produced, commercially compiled resources, but we have competition:

- Other groups and individuals have been busy developing alternatives to commercial resources;
- the Internet enables scholars, researchers, and practitioners to share information among themselves in ways that decrease their need for libraries;
- the open Web houses plenty of factual and authoritative information for students, researchers, professionals, and consumers who know how to find it; and
- options for obtaining targeted resources using micro-payments or reasonably priced personal subscription services are attractive to some users if the services clearly save their time.

For the library to remain relevant to its users in this changed environment, it is crucial to understand information-seeking behavior in general. You may want to review Chapter 2.

INFORMATION-LITERACY ASSUMPTIONS

As we know, people are not born knowing how to evaluate information resources, identify the most relevant or the most authoritative information, locate obscure information, or deal with information overload. In an ideal world,

- the K-12 curriculum would provide a strong information-literacy foundation;
- college students would be taught more advanced information skills as part of their composition courses or orientation activities;
- upper-level and graduate courses would cover the characteristics of the information environments of each discipline; and
- advisors would coach their thesis and dissertation students in online information retrieval.

In the real world,

- a small minority of students gain information-literacy skills in the classroom or through library instruction or independent experiences;
- many K-12 teachers lack technological literacy;
- some college instructors have not updated their research skills or they do not want to devote class time to the basics of the literature review.

The majority of college and university courses are textbook- and lecture-based, and supplemental articles are frequently preselected for students and compiled in a course pack or placed on reserve at the library. So when a student is required to find articles for a research paper, he or she may not have a clue about where to begin. Graduate students may not get much assistance from their advisors on thorough searching, and researchers who are entering unfamiliar territory may not know how to use online resources—or even that some of them are available.

You cannot assume information literacy on the part of your users, even though they might have a good mastery of technology. Most high school and college students have an impressive amount of experience with computers, but they may not have any experience with searching for certain types of information. You may never see them in your library, though you may be able to help them find your library resources using online means. You can enhance your users' information-literacy skills somewhat through the way you present and organize your resources. Users could start anywhere, so your electronic journals should be there, wherever "there" is.

WHERE USERS BEGIN

To make your e-journals accessible through any possible approach by users, you should provide ways to

- search appropriate databases for articles by subject,
- link to the full text of your journals from bibliographic databases,
- browse journals within appropriate categories, or
- find a known article.

You will want to support all of these approaches by activating pathways for navigation and ways for users to build upon their results. Wherever they start, you will want to give users a chance to end up somewhere even better for their needs.

Subject Searching

We can assume that the majority of K-12 users, public library users, and lower-division undergraduates will take a subject approach to articles in electronic journals. In a common situation, they may need a few good articles on their topic for an assignment or project, or to help with a decision. Researchers will use this approach less often. One study (Tenopir et al., 2003) indicates that scientists do article searches for

- new topics,
- old articles,
- primary research, and
- their own articles.

Your library catalog is not the place for subject searchers to begin their search for articles. They belong in a general or specialized database that aggregates many articles from different sources, preferably a database that contains the full text of the articles. If you catalog your databases, and your users happen to know the exact name of the database they should use, they might be able to get to the database through your OPAC. But in general, your library's Web site will be the appropriate gateway to your databases. Many of them will not know that they need articles, or how one goes about finding articles. In serving users looking for articles by subject, you face two big challenges:

1. To guide them to the right database(s)
2. To enable them to link to the full text of articles from non-full-text databases

The sections on Web access, linking, and federated searching below will help you meet these challenges on behalf of your users.

Browsing

Browsing journals is a time-honored practice, demonstrated by the common presence of current-periodicals areas in libraries of all types. Some types of browsing behavior transfer well to electronic journals that are presented optimally (see "Web Access" in this chapter). Tenopir (2003) has noted that scientists browse

- core titles in their disciplines,
- current issues of selected journals,
- for background information, and
- for current awareness.

If browsing journals is a fundamental requirement of their academic work and if print journals are no longer available to them, faculty will adapt to the electronic environment, and some of them will prefer it. In a library reading room, print issues may be missing or in use, whereas on a library's Web site, all online issues will be available for concurrent use, in some cases earlier than print issues would be available on the shelves. For browsers, looking through articles in current issues is even more fruitful and appealing when they are able to link directly to related articles that are referenced in the articles they browse.

Students and the general public browse more broadly for current awareness purposes, perhaps in a news weekly or a popular magazine that relates to their interests. A student who is browsing through *Time, Ms, The Rolling Stone* or *Runner's World* between classes may or may not continue to browse the online version if the print version is no longer in the library.

Most libraries with electronic journals will continue to subscribe to their most heavily used print magazines, especially those that are inexpensive, to satisfy an obvious need. However, they may choose not to bind or even keep the older issues of periodicals that are available to users online, since most users who are looking for specific older articles or a subject that is represented in older issues will prefer to find and use them through online means.

Finding a Known Article or Journal Issue

Some users will approach your electronic journals with a citation in hand, looking for a specific article or a specific issue of a journal. You might expect them to search for the title of the journal in your online catalog and connect to the journal through the record they will retrieve, and some will. But if they know they are looking for a journal that is electronic, and if they think that your catalog describes your library's inventory (assuming they know about your catalog at all), they may not automatically assume that something on the Web will be represented in your catalog. You will want them to be able to locate that journal issue through your Web site, outside of your catalog as well as in your catalog—wherever they think to look.

Integration with Courseware

For college students, course-oriented Web experiences increasingly take place within an environment created with "courseware," or course-management software designed for conducting course-related communication online. The most popular courseware products are Blackboard and WebCT, though there are others. Designed originally for distance education, courseware is now a popular tool for enhancing on-site courses. Students might go to lectures as usual, but they log on to WebCT or Blackboard to consult their syllabus, discuss topics in an online forum or real-time chat session, work on group projects, receive and submit assignments, take quizzes, and exchange e-mail messages with the instructor. It only makes sense that within this specialized online environment students should be able to read electronic journal articles.

WEB ACCESS

All access to your e-journals will be through your Web site, even if that means going through your Web OPAC. In most cases, the library's home page will connect users to the catalog as well as other resources. The ways in which you guide them to your e-journals will be very much a function of your library's Web design. One of the most important and challenging aspects of library Web design is to use the terminology and structures that make sense to users; that is often very different from what makes sense to librarians. Keep these basic principles in mind:

- Your goal is not to get your users to "think like librarians"; your goal is to "think like users."
- Although you may serve several kinds of users, your experienced or specialized users can navigate a complex site more easily than inexperienced or general users; design simple paths for the latter.

- Design primarily for your primary users; simplify their choices.
- Emphasize what your primary users will most want—in most cases, the full text of articles.
- Think of your catalog as one of many databases; remember that articles aren't represented in your catalog. Most of what is represented there has lost its attraction. Don't hide it, but don't make it the centerpiece or the obvious first choice.
- Minimize the intermediate pages between your home page and full text; the fewer clicks, the better.
- Avoid terms like "databases," "periodicals," "bibliographic," and be careful with "catalog" and "electronic journals" (explain what you mean, somehow—e.g., with mouse-over, pop-up text).
- Talk to users about their information needs; listen carefully for the terms they use.
- Think in terms of functions, like "find books, journals, videos, DVDs, and other materials"; "find online articles on your subject"; "find information by subject."

FULL-TEXT AND BIBLIOGRAPHIC DATABASES

As studies have shown, the largest number of prospective e-journal users are looking for articles on a certain topic, and they usually don't care which journal has the article(s), though they may be required to use journals that meet certain specifications (often scholarly or peer-reviewed). If they end up on your library's page, unless yours is a specialized library, you will want to provide an easy pathway to "a few good articles." On most library sites, they would feel overwhelmed by the choices. The choices are necessary for your users who need specialized information, but those users are a "captive audience," who will be willing to invest some time in exploring what is available. Consider your "fleeting audience," who will leave your site if they can't easily and immediately find what they need.

Think about your best full-text database for the primary needs of your primary users. For example, if your library serves a university community that is primarily undergraduates, many of them will be looking for articles in scholarly journals that are readable by nonspecialists. They would be better off in one of the general indexes:

- Gale's InfoTrac Expanded Academic ASAP
- ProQuest Research databases

- One of EBSCO's Academic Search or MasterFile databases
- Wilson OmniFile or WilsonSelect

If you can provide a direct link on your library's home page to the "simple search" or "basic search" screen of your best database for your inexperienced primary users, configured to look and act like Google, you will increase their success rate and reduce the chances that they will retreat to Google itself. Remember that according to studies, at least 70% of college students are reportedly satisfied with Google for their research papers.

If the database has a mixture of full-text articles and non-full-text bibliographic records, you may want to set default options to retrieve only full-text articles, if that is something you can configure locally. In an academic library, it might be appropriate to set default limits for scholarly or peer-reviewed articles, if you have that option.

Other users will want to use subject-specific databases for a more specialized search. Most of these users would also prefer to retrieve online full-text articles, but you will not want to limit their options, since many of them will use print journals or wait for interlibrary loan if there is no other option. Non-full-text databases often include a system that will link users to your licensed full-text journals from other sources, either internally or through an external link-resolver service, such as SFX. But you will increase their success of retrieving full-text articles by organizing Web lists of databases by subject and indicating on those lists which ones include full-text articles and which ones can connect to full text through your link resolver, if you have one.

E-JOURNAL PAGES

Most libraries now provide Web pages that aggregate titles of individual journals, no matter how they acquire them:

- packages from publishers
- licenses for individual journals
- consortial licenses
- aggregator databases
- identification of freely available titles

Studies of users' preferences indicate that these cumulated lists are used and appreciated, even if the e-journals are also represented more thoroughly in the library catalog. These pages might include alphabetical lists of e-journals, lists organized by subjects, search boxes that allow simple or complex searches for an e-journal, or links to other resources:

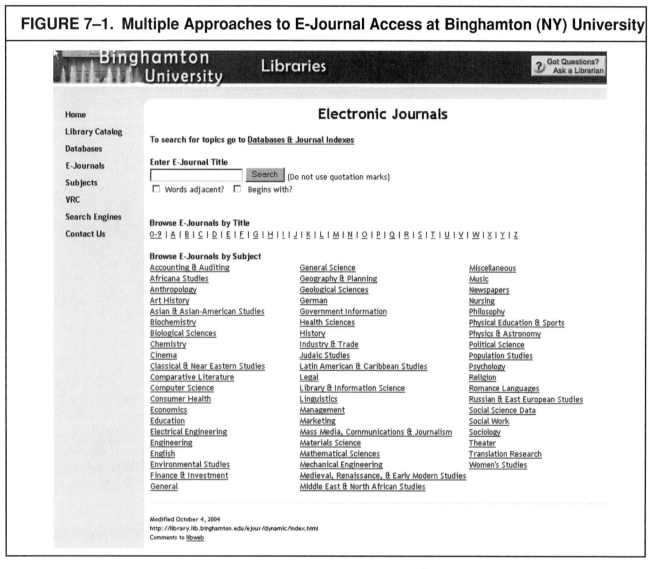

FIGURE 7–1. Multiple Approaches to E-Journal Access at Binghamton (NY) University

- Various aggregations of e-journals
- Instructions for accessing journals from off-site
- The latest version of Acrobat Reader to download
- General license terms
- Technical support
- Other information related to electronic journals

Through the use of text colors, fonts, font sizes, graphics, icons, and layout, you can convey a lot of information on your Web pages about electronic journals without confusing your users, enabling them to navigate a course that fits their needs. Figure 7–1 gives an example of a well-designed e-journal page from Binghamton University Library. See it live at http://library.lib.binghamton.edu/ejour/dynamic/ to view the colors.

With simple Web-editing software or basic knowledge of

HTML, it is not difficult to construct a Web page listing your e-journals. But keeping your lists up-to-date is not a simple matter. Making title-by-title changes to static lists is not practical, especially if a journal is listed on more than one Web page. You will need one or more of the following:

- An acquisitions database that includes individual titles (see Chapter 6)
- All of your e-journals in your library's online catalog and the ability to output them in a delimited format
- A spreadsheet or database with all your titles from a vendor such as Serials Solutions, TDNet, or Gold Rush or from your consortium headquarters
- A master spreadsheet maintained locally
- A master database maintained locally
- An e-journal "knowledge base" from a link resolver such as SFX and the ability to export and manipulate title information

You will probably have to customize any spreadsheet or database that you receive from a third party to include the elements (and perhaps additional titles) that will be meaningful for your own users, such as the subject codes that will help you create subject lists. If you don't get customized lists from an e-journal management vendor, you will need to download and standardize lists from each of the aggregators and publishers from whom you license multiple journals. Appendix B provides detailed information about this process.

Once you have a database or spreadsheet that represents your library's e-journal holdings, you can query it or sort it in ways that will allow you to create updated lists of journals as often as you can manage. You can either turn them into text files that can be pasted into template-based pages or automate the procedure with a database-driven Web-site process (see Thomas, 2002, for several libraries' approaches). Your database or spreadsheet can also be used to generate simple MARC records for your catalog.

Appendix E shows a simple way to turn a spreadsheet into an HTML list that can be inserted into a Web template. This is a simple way to begin providing access to your library's e-journals, but once you have thousands of them and you want to provide more information, such as holdings and publishers, and especially if you plan to have some of your journals on more than one subject page, you will save time and frustration by migrating your master spreadsheet to a master database.

If your library has a database-generated Web process in place, or if you have the expertise or local assistance to create dynamic Web pages from your database, you will be able to save a great deal of maintenance time and give your users up-to-date e-journal information at the same time. Libraries have used a variety of tools to create a dynamic Web presence for their electronic journals. You will need these three tools:

- A database application such as Microsoft Access or Microsoft SQL Server; Access is limited in the number of simultaneous users it can comfortably support
- An application server, either Active Server Pages (ASP) or ColdFusion
- A user interface

ALPHABETICAL LISTS

Alphabetical e-journal lists require the least amount of processing to be made available on a Web site. However, they still take some thought and require some advance decision making.

Presentation

Most libraries that have alphabetical lists display the alphabet, or a segmented alphabet, in various places on their e-journal pages (including subject pages) with links to the appropriate section on one list or to the appropriate page when there is more than one page. An alphabetical header is easy to insert on every page in your complex of e-journal pages and will serve as a navigational shortcut for users who may have ended up in the wrong place during a search for a particular electronic journal.

Detail

Often libraries will start with a simple list of linked titles, such as this:

- Academic Psychiatry
- Accounts of Chemical Reactions
- AJR: American Journalism Review
- American Journal of Geriatrics

But after becoming comfortable with the process of using a database report or a spreadsheet to update Web pages, perhaps in response to requests from users, they will want to provide more information, such as the dates of full-text coverage for each journal. Figure 7–2 shows two levels of detail for two types of e-journals. Full-text coverage dates are provided for stable journals

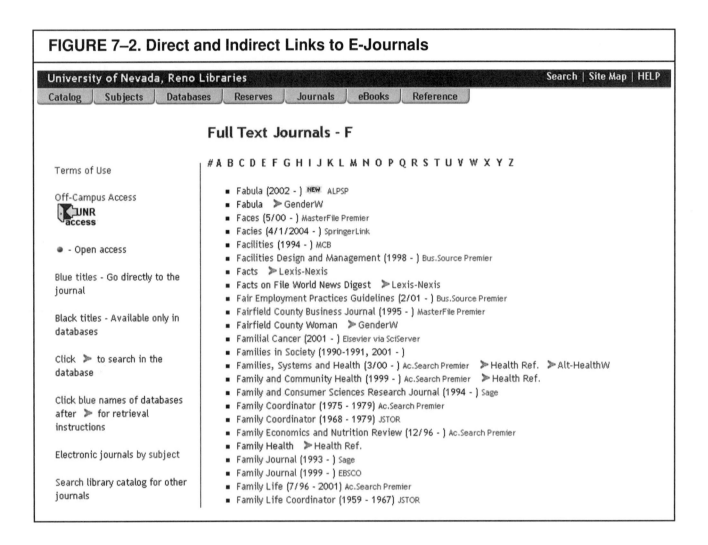

FIGURE 7–2. Direct and Indirect Links to E-Journals

acquired from publishers or individually and for those in aggregator databases that provide persistent links to tables of contents, but dates are not included for those in aggregator databases that don't provide direct links to journals.

If a large number of your e-journals come from more than one source, you may want to unobtrusively identify the source for each, for example

- <u>Black Issues in Higher Education</u> **Ethnic NewsWatch**
- <u>Black Issues in Higher Education</u> **Expanded Academic Index**
- <u>Black Issues in Higher Education</u> **Education Index**

Or, to keep your list shorter, you may want to present the links another way:

FIGURE 7–3. Serials Solutions Display

ABA banking journal (0194-5947)
from 01/01/1979 to present in <u>Business Source Premier</u>
from 01/01/1980 to present in <u>LexisNexis Academic</u>
from 01/01/1987 to present in <u>ABI/INFORM Complete</u>
from 2003 to present in <u>Wilson OmniFile: Full Text Mega Edition</u>

ABA journal (0747-0088)
from 01/01/1975 to present in <u>Academic Search Premier</u> and <u>Business Source Premier</u>
from 01/01/1982 to present in <u>LexisNexis Academic</u>
from 02/01/1988 to present in <u>ABI/INFORM Complete</u>

Abacus (Sydney) (0001-3072)
from 09/01/1965 to 1 year ago in <u>Business Source Premier</u>

FIGURE 7–4. Serials Solutions Spreadsheet

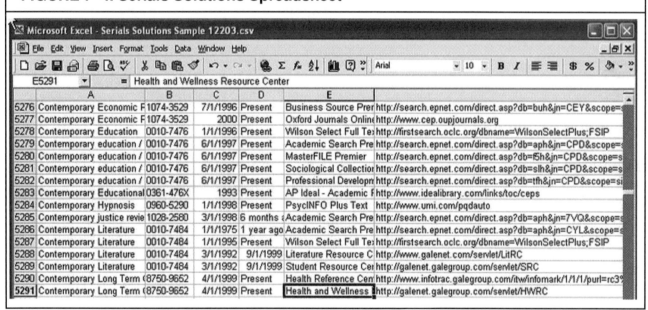

- **Black Issues in Higher Education**; in <u>Ethnic NewsWatch</u>
  - <u>Expanded Academic Index</u> • <u>Education Index</u>

If your library is a Serials Solutions customer, you might receive a Web-ready list that looks like Figure 7–3.

Serials Solutions will also send a "report" in spreadsheet form that can be adjusted for a customized Web display (Figure 7–4).

If your library is a TDNet customer, your e-journal Web pages

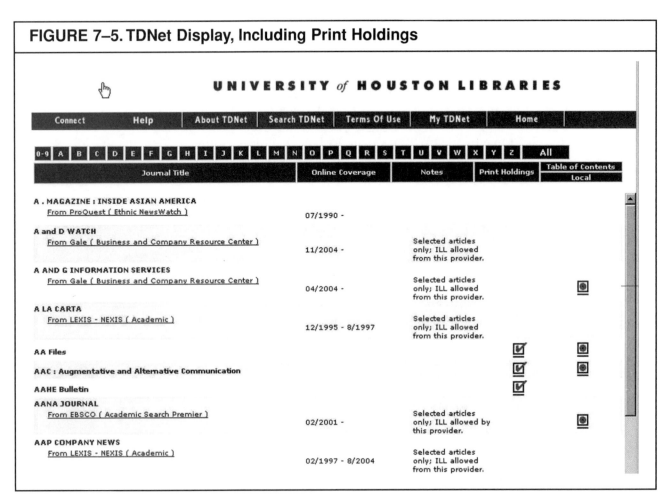

FIGURE 7–5. TDNet Display, Including Print Holdings

might look something like those of the University of Houston Libraries (Figure 7–5). Note that print holdings are also indicated. Both TDNet and Serials Solutions allow you to include your print holdings in Web-page products if you provide the information in a format that can be integrated with the e-journal information they provide.

Prioritization and Synchronization

If your alphabetical e-journal lists will contain journals included in more than one aggregator database, you will have some duplication of titles that are available from more than one source. Since some commercial database interfaces make it easy to get directly to issues and tables of contents of a given journal, and other interfaces make it difficult or impossible, you will probably want to prioritize the display order to favor the direct connection, or even exclude some sources if journals are available from better sources.

FIGURE 7–6. EBSCO A-to-Z Service Display

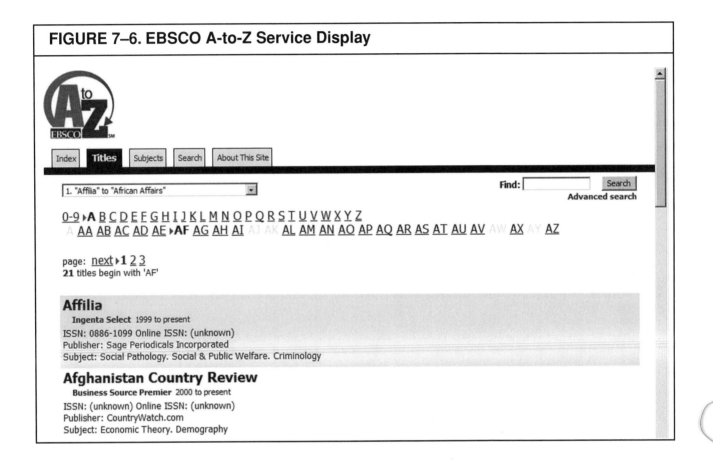

Some libraries' e-journal management systems have a built-in ranking system. In Journal Finder, developed by the University of North Carolina, Greensboro, "When there are multiple electronic access points the best links appear first and the worst appear last." This is a sophisticated system, with a great deal of support from a library systems department. If you have a simpler system for maintaining your e-journal pages, you may need to rely on a "sort" process in order to rank your duplicated titles.

If you compile your own spreadsheet or database from vendors' lists, you will need to "normalize" or synchronize titles in order to group them. Some vendors use initial articles, especially "The," and others don't. For help with this process, see Appendix B.

SUBJECT LISTS

E-journal lists organized by subject provide a wonderful service to those who want to browse what is available in a certain discipline, but they have their challenges. Targeted and specialized lists

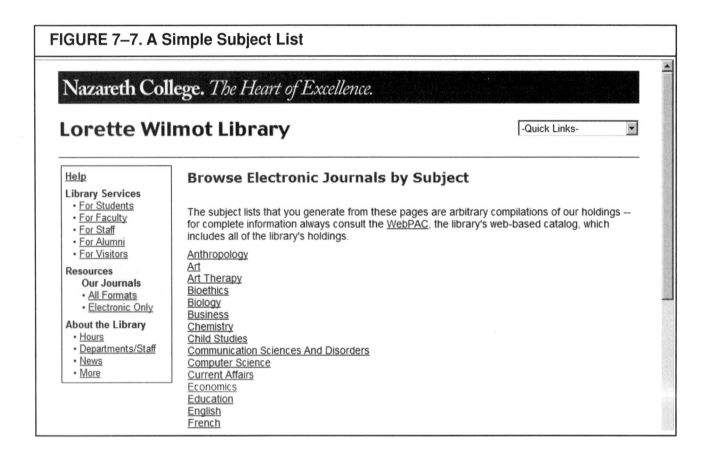

FIGURE 7–7. A Simple Subject List

Nazareth College. *The Heart of Excellence.*

Lorette Wilmot Library

-Quick Links-

Help
Library Services
- For Students
- For Faculty
- For Staff
- For Alumni
- For Visitors

Resources
  Our Journals
  - All Formats
  - Electronic Only
About the Library
- Hours
- Departments/Staff
- News
- More

Browse Electronic Journals by Subject

The subject lists that you generate from these pages are arbitrary compilations of our holdings --
for complete information always consult the WebPAC, the library's web-based catalog, which
includes all of the library's holdings.

Anthropology
Art
Art Therapy
Bioethics
Biology
Business
Chemistry
Child Studies
Communication Sciences And Disorders
Computer Science
Current Affairs
Economics
Education
English
French

are most useful, so you will be tempted to create lists for subdisciplines and specialized programs. The more subject lists you create, the more difficult they will be to maintain, though one of your goals should be to automate your updating process as much as possible.

Your Subject Menu

Your most important consideration should be to make it easy for your users to find their subjects. Having to scan through a list with dozens of subjects will irritate some users, whereas other users will be confused by categories of subjects if they don't understand your system. Different libraries use different approaches, and some offer a choice of ways to approach electronic journals by subject. Part of a simple subject list is displayed in Figure 7–7.

Because some users may be uncertain about which of your subject lists relates most closely to their subject, it is good to allow them to see all of your subjects at a glance. A column display (table construction) is a little more difficult to manage than a run-

FIGURE 7–8. E-Journal Subjects at a Glance

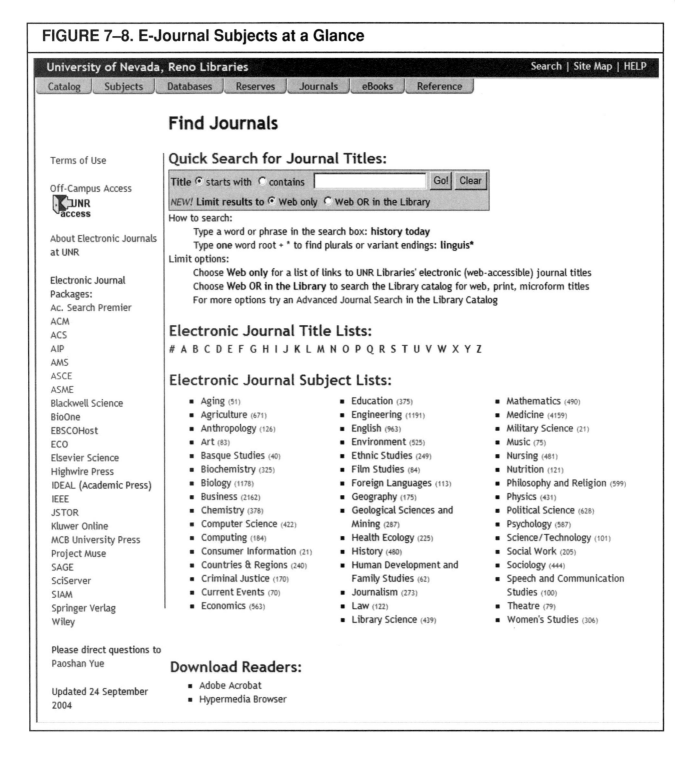

ning list, but provides a better service to your users. (See Figure 7–8.) Drop-down menus conserve space on a page, and for that reason they might be the best choice in some cases, but they require scrolling unless the selection is very small.

The optimal number of subject categories will vary among libraries. Too many subjects make it difficult for users to zero in on a particular subject. Too few subjects make the individual lists broad and long, and not as useful for browsing. A reasonable number would be somewhere between 45 and 55. No two libraries would have the same choice of subjects (except for those that use the same vendor that provides pre-selected subjects). The University of Nevada, Reno, may be the only U.S. library that would have a subject page for Basque Studies, and "Health Ecology" would be meaningless if it weren't the name of a department. See Appendix C for more information about the subject classification of e-journals.

Some libraries display subcategories of subjects. Whether this is a good choice will depend on the sophistication of your users. If they understand the concept of humanities or social sciences or fine arts or other general groupings, then you can filter the number of subjects they will have to browse in order to find their own subjects. But if you are designing for the average undergraduate, you may want to present your subjects in one group that corresponds to the departments in your university. Students know the departments that their classes are in, but studies show that they may not know the college that houses departments, even their major department, even though they may know where to go on campus to get a signature from their office or the dean of their college.

Public Libraries and Subject Menus

At this point, only a very few public libraries have provided subject categorization of electronic journals, but undoubtedly, public library users would appreciate such a service if it were made available to them. If your public library subscribes to one or more full-text databases, you can organize the e-journals within the database(s) by subject categories that are appropriate for your users for their browsing convenience. These are some suggested categories:

- Art & Music
- Business & Investments
- Children's
- Computing and Electronics
- Consumer Issues
- Government & Politics
- Health
- History & Geography
- Hobbies & Recreation
- Literature

FIGURE 7–9. Subcategorized E-Journal Subjects

Bryn Mawr | Haverford | Swarthmore

Tri-College Libraries:

Electronic Journals by Subject

Tripod Home
Databases
ILL Requests
LiveHelp
Other Libraries
Your Record

JSTOR | Project Muse | Science Direct | Kluwer | BioOne

Do an **Online Journal Title Search** to look for a specific electronic journal title in Tripod.

HUMANITIES	SCIENCES	SOCIAL SCIENCES
• Archaeology • Art/Art History • Cities • Classics • Dance • Film & Media • Libraries • Languages & Literature • Music • Philosophy • Religion • Theater	• Astronomy • Biology • Chemistry • Computer Science • Engineering • Geology • Mathematics • Medicine • Physics • Statistics	• Anthropology • Business • Economics • Education • History • Law • Linguistics • Political Science • Psychology • Social Work • Sociology

INTERDISCIPLINARY STUDIES

• Africana • Black • Asia • Cultural	• Environmental • Gender • Hebrew/Judaica • Latin America	• Medieval • Peace • Public Policy • Urban Policy

Please note: Some ejournals are available at all three colleges while others are restricted to specific colleges.

- Education
- Entertainment
- News, Current Events, People
- Science & Technology

SEARCH BOXES

As your library's lists of electronic journals get longer, users will lose patience with scrolling to find a journal title. Or they may not remember the exact title of a journal even though they remember some of the significant words. Occasionally, someone will want to retrieve a list of all the journals that have a certain word in the title, such as Africa or nanotechnology, or they may

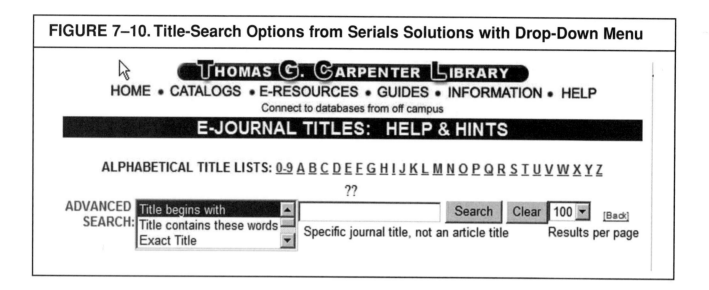

FIGURE 7–10. Title-Search Options from Serials Solutions with Drop-Down Menu

tire of jumping around on your multiple alphabetical lists. There-fore, it is a good idea to give them the opportunity to search your title list. If you use a database to generate your lists, you can sim-ply make your database Web accessible. Figure 7–10 shows the search screen provided to Serials Solutions (SS) customers. Users would search the master database on the SS server, limited to the journals of the subscribing library.

A search box takes up little space, so you can add one to any of your e-journal pages.

Citation Linker

Libraries using SFX as a link resolver can take advantage of the Citation Linker feature, posting a form (Figure 7–11) that allows users to enter information from a complete or incomplete cita-tion to retrieve the full citation from the SFX Knowledge Base with links to the article itself if the library subscribes to the e-journal.

RELATED INFORMATION

Web pages containing lists of your e-journals, whether displayed alphabetically or by subject, can convey a great deal of informa-tion to your users in addition to information about and links to the journals themselves. The subject gateways shown in Figures 7–7 and 7–8 provide links on the left side of the page to affiliated information. Electronic journal Web pages can provide links to many types of related information:

FIGURE 7–11. Citation Linker

- Information about off-site authentication
- The Adobe site for downloading the latest version of Acrobat Reader
- Subject-specific, searchable, full-text databases of electronic journals
- Information about link-resolver system (such as SFX)
- A search box for print journals in your catalog
- A form to report problems accessing an e-journal
- General license terms for using e-journals
- A journal abbreviation list
- Interlibrary-loan or document-delivery forms
- A chat icon to connect users with a librarian
- Any other information that would help your users

Some librarians have found that some of their users are interested in behind-the-scenes issues regarding the library's e-journals. Provide background information in such a way that it is avail-

---

FIGURE 7–12. Arguments for and against the Catalog as a Gateway to E-Journals

Library-Centric Arguments for the Catalog as Gateway to Electronic Journals	User-Centric Arguments *against* the Catalog as Gateway to Electronic Journals
"Libraries need to continue benefiting from the work they have previously invested in their OPACs." (McCracken, 2003, p. 102). "The catalog, or index of the library's collection, is an integrated directory to the collected information, regardless of format. This 'gathering function' is fundamental in providing ideal access to information through the organization of the catalog." (Bevis and Graham, 2003, p. 115). "Including electronic resource records in the OPAC helps to bring users back to the collections for which the library has already spent revenues by leading them to electronic and traditional (print, media, etc.) resources simultaneously" (James Veatch, quoted in Hinton, 2002, p. 54). "There is a sense (realistic or not) that libraries may just fade away in time as more of the world's information becomes digitized. Expanding the traditional role of the catalog and finding new ways to adapt it may go a long way in revitalizing the role of the library" (Hinton, 2002, p. 65).	"The integrated library system should be a complete and accurate recording of a local library's holdings. It should not be presented to users as the primary system for locating information. It fails badly at that important job." (Tennant, 2003, p. 28). "Links on home pages can easily be enhanced with such features as commentary, annotations, or directions for use, as well as special fonts and formatting . . . . However, creating user-friendly bibliographic records that include these useful features is difficult, if not impossible, when using the MARC bibliographic format" (Briscoe, Selden, and Nyberg, 2003, pp. 157–158). "Users want to get directly to quality full-text resources as easily as possible. Your Web design should not lead them to believe that the library catalog is the place to start their search. If they conduct a subject or keyword search in most catalogs they will retrieve a high proportion of records for print materials. If they are able (if the system allows it, and if they figure out the procedure) to limit their catalog search to online resources, they will still not find articles in journals" (Curtis and Greene, 2002, p. 53).

able to those who are interested without adding to the "noise" on a page that needs to be as simple as possible for other users.

WEB LINKS TO THE LIBRARY CATALOG

Through instruction and the organization of their Web sites, some libraries emphasize the catalog as a gateway or portal to all of their resources, including electronic journals. If electronic journals are included in your library catalog, it may seem logical to direct your users to the catalog rather than to your Web lists. Each source has its strengths and weaknesses, and if the catalog has records for journals that are not represented on your Web lists, you should encourage the use of both. But the catalog will be unfamiliar and confusing territory to many of your users, so when you direct them there it should be for the right reasons. Unfortunately, librarians sometimes promote the use of the catalog as a gateway to their online resources for reasons that do not make sense to users or for users. See Figure 7–12 for arguments for and against using the catalog this way.

CATALOG ACCESS

Even though some users (perhaps the majority) will access your library's electronic journals through other means, and even though you might choose to emphasize (1) your full-text databases for searching for articles by subject and (2) your Web lists for browsing, e-journals should be represented in your online catalog. Studies of usage statistics in several libraries have shown that the use of their electronic journals increased dramatically after they were represented in the catalog. At California State University (CSU) Northridge, the usage of Academic Search Elite (ASE) more than doubled shortly after records for individual ASE journals were added to the OPAC (Wakimoto, 2003), and CSU Sacramento had the same experience (Bevis and Graham, 2003). Jill Emery reported at the North American Serials Interest Group (NASIG) meeting in 2003 that a University of Houston study showed that the use of electronic journals tripled after their titles went into the catalog. A number of reasons will account for the increased use of cataloged e-journals:

- Inexperienced library users can end up in any database, including your catalog.
- Experienced library users who are accustomed to using the catalog and who understand about library-licensed e-resources may automatically begin their search in the catalog, and they will appreciate being able to find all resources in one place; they might not know or think to look elsewhere.
- Detailed information about all of your journals will be in one place; those looking for journals will be sure not to miss your electronic journals (this is especially important if you are canceling print journals).
- The catalog increases a user's chances of finding a particular e-journal; it can more easily provide cross-refer-

ences and access points—title variations, title translations, publishers, corporate body (association or society), ISSN.
- Some bibliographic databases have a "check library's holdings" feature that links to libraries' online catalogs, giving users the ability to get to the full text of articles through the catalog record.

BASIC CONSIDERATIONS IN CATALOGING E-JOURNALS

Cataloging electronic journals is new territory for everyone, so whoever has the responsibility will be faced with challenges in redesigning the work flow and establishing new policies and procedures.

Shifting Cataloging Resources and Priorities

Creating access to electronic journals through your library catalog is time consuming and labor intensive, and requires a long-term investment of staff resources. Libraries that do not receive new staff positions to help them meet the challenge will be required to shift resources and priorities quickly (see Chapter 3). Your serials cataloger(s) cannot manage this task alone. "One day you have a backlog of thirty or forty titles, and the next day you have three thousand," observes Wayne Jones (2003, p. 23). In some libraries, e-journal cataloging may be assigned to staff who have never cataloged serials. Even serials catalogers will have some new issues to contend with in cataloging e-serials. It may help to step back a bit and take a global view of your primary objectives in cataloging electronic journals.

Policies and Procedures

As with any aspect of managing electronic journals, a written policy will help minimize confusion and maximize consistency, especially in a cataloging department with staff turnover. Written procedures will help with training and with day-to-day questions.

For experienced catalogers, familiarity with other formats will not always apply. Indeed, established cataloging rules and standards have proved to be inadequate for properly describing and providing access to e-journals, resulting in a recent revision of *AACR2* and new record types from CONSER. Even in following the updated procedures, rules and guidelines, however, catalogers of e-journals will sometimes find themselves having to make some difficult decisions and judgment calls on their own.

Some libraries apply limits to the electronic journals that will be represented in the catalog. The most common restriction is to catalog only those journals that the library pays for. If your li-

---

FIGURE 7–13. Examples of Academic Library E-Journal Cataloging Policies and Procedures

University of North Carolina at Chapel Hill Libraries
Catalog Department—Cataloging Electronic Journals, Copy and Original
www.lib.unc.edu/cat/localdocs/ejproc.html

Virginia Tech University Library (Virginia Polytechnic Institute and State University, Blacksburg)
Electronic Serials Accessed via Internet: Cataloging Procedure
http://techserv.lib.vt.edu/Cataloging/ElectronicResources/Ejournal8.html

Rutgers University Library, New Bruswick, NJ
Cataloging Electronic Journals
www.libraries.rutgers.edu/rul/staff/cataloging/policies/e-ejour.shtml

University of Arizona Library, Tucson
Procedures for Cataloging Electronic Journals Titles that we don't own in paper
www.library.arizona.edu/library/teams/tst/ejourn2.htm

Note: Some of these policies may no longer be current for these libraries.

---

brary has such a policy, you may want to reconsider it, given the surge in publication of high-quality, open-access journals. In some cases, though, if cataloging is tied to the order process, cataloging free electronic journals may require an adjustment to the work flow.

In making decisions about local procedures or interpreting cataloging rules for electronic journals it is essential to keep three major considerations in mind:

1. Display: What will users see? What makes sense to us may not make sense to them, and sometimes default labels in an OPAC are not helpful; seek the input of public services librarians or, even better, users themselves.
2. Search and retrieval: How are users most likely to search, and what will intermediate screens look like?
3. Interoperability: If a database vendor's linking system takes users to your catalog, will they find electronic journals whether the linking is based on the print ISSN, the e-ISSN, or the title? Will you be able to output information from your e-journal records for other kinds of access?

Another less crucial consideration is whether your catalog records can support administrative uses—will your catalog records be useful in running reports for administrative purposes? Relaxed standards and new technology allow libraries a certain amount of new freedom to customize catalog records, but if you are going to stray very far from traditional pathways, you will want to put a great deal of thought into the results of your efforts. You will save backtracking time in the future if you have carefully anticipated the needs of your users and your staff.

Training and Continuing Education

Many libraries experience the need for some outside help in preparing staff for new responsibilities in cataloging electronic journals. That help can come from a variety of sources:

- The Serials Cataloging Cooperative Training Program (SCCTP) at the Library of Congress provides support and instructors for local workshops, including "Electronic Serials Cataloging," which are sponsored by other groups, such as library associations and bibliographic utilities. A trainee manual can be purchased at the SCCTP site, which also lists workshops in the U.S. (www.loc.gov/acq/conser/scctp/home.html).
- Discussion lists such as AUTOCAT and ERIL (see the "Staff Training" section in Chapter 3) provide a forum for sharing information about cataloging e-journals.
- OCLC and RLIN provide workshops and training materials for member libraries.
- The North American Serials Interest Group (NASIG) provides continuing education resources for its members (www.nasig.org).
- Preconferences and conference workshops often provide basic resources and a place to network and ask questions. The NASIG annual conference focuses heavily on practical aspects of managing electronic journals.
- CONSER, the Cooperative Online Serials cataloging program based at the Library of Congress, maintains standards, guides, and training materials (www.loc.gov/acq/conser/homepage.html).
- Professional journals with frequent articles about cataloging electronic journals, for example:
  o *Cataloging and Classification Quarterly* (Haworth Press)
  o *Library Collections, Acquisitions and Technical Services* (Elsevier)

FIGURE 7–14. Single Record Display

Title	Annual Review of Biochemistry
Issues held	Full-text on Web
Publ info	Palo Alto, Calif

Click the following to view:
(1996 – present) via Annual Reviews (UNR users only)
(1997 –) [excluding most recent 12 months] via Academic Search Premier (UNR users only)
[selected articles only] via Health Reference Center search engine (UNR users only)

Location	Medical Lib Jrnl Stacks
Library Has	**Paper:** v.1(1932)-v.72(2003)

LOCATION	CALL #	STATUS
World Wide Web		ONLINE
Medical Lib Jrnl Stacks	v.4 1935	NOT CHK'D OUT
Medical Lib Jrnl Stacks	v.5 1936	NOT CHK'D OUT
Medical Lib Jrnl Stacks	v.6 1937	NOT CHK'D OUT
Medical Lib Jrnl Stacks	v.7 1938	NOT CHK'D OUT
Medical Lib Jrnl Stacks	v.8 1939	NOT CHK'D OUT

o *OCLC Systems and Services* (MCB)
o *Serials* (United Kingdom Serials Group)
o *Serials Librarian* (Haworth Press)
o *Serials Review* (Elsevier)

SINGLE RECORD OR SEPARATE RECORDS?

A big debate topic in libraries and one of the most difficult decisions a library will have to make in cataloging e-journals is whether to create separate records for electronic journals or whether to use a single record for all formats of a journal, adding to the record already in the catalog for the print version. To complicate matters, an e-journal can be available to your users from several sources, often aggregator databases.

Library approaches can fall along a continuum of possibilities, at one end being a rigid adherence to the principle of using one record for every version of a work, and at the other end, the use of a separate record for each unique instance of the journal. In between are libraries that might use combinations:

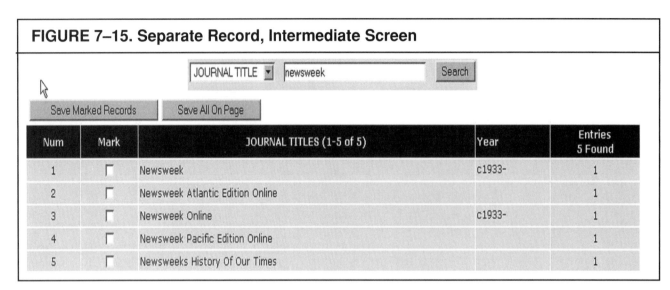

FIGURE 7–15. Separate Record, Intermediate Screen

- The single record approach for e-journals from stable sources, attaching URLs to print records for those, while having separate records for those from aggregator databases (because the library obtains separate MARC records from a vendor or vendors, or because they want to be able to update an aggregator's records en masse by replacing all of them whenever an update list is available);
- One record for the print and microform versions and another "aggregator neutral" record for an e-journal, with links in that record to all e-sources, using MARC tags that allow global updates to records;
- One approach for the library's own records but another approach for consortial records in the library's catalog; or
- Mixed records because of a change of approaches based on local considerations or changes in standards

Keeping up-to-date:

CONSER *(Cooperative Online Serials)*

www.loc.gov/acq/conser/

MARBI *(Machine-Readable Bibliographic Information Committee)*

www.ala.org/ala/alcts/ divisiongroups/marbi/ marbi.htm

The separate-record approach was the standard for many years until CONSER, the Cooperative Online Serials organization based at the Library of Congress, began allowing the single-record approach in 1996. The CONSER database contains separate records for e-journals from most sources for libraries that want to use the separate-record approach.

The single-record approach can be either more or less time consuming and labor intensive than the separate record approach, depending on the practices in your library. If you acquire MARC records from a vendor, or if you create your own database or spreadsheet of records downloaded from vendor sites and then converted to simple MARC records, you should be able to get separate records in and out of your catalog easily. But if you cata-

---

FIGURE 7–16. Single-Record Approach versus Separate-Record Approach

Single-Record Approach	*Separate-Record Approach*

Advantages
• On a one-by-one basis, faster to catalog by adding some fields than to create a new record
• Keeps holdings together, less chance of missing one of the formats
• Ease of maintenance—revisions such as title changes need only be updated in one record
• Consistent with GPO records
• Reduces the number of records that users have to deal with
• Increases users' chances of finding issues that are available to them in print but not online
 	
Disadvantages
• Unwieldy, bulky records can be difficult to scan
• Not always easy for catalogers to determine equivalence of print and electronic versions
• Confusing if the print version ceases
• Difficult in a consortial environment
• Eliminating duplicates can be problematic
	Advantages
	• Consistency in the format of records for e-journals; easier to read
	• Easier to add (or delete) multiple records in batch mode
	• Ability to limit search to online-only serials
	• When a license or library policy prohibits lending through ILL, the library may decide not to include the OCLC symbol in the e-record.
	• Option to use minimal records for ease of cataloging and simplicity for users
	
	Disadvantages
	• Multiple sources can be confusing to users.
	• Will not always list the online and print titles next to each other on browse screens in the catalog, even when monographs are excluded, as happens with the journal *Nature* in this example:
	    Nature
	    Nature Biotechnology
	    Nature Biotechnology Online
	    Nature Conservancy
	    Nature Online
	• More records in the catalog might slow some processes
	• Brief records can be misleading to users (lack of links to previous titles, etc.)

log your e-journals individually, it will be much easier to add information to a few fields in the print record than to create new records. (See Figure 7–16 for a summary of single records versus separate records.)

For users, it is generally considered to be most helpful if information about all formats appears in the same record. But that will depend on your users and the searching and display functionalities of your OPAC. Neither method will serve all types of your users equally well.

Single-Record Approach

Using the single-record approach, you will generally add information to a record that is already in the catalog for a print journal. CONSER makes a clear recommendation for when it is appropriate to use the single-record approach (which they refer to as the "non-cataloging approach"), based on the principles:

From the CONSER Cataloging Manual, 2002 Edition, pp. 14–15
31.2.3. Access to online versions

If the bibliographic record for the original version (print, CD-ROM, etc.) provides sufficient access for the online version, no matter what the differences are between the two, the single-record approach is a good alternative. If the desired access points for the online and the original version differ, separate records may be more useful. Separate records are always a permissible option.

- The single-record approach is considered most valid when the online version contains sufficient full-text to be a satisfactory substitute and has no significant additional content. That is, the single-record approach works best when the original and online versions can be considered equivalent manifestations.
- The single-record approach is also commonly applied when the online version lacks full-text or has only selected full-text from the original, and is therefore not considered to be an adequate substitute. The online site may not be considered worth cataloging separately in many such cases, so its existence and electronic location are noted on the record for the original, with appropriate indication of its relationship to the original version.

Available at www.loc.gov/acq/conser/Module31.pdf

With proper training and backup, a lower-level staff position could be responsible for this process, which has several steps:

1. Identifying the correct record.
2. Comparing the content of the online journal with the print journal for equivalency.
   - PDF files or other scanned images are generally identical to the print counterpart; hypertext links, home pages, advertisements (or lack of them), licensing information, etc., would not be considered in the determination of equivalency.
   - Omission or inclusion of announcements, job ads, reader comments, corrections, incidental illustrations, or other ephemeral data will not affect the equivalency between print and electronic versions.

- Electronic journals that are missing some of the articles in the print version would be considered a "related site" instead of an equivalent serial, but could be part of the single record.
- If the online version has significant additional content it would be a "related electronic serial."
3. Adding the e-journal's URL or URLs to the 856 field of the record.
4. Putting a note in the 530 field indicating the presence of the online format.
5. Adding holdings notes.

Figure 7–17 shows an example of a single local MARC record for multiple versions of a journal (public display shown in Figure 7–14).

Separate Records /Aggregator-Neutral Records

In the not-too-distant past, the separate-record approach was the accepted standard. Now, CONSER recommends it primarily "when the online version has significant additional content not present in the original," but acknowledges that "different libraries may choose separate-record or single-record approaches in the same cases, according to needs" (CONSER 2002, 31.2.5). The choice is often made on the basis of work flow considerations.

A catalog record for an electronic journal can be either brief or complete. Figure 7–18 shows an example of a simple separate catalog record for an e-journal, along with the public display (the intermediate screen for this journal is shown in Figure 7–15).

The aggregator-neutral record was implemented by CONSER in 2003 to consolidate information about e-journals from multiple sources by providing the basic stable bibliographic information for journals that are included in publisher packages and third-party aggregator databases, without information about the means of access. This format is not intended for use in catalogs that adhere to the single-record approach; but for those catalogs that include separate records for electronic journals, the aggregator-neutral record provides a way to reduce local maintenance. CONSER libraries create these records for bibliographic utilities such as OCLC and RLIN. For copy cataloging using these records, libraries need only add information about their own sources.

OCLC has adopted the use of the aggregator-neutral record and is collapsing the separate records that were in use before. Use the CONSER aggregator-neutral records for copy cataloging if you have a choice. See Appendix D for information about adapt-

---

FIGURE 7–17. Single Record

```
B1041203/                Last updated: 05-28-04 Created: 06-14-89 Revision: 66
01 LANG: eng        03 LOCATION: multi 05 BIB LVL: s      07 SUPPRESS: 4
02 SKIP: 0          04 CAT DA:06-12-89 06 MAT TYPE: s     08 COUNTRY: miu

09 001        BRUG0003928
10 008        751230c19759999miubr1p       0uuua0eng  cas
11 010        75647252
12 022   0    0099-1333
13 042        lc|ansdp
14 049        |onep
15 050   0    Z671|b.J58
16 090        Z671|b.J58
17 093        A
18 093        b
19 222   0 4  The Journal of academic librarianship
20 245   0 0  Journal of academic librarianship
21 260   0 0  [Ann Arbor, MI, etc.,|bMountainside Pub.]
22 300        v.|bill.|c28 cm
23 362   0    v. 1-  Mar. 1975-
24 530        Also available on the World Wide Web
25 599   1    |tJournal of academic librarianship (Online)
26 599   1    |tJournal of academic librarianship
27 650     0  Library science|xPeriodicals
28 650     0  Academic libraries|vPeriodicals
29 690        Electronic journals|xLibrary/information science
30 740   0    Journal of academic librarianship (Online)
31 770   0    |tLibrary issues|x0734-3035
32 856   4 1  |uhttp://search.epnet.com/direct.asp?db=aph&jid=%22ALN%22&
              scope=site|z(3/77 - present) via Academic Search Premier (UNR users
              only)
33 856   4 1  |uhttp://sciserver.lanl.gov/cgi-bin/sciserv.pl?collection=journals&
              issn=00991333|z(1995 - present) Elsevier via SciServer (UNR users
              only)
34 949        |bFull-text on Web
35 949        |bUNR Main =|cta|dZ671 .J58 =|gv.1(1975)-v.28(2002)|zHoldings
              verified 2/04
36 973        AcadSearch|f2925321
37 973        Elsevier|bAISTI|cSciServer|f3305752|iPrint
38 INNOVACQ #    .b1065683
39 LOCATIONS     m,net
```

ing or creating your own aggregator-neutral records. Figure 7–20 is an example of a fully-cataloged aggregator-neutral record in a local catalog.

FIGURE 7–18. Aggregator-Neutral Record (Minimal Cataloging)

```
B21767713          Last updated: 09-10-03 Created: 07-30-03 Revision: 3
01 LANG: eng       03 LOCATION: net   05 BIB LVL: s      07 SUPPRESS: 4
02 SKIP:  0        04 CAT DA:07-30-03 06 MAT TYPE: s     08 COUNTRY:
09 001     SEREJ
10 022     0163-7053
11 049     NNYO|opwy|oshx
12 245  0 0 Newsweek (Atlantic Edition) (Online)|h[electronic resource]
13 599  1   |tNewsweek (Atlantic Edition) (Online)
14 690      Electronic journals|xCurrent events
15 856  4 0 |uhttp://search.epnet.com/direct.asp?db=f5h&jid=%222SU%22&
            scope=site|z(1998 - present) via MasterFile Premier (UNR users only)
16 949      |bFull-text on Web
17 973      MasterFile|2925321001
```

Title	Newsweek (Atlantic Edition) (Online) [electronic resource]
Issues held	Full-text on Web

Click on the following to view:
(1998 - present) via MasterFile Premier (UNR users only)

LOCATION	CALL #	STATUS
World Wide Web		ONLINE

Subject	Electronic journals -- Current events

FIGURE 7–19. Advantages and Disadvantages of Aggregator-Neutral Records

Advantages

- Less confusing for some users than a single record with information about all formats.
- Less confusing for users than multiple records for duplicate online content.
- On a record-by-record basis, maintenance is less burdensome than with separate records; CONSER members are no longer required to maintain multiple bib records for one e-serial.
- Libraries using the single-record approach can use it as their single record for electronic-only journals.
- Vendors and consortium managers can customize these records for customers and participants.

Disadvantages

- Resists automation. Merging records already in the catalog and maintaining the holdings in aggregator-neutral records requires high-level manual work.
- Print and online versions of individual titles still may not display together on intermediate screens.

FIGURE 7–20. Fully Cataloged Aggregator-Neutral Record

```
B16835566              Last updated: 12-16-03 Created: 08-06-98 Revision: 27
01 LANG: eng        03 LOCATION: multi 05 BIB LVL: s     07 SUPPRESS: 4
02 SKIP: 0          04 CAT DA:08-09-99 06 MAT TYPE: s    08 COUNTRY: nyu
09 001      ocm41970220
10 003      OCoLC
11 005      19990809094753.0
12 006      m        d
13 007      crumnu
14 008      990728c19uu9999nyuuu p      0      0eng dnasIa
15 022      1387-7003
16 040      OH1|cOH1
17 049      NNYO|oart
18 090      QD146|b.I52
19 093      4
20 093      q
21 130   0  Inorganic chemistry communications (Online)
22 245   0 0 Inorganic chemistry communications|h[electronic resource]
23 260      New York, NY :|bElsevier Science Pub. Co.,
24 362   1  Coverage as of July 26, 1999: Vol. 1, issue 2 (Feb. 1998)-
25 500      Description based on: Vol. 1, issue 2 (Feb. 1998); title from
            general information screen (viewed July 26, 1999)
26 506      Subscription and registration required for access
27 516      Abstracts, tables of contents, and citation information are
            HTML encoded; articles are available in portable document format (PDF)
            and as Postscript Level 2 files
28 530      Online version of print publication
29 538      System requirements: Internet connectivity, World Wide Web
            browser, and Adobe Acrobat reader
30 538      Mode of access: World Wide Web
31 599   1  |tInorganic chemistry communications (Online)
32 650     0 Chemistry, Inorganic|vPeriodicals
33 650     0 Organometallic chemistry|vPeriodicals
34 650     2 Chemistry, Inorganic|vperiodicals
35 690      Electronic journals|xChemistry
36 780   1 1 |tInorganica chimica acta (Online)
37 780   1 1 |tPolyhedron (Online)
38 780   1 1 |tJournal of organometallic chemistry (Online)
39 856   4 0 |uhttp://sciserver.lanl.gov/cgi bin/sciserv.pl?collection
            =journals&issn=13877003|z(1998 - present) Elsevier via SciServer (UNR
            users only)
40 949      |bFull-text on Web
41 973      Elsevier|bAISTI|cSciServer|f3305752|iPrint
42 LOCATIONS   net,phy
```

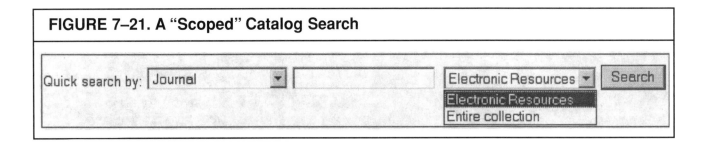

FIGURE 7–21. A "Scoped" Catalog Search

Scoped Searching

Some online catalogs have a feature that allows users to limit their search by the location of materials (the Web would be a location that would allow them to search only electronic resources) or type of materials (journals, videos, books) or both (see Figure 7–21). The so-called "scoped-search" function may be an add-on feature with add-on costs, or something that needs to be activated by your ILS vendor. Scoping uses designated MARC fields, so you will need to understand the way your system works before making the final decision about using single records or separate records. In order to enable your users to limit their catalog search to electronic journals, you may need to add special codes during cataloging. Check with your local systems expert or your vendor for the details of your system.

RULES AND STANDARDS

Rules and standards have always dictated the approaches for cataloging a library's materials. Although serials cataloging rules have changed in some major ways recently, they are still in place, accomplishing their enduring purpose, which is to ensure uniformity for interchangeability.

Dealing with Limitations of MARC

The standards for metadata exchange have changed dramatically with the advent of the Internet—and flat MARC records are interchangeable only in a MARC-centered silo of the library-to-library environment. To prevent library catalogs from being seriously marginalized in the much larger electronic information world, radical measures that will alter cataloging forever are being implemented on an experimental basis. The conversion of library catalogs from MARC-based to XML-based schema will allow for many different kinds of input formats and for many kinds of representations inside and outside of the catalog. If MARC remains alive as an element in the new catalog, it will be

Keeping up-to-date:

OCLC Research Activities

http://www.oclc.org/research/projects/

Standards at the Library of Congress

www.loc.gov/standards/

a transformed MARC. Since MARC represents "MAchine Readable Cataloging," MARC records are easily converted to other formats that are more compatible with other metadata formats. There are two developing standards you will want to watch:

- Metadata Object Description Schema (MODS): an XML standard for bibliographic elements; intended to be able to carry selected data from existing MARC 21 records as well as for use in creating new records
- Metadata Encoding and Transmission Standard (METS): an XML standard for encoding descriptive, administrative, and structural metadata regarding objects within a digital library.

Tools for large- or small-scale conversion of MARC records are available at the Library of Congress as free downloads (www.loc.gov/marc/marctools.html).

Current Standards

The most recent revision of *AACR2* and the *Library of Congress Rule Interpretations* (*LCRI*) govern the creation and modification of MARC records. The CONSER cataloging manual is the bible for many serials catalogers—you can find it online at www.loc.gov/acq/conser/Module31.pdf. Keep in mind that the CONSER standards are high. Locally-created minimal records for e-journals may not meet the CONSER standards, but would be perfectly acceptable under OCLC guidelines for Level K.

Libraries that contribute records to WorldCat are required to follow the OCLC-MARC Coding Guidelines for Electronic Resources (www.oclc.org/support/documentation/worldcat/cataloging/electronicresources/) for fixed-field elements, particularly the Type of Record and Type of File codes.

Full Records/Minimal Records

Many catalogers believe that when it comes to OPAC records, "more is better" and full records are always better than brief records. In the case of physical materials, a complete description can help a user decide whether or not to come into the library and check out the item. But for electronic journals, a lengthy description may actually hinder access, for the following reasons, among others:

- Timeliness: It can take much longer to catalog each item by modifying an existing record than to add multiple new brief records in a batch mode.

- Subject access: Full cataloging requires the use of Library of Congress or Dewey subject headings, which are generally not appropriate for electronic journals. Minimal records can have local headings that will be more meaningful for users and that can be used to set up canned searches or to generate Web lists.
- Too much information: Having to scan through information that is not of interest to the vast majority of users makes it more difficult to find the information that is of interest, including the link to the full text (if the catalog records are full of hyperlinks). Compare the public record shown in Figure 7–18, with two links (to the journal itself and to a list of other e-journals that have been classified locally as "current-events" journals) with the record in Figure 7–14, which has 14 links that are circular or lead to item records for print journals, in addition to the three links to the online journal.

If you are uncomfortable about adding records without some of the customary descriptive information, keep in mind that the resource itself is a click away for the small minority of users who would benefit from more detail.

If you do use full records for electronic journals in copy cataloging, look for "core records." These records are kept up to date and have been authenticated by CONSER members according to CONSER guidelines.

"MACHINE-GENERATED" RECORDS

Some libraries have developed a semi-automated process to develop brief MARC records in a "batch" mode. This is done by running reports from their local e-journal master database or downloading lists from vendors, followed by several steps that will result in individual brief records that can be imported into their catalog. There are tools developed for this purpose.

Process Overview

Most of the initial batch work can be done with a cursory knowledge of Word and Excel. Specialized programs are freely available to complete the process. (See Appendix E for details.) The basic process has seven steps:

1. Compile, export, or download a list of electronic journals, with or without ISSNs, holdings, and provider information, but with URLs for each journal.

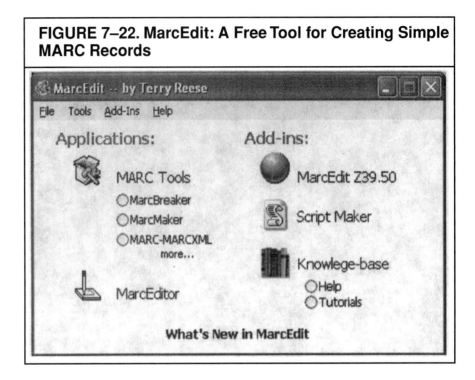

FIGURE 7–22. MarcEdit: A Free Tool for Creating Simple MARC Records

2. Use Word to clean up records.
3. Use Excel to organize the data elements (columns represent MARC fields).
4. Add MARC tags in inserted Excel columns or using Mail Merge in Word to insert them.
5. Save Excel or Word document as text with appropriate delimiters after each item, and re-open with Word.
6. Use MarcEdit to convert Word file to MARC records.
7. Import records into the catalog.

MarcMaker and Auxiliary Tools

MarcMaker and MarcBreaker are programs developed at the Library of Congress (LoC), and are available at the LoC site as free downloads, along with a user's manual, at www.loc.gov/marc/makrbrkr.html. MarcBreaker translates MARC records into text files that can be edited. MarcMaker translates an edited file into the arcane machine-readable format required by the architecture of our online catalogs.

Terry Reese at Oregon State University (Corvallis) has developed MarcEdit (Figure 7–22), a user-friendly utility that acts as an interface to and goes beyond MarcMaker. Download MarcEdit, which is free, at http://oregonstate.edu/~reeset/marcedit/html/.

PURCHASING MARC RECORDS

One easy way to add records to your catalog for e-journals is to acquire MARC records from a primary or secondary vendor. Several database vendors sell or freely provide files containing records for the full-text journals in their databases, and e-journal management companies such as Serials Solutions also provide aggregator-neutral records, with your local holdings information, as an add-on service. In considering this option, there are certain attributes you will want to look at:

- The quality of the records: Do they meet the standards you have established for your catalog?
- Currency: How often are updates issued? At any one time, how well do they correspond to the journals currently represented in the database?
- Maintenance: How easy is it to update your catalog to reflect changes in database content? Can you globally update records, or must you edit them or remove them one-by-one? Do new records overlay old records?
- Cost: Is this cost effective for your library and can you afford it?
- Compatibility: Are the records compatible with local standards and practices?
- Customization options: Will they meet your local needs?

Acquiring records from an outside source requires clear communication about the exact type of MARC record that is compatible with your catalog and what field your library uses for local holdings.

Things can get messy in the catalog of a library that has experimented with multiple ways of cataloging e-journals. For example, you may have tried the single-record approach, adding links in print journal records for e-journals in an aggregator database, and subsequently realized that your staff could not keep up with the maintenance tasks. If you then acquire MARC records from the vendor, it will be time-consuming to remove the original links. It may be necessary to leave them intact, at least for a period of time, while simultaneously providing access to those same e-journals through the new separate records. Remember that your users are accustomed to the results from Web search engines, so they can tolerate some duplication. Your most urgent task will be to identify the records that include links to journals that are no longer included in the database and remove *those* links so that your catalog is accurate. Use the ISSN to match records whenever possible, keeping in mind, however, that some journals in aggregator databases do not have ISSNs.

Vendors will be able to do some customizing for you, but you will need to take care of other modifications that will customize and optimize the records for your catalog. Terry Reese has developed a freely downloadable application to support the management of vendor-supplied MARC record sets, "to take multiple aggregator record sets and produce a single, de-duplicated data set containing custom MARC data defined by the individual library" (Reese, 2003). Although it is known as ERW (EBSCO Records Wizard), the tool works with record sets from several vendors. It can be downloaded from http://oregonstate.edu/~reeset/ebsco/html.

MAINTAINING CATALOG RECORDS

Adding e-journal records to your catalog is relatively easy. Maintaining e-journal records, though, especially for journals in aggregator databases, is much more challenging. The CONSER Task Group on Journals in Aggregator Databases identified six types of record maintenance (French, 2002):

- Added and dropped titles in the aggregator package
- Changes in the volume coverage
- Completeness of content for volumes covered
- URL maintenance
- Conventional title changes
- Cancellation or change of subscription necessitating removal of records from OPAC.

Global Updates for Aggregator Titles

Libraries use various approaches for keeping e-journal records up-to-date in their catalogs, depending on the ways in which they have cataloged the journals in the first place, and whether they work with a serials management vendor. Libraries using the single-record approach will have a more difficult time maintaining accuracy in the records that contain links to journals in aggregator databases. Separate records are more easily added, deleted, or overlaid in batch mode. See Bland, Carstens, and Stoffan (2002) for one approach that has been developed for use in a shared catalog with separate records.

Elements of single records can also be edited automatically with locally developed or locally adapted programs such as ERW (described above), which allow for batch edits and overlays of designated fields in MARC records. Your method will depend on

"In the initial planning, staff assumed that the number of record changes, deletes, and additions would not be so great over a two-month period as to make manual editing of the update file impractical. That assumption proved incorrect, however."

—Bland, Carstens, Stoffan
(2002)

the technical sophistication of your staff or the technical assistance that is available.

Updates for Publisher Packages

Electronic journal subscriptions directly from publishers are certainly more stable than the journals in aggregator databases, but they are by no means maintenance free. Journals cease publication and new journals are born after a license is finalized, publishers merge, and individual journals move from one publisher to another.

Depending on the arrangements between publishers and the terms of your licenses, earlier volumes of a journal may stay with the original publisher or move to the new publisher's site. The library's access to migrating journals may be uncertain, and keeping track of the changes and updating the library's access to these journals can be a challenge for catalogers. Sometimes several years of backfiles might be made available without the library's knowledge.

Most large publishers have established methods for notifying their subscribers of changes in their collections. Publishers' newsletters, both online and in print, keep subscribing institutions updated on title changes, new titles, transferred titles, and discontinued titles. Librarians can sign up for special alerts for changes in the collection as well. It takes considerable effort on behalf of the library to be kept informed about changes in publishers' holdings. Most publishers have developed a page called "Resources for Librarians" or "Services for Librarians," which will allow you to register for e-mail updates. Some examples of publishers sites for updating libraries are

- ScienceDirect: www.info.sciencedirect.com/sd_updates/
- Blackwell Publishing: www.blackwellpublishing.com/librarians/?site=1
- JSTOR: www.jstor.org/resources/index.html

PURLS

One of the irritating facts of life for those who maintain access to electronic journals is the frequency with which their URLs can change, sometimes without any notice. It is common for freely available e-journals in particular to move from one site to another. Even if a URL changes slightly because the publisher moves the files to a new server, all the libraries that provide access to that journal will have to update the links in their catalogs and on their Web pages. Once again the serials community has come up with a cooperative means of reducing work and maintaining quality control for access to e-journals through libraries.

OCLC has provided a PURL server for CONSER-member libraries to use as a way to stabilize URLs for freely available resources in WorldCat (http://bibpurl.oclc.org/). PURL stands for "persistent URL," meaning that any library that uses an OCLC/CONSER record containing a PURL instead of the publisher's URL will not have to change any links if the publisher's URL changes. The PURL server redirects the user to the actual URL, and if the actual URL changes, it will be changed only once—in the PURL server. CONSER libraries that use the PURL server have accepted the responsibility for assigning PURLS and keeping the actual URLs updated. An automated URL-validation system helps with updating.

Besides reliability, using a PURL provides other benefits. A PURL is generally much shorter in length than the journal's actual URL. A short URL is less likely to contain typos, and a long URL can cause display or access problems in some catalogs.

The OCLC PURL server is reserved for nonsubscription journals, which limits its value. However, some libraries maintain their own PURL servers. A broken URL needs to be repaired in only one place—the PURL table. Another advantage of a local PURL server is that each redirect can be logged, offering a local means of gathering simple usage statistics for your electronic journals. The major disadvantages of a local PURL server are that

- the redirection will add some time to the connectivity between the user and the full text, and
- if the PURL server goes down, you will lose access to all of your electronic journals.

ELECTRONIC RESERVES

Students have benefited lately from the automation of libraries' course reserves systems. Instead of having to come to the library to get homework solutions or read an article that a professor has put on reserve (that might be checked out to someone else), students can now access many of their course reserves through the Internet, even when the library is closed. If your library has not yet activated electronic course reserves, you will be able to take advantage of the experiences of many libraries that have gone before you and use some of the tools that others have developed.

Keeping up-to-date:

*Electronic Reserves
Clearinghouse*
www.mville.edu/
Administration/staff/
Jeff_Rosedale/

If you have a system in place, you can easily add articles from your electronic journals. Some e-reserves items, such as instructors' notes or practice exams, articles from print journals and chapters from books, will need to be scanned, and the files must be kept on a library server. But for an electronic journal to which the library subscribes, a link to an article on the provider's site (known in the e-reserves world as "deep linking") will be sufficient. For articles that don't have persistent links within a database, some vendors provide tools for creating them. Check with your vendors. If there isn't any way to link directly to an article in a database, you may be able to download or e-mail the article to yourself and provide access to it on your library's server. As a last resort, you can copy the text from the article in the database and paste it into a new document. Be sure to check each item that is on reserve to make sure students can retrieve it. One bad link for a key resource can seriously damage the library's reputation.

E-RESERVES AND COPYRIGHT

Ensure that you do not violate copyright law or terms of a license agreement:

- Be aware of any e-journal license agreements that prevent the use of content for electronic reserves.
- Limit access to articles from licensed resources only to users at your institution. Articles from journals your library does not subscribe to can usually be made available online if the use is restricted to students in a particular class, just as a photocopied article brought in by a professor could be placed on reserve in a folder.
- Terminate access through the reserves system at the end of the term, or after students have completed the course.

ABDICATING E-RESERVES

Some academic libraries have deliberately transferred the responsibility for electronic reserves to instructors. In other cases, instructors have taken it upon themselves to use their own Web pages to provide access to supplementary materials in electronic format rather than involving the library. Print resources can only be in one place, and the library has a way to manage their orderly circulation. But scanned files can be on any server, and links to files on servers (including articles on publishers' servers) can be on any Web page.

It is tempting to get out of the e-reserves business or not get into it in the first place. With so many new issues to deal with, libraries need to find things they don't need to be doing. But electronic reserves are best handled in the library for several reasons. The library can

- realize efficiencies in the purchase of equipment and software and training of staff through a centralized approach to digitization and link management;
- prevent inadvertent violations of license agreements and copyright law by using an authentication system that is already in place and extending regular reserves practices to e-reserves;
- maintain quality control, ensuring a more reliable and uniform experience for students using e-reserves;
- provide in one place, through its ILS, information about the availability of print reserves and access to electronic reserves for a given course; and
- create persistent URLs for articles in library-licensed e-journals (see below).

Electronic reserve modules are now available for all major integrated library systems. To circumvent or reduce e-reserve anarchy on your campus, your library must publicize, promise, and deliver

- fast turnaround time for processing e-reserves requests, regardless of the time of year (which will probably require temporary reallocation of staff resources at busy times);
- consistently readable files that load as quickly as possible with every kind of connection and browser.

INTEGRATING ARTICLES WITH COURSEWARE

Bringing electronic journals into the course reserves system at a university library is a natural step in the progression from print to electronic materials and services. But the library's licensed electronic resources may not be as easily incorporated into all Web-based course-management software, or courseware. That is because the library is often left out of discussions and decisions about a university's acquisition and implementation of courseware.

Libraries have also been left out of the design and development of the courseware that is on the market; however, recently this oversight has been recognized and remedied by some vendors. For example, the Blackboard Content System includes a Library Digital Asset Management component:

> Many academic institutional libraries contain a wealth of rich content and resources. However, most libraries do not have an effective way of making relevant, valuable digital content available to faculty for use in their courses. Using the Blackboard Content System, librarians can make subject-specific library content such as eReserves available to courses (www.blackboard.com/products/academic/cs/index.htm).

Web-based instruction represents such a radical departure from traditional instruction that academic decision makers will naturally be interested in tools that make the transition as easy as possible for instructors and the institution. Self-contained systems sometimes include information content as well as communication tools and an organizational structure for the instructor's content. For example, WebCT, another major courseware vendor, includes digital content called "e-Packs." Most of the components of WebCT e-Packs appear to be parts of textbooks or specially developed course materials rather than electronic journal articles. However, several of the "Content Development Partners" are publishers that do business with libraries, developing yet another academic market. Libraries, however, are not mentioned in the discussion of digital content. Nor is the library recommended as a source of help. This is the advice from the WebCT FAQ:

> **Is there someone on my campus who can help me with digital content?** It is likely that either your WebCT Administrator or helpdesk on campus can assist you. You can also consult <u>WebCT customer Care for Digital Content</u> on our Web site (www.webct.com/content/viewpage?name=content_faq#q14).

A university that buys content-laden courseware may be paying a premium for content the library has already licensed (or content that is similar to what the library has licensed) for the university community. It is important for someone from the library to work closely with campus courseware administrators and those who provide support to courseware users to let them know how the library can "help with digital content" that is already available. It is also important for library people to become familiar with the courseware in case they are contacted by faculty for assistance with content.

COURSEWARE AND E-RESERVES

Commercially licensed courseware and some locally developed courseware systems have an authentication component to protect the intellectual property of faculty and the privacy of students. Authentication for courseware usually involves the use of a unique password for each course, distributed to students taking the course. Some systems will allow students to use their own IDs to log into the courses they are taking. Whatever method is used, those who are able to access courseware modules through their enrollment in a course offered by your university will undoubtedly meet the definition of authorized users of licensed electronic resources. To require them to authenticate again in order to access electronic reserves is an unnecessary irritation.

You may want to work with faculty who use courseware and technical administrators to circumvent the usual procedures for accessing e-reserves provided by the library. Because faculty who use courseware have easy access to server space, it might be best to let them provide their own reserves within the courseware environment. In such cases, libraries sometimes digitize items and send the files or send links to articles in electronic journals for access through pages that are used by authenticated students.

PERSISTENT URLS FOR ARTICLES

Sometimes the only way to retrieve an article in an electronic journal is through a database, whether provided by a full-text aggregator or a publisher. Frequently in databases articles will not have assigned and stable URLs. The URL that appears in the address bar will include information about the search that retrieved it, and if you save and try to re-use that URL you will get an error message rather than the article. Whether the library is providing access to designated articles through its own e-reserves system or helping a faculty member incorporate articles into a courseware system, you will need to know how to establish a reusable URL for the article.

With most of these databases it is possible to create a "stable" or "durable" or "persistent" link to the article, after going through a few steps. Librarians might become adept at creating these links, but someone who is less familiar or experienced with the database could have some trouble figuring out the process, which of course is different for each database. Your faculty will appreciate a "how-to" page on creating persistent links (see www.library.unr.edu/

services/online.html#inst, for an example). In some databases there isn't a way to create a persistent URL, so your only option will be to download the article and save it on a library server that is accessible only through authentication with a locally-assigned URL.

CONTEXT-SENSITIVE LINKING

From the e-journal user's point of view, being able to move seamlessly from a record in a bibliographic database to the full text of an article at another site is one of the most valuable services a library can provide. Chapter 1 explains the many variations of links between electronic resources. Technical details are beyond the scope of this chapter, especially since these vary from product to product. Articles under "More Information" will provide more information. For this chapter, suffice it to say that the selection, configuration, and maintenance of a link resolver is a key element in "delivering electronic journals and maintaining access channels." Libraries that are not ready for that additional work load (which can be significant) should at least take advantage of opportunities to activate links through database vendors. See Grogg (2002) for an overview of linking issues.

SOURCES AND TARGETS

The basic concept for every system that links from one electronic resource to another is that a *source* (e.g., a record in a bibliographic database or list of references at the end of an article) will connect to a *target* (ideally the full text of an article, but it could be information about an article or book and how to find it or receive it). These connections between sources and targets are based on two major protocols and on various technology. The connection process may take place through remote servers or through a library server. Usually (but not always), a database of targets, sometimes called a knowledge base, is part of the process.

DOI AND OPENURLS

Two parallel approaches to providing links between resources are now interoperable, but it is important to understand the basic concepts and distinctions between the digital object identifier (DOI) approach and the OpenURL approach. Both approaches use the ISSN for the journal and standardized formats for article information.

Digital Object Identifier

The DOI concept was developed by the CrossRef organization (www.crossref.org), a group of e-journal publishers and database providers. The concept is simple: article providers will identify each article with a unique identifier that can be used by others to link directly to any of their articles. Some e-journal publishers activate DOI links in their articles' reference lists, and some database producers use the CrossRef DOI database to link from their records to journals at the publishers' site. However, if a library has licensed access to e-journal content from a source other than the publisher's site (such as an aggregated database), another step will be involved in getting the user to the right site (referred to in the literature as the "appropriate copy"). See O'Leary (2003) for more information about CrossRef.

OpenURL

The OpenURL protocol, developed at Los Alamos in the late 1990s, was quickly adopted as the standard for "context-sensitive" linking, and further developed by several commercial vendors (see the "Scholarly Access and Publication Chain" section in Chapter 1 for a list). OpenURL software allows libraries to produce "on the fly" links from sources to targets, including services and information as well as the full text of articles. For these links to be generated, or "resolved," citations must be in a standardized format ("OpenURL enabled") at the source site, and a database must be kept current by the library or the link-resolver vendor. The DOI can be part of the OpenURL, but to use it in a local system, your library might have to become a CrossRef member (see www.crossref.org/03libraries/index.html). When links can't be resolved by the software, users may get links to the issue level for the journal or to the journal level. Most link resolvers provide the opportunity to enable links to multiple sources for e-journals if you have access from more than one provider.

MAINTAINING LINKS

A library might contract with an organization to provide an "OpenURL link resolver," or may develop one locally. Without a link resolver, it is still possible to work with database providers to allow your users to link from database records to your licensed full-text targets at other sites. For links to be accurate, libraries

Keeping up-to-date:
DOI at CrossRef
www.crossref.org

Keeping up-to-date:
NISO OpenURL Standards
www.niso.org/committees/
committee_ax.html

must be vigilant in keeping their systems up to date.

Activating Links with Vendors

Most of the major database vendors offer a linking service that can be customized by libraries to show only links to the targets to which the library subscribes. Some database providers use DOI protocols and others use the OpenURL. Some will ask you to send a list of your full-text resources so that they can enable your links, whereas others will allow (or require) you to activate and deactivate your own links on an administrative site. In a few cases, a database vendor may offer only links to the library's catalog, so if your e-journals are cataloged, your users will be able to get to the journal, though not to the individual article. They will also see your print journals.

Maintaining links to your e-journals through each database vendor is a relatively simple duty, but like every other e-journal duty, it requires ongoing and frequent attention.

Selecting, Configuring, and Maintaining a Link Resolver

When choosing a link-resolver system, consider your resources. If you don't have an adequate staff to maintain a local server, you may want to select a vendor that will do it for you. However, the annual cost will be higher. If you plan to maintain your own link resolver, you will need to make more of an investment in training and technical support the first year. Either way, information about your licensed content must be kept current, and that will require staff time and effort.

See Collins and Ferguson (2002) for information about four major link-resolver systems. Products evolve, and new products come along. Most of the major ILS vendors have developed (or are developing) modules for resolving links. Your vendor might give existing customers a discount, and a module that is designed by your ILS vendor may require less configuration work, especially if you have other digital-resource modules.

SERIALS CATALOGING AND ACCESS ACRONYMS AND INITIALISMS

The serials cataloging world is full of insider codes:

AACR2R—*Anglo-American Cataloguing Rules*, 2nd Edition Revised: The 1998 revision of this cataloger's bible has significant changes that accommodate e-journals.

ALCTS—Association for Library Collections and Technical Services: a division of the American Library Association (ALA).

CC:DA—Committee on Cataloging—Description and Access: responsible for developing official ALA positions on additions to and revisions of AACR2.

CONSER—Cooperative ONline SERials cataloging program: a component of the PCC (see below); source of bibliographic records for serials, residing within the OCLC database.

DOI—Digital Object Identifier: a coded URL that uniquely identifies a single article within a database.

FRBR—Functional Requirements of Bibliographic Records: a 1998 recommendation of the International Federation of Library Associations and Institutions (IFLA) to restructure catalog databases to reflect the conceptual structure of information resources.

ISBD (ER)—International Standard Bibliographic Description (Electronic Resources): a means of international standardization of descriptive cataloging. Allows for different formats of a work to be described in one record.

LCRI—Library of Congress Rule Interpretations

MARBI—MAchine-Readable Bibliographic Information Committee: develops official ALA positions on standards for the MARC format.

MARC21—MAchine Readable Cataloging: the current version of the MARC data format, which became USMARC in the 1980s and then MARC 21 in the late 1990s.

METS—Metadata Encoding and Transmission Standard

NASIG—North American Serials Interest Group

ONIX—Online INformation Exchange: international standard for representing book and serials industry product information for machine transmission.

PCC—Program for Cooperative Cataloging: an international cooperative program coordinated jointly by the U.S. Library of Congress and international participants.

SCCTP—Serials Cataloging Cooperative Training Program: sponsored by CONSER; provides materials and trainers, and trains trainers.

USMARC—U.S. MAchine Readable Cataloging: a bibliographic record format developed by the Library of Congress and originally called LC-MARC.

REFERENCES

Bevis, Mary D., and John-Bauer Graham. 2003. "The Evolution of an Integrated Electronic Journals Collection." *The Journal of Academic Librarianship* 29, no. 2: 115–119.

Bland, Robert N., Timothy Carstens, and Mark A. Stoffan. 2002. "Automation of Aggregator Title Access with MARC Processing." *Serials Review* 28, no. 2: 108–115.

Briscoe, Georgia, Karen Selden, and Cheryl Rae Nyberg. 2003. "The Catalog vs. the Homepage? Best Practices in Connecting to Online Resources." *Law Library Journal* 95, no. 2 (Spring): 151–174. Retrieved Sept. 21, 2004, from http://www.aallnet.org/products/2003-10.pdf.

Collins, Maria D. D., and Christine L. Ferguson. 2002. "Context-Sensitive Linking: It's a Small World after All." *Serials Review* 28, no. 4: 267–282.

Curtis, Donnelyn, and Araby Y. Greene. 2002. "Presenting the Virtual Library." In *Attracting, Educating and Serving Remote Users through the Web: A How-To-Do-It Manual for Librarians*, ed. Donnelyn Curtis, 39–71. New York: Neal-Schuman.

French, Pat. 2002. "Taming the Aggregators: Providing Access to Journals in Aggregator Databases." *The Serials Librarian* 42, no. 3/4: 157–163.

Grogg, Jill E. 2002. "Thinking about Reference Linking." *Searcher* 10, no. 4 (April): 56–62.

Hinton, Mellissa J. 2002. "On Cataloging Internet Resources: Voices from the Field." *Journal of Internet Cataloging* 5, no. 1: 53–67.

Hirons, Jean. 2003. "From the Editor." *ConserLine: Newsletter of the CONSER Program* 22 (Winter). Retrieved Sept. 20, 2004, from www.loc.gov/acq/conser/consln22.html#editor.

Johnson, Kay, Maribeth Manoff, and Rebecca Sheffield. 2003. "Report of the Death of the Catalog Is Greatly Exaggerated: The E-Journal Access Journey at the University of Tennessee." *The Serials Librarian* 44, no. 3/4: 285–292.

Jones, Wayne. 2003. "A Personal Mini-History of E-Serials Cataloging. E-scape: A Column about E-Serials Cataloging. *The Serials Librarian* 43, no. 3: 21–24.

Knudson, Frances L., Nancy R. Sprague, Douglas A. Chafe, Mark L. B. Martiniz, Isabel M. Brackbill, Vicky A. Musgrave, and Kathleen A. Pratt. 1997. "Creating Electronic Journal Web Pages from OPAC Records." *Issues in Science and Technology Librarianship* 15 (Summer). Retrieved Sept. 20, 2004, from www.istl.org/97-summer/article2.html.

McCracken, Peter. 2003. "Beyond Title Lists: Incorporating Ejournals into the OPAC." *The Serials Librarian* 45, no. 3: 101–108.

O'Leary, Mick. 2003. "Publishers Forge New Access Tool with CrossRef." *Online* 27, no. 1 (January/February): 64–66.

Online Catalog Group [OCG]. University of Sydney Library. *Maximising Access to the Library's Electronic Journals, A Discussion Paper*. Retrieved Sept. 21, 2004, from http://staff.library.usyd.edu.au/ocg/ejournals.html.

Parks, Bonnie. 2002. "Serial Conversations: An Interview with Steve Shadle." *Serials Review* 28, no. 4: 321–326.

Paul, Kathryn, Elena Romaniuk, and Daisy T. Cheng. 2004. "Using the Library's OPAC to Dynamically Generate Webpages for E-Journals." *The Serials Librarian* 46, no. 3/4: 301–308.

Reese, Terry. 2003. "Aggregate Record Management in Three Clicks." *D-Lib Magazine* 9, no. 9 (September). Retrieved Sept. 9, 2004, from www.dlib.org/dlib/september03/reese/09reese.html.

Rothman, Jonathan. 2002. "Bridging the Gap between Materials-Focus and Audience-Focus: Providing Subject Categorization for Users of Electronic Resources." *Journal of Internet Cataloging* 5, no. 4: 67–80.

Tennant, Roy. 2003. "Library Catalogs: The Wrong Solution." *Library Journal* 128 no. 3 (February 15): 28. Retrieved Sept. 20, 2004, from www.libraryjournal.com/article/CA273959?display=searchResults&stt=001&text=tennant.

Tenopir, Carol. 2003. *Use and Users of Electronic Library Resources: An Overview and Analysis of Recent Research Studies*. Washington, DC: Council on Library and Information Resources. Retrieved Sept. 18, 2004, from www.clir.org/pubs/reports/pub120/pub120.pdf.

Tenopir, Carol, Donald W. King, Peter Boyce, Matt Grayson, Yan Zhang, and Mercy Ebuen. 2003. "Patterns of Journal Use by Scientists through Three Evolutionary Phases." *D-Lib Magazine* 9, no. 5. Retrieved Sept. 20, 2004, from www.dlib.org/dlib/may03/king/05king.html.

Thomas, Nancy. 2002. *Researching Database-Driven Library Web Sites*. College of DuPage Library [Glen Ellyn, IL]. Retrieved Sept. 20, 2004, from www.cod.edu/library/libweb/thomas/DatabaseReport.htm.

Wakimoto, Jina Choi. 2003. "Electronic Resources: Approaches in Providing Access." *Journal of Internet Cataloging* 6, no. 2: 21–33.

Watson, Paula. 2003. "E-Journals: Access and Management." *Library Technology Reports* 39, no. 2 (March/April): 44–69.

MORE INFORMATION SOURCES

Bradley, Lynne E. 2003. "Washington Hotline." *College and Research Libraries News* 64, no. 11 (December): 756–757; 771.

Brandsma, Terry W., Elizabeth R. Bernhardt, and Sally M. Dana. 2002. "Journal Finder: A Solution for Comprehensive and Unmediated Access to Journal Articles." *Serials Review* 28, no. 1: 13–20.

Blake, Miriam E., and Frances L. Knudson. 2002. "Metadata and Reference Linking." *Library Collections, Acquisitions, and Technical Services* 26, no. 2: 219–230.

Bross, Valerie. 2003. "The PCC/CONSER PURL Project: Improving Access to Free Resources." *The Serials Librarian* 45, no. 1: 19–26.

"Cataloging Electronic Documents." University of North Dakota. http://www.und.edu/dept/library/Departments/abc/Catedocs.htm.

Chen-Gaffey, Aiping. 2003. "MARC Standards and OPAC Display of Records for Web-Based Resources." *The Serials Librarian* 43, no. 4: 23–28.

Cohen, Laura B., and Matthew M. Calsada. 2003. "Web Accessible Databases for Electronic Resource Collections: A Case Study and Its Implications." *The Electronic Library* 21, no. 1: 31–38.

CONSER Working Group. 2003. "Single or Separate Records? What's Appropriate When [rev]. Retrieved Sept. 21, 2004, from wwwtest.library.ucla.edu/libraries/cataloging/sercat/conserwg/.

Duncan, Robert E. 2001. "Dynamic Publishing of Links to Web Resources Using FileMaker Pro." *OCLC Systems and Services* 17, no. 4: 178–186.

Grogg, Jill E., and Christine L. Ferguson. 2003. "Linking Services Unleashed." *Searcher* 11, no. 2 (February). Retrieved Sept. 20, 2004, from www.infotoday.com/searcher/feb03/grogg_ferguson.shtml.

Hirons, Jean, and Adolfo Tarango. 2003. "CONSER Begins Defining the 'Aggregator-Neutral' Record." *ConserLine: Newsletter of the CONSER Program* 22 (Winter). Retrieved Sept. 20, 2004, from www.loc.gov/acq/conser/consln22.html#aggrec.

Ho, LeVu, Siu Cheung Hui, and A. C. M. Fong. 2003. "Monitoring Scientific Publications over the WWW." *The Electronic Library* 21, no. 2: 110–116.

Integrating Access to VIVA Collections: Report of the Content Linking Committee. 2003, June 5. Retrieved Sept. 20, 2004, from www.vivalib.org/tech/cat/link/content_linking_2003_June.pdf.

Robbins, Laura Pope. 2002. "Creating an Integrated Periodicals Listing using Microsoft Access and ASP Scripts." *OCLC Systems and Services* 18, no. 1: 24–31.

Shemberg, Marian. 2003. "The Role of the ISSN in the Electronic Linking Environment." *Serials Review* 29, no. 2: 89–96.

Warren, Scott. 2004. "Deeplinking and E-reserves: A New Generation." *Journal of Interlibrary Loan, Document Delivery and Information Supply* 14, no. 2: 65–81.

Young, Naomi Kietzke. 2003. "The Aggregator-Neutral Record: New Procedures for Cataloging Continuing Resources." *Serials Librarian* 45, no. 4: 37–42.

8 SUPPORTING USERS AND FOSTERING THE USE OF ELECTRONIC JOURNALS

CHAPTER OVERVIEW

- The Importance of User Services
- Attracting and Informing Users through Marketing
- Delivering Instruction
- Providing Technical Support: Helping Users in Trouble
- Helping Users inside the Library
- Serving Users with Disabilities

If you have read the preceding chapters of this book, you should understand the importance of considering the needs, practices, preferences, and expectations of users when you are designing a system for delivering electronic journals. Chapter 2 and the first part of Chapter 7 provide insights into users of the Web in general and e-journals in particular. But implementing a user-centered system is only the beginning.

This chapter will not revisit earlier references to the large body of research that identifies the disconnect between users' expectations and the complexity of accessing and using licensed e-journals and databases provided by libraries. Even with the very best user-centered e-journal delivery system, some of your users will need help and guidance, and designing effective user services is an essential aspect of providing e-journals. The focus in this chapter is on attracting and supporting users and ensuring their success. The importance of the service dimension of providing electronic journals cannot be emphasized strongly enough.

THE IMPORTANCE OF USER SERVICES

Different kinds of users require different types of services. Those who are experienced with traditional print resources and the conventions of library research may be more patient with navigational and searching processes but could run into problems in viewing or printing results. Some of these experienced library users will use help files and read written instructions; and they may not expect an instant response to a request for help.

New users of library resources, on the other hand, will generally expect simplicity, will be unwilling to deal with technical obstacles, and will not understand library terminology. They don't know whether what the library has to offer is worth the effort of finding and retrieving it, and if they request help, they will want it immediately.

TIME CONSTRAINTS AND INFORMATION OVERLOAD

Lack of time is a constant and universal complaint of all types of e-journal users, but information overload may be the actual unrecognized problem. Most users do not see the overabundance of available information as a factor in their struggles against deadlines, time constraints, and competing demands. They may not be aware of the extent to which sifting through a large quantity of off-target, sloppy search results eats up valuable time. But they may come to you in desperation if they run out of time before finding what they need, or if they are having technical difficulties that threaten to consume even more of their time. In addition to making your resources as obstacle free and easy to use as possible, you will want to offer assistance that is as efficient, effective, context sensitive, and brief as possible.

CUSTOMIZED, TARGETED, AND REMOTE SERVICES

Most libraries already have a strong service orientation, but serving users of electronic journals (and other electronic resources) is challenging because you will be creating communication conduits and a support system for users you will never see. Service considerations for remote users could fill a book! (See Curtis, 2002.) Your Web design and help screens can adequately serve most users with most types of information needs and problems, but individual users will have individual situations with which they need individual assistance. Just as most users of the physical library can serve themselves, some will require reference or other types of assistance from staff. Individualized services to assist with e-journals and maximize their use can take several forms:

- responsive, human help (by phone, e-mail, or chat)
- cookies that will remember users' preferences from one session to the next and use their online choices to make recommendations (the Amazon model)
- alerting services, automatic or manual

Proactive, targeted assistance can also be off
ating visits to e-journal users in their computi   ...ılıs.
This allows you to help individuals with access problems and
market your resources selectively, and at the same time you are
getting direct input on users' needs, preferences, and practices.

ATTRACTING AND INFORMING USERS THROUGH MARKETING

One of the most basic e-journal services is to provide awareness
and promote your collection to prospective users. Academic libraries have a "penetration factor" of approximately 48%, which
is considered high for a service organization (Outsell, 2003). But
that means more than half of the faculty and staff at an average
university never use library resources for their teaching, learning,
or research.

Just because most libraries are nonprofit organizations that do
not charge fees for use of their resources does not mean they don't
have to "compete for customers." Libraries developed their traditional services when information was scarce and they were the
most prominent information providers; but, as we know, that is
no longer the situation. Information of all kinds is so abundant
today that the library needs to "sell" what it has to offer, to convince prospective users of the value of online resources provided
by the library.

LEVERAGING YOUR WEB PRESENCE

The last chapter focused on how to provide organized and optimal access to e-journals within the library's self-contained Web
site. Now it is time to step back and strategize about directing
users to those Web pages.

The Library Home Page and Internal Pages

Your library's home page design should be "sticky" enough to
capture casual visitors and let them know about your electronic
resources, and it should be organized logically enough to ensure
their success in getting to these resources. At the same time, the
overall purpose of your library's home page is to serve a number
of different kinds of users with a range of needs, and your challenge is to get each of them to the most appropriate resources
and services for their purposes. For example:

FIGURE 8–1. Clean and Simple Home-Page Design

- Freshman English students writing their first college research papers should be guided to a general full-text database rather than to a list of e-journals or the library catalog.
- Someone looking for books or videos would not be given the impression that the library has nothing but full-text electronic resources.
- The library's hours of operation and policies should be easy to find.

There are many reasons to visit a library Web site other than to use e-journals, but you do want them to be easy to find. Too much explanation on one page will undermine your purpose. Try to provide a sense of the richness of content on your site while directing each type of user to a suitable path without unnecessary words (Figure 8–1). Figure 8–2 shows an example of a library home page that serves many types of users.

If you don't already have a "What's New" area on your home

FIGURE 8–2. Home Page for a Multitype Library

page, consider adding one and using it to publicize your e-journals (see Figure 8–3).

Internally, your library's subject guides and other specialized Web pages can link to appropriate e-journal subject pages, and your e-journal subject pages can link back to broader resources. Some libraries maintain a blog that keeps users apprised of new and interesting resources (see Fichter, 2003).

Branding Your Resources

Although it may be hard for us to imagine, many of our prospective users have never thought to visit the library's Web site. Since every university department and city agency and organization in the universe has a Web site, your constituents would expect the library to have one that would give information about its location, hours, and on-site features, services, and collections. They might even expect an online catalog in the form of an inventory database, similar to Amazon's or Blockbuster's.

But the idea of going to the library's Web site to access resources

FIGURE 8–3. What's New

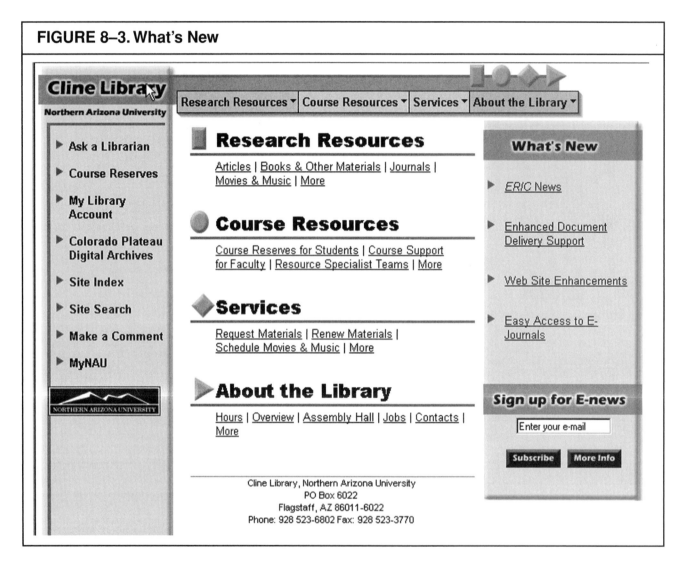

that are available elsewhere on the Web is not an intuitive concept. In fact, they may even use resources that are provided by your library without realizing that their status as a member of the community your library serves gives them free access to resources that would otherwise be unavailable to them. For example, users on a university campus might be able to retrieve articles from the Institute of Electrical and Electronic Engineers (IEEE) journals through a Google search without even realizing that the IP address of their office or lab computer was recognized at the IEEE site as a result of their library's license agreement. This scenario will become increasingly common as Web search services strive to expand their offerings of high-quality, scholarly full-text resources.

Once your users realize that they have come across a quality

FIGURE 8–4. Library Branding

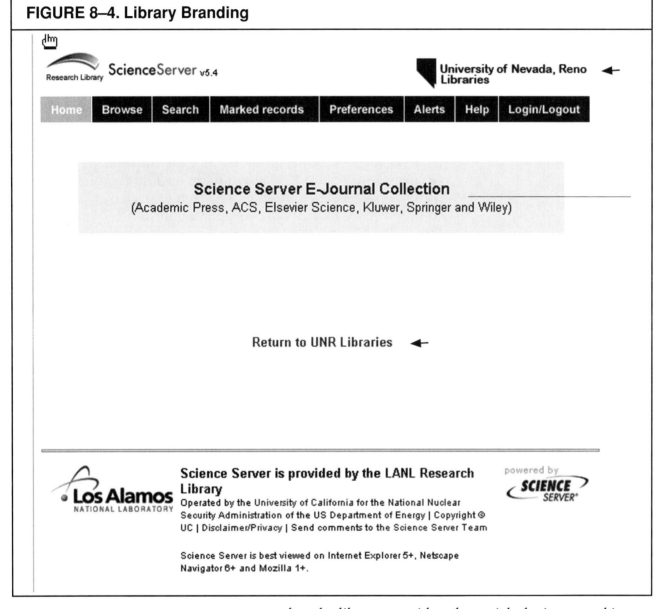

resource that the library provides, they might be interested in seeing what else you offer. One way to help them make a connection between resources they are already using and the library that makes their access possible is to take advantage of options to "brand" the pages with your library's logo. Most vendors offer the opportunity to configure the user interface to include a library logo (or name) that might link to a designated URL. For example, for Science Direct "You can customize the User Interface by placing a header banner at the top of every page saying: 'Brought to you by NAME INSTITUTE' and/or you can have your institute's logo displayed at the bottom of every page." See Figure 8–4 for a similar example. License agreements usually ask for the library's "technical contact person," and whoever is listed should have the password and instructions for accessing the administrative site where branding is made possible.

Your Parent Organization's Web Site

An even better way to lure unsuspecting members of your community to your electronic journals is to arrange for links to be embedded in appropriate areas of your university's, city's, or company's Web site. A 2001 study showed that over 25% of the members of the Association of Research Libraries (ARL) are part of a university that doesn't have an "immediately visible active link to the library" (Astroff, 2001, 98). The Webmaster of your parent organization faces the same problem that the library faces in needing to direct many kinds of home-page visitors to many different resources and services. But a link to the library isn't too much to ask of them, and you should lobby for at least a small piece of that prime real estate.

However, even a prominent link to the library on a page with high traffic won't be used by information seekers in your community if they don't know what the library has to offer. You should also think about targeted links on strategic inner pages of the larger domain:

- University department pages could have links to subject listings of the e-journals supporting those disciplines.
- Online course syllabi could link to e-journal pages (or customized library pages that list resources, including e-journals, that are appropriate for that course).
- A city or county health department page could have a link to the public library's compilation of health-related online resources.

MARKETING YOUR RESOURCES

Members of your user community will be much more likely to visit your library's Web site if they know in advance what you have to offer, which may require some re-education, through an advertising blitz or targeted marketing. Libraries are not accustomed to advertising, but we have no choice if we want to compete in the information marketplace and satisfy the needs of our constituents. You can get their attention at first by making a big point about how things are changing in a major way.

A Marketing Plan

Any marketing effort will be more successful if it follows a carefully developed plan. A marketing plan is based on market research, meaning that you should know who you are trying to reach and what they need. If this seems foreign and difficult, consider using the services of a consultant. Perhaps a marketing or public relations class in your university might be able to take you on as a project.

Marketing inside the Library

Habitual or occasional visitors to your library might notice the proliferation of computers and a decrease in the number of current periodicals on the shelves, but how would they know that a large number of electronic journals are now available for use in their homes or offices? You have to take advantage of every opportunity to let them know:

- Put signs in your periodicals browsing area.
- Put stickers on individual issues of journals: "also available online at [your URL]."
- Hang a banner on the outside or inside of your building with the library's URL.
- Blanket the library with posters.
- Put a brief message on table tents.
- Hand out bookmarks or other printed materials with brief information. Emphasize new online content and how to get to it rather than details.
- Have date-due slips printed with "Check out the library's electronic journals at [your URL]."
- Host events to demonstrate new resources (see the "Instruction" section, below).
- Mention e-journals to information-seekers at service points whenever possible.

If you have departmental branch libraries or subject-oriented sections of your library, try using targeted posters or flyers that read, "Do you read the Journal of ...? Now you can read it online in your home or office at [your library's URL]!"

Marketing outside the Library

Of course, you will never see most of your prospective users, especially the younger ones. When they need information, they use "the Web," and most of them are perfectly satisfied with what they find. You will have to reach out and give them a taste of what they are missing, using every possible ploy to sell them on your product:

- Post flyers and posters in appropriate areas—departmental bulletin boards, the student union, computer labs, dormitories (or city council chambers, food co-ops, hospitals . . .).
- Use interdepartmental mail to distribute flyers.
- Establish an opt-in or opt-out e-mail newsletter from the library (note: keep issues short and articles lively).
- Send occasional focused e-mail messages to appropriate groups (faculty in a department, administrators in a unit, professionals in an organization).
- Invite yourself to meetings of prospective users; ask for 5 or 10 minutes, bring handouts and business cards and provide a quick demo if the location allows it; follow up with an e-mail message to those attending.
- Conduct market research and outreach at the same time; interview some users.
- Visit prospective users in their offices; ask to bookmark the page that is most suitable for their e-journal needs.
- Nurture evangelists. If some of your users are especially excited about your electronic journals, encourage them to spread the word, and keep them posted about new developments.

USING PROMOTIONAL MATERIALS FROM PUBLISHERS AND VENDORS

Many publishers and other e-journal providers have made promotional materials freely available to librarians through their Web sites (see, for example, the "Promoting Emerald Fulltext" section on the "Librarian Toolkit" page at www.emeraldinsight.com/usagetoolkit, and "Librarian Services" from Elsevier at www.info.sciencedirect.com/librarian_help/index.shtml). They will also mail marketing items to you in the form of bookmarks, posters, or brochures. The problem with materials such as these is that they are designed to increase the use of that vendor's products, promoting only a segment of your e-journals, and their focus is on promoting brand recognition of their products, which may be counterproductive for the library. However, some of the online materials can be adapted for more generic use, allowing you to use professionally developed marketing materials to promote all of your own library's electronic products.

FIGURE 8–5. E-Journal Newsletter Sign-Up Form

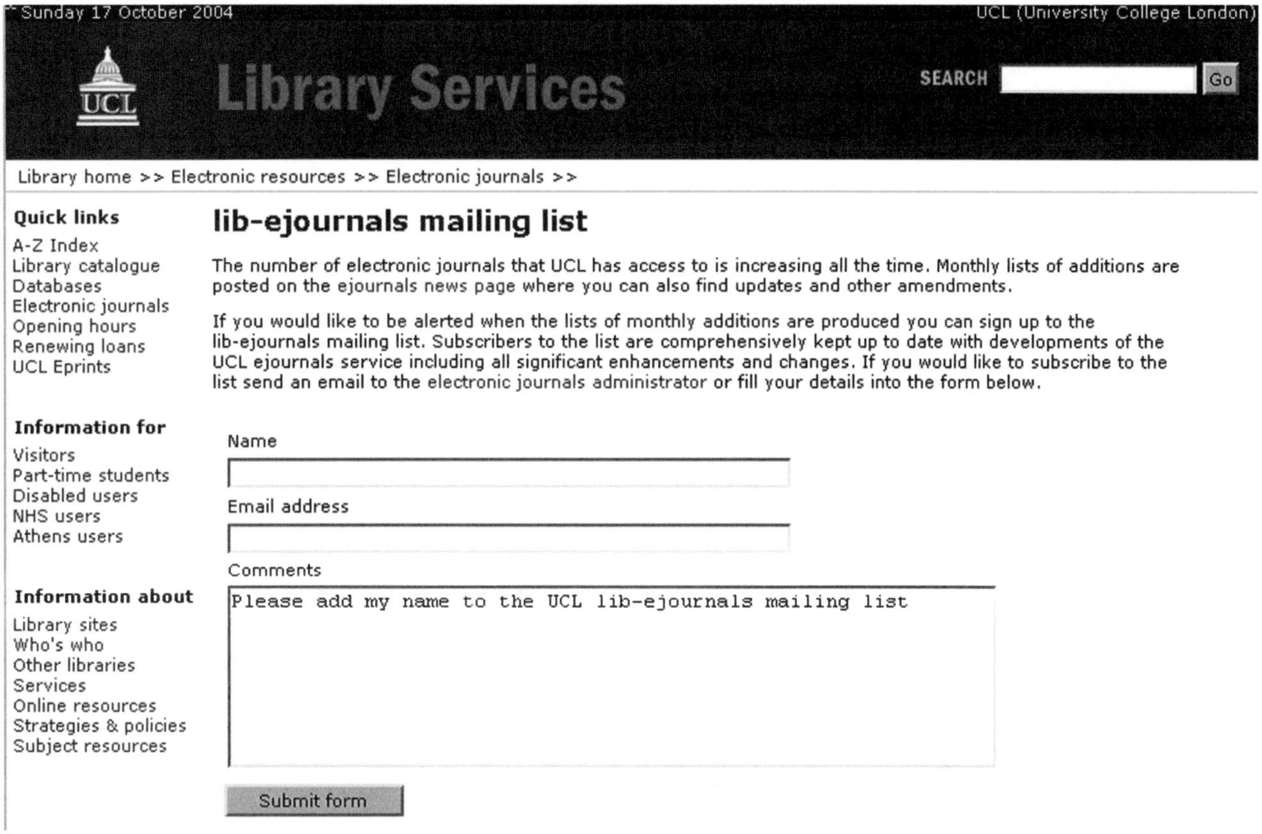

Sunday 17 October 2004

UCL (University College London)

UCL Library Services

SEARCH Go

Library home >> Electronic resources >> Electronic journals >>

Quick links
A-Z Index
Library catalogue
Databases
Electronic journals
Opening hours
Renewing loans
UCL Eprints

Information for
Visitors
Part-time students
Disabled users
NHS users
Athens users

Information about
Library sites
Who's who
Other libraries
Services
Online resources
Strategies & policies
Subject resources

lib-ejournals mailing list

The number of electronic journals that UCL has access to is increasing all the time. Monthly lists of additions are posted on the ejournals news page where you can also find updates and other amendments.

If you would like to be alerted when the lists of monthly additions are produced you can sign up to the lib-ejournals mailing list. Subscribers to the list are comprehensively kept up to date with developments of the UCL ejournals service including all significant enhancements and changes. If you would like to subscribe to the list send an email to the electronic journals administrator or fill your details into the form below.

Name

Email address

Comments

Please add my name to the UCL lib-ejournals mailing list

Submit form

E-JOURNAL NEWS

Some libraries maintain a Web page for news about electronic journals—primarily for the announcement of new titles or licenses, but also to report any changes in services or new forms of access. University College London provides such a page, and also maintains an e-journal mailing list (Figure 8–5 shows the sign-up form). You don't want to irritate constituents by sending e-mail messages they might not want to receive; however, every few months a brief announcement inviting them to subscribe, with a sample announcement chosen carefully for its broad appeal would be an appropriate reminder that your library's e-journal collection is growing and your services are improving.

DELIVERING INSTRUCTION

A large-scale study of undergraduates, graduate students, and faculty members from a wide range of academic institutions (commissioned by the Council on Library and Information Resources [CLIR]) found that 38.4% of respondents believed that having insufficient training on how to search for information was an impediment (Friedlander, 2002). Many users of electronic information resources in public libraries would also benefit from training opportunities. Providing instruction is one of the most important ways that libraries can support the users of their electronic journals, but only if users or their instructors are receptive.

UNDERGRADUATE LIBRARY ORIENTATIONS

If your library has an established and successful instruction program in place, you will want to include information about electronic journals in ways that are appropriate for each audience. Many libraries these days have fewer opportunities than they once had to introduce students to e-journals with formal instruction. Library instruction, like so many other library functions, is being reinvented to serve new purposes in a transformed educational and information environment.

Teaching about electronic journals during formal instruction sessions for undergraduates will be most successful if you can

- relate the process of searching for articles to the students' Web-searching experiences,
- emphasize full-text databases for subject searching,
- keep the instruction short and simple,
- cover a few main points, and
- demonstrate the process of connecting from a remote site, including how to authenticate.

TAKING LIBRARY INSTRUCTION OUT OF THE LIBRARY

For classes of students who are more likely to use electronic resources than print resources (most, if not all, undergraduates), and especially for students who are likely to become remote users, it can be more effective for a library representative to visit their classroom than to have the students come to the library. Demonstrating how to access e-journals from outside the library will prove that it is possible.

Wired classrooms, wireless technology, and portable comput-

Keeping up-to-date:

Library Instruction Round Table (LIRT)

http://www3.baylor.edu/LIRT/

LOEX Clearinghouse for Library Instruction

http://www.emich.edu/public/loe/loex.htm

ers and projectors extend the potential of library instruction to reach larger classes than would fit into traditional library-instruction venues. When approaching instructors for the first time to propose a visit to demonstrate the library's electronic resources, you will be more successful if you ask for a short period of time, 10 or 15 minutes.

It is possible in a brief presentation to convey these fundamental concepts:

- The library provides high quality resources that are especially useful for a particular class;
- These resources can be accessed through the web, but they require an authentication process; and
- Help is available when needed.

A very short presentation will be more sucessful if supplemented with a Web page that reinforces your main points and provides more information.

WORKSHOPS

Many libraries have had at least one experience with scheduling workshops or training sessions that were not well attended, even though they may have been designed in response to clamorous requests and earnest promises to attend. When the time comes, other activities and commitments take precedence, nobody shows up, and librarians get discouraged.

Workshops for Faculty and Researchers

Workshops for faculty tend to be more successful if they are held in conjunction with other events; for example:

- A new-faculty orientation
- An information-technology fair
- A series of university-wide programs that have developed a following
- Any technology-oriented event on campus, especially one that is designed to foster the use of technology in the classroom

If a special event such as a reception to honor award winners is held in the library, you may be able to take advantage of a captive audience and lure some of them into a nearby computer classroom for a demonstration of the library's newest electronic products. A workshop for faculty and researchers will be more successful if you can

- get them excited about the new content that is available to them through library licenses,
- relate searching for articles in e-journals to traditional forms of searching for library resources,
- focus on browsing and searching strategies that are thorough and efficient, and
- provide some (but not too much) contextual information about producers and providers, embargoes, moving walls, and costs to the library.

Researchers will also want specific information:

- Technological requirements for access
- How to get help if they run into problems
- How to create persistent links to articles for their students
- How to request electronic reserves
- How to recommend new e-journals
- How to subscribe to current awareness services
- Where to find instructions for authors and other front-matter information, such as listings of editorial boards

Health sciences libraries appear to be more successful than academic libraries in attracting faculty and researchers to their e-journal workshops. Stewart Brower (Emery, 2003) presents an outline for a 40-minute session in a health sciences library where users are interested in topics like differences in types of publishers and the advantages and disadvantages of different types of formats. Brower suggests giving students in the class some freedom to define what they feel is important to learn.

Workshops for Graduate Students

Graduate students have a higher level of intrinsic interest in library-provided resources than undergraduates and more incentive than faculty to learn how to use them. Specialized workshops for graduate students tend to be well attended, partly because many faculty advisors are unable to guide their graduate students through a high-tech contemporary literature review. Graduate workshops can be longer in duration and more in-depth. In addition to covering everything you would cover in both undergraduate instruction sessions and faculty workshops, you will want to cover the following:

- Introduce appropriate subject databases.
- Discuss how to get to the full text of articles from bibliographic databases.

- Suggest a personalized consultation with a library subject specialist.
- Present "advanced-searching" functionality for databases.
- Include information on how to cite articles from electronic journals.

Citing electronic journals causes a certain amount of confusion and consternation. According to a 2002 NASIG workshop by Janice Krueger, well described by Jill Emery (2003), it is important to know certain basics:

- How to tell the difference between the producer and the publisher,
- How to handle a lack of pagination and occasional uncertainty about dates, and
- How (and when) to include the URL in the citation according to different style manuals

Partnering with Systems and IT Units

"Electronic Journals" as an academic-library-sponsored workshop might not attract as large a crowd as an "Information Technology Update" session sponsored by the university's IT division. Partnering with IT colleagues will guarantee the marriage of content with technology, and faculty and staff who attend will get a more complete picture of the value of the technology that can support their teaching and research.

Sometimes library systems offices provide public services outreach for the library. The Information Technology Arcade (or Info Tech Arcade) at the University of Illinois at Chicago (UIC), staffed by three librarians, provides Web consulting, a multimedia teachers' lab, server hosting, and seminars. When electronic journals were introduced at UIC, the Info Tech Arcade held special classes to introduce them (Fu, 2002).

The Spencer S. Eccles Health Sciences Library at the University of Utah (Salt Lake City) holds an annual InfoFair that is open to the public and also broadcast in real time on the Web (Figure 8–6). The Webcasts are archived. The goal of the popular InfoFair is "to provide up-to-date information on computer applications, resources and services as well as a glimpse into the future of computers and computing in the health science." One of the sessions for 2004 was "New Technology Hands On!—Presentations, demonstrations and try it!" The library's electronic journals feature prominently in the presentations and demonstrations every year. For more information see the Web site at http://medlib.med.utah.edu/library/infofair/infofair.html.

FIGURE 8–6. InfoFair 2004

INSTRUCTION FOR DISTANCE STUDENTS

For distant students without a library nearby, e-journals are a lifeline to scholarly information resources. Access to e-journals can make a significant difference in the quality of their work, and in the quality of their online education, for that matter. But remote students are less likely than local students to have technical support on hand, and more likely to run into telecommunication and authentication problems. For example, if your authentication system requires information that is on a library card, your remote students may not have a library card. If distance education is new in your institution, you will run into a number of unique situations with distance students that will need to be resolved.

Electronic journals are well suited for inclusion in a library's online tutorials or distance-education modules. Developing and maintaining an online tutorial is a lot of work—keeping one up-to-date as interfaces change is quite a challenge, and some libraries have abandoned the attempt, especially since tutorials have not proved to be popular with on-site students. However, if your library supports a large number of distance students, a tutorial could be your best approach for teaching them how to take advantage of your electronic journals and databases. Students in distance programs will be more motivated to use (and more accustomed to using) online support.

PROVIDING TECHNICAL SUPPORT: HELPING USERS IN TROUBLE

Even if your e-journal delivery system is well designed and you have done an excellent job with marketing and instruction, some of your users will have trouble accessing your electronic journals. Whether the problem originates with the vendor (a server is down, IP recognition fails); the user (unwilling or too panicked to read instructions, lost user ID); or your library (complex authentication requirements, an error in the patron database, an incorrect URL), your entire public services staff should be prepared to diagnose and solve individual users' problems.

Each time a problem is reported you will have the opportunity to prevent it from happening again. Responsive service goes beyond the resolution of individual problems, and even if a recurring problem is not preventable, you can describe it on your FAQ page, along with suggestions for handling it. Some users will have problems with e-journal access when the library is closed. How will you help them?

STAFF READINESS

"Solving" a problem may ultimately involve referring it, but good user support means that if anyone calls the library with a problem related to e-journals, the person who answers the phone will be able to discuss the problem intelligently, solve it on the spot or take the responsibility for getting it solved, and follow up to ascertain user success. That's a tall order. Front-line user services staff will most likely require specialized training to be able to provide this level of service.

The best methods for training your staff to provide technical support will depend on the size of your staff, the level at which they are beginning, and other factors. You will probably use a combination of some of these methods:

- Formal workshops
- A public services e-mail group for sharing experiences
- Real or simulated hands-on experiences with various browsers, operating systems, and modes of connectivity

- Competencies checklists
- Troubleshooting exercises
- Update sessions in public services meetings
- Training-related goals in job descriptions, linked to your evaluation process
- An intranet site for internal-training resources
- Clearly defined modes of communication for updating staff on new resources
- The use of vendors' trainers
- A knowledge base that reports and tracks questions and answers

You may need to extend your training activities beyond the library public services staff. If it is likely that questions about e-journal access will go to a university help desk or to distributed system administrators in your parent organization, you will need to make sure that those computing-support people can recognize and respond to questions about access to library resources. If a student assistant at a help desk gets a call about someone who is having trouble with SFX links from GeoRef, they should know enough library terminology to recognize that it is a library situation. Invite yourself to a regular meeting of the user services staff in the IT department, or perhaps a meeting of systems administrators, to talk about the most common problems with library resources and show them your help pages or FAQs.

RESPONSIVE ONLINE SERVICE

Every time a user reports a problem, you can be sure that several other users have experienced or will experience the same problem. So you will want to be sure to respond in such a way that the silent users will be helped as well. For example, if you find out that a journal provides supplemental materials in a format that requires a special plug-in, you may want to put a link to the download site where the latest version is available in addition to sending that URL to the person who reported the problem.

COMMUNICATING WITH USERS

Some of the advantages of electronic journals are also some of their disadvantages, when it comes to supporting them. They are available to your users 24 hours a day, seven days a week from anywhere in the world, but your staff is probably centrally located and available at limited times of the day and night. On Sunday night at 11:00 p.m., a user is unlikely to get real-time support with e-journal problems. So in addition to providing direct help,

---

FIGURE 8–7. Contacts and Help Page

KING'S College LONDON
University of London

Text only

ISS: Information Services and Systems

| Services | Information gateway | Locations/hours | Contacts/help | About ISS |

Electronic Journals Contacts & Help

Help with electronic journals

- Introduction to electronic journals at KCL
- Searching a list
- Troubleshooting
- Do I need a password?
- Can I access ejournals from outside the KCL computer network?
- What if I have technical problems?
- What if the journal I want isn't listed?
- Can ejournals help me keep up to date?

Passwords

Who to contact for further help

Recent news updates about ejournals

Back to the journals homepage

---

you will also need to give your users some other ways to find information and communicate with you. Most of us like to have someone available to answer our questions when they come up, but we understand that it isn't always possible.

Synchronous Communication

You should make it easy for your users to contact someone directly during regular service hours, whatever those hours might be (the longer, the better, of course). You should prepare for and welcome in-person visits (especially from the growing number of

practitioners of mobile computing who can bring their computers along), phone calls, and (ideally) chat visitors. Your e-journal
Web pages could link to a "Contacts and Help" page that might
look like the one in Figure 8–7.

Your contact information for real-time help would include

- locations of help desk(s) or other service points;
- a reliable phone number that will connect to a knowledgeable person during service hours;
- phone numbers of specialists, if appropriate;
- hours when service is available.

If your library participates in a cooperative chat service, you
probably won't want to direct your users to a chat operator at
another institution who won't be familiar with your library's electronic products or authentication processes. However, if your library has a self-contained chat service, think about offering
customized links on your e-journal pages for "live help with e-
journals." Make sure that chat operators are trained to troubleshoot your most common problems and that they will be able to
refer more difficult problems to the appropriate support channels.

Asynchronous Communication

Even during your service hours, some users will prefer to use a
more indirect mode of help, and when no one is around to help,
of course, they will have no choice. For these times, "self-help"
methods will be the most useful, but you will also need to provide ways for users to ask a question or report a problem and
receive an answer or help in response:

- If possible, configure your help line to receive voice-mail
  messages after hours—but only if they can be retrieved
  and managed in a timely way.
- Configure forms to gather facts that will help you solve
  the problem.
- Channel your forms and e-mail messages to an account
  that can be accessed by more than one individual; establish clear procedures for responsive retrieval and quick
  turnaround time and follow-through.

Forms for technical support can be very effective for users and
efficient for the support operation. Without requesting unnecessary information, you might consider asking for the following,
using a combination of radio buttons and text boxes:

FIGURE 8–8. Technical-Support Form

University of Nevada, Reno Libraries   Search | Site Map | HELP

| Catalog | Subjects | Databases | Reserves | Journals | eBooks | Reference |

Technical Support

First contact for all computing problems
- Campus Computing Help Desk
  775-784-4320

Off-campus access to Library resources
- **Please read these** INSTRUCTIONS
- Technical support: Campus Computing Help Desk, 775-784-4320
- Library card or account questions: Library Circulation, 775-784-6500 ext. 238
- Problems with a **specific** licensed service: Araby Greene, 775-784-6500 ext. 343

Report a problem or broken link
This report is e-mailed to the library webmaster. You will receive a response within 24 hours regarding the status of your request. Please fill out the form as completely as you can. Name and E-mail are required.

Your Name:	[_____] (Required)
Your UNR library account or card:	○ Current UNR student/ faculty/ staff ○ Community Borrower ○ Do not have a library card ○ Not sure if I have a library card
Your E-mail:	[_____] (Required)
Type of problem:	○ Broken link ○ Cannot access Course Reserves ○ Cannot access any database or electronic journal ○ Cannot access specific database or electronic Journal ○ Other problem

Broken Link Details, if applicable:

Broken link name or displayed text:	[_____]
Where did you find the broken link:	[_____] Web page title or description

Details that help us identify your problem:

When problem occurred:	[_____] Date, approximate time
Where:	○ On-campus ○ Off-campus, at home ○ Off-campus, at work
If off-campus access problem:	How do you connect to the Internet: ○ AOL Dial-up or Broadband ○ MSN Dial-up or Broadband ○ Other Dial-up ○ Other Broadband ○ Not sure What browser were you using: [—Please select from list— ▼]
If an error message displayed:	[_____] Number or description

Problem Description. Please include details not covered above:

[   ]
[   ]
[   ]

[Send Report]   [Start Over]

- The location of the computer used to access e-journals (home, work, on-site)
- The IP address of the computer (if known)
- The type of problem—offer some choices
- Error message received
- Broken-link name or URL (if applicable)
- Type of Internet connection—offer choices (AOL, dial-up, MSN, DSL)
- Type of browser and version
- Operating system (Windows, Macintosh, other—specify)
- Problem description
- Contact information

See Figure 8–8 for an example of a technical-support form.

One advantage of using an e-mail form is that you will receive the correct e-mail address of the person asking the question. There is nothing more frustrating than writing a complicated response or set of individualized instructions that are undeliverable because the e-mail address provided was not correct.

SUPPORTING SELF-HELP

Assuming that many of your users will have problems requiring information rather than intervention, they will appreciate detailed explanations of how to solve the problems on their own, particularly during the hours when no human support is available. In addition to detailed instructions for how to authenticate from off-site (discussed below), it would be appropriate to offer written explanations for optimizing browsers for the best use of e-journals, for downloading and installing plug-ins, and to answer any question that has come up by phone, chat, e-mail, or at a service desk. In fact, FAQs can be generated from a database or spreadsheet of logged questions.

Troubleshooting guides or flowcharts to help identify problems can be very useful for user self-help as well as for staff use. It is well worth your time to document the route an expert would take to pinpoint a problem and share that process with interested users. A troubleshooting guide can be wide ranging or specific to one type of problem. On a Web guide, you can include links to other guides or sets of instructions for certain types of problems. See Figure 8–9 for one example of a troubleshooting guide. Other troubleshooting guides can be found on the Web, for example:

- "Troubleshooting Off-Campus Access to Library Subscription Services"—University of Nevada, Reno (www.library. unr.edu/authenticate/proxytrouble.html)

FIGURE 8–9. Troubleshooting Guide

Electronic Resources Help

Troubleshooting connection problems

If you have problems linking to a database or journal, or your browser does not respond as expected when you click on a link to try to pinpoint what the problem might be, try:

- Clearing the cache, history and cookies from your browser
- Using another browser (e.g. Opera from **www.opera.com**)
- Checking your Windows privacy settings (Win2000,Me,XP) to make sure they are not set to block all cookies
- Checking your Windows or third party firewall settings to make sure connections via port 2048 are permitted
- Checking to make sure your browser accepts cookies

If none of the above helps, see if the same problem occur if you try using a different computer located somewhere else? Are you linking to the library's electronic resource search page **http://micro189.lib3.hawaii.edu/ezproxy/** and then selecting a resource, rather than using a previously bookmarked link? If you have the same problem on different PCs and different resources, even after clearing files, changing settings and browser, please send more information via the **Feedback Form**

- "OhioLINK Databases Troubleshooting Guide"—OhioLINK (www.ohiolink.edu/ostaff/ref/troubleshooting.html)
- "EZProxy Troubleshooting Guide"—University of New England, Biddeford, Maine (www.une.edu.au/library/ elecres/ezproxy_help.htm)

A Google search for "troubleshooting guide" "electronic journals" will provide many other models.

Not all users' questions are technical. When we think of "problems" we tend to think in terms of malfunctions and connectivity obstacles, but for inexperienced e-journal users, understanding what they should be doing and how to do it may pose a huge problem. Questions and answers in your FAQ should be both technical and procedural. The most usable FAQs have the questions listed at the top of the page with links to the answers, even if the answer is on the same page. Most FAQs have the most frequently asked questions at the top of the list, but if you have more than 20 questions, you may want to group them by topic. It can be difficult to think in terms of the types of questions users might ask and the words they might use—instead of what we want them to know, in the words that we use. There are, however, some frequently appearing questions on libraries' e-journal FAQs that you'll want to consider:

- What are e-journals?
- What is the quickest way to find an article in an electronic journal?
- How can I get help right now?
- How do I retrieve full text while searching a database that doesn't have full text?
- Who can access e-journals?
- The PDF file is blank when I display it, what can I do?
- What do I do if I can't print a PDF file?
- Can I save a PDF file?
- How can I use e-journals from off-campus?
- How do I recommend an electronic journal?
- Why do you list electronic journals more than once?
- Are there journals I can use off-campus if I am not a student?
- What is SFX?
- What is the password I am supposed to use when I am trying to use a database?
- What should I do if I am asked to accept cookies when trying to see a full-text article?
- Will older print issues of electronic journals eventually become available in electronic format? How far back in time are electronic journals available?
- Can I download e-journal articles to create my own database or to share them with colleagues?
- Why do some e-journals in the A–Z listing link directly to the journal title, while others link to a database search screen?
- Does an e-journal provide the same information as the print version?
- Why aren't all journals available electronically?
- Why can I find only older issues of some journals in an electronic format, but not the most recent issues?
- What can I do if I need an article that's not available electronically?

You will probably have some questions that are specific to your library regarding off-site authentication procedures or other unique circumstances. And some of the questions listed here will not apply to your library.

Some libraries offer printed or printable guides to walk users through procedures or answer questions that they might have while using electronic journals. It makes sense to have something that is not on the computer to refer to while using the computer. Not all users are as adept at multitasking on their computers as librarians have come to be. A study by Ashcroft (2002) indicated that UK libraries promoted e-journals with database-specific, hard-copy user guides at a significantly higher rate than did North American libraries. An example of a printable guide to electronic journals is from University College, London, at www.ucl.ac.uk/library/ejournal/HowfindJournal.doc.

SUPPORTING OFF-CAMPUS ACCESS

As Chapter 5 has illustrated, authentication is still complicated, no matter what method your library uses. In order to let authorized users in and keep the rest of the world out, a system requires a certain amount of complexity. It is probable that the most common complaint from off-site users will be problems with authentication.

Web-Based Instructions

Instructions and explanations about your authentication system should be available to your users through prominent links on every page that links to licensed resources. Even then, some users will not notice the link or will not realize that they have to do anything special to use certain resources. At the University of Nevada, Reno, we get their attention with a pop-up message that appears one time per day the first time an off-campus user opens any page that has licensed resources. For this method to work, those designated pages must be in a special directory on our Web site. See Figure 8–10.

Instructions should be written with as much detail as is necessary and as few words as possible. Illustrations are much more valuable. Using screen shots or simulations will help users. For example, if your process requires users to use a number on their library card, it is more helpful to show what that number looks like than to describe where it is located (as in Figure 8–11).

If there are differences in your authentication process for various browsers or operating systems or databases, even if those differences are minor, it is better to prepare separate instruction sheets for each instance rather than to try to explain the differences in the basic instructions. For authentication at the University of Nevada, Reno, we provide separate instruction pages (accessible through a menu) for the following and operating systems:

- America Online (AOL) or CompuServe
- Customized Browsers (MSN, Juno, NetZero, free Internet services)

FIGURE 8–10. Pop-Up Reminder to Authenticate

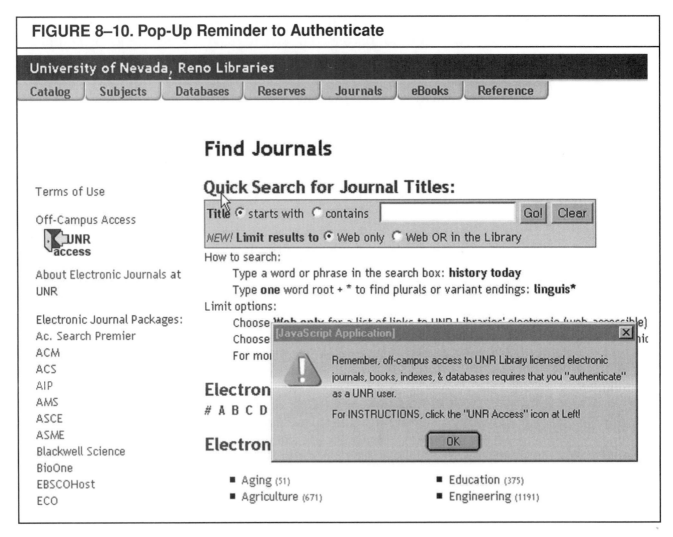

FIGURE 8–11. Illustrating Instructions

- Internet Explorer
- Internet Explorer with DSL, cable, or satellite
- Netscape
- Netscape with DSL, cable modem, or satellite
- Safari for Mac OS X.2 (Jaguar) or Mac OS X.3 (Panther)

If your authentication instructions have several steps, it can be useful to number them. When working with users over the phone, you may want to refer to one of the steps by number.

Many users will want to print complex instructions to make it easier to follow the steps, so be sure that your instruction pages are the right width for printing, even though the instructions may be too long to fit on one page. If the user needs to enter a lengthy password or a proxy URL as part of the process, use HTML for that part of the instructions rather than an image format so it is easier for the user to copy and paste the string of characters into a browser.

Troubleshooting Access Problems

A remote user who is having a problem accessing your e-journals will want it solved right away. The best way to get help will depend on the user's preferences, the time of day, the day of the week (weekday or weekend), the type of problem, and the technology at hand. Someone with a dial-up modem connection, for example, may not conveniently be able to make a phone call, but for another user, a phone call might be the most effective way to troubleshoot the problem. You can increase the chances for a successful resolution of the problem if you provide

- multiple formats for Web-based instructions (a step-by-step guide, an FAQ, targeted help files);
- multiple ways to obtain assistance (forms, phone numbers, an e-mail address, a chat connection, directions to a service point);
- a Web-accessible list of already-asked (not just frequently asked) questions and answers, sorted by frequency;
- a form that is designed to capture information that will help identify the problem and be delivered to a responsive party;
- a phone number that connects with a person or an assistance queue rather than voice mail;
- an e-mail address for an account that is checked regularly, including at night and on weekends, if possible;
- a phone number for a service point that has long hours and knowledgeable staff;
- a way to track the progress of the solution of problems.

If the user has a major access problem, nonlibrary technical-support staff in your organization should be able to solve it as well as librarians, and perhaps better, in some cases. But if they receive requests for help from users directly, you should encourage them to refer certain types of requests to library personnel.

- The library will probably need to fix an error in a patron record if access to library resources is linked to the library's circulation system.
- If there is a problem with access to some resources but not others, a librarian can suggest the best alternative.
- If the problem is at the vendor's end, the library will want to contact the vendor's technical-support network.
- Sometimes a user will ask a question about navigating or searching e-journals immediately after the access problem is resolved.

Good communication and a cordial relationship between library staff and other IT personnel in the organization will result in many benefits for your users.

THE INTERMEDIARY ROLE

Often a user will report a problem that originates with the vendor; for example:

- a server is down,
- your institution's IP addresses are no longer recognized, or
- a significant amount of licensed content is missing.

It is good to find out about such things as early as possible, not only for the sake of the individual who reported it, but for your other users as well. Serving as an intermediary with vendors is an important aspect of user support. Many libraries designate one person to contact vendors to report and resolve technical problems with electronic journals and databases. The designated communicator could be from reference, serials, systems, acquisitions, or any of a number of departments in the library. Important qualities for this duty are an interest in doing it, a sense of responsibility, determination, follow-through, willingness to work on problems during off-hours, and an understanding of technology issues. Your library will be more successful in solving vendor-related problems quickly if you take the following steps:

- Make sure your designated intermediary is a member of your "first-alert" communication network.
- Designate a backup contact if the primary person is unavailable.

- Keep a log of reports and problems and how they were resolved.
- Clarify technical-support procedures with vendors during the licensing process; specify an acceptable level of support in your contract, if possible.
- Manage an up-to-date list of contact people for each vendor, with phone numbers and e-mail addresses; include names of responsive support people, even if they are not your designated contact.
- Report unsatisfactory levels of support through your vendor's chain of command until you are satisfied with the improvements.
- Report recurring or irresolvable problems with vendor support on discussion lists such as Liblicense-l as a last resort (resolution will almost always follow, at a cost to the vendor's reputation).

If a problem with a vendor's site or services cannot be resolved immediately, it is important to communicate the nature of the problem (and the projected duration) to all public services staff and any technical support personnel who might receive calls.

The best way to communicate the problem to users is through alerts on your menu pages for e-journals. Red type is good for catching their attention. You won't catch all readers, since some of them will have bookmarks directly to the journal or the vendor's site, but you will have done what you could. Then, of course, you will have to remove all those messages as soon as the problem is fixed . . . .

WEB BROWSERS

The best way to prevent users' problems with out-of-date or out-of-the-ordinary browsers is to test your Web pages and e-journals with as many versions of as many browsers as possible, including Mozilla and Opera. Following the latest Web standards will prevent many problems. You can test a page for compliance by going to http://validator.w3.org/check/referer when your page is on the screen. If you use Cascading Style Sheets (CSS), you can validate your pages against the CSS standard at http://jigsaw.w3.org/css-validator/check/referer.

Some of your most difficult-to-solve browser incompatibility problems will stem from noncompliant code on vendors' sites. The library, serving as the gateway, has no direct control over problems that originate on an external server, but as the paying customer the library can work with the vendor on behalf of users, and any resulting improvements will benefit users everywhere, not just the one who brought the problem to your attention.

Keeping up-to-date:

Web Standards and Validators
http://www.w3.org/

Some e-journals will not display unless the user has enabled JavaScript or cookies. If you explore the vendor's site, you may find some help files that will help you troubleshoot some users' problems.

PLUG-INS/VIEWERS/READERS

As more and more e-journal providers enhance their articles with multimedia and other supplementary content, the library will need to provide support in the form of links to specialized browser plug-ins that users will need in order to view or interact with that content. Some new Web users may also need to install Adobe Acrobat Reader in order to read common PDF articles.

Windows operating systems support some seamless integration of multiple file formats, particularly between the Internet Explorer (IE) browser and files created using Microsoft products. However, some e-journal providers will not have tested the usability of their system with Apple or Linux operating systems. And as publishers compete with each other to provide exciting e-journal features, some will require special plug-ins that are uncommon.

Frustrated users should be able to contact the library for help with accessing supplemental materials. Kichuk (2003) provides a good list of URLs for free downloads of plug-ins and viewers. You will want to strike a balance between making specialized plug-ins easily available and keeping your e-journal pages simple and navigable. On e-journal menu pages, you may want to provide links to the most commonly needed plug-ins, such as Acrobat Reader, and another link to a page with links to more specialized downloads. You should check your download links frequently to be sure they are viable. It is better to link to a page that will present the latest version of the download than to link to a page for a specific version that may become outdated.

Portable Document Format (PDF)

The PDF format is so pervasive and popular among e-journal formats that your users will have no choice but to download and install it on their computers. PDF is not an optimal format for electronic journals, but as long as electronic journals preserve the look of print journals, and as long as users prefer to print articles for reading, PDF will remain popular. It was designed for standard-size paper and not for a computer screen, which has different proportions. Some of your users might report problems reading PDF files:

- If they have a very old version of Acrobat Reader, they may need to upgrade to a newer version to read some electronic journals, but an older computer or an older operating system may not be able to accommodate it. The Adobe site (www.adobe.com) lists the system requirements for each version.

- Files consisting of print facsimiles are large, and these big content chunks can take a long time to load. Users with a low-bandwidth Internet connection might complain about the amount of time it takes for a PDF article to load, and in some cases their system might even time out before they can load an article. In this case, you might want to suggest that they save the files and use Acrobat to open it from their own computers.

- Adobe Acrobat contains its own environment, with its own print, save, and find features. Using the browser print function for a PDF may result in blank pages. This problem is more common for users than you might expect.

Math Characters

Mathematics publishers use a system known as TeX (with many variations) for typesetting mathematical material. PDF versions of math journals will view and print with no problem, but sometimes TeX publications are brought to the Web in such a way that they require special readers. The output format, known as DVI (device independent), requires a helper application that is easily downloaded and installed. IBM developed the Techexplorer reader for this purpose, now available from integre, at www.integretechpub.com/techexplorer/.

Multimedia

Multimedia is used for more than entertainment in electronic journals. Scientific visualization techniques often involve animation, streaming video, sound, and the use of 3D. Sometimes the only clue to the identity of the required plug-in will be the file extension. Figure 8–12, a table compiled by Diane Kichuk of the University of Saskatechewan for an article in *Serials Review* (2003), shows some of the file types for supplemental content in journals licensed by the Canadian National Site License Project and the plug-ins needed to read them.

MANAGING E-JOURNAL SEARCH RESULTS

Some of the most frustrating problems for users come at the end of what may have been a tortuous journey. They may have successfully chosen and narrowed a topic, found the right database to search, entered appropriate terms, and conducted a search cor-

Keeping up-to-date:

Document Viewers recommended by the AMS

www.ams.org/publications/ viewers.html

FIGURE 8–12. Plug-Ins and File Extensions

Plug-in/viewer	Developer	Description	File extension
Acrobat Reader	Adobe	Portable Document Format viewer	.pdf
Chem3D Net Viewer	CambridgeSoft	Basic 3D model viewer	.c3d
ChemDraw Net Viewer	CambridgeSoft	Basic chemical structure viewer	.cdx, .chm
Chime	MDL Information Systems	Chemical structure interactive visualization plug-in; view, for example, 3D rotatable molecules, IR spectra, and crystallographic models	.csml, .csm, .xyz, .mol, .pdb, .jdx. .dx
COSMO Player	COSMO Software	View and manipulate 3D objects and worlds—virtual reality files (Virtual Reality Modeling Language [VRML])—using keyboard and mouse	.wrl, .wrz
Cortona	Parallel Graphics	View and manipulate 3D objects and worlds (VRML files)	.wrl, .wrz
DVIscope	Personal TeX, Inc.	View DVI (Device Independent) files	.dvi, dvz
Excel	Microsoft	Spreadsheet software (commercial)	.xls
Flash	Macromedia	Interactive streaming video, animation, audio, vector graphics, and bitmap graphics	.spl, .swf
GhostScript/GSview	Aladdin	PostScript interpreter and viewer	.ps
QuickTime	Apple Computers	Multimedia viewer for animations, music, MIDI, audio, video, and VR panoramas and objects	.aif, .aiff, .au, .qt, .mpeg, .wav, .midi, .tif, .tiff, .bmp, .ptng, .png, .avi, .fli, .flc, .mov
Gzip		Compression software	.gz, .tar
Internet Explorer	Microsoft	Web browser; enables viewing text files, Web pages, and image files	.cif, .gif, .jpg, jpeg, .html, .xml
ISIS/Draw	MDL Information Systems	Drawing package	.mol, .rxn, .tgf
Media Player	Microsoft	Multimedia player	.aiff, .asf, .au, .avi, .midi, .mp3, .mpeg, .mpg, .rmi, .vod, .wav, .wma
Netscape Navigator	Netscape	Web browser; enables viewing text files, Web pages, and image files	.gif, .jpg, .jpeg, .html, .xml
RasMol	Roger A. Sayle	Molecular structure viewer	.mol, .pdb, .xyz
RealOne Player/ RealPlayer	Real Networks	Streaming audio and video player	.mpg, .ram, .rm, .rpm
Shockwave Player	Macromedia	Multimedia and 3D player	.dir, .dxr, .dcr
Techexplorer	IBM	TeX, LaTeX, and MathML document and multimedia interactive browser	.tex, .gif, .jpeg, .wav, .avi
WebLab Viewer		Lite version of 3D molecular structure viewer and creator with analytical functionality	.gif, .jpg, .jpeg, .html, .xml
Winzip Inc.	Winzip Computing, Inc.	Compression file or file archives utility	.zip (PC), .gz
Word	Microsoft	Word processing software (commercial); view text, tables, and data files	.doc, .rtf, .txt
WordPerfect	Corel Corporation	Word processing software (commercial); view text, tables, and data files	.wpd, .txt
ZipIt	ZipIt	Compression file or file archives utility	.zip (Mac)

rectly so that they have found results that will be suitable for their project. Or they have tracked down an elusive citation or an article that has exactly the right piece of information. And then . . . it can't be captured. It is on the screen, but it doesn't print. Or it looks as though it is possible to e-mail it, but the process doesn't work. And it can't be downloaded to a disk. Or the user wants to use a long quotation from an article but is unable to copy it and paste it into a document. By helping to solve these problems you can be a hero. Some of the problems (and solutions) are specific to Adobe Acrobat Reader. You may want to keep the user's guide handy, or at least the FAQ contained within. It can be obtained on the Adobe site, www.adobe.com. Adobe also maintains a support page for Reader that deals with "top issues," troubleshooting problems that are specific to browsers and operating systems.

Printing

Studies shows that users generally print out articles to read them. To "take possession" of an article for his or her own later use, a user will generally want something tangible, although some researchers file electronic articles on their computers or maintain their own bibliographic database for articles of interest.

Printing e-journal articles can be more problematic than photocopying from a print journal:

- Hyperlinked articles in HTML format may be too fragmented for easy printing—graphics may be linked or separate files, or long articles might be presented in separate parts.
- Some HTML articles that are readable on the screen are not formatted correctly for printing, and part of each line might be missing from the printed version.
- A browser's print function may not work well (or in some cases at all) with PDF articles.

Be sure that all public services and technical support staff are trained to help with these problems, and consider providing an online FAQ for printing questions.

The most common solution for PDF-printing problems is to use the Print function within Acrobat Reader instead of the browser's print function. But since PDF files are large, and the Acrobat Reader Print function may not be compatible with certain equipment, it may be necessary to do some troubleshooting. The Acrobat Reader troubleshooting page suggests that you try the following, among other things:

- Try to print another type of file, such as a .txt or .doc file to be sure the printer is working.
- Try to print another PDF file; if that works, the target file may be damaged.
- Restart the printer after turning it off for at least 15 seconds.
- Exit from other applications to optimize memory.
- Print from another computer and/or another printer, if possible.
- Print the file as an image (though it will print more slowly).
- Save the file and print it from the local computer.
- Download the file again.
- Print the document in batches.
- Re-set the Acrobat Reader default printing settings.

For PostScript printing problems, you may want to refer your users to more advanced technical support or use the Adobe Knowledgebase Support pages at www.adobe.com.

Macintosh computers need to have the OS X v10.2.2 or later to print using Adobe Acrobat Reader 6.0. In addition to the suggestions listed above, Mac users who are having trouble printing PDF files can try reducing the monitor resolution to 800   600 (Mac OS 9.x only).

Downloading

The word "download" can cause confusion because sometimes it is used to mean bringing the article to the screen (downloading it from its server), and other times it means to save it locally, on a hard drive or a portable device, from the screen, as it were. If a user claims to be having trouble downloading an article, you will need to determine whether the article appears on the user's screen or not. If not, the user could have one of several problems, needing for example:

- A newer version of Acrobat Reader
- An earlier version of Acrobat Reader (if the system doesn't meet the requirements for the newer version)
- To refresh the screen
- To change a setting to accept cookies
- For the ActiveX plug-in to be in the correct location
- To restart the computer
- A different browser

For Windows users, Acrobat and Adobe Reader are automatically configured to open files within the browser window, but if there are problems, the user may want to change the settings in the browser to open PDF files in a separate window. Macintosh users will have to configure IE or Netscape Navigator to use Reader as a helper application.

Saving a PDF file to a disk is straightforward. For **Internet Explorer** (IE) and **AOL** on **Windows**:

1. Right-click the link to a PDF file, and then choose Save Target As from the pop-up menu.
2. In the Save As dialog box, select a location on your hard drive, and then click Save.

For **IE** on **Macintosh**:

1. Control-click the link to a PDF file, and choose Download Link To Disk from the context menu.
2. In the Save As dialog box, specify a location on the hard disk, and then click Save.

System freezes that prevent PDF articles from displaying or printing require more complex troubleshooting—see the Support Knowledgebase at www.adobe.com.

E-Mailing

E-mailing an article from a database or electronic journal package can be quite convenient for someone who wants to print it at another site or save it for later use. However, not every database allows the user to e-mail articles. This is a special feature that is available only with certain databases. And not every computer will allow it, either—a browser needs to be configured with an e-mail address from which the article will be sent. Each type of browser has its own ways of doing this, so check browser help files.

Copy/Paste

Some instructors would rather not have their students copy and paste anything from the Web into their own papers; nevertheless, there are ethical and legitimate uses for the copy and paste functions, which are exceedingly popular.

Users generally do not have problems copying and pasting text from an HTML article, but frequently run into problems with

FIGURE 8–13. Adobe Toolbar

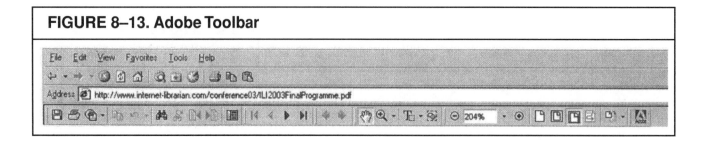

PDF files. They may not know about the Acrobat-specific text-selection and image-selection tools (Figure 8–13) or how to use the column-select tool available in the later versions of Acrobat Reader. However, even when they choose the correct tool, they may be blocked from using it by settings the author has established. When copying is restricted, the tools will be grayed out. Sometimes the tool will not be grayed, even though text cannot be captured because of the settings used during scanning.

If you include tips or explanations about copying/pasting in your help pages or FAQ, you have an opportunity to link to another page that could explain what is plagiarism and what is not, how to give credit to authors being quoted, and generally how to copy and paste responsibly and ethically.

MOBILE USERS

Users of your electronic journals no longer need to be tied to a computer on a wired network. Wireless computing and online handheld devices give you a seemingly infinite number of locations where users could need help. Despite their freedom from wires, mobile users have a few more technical obstacles in connecting to electronic library resources.

Wireless Computing

The increasing use of wireless networks in libraries and other organizations provides new possibilities and new complications for users wanting to access electronic journals. Your users will need to have mobile networking cards (and drivers for the cards) that are compatible with the wireless networks they are using to access your e-journals and some way to log in to the network. These are not problems you will be expected to solve unless you are providing the wireless network (see below). On a wireless campus, your users should be able to count on getting help from library staff when connecting to the network to use the library's electronic journals, especially if the library is a wireless "hot spot."

Keeping up-to-date:

The Wireless Librarian

http://people.morrisville.edu/ %7Edrewwe/wireless/ index.htm

It would be your responsibility to acquire the necessary knowledge from the IT professionals on campus.

PDAs and PocketPCs

PubMed on handheld, wireless devices
(abstracts of articles in medical journals)

www.nlm.nih.gov/pubs/ techbull /ja03 _pda.html

Medical professionals who have become accustomed to having access to a deep store of reference information through their personal digital assistants (PDAs) with wireless capabilities may ask for help reading e-journals on their teeny-tiny screens. Some publishers are beginning to offer selected full text of their e-journals in PDA-viewable formats, and we can expect this technology to change rapidly. Several Highwire Press journals are compatible with PDAs, for example, with tables of contents, abstracts, and selected full text available, but to use them requires free registration and specialized software that can be downloaded at the Highwire site.

Despite their small screens, PDAs are popular for several reasons, including their portability and their immediacy. There is no waiting for them to power up. The need to help users with PDA-oriented problems will increase, so public services staff should become familiar with this tool. Adobe has a version of Acrobat Reader for the Palm Operating System, but before users can read e-journals with their handheld devices, they need client software that is compatible with a wireless LAN. You may need to work with your computing support colleagues initially to help PDA users with their access problems. Pocket PCs, Tablet PCs, and other variations of very small, lightweight, and versatile handheld computing devices will continue to fill in the gaps between laptop computers and PDAs for mobile access to electronic information.

HELPING USERS INSIDE THE LIBRARY

Electronic journals and other Web-based electronic resources change the landscape of in-house user services considerably, though each library experiences its own variations of the changes brought about by the Web. Some libraries are noticeably less visited, and others are still very busy serving users who are using the library in ways different from the ways they did in the past. Most libraries have experienced a decrease in the number of reference questions, and some libraries are receiving an increased number of reference queries by phone. Libraries with public-access computers near the reference desk generally have a demand for assisting users with finding articles in electronic journals. As

---

FIGURE 8–14. A Wireless Glossary

A Wireless Glossary

Access Point (AP) — Wireless LAN transmitter/receiver that acts as a connection between wireless clients and wired networks.

Bluetooth — A short-range wireless specification that allows for radio connections between devices within a 30-foot range of each other.

Client — Wireless device that accesses the WLAN. Can be a computer, PDA, or other handheld device with a wireless connection.

HiperLAN — High-performance radio local area network. Developed by the European Telecommunications Standards Institute, set of WLAN communication standards used chiefly in European countries.

Network Interface Card (NIC) — hardware installed in computing device that enables it to communicate on a network.

PC Card — A removable, credit-card-sized memory or I/O [input/output] device used primarily in PCs, portable computers, PDAs, and laptops. PC Card peripherals include Wi-Fi cards, memory cards, modems, NICs, hard drives, etc.

Wi-Fi (Wireless Fidelity) — High-rate transmission that meets the **IEEE Standard 802.11** for interoperability.

Wireless Application Protocol (WAP) — Set of protocols that lets users of mobile phones and other digital wireless devices access Internet content, check voice mail and e-mail, receive text of faxes, and conduct transactions.

Wireless Local Area Network (WLAN, Wireless LAN) — Uses radio-frequency technology to transmit network messages through the air for relatively short distances, like across an office building or college campus.

Wireless Markup Language (WML) — Similar to HTML, WML is based on XML and will run with its own version of JavaScript. Wireless application developers use WML to convert content for wireless devices.

11a — refers to IEEE Wi-Fi Standard **802.11a** (in the 5 GHz spectrum, operating at a maximum speed of 54 Mbps transfer rate); higher-speed "11a-only" products won't work with 11b or 11g networks. There is less interference in the 11a band.

11b — refers to IEEE Wi-Fi Standard **802.11b** (in the 2.4 GHz spectrum, operating at a maximum speed of 11 Mbps).

11g — refers to IEEE Wi-Fi Standard **802.11g** (in the 2.4 GHz spectrum, operating at a maximum speed of 54 Mbps). Newer standard; 11g products are all back-compatible with 11b.

Adapted from The Wireless Librarian Glosssary
http://people.morrisville.edu/~drewwe/wireless/glossary.htm

the number of electronic journals in a library grows, photocopying drops off sharply. Depending on the proportion of in-house to remote users of your e-journals, the amount of printing may increase sharply.

REFERENCE QUESTIONS

Some reference librarians have noted that questions coming to the reference desk are more complex than in the past because of the wide availability of information on the Web. People with access to the Web do not need the library for factual answers to straightforward questions, or even for background information on most subjects. It is when they are unsuccessful in their self-service quests that they tend to turn to the information professionals at their library. This gives you a perfect opportunity to introduce the library's electronic journals as a deep pool of content that is largely unavailable on the open Web. With a reduced number of reference transactions, you should have the time to give in-depth assistance to individuals who come to you.

NEW SKILLS FOR PUBLIC SERVICES STAFF

Only a few short years ago, salesmanship was not thought to be an essential qualification for librarians. But in the electronic information environment, approachability is no longer enough for public services staff—they will need to be effective in marketing the library's wares. "Consider adding outreach and public relation duties to librarians' job descriptions" and "consider having librarians make one-on-one contact with and offer assistance to students in not just reference areas but also in other areas of the library (book stacks, computer labs, cybercafé)" suggest Harley, Dreger, and Knobloch (2001).

A librarian's proactive offer of assistance will only be appreciated and meaningful if it includes troubleshooting and aids in overcoming technological obstacles. Public services staff will need to keep up with the rapid changes in information technology to be able to give specialized on-site help at the point of need.

OPTIMIZING LIBRARY COMPUTERS FOR E-JOURNALS

The digital-divide studies show that many households do not have computers or access to the Internet and that libraries provide a popular gateway to the Internet. Even those who do have their own connectivity will sometimes use the computers in the library. For example:

- Students who stay on campus between classes might work on a research paper.

- Faculty and other researchers may want to use online journals in conjunction with their use of print journals in the library.
- Some academic libraries have a mission to serve their larger unaffiliated community by providing walk-in access to licensed electronic resources that would be unavailable off-site.

Make it as easy as possible for all of your on-site users to use your e-journals. If at all possible, consider keeping part of the library open 24 hours.

Configuration of Library Computers

Setting up an optimal computing environment in the library is beyond the scope of this book, but you should consult one of the several excellent books on the subject. To optimize public access computers for electronic journal users, you may want to consider the following:

- Install the latest versions of the most commonly used browser plug-ins and other client software required for viewing e-journal articles or supplemental material.
- Monitor and respond to the popularity of browsers; the majority of your users will be most comfortable using Internet Explorer on library computers, since it is by far the most popular browser.
- Provide a means for saving large files (3.5 inch floppy disks will not hold some PDF articles); consider CD-writers, DVD-writers, zip drives, or front-of-computer USB ports for storage devices (or a range of these options), and sell the storage media on-site.
- Save your users' time by offering one-stop shopping on library computers; include productivity software, such as Microsoft Office applications
- Foster a hospitable environment by minimizing restrictions on Internet use in the library.
- Protect the library from liability for infringement of license terms by requiring a log-in process for library computers.
- Secure your settings, shield your hard drive, and protect users' privacy by configuring computers to restore default settings (the computer's image) after each use, deleting modifications to the image and other results of users' actions.

- Have computers reboot after a designated period of inactivity.

Printing

In addition to the common printing difficulties mentioned above, public services staff have found that electronic journals present new challenges for printing services in the library. Libraries that for years provided free printing from public-access computers find they can no longer afford the cost of paper and ink once their users have access to electronic journals. But to add charging capabilities to library printers requires extra staffing or a capital investment for card readers and queuing software. E-journal users will have one more procedure to deal with in retrieving and paying for articles they print in the library, so you will want to make your system as simple and reliable as possible. Don't let your printers run out of paper!

Some libraries have dealt with the increasing cost and complexity of supporting printing by eliminating printers altogether. Staff in the Libraries of the University of Missouri, St. Louis, refer users to campus computer labs for printing, and encourage them to download articles onto their own diskettes (which the library sells to those who need them). Other libraries have acquired card readers and commercial printer-management software, for example:

- GoPrint (www.goprint.com)
- Pharos Uniprint (www.pharos.com/products/uniprint.asp)
- Print Queue Manager (www.whitehatinc.com/w2ktools/printqueue/)
- Qview Pro (www.sdesign.com/)
- LPT:One (www.envisionware.com)
- Printer Accounting Server (www.metrics.com)
- Pcounter (www.pcounter.com)
- OCS (www.vasinc.com)

Wireless Laptop Checkout

If space for more computers is a problem in your library, or even if it isn't, you might want to purchase a fleet of circulating laptop computers for in-library use. This is an increasingly popular library service that allows users to sit where they are most comfortable, and should increase the use of your electronic journals. There are some challenges in checking out laptops, however:

- Users will be farther from service points; you may want

staff to do more roving throughout the library to make themselves available to help.

- If a wireless network is not available throughout the library building, you will need to convey that information through signage or other types of communication.
- Users will need to save their work on their own storage devices or transfer it to another computer through e-mail or ftp, and they may need help with that process.

Checking out laptops may seem like a radical departure from traditional library services, but the public relations aspect is well worth the effort of solving some of the problems it might cause. Furthermore, through configuration of the laptops you can promote the library's Web site and electronic resources.

SERVING USERS WITH DISABILITIES

Depending on how they are presented, electronic resources can greatly improve or greatly complicate the lives of users with disabilities. Computers have enabled great strides in assistive technology, and the Web has opened the world to many who are homebound or institutionalized with disabilities. An estimated 20% of Americans, including 6–8% of college freshmen, have a disability as defined by the Americans with Disabilities Act of 1990. Fortunately, there are many excellent and free resources for librarians to consult in serving these users. For example you might want to look at the readings by Mates, Burgstahler, and Minow at the end of this chapter.

INSIDE THE LIBRARY

A barrier-free library will have eliminated obstacles that might make it difficult for users with all types of disabilities to use library resources. In terms of electronic journals, you will want to have computers that can be used by people with limited mobility, visual disabilities and learning disabilities, and service desks that are wheelchair accessible.

For users with disabilities to have equal access to electronic journals inside your library, you will need to provide screen readers and other assistive devices. Sheryl Burgstahler (2004a, 2004b) of Project DO-IT (Disabilities, Opportunities, Internetworking, and Technology) recommends the following assistive equipment

Keeping up-to-date:

The Alliance for Technology Access

www.ataccess.org/

Web Accessibility Survey Site

http://library.uwsp.edu/ aschmetz/Accessible/ websurveys.htm

EASI—Equal Access to Software and Information

www.rit.edu/~easi/index.htm

for libraries and computer labs to be equipped minimally to serve users with disabilities:

- An adjustable table for each type of workstation
- A large monitor
- Large-print key labels
- A speech output system
- Wrist rests and forearm rests
- Trackballs
- Software to enlarge screen images

Ideally, the library will also supply at least some of the following equipment:

- Braille-printer and Braille-translation software
- Word-prediction software
- Hearing protectors
- Keyboard guards to assist those who have limited fine-motor skills
- Alternative keyboards, mini-keyboards, or extended keyboards for users with mobility impairments
- Software to modify keyboard response, such as sticky keys, repeat rate, and keystroke delay
- One-handed keyboards or "keyboard-layout" software

Adaptive technology can be expensive, so make your choices carefully. Talk to users with disabilities about their preferences and their experience with technology in other environments. Read reviews and studies in library publications and in other sources.

WEB ACCESSIBILITY

As a gateway, your library has only partial control over whether electronic journals are accessible to visually impaired users. The library can follow accessible-design guidelines for its own Web site, but if e-journal providers do not follow guidelines for accessibility, then users with disabilities will not be able to use your electronic journals without your intervention. If your library is committed to providing equal access for all of your users to all of your materials, including materials that are not accessible with adaptive technologies, you will need to develop services that will further process those parts of the electronic collection to make them accessible or provide individualized research assistance with electronic resources.

Accessibility Standards for Library Sites

Although libraries are becoming increasingly aware of the importance of designing their Web pages for accessibility, studies show that the majority of library sites do not meet minimal standards (see issues 2 and 4 of *Library Hi Tech*, vol. 20, 2002). You can check your pages for accessibility using the Bobby software that was developed by the Center for Applied Special Technology, available at bobby.watchfire.com/bobby/.

The Content Accessibility Guidelines developed by the World Wide Web Consortium (W3C) are available at www.w3.org/tr/wai-webcontent/. To help you improve the accessibility of your library's site, the Trace Center has compiled a resource center at www.trace.wisc.edu/world/web/.

Product Compliance

Database vendors and publishers comply with accessibility guidelines to varying degrees. To remain competitive, they develop features that are in demand, and if the marketplace demands products that can be used with adaptive software, then their products will include that feature. However, a concern for users with disabilities typically does not enter into the process of selecting electronic journals; other considerations weigh more heavily. Even if a library's collection policy (or governing regulations) require that products meet accessibility guidelines, it is sometimes difficult to determine whether they comply. There are a few things you can do to help improve vendors' efforts in making their e-journal accessible to all of your users:

- Become familiar with the W3C Web Access Initiative (WAI) design guidelines.
- Make product accessibility an issue among your colleagues.
- Test products before purchase using your library's assistive technology.
- Talk to e-journal providers at conferences and during sales visits to your library about the importance of product accessibility for all users.
- Include accessibility requirements in RFPs for statewide and large consortial contracts for full-text databases.

REFERENCES

Ashcroft, Linda. 2002. "Issues in Developing, Managing and Marketing Electronic Journals Collections." *Collection Building* 21, no. 4: 147–154.

Astroff, Roberta J. 2001. "Searching for the Library: University Home Page Design and Missing Links." *Information Technology and Libraries* 20, no. 2 (June): 93–99. Retrieved Sept. 17, 2004, from www.ala.org/ala/lita/litapublications/ital/2002astroff.htm.

Burgstahler, Sheryl. 2004a. "Equal Access: Computer Labs." Project DO-IT. Retrieved Sept. 17, 2004, from www.washington.edu/doit/Brochures/Technology/comp.access.html.

———. 2004b. "Equal Access: Libraries." Project DO-IT. Retrieved Sept. 17, 2004, from http://www.washington.edu/doit/Brochures/Technology/libsrv.html.

Curtis, Donnelyn, ed. 2002. *Attracting, Educating, and Serving Remote Users through the Web: A How-To-Do-It Manual for Librarians.* New York: Neal-Schuman.

Emery, Jill. 2003. "Teaching Electronic Journals: Finding, Using, and Citing Them." *The Serials Librarian* 44, no. 3/4: 189–194.

Fichter, Darlene. 2003. "Why and How to Use Blogs to Promote Your Library's Services." *Marketing Library Services* 17, no. 6 (November/December): 1–4. Retrieved Sept. 21, 2004, www.infotoday.com/mls/nov03/fichter.shtml.

Friedlander, Amy. 2002. *Dimensions and Use of the Scholarly Information Environment: Introduction to a Data Set Assembled by the Digital Library Federation and Outsell, Inc.* Publication 110. Washington, DC: Council on Library and Information Resources. Retrieved Sept. 17, 2004, from http://www.clir.org/pubs/abstract/pub110abst.html.

Fu, Li. 2002. "Information Technology Outreach in the UIC Library." *Technical Services Quarterly* 20, no. 2: 33–39.

Harley, Bruce, Megan Dreger, and Patricia Knobloch. 2001. "The Postmodern Condition: Students, the Web, and Academic Library Services." *Reference Services Review* 29 no. 1: 23–32.

Kichuk, Diana. 2003. "Electronic Journal Supplementary Content, Browser Plug-ins, and the Transformation of Reading." *Serials Review* 29, no. 2: 103–116.

Outsell. 2003. *The Changing Roles of Content Deployment Functions: Academic Information Professionals.* Burlingame, CA: Outsell.

MORE INFORMATION SOURCES

Boerner, Gerald L. 2002. "The Brave New World of Wireless Technologies: A Primer for Educators". *Syllabus Magazine* (October): 19–20, 22, 30. www.syllabus.com/article.asp?id=6771.

Bowen, Jennifer, Judi Briden, Vicki Burns, David Lindahl, Brenda Reeb, Melinda Stowe, and Stanley Wilder. 2004. "Serial Failure." *The Charleston Advisor 5*, no. 3: 48–50. http://www.charlestonco.com/features.cfm?id=146&type=ed.

Gray, Edward, and Anne Langley. 2002. "Public Services and Electronic Resources: Perspectives from the Science and Engineering Libraries at Duke University." *Issues in Science and Technology Librarianship* 35 (Summer). Retrieved Sept. 17, 2004, from www.istl.org/02-summer/article2.html.

Horton, Sarah. 2001. "Practical Accessibility: Core Concepts." Web Teaching at Dartmouth College. Retrieved Sept. 17, 2004, from www.dartmouth.edu/~webteach/articles/access.html.

Keating, John J. III, and Arthur W. Hafner. 2002. "Perspectives on . . . Supporting Individual Library Patrons with Information Technologies: Emerging One-to-One Library Services on the College or University Campus." *Journal of Academic Librarianship* 28, no. 6: 426–429.

Mates, Barbara T. 2000. *Adaptive Technology for the Internet: Making Electronic Resources Accessible to All.* The Online Version. Chicago: American Library Association. Retrieved Sept. 17, 2004, from www.ala.org/ala/productsandpublications/books/editions/adaptivetechnology.htm.

———. 2001. "Accessibility Guidelines for Electronic Resources." *Library Technology Reports* 37, no. 4 (July/August) [entire issue].

———. 2004. "Computer Technologies to Aid Special Audiences." *Library Technology Reports* 40, no. 3 (May/June) [entire issue].

Minow, Mary. 1999. "Does Your Library's Web Page Violate the Americans with Disabilities Act?" *California Libraries 9*, no. 4 (April): 8–9. Retrieved Sept. 17, 2004, from www.librarylaw.com/ADAWebpage.html.

9 ANALYZING ELECTRONIC JOURNAL USAGE AND EVALUATING SERVICES

CHAPTER OVERVIEW

- Why Gather Statistics?
- Defining Management Information Needs
- Acquiring Usage Data
- Standards and Guidelines
- Processing and Analyzing Usage Data
- Describing, Distilling, and Presenting Data

Libraries, especially those that are publicly funded, are increasingly called upon to justify their expenditures and priorities. After implementing major changes in library services, it is especially important to be able to measure the results of the changes. One of the more anticipated capabilities of electronic journals was the accurate measurement of usage. But like other capabilities of e-journals, it has been only partially realized. Nonetheless, the outlook is improving. Standards for reporting usage data have been developed and are being implemented, and a growing number of vendors are making statistics available in a usable form. Even so, to collect and analyze data and to communicate the results is challenging and time consuming. This chapter will help your library develop a reasonable and manageable approach to tracking the use of your electronic journals within the larger context of other services you provide. Once you have analyzed the use of your electronic journals, you can apply the knowledge to the improvement of your library's collections and services.

"Usage statistics represent a huge opportunity to transform the profession."

—Thomas A. Peters (2002)

WHY GATHER STATISTICS?

Dealing with usage statistics is undoubtedly the least-practiced aspect of managing electronic journals in libraries, because it tends to be treated as optional. Given the challenges of acquiring e-journals and making them accessible to users, analyzing their use falls to the bottom of the "to do" list in most libraries. Even when we realize the value of usage statistics, in the early stages of the transition to electronic journals, more urgent tasks will take precedence. But eventually the new work flow settles into place, e-journal management becomes routine, and there will be time to stand back and appraise and adjust (and admire) your work. There are many functions that analyzing usage of electronic journals can help you with:

- Making the best use of your budget
- Documenting the return on your investments
- Tracking change
- Accountability to external stakeholders/parent bodies
- Making day-to-day operational decisions (what to cancel, what to buy less or more of, what to promote)
- Required internal reporting (annual reports, etc.)
- Strategic planning
- Standard external reporting for aggregation of data
- Comparison with other libraries (ARL, peers, etc.)
- Assessment of quality

There are some things that statistics can't tell you—such as whether your users were successful and satisfied with their use of e-journals. Value to users must be determined in other ways.

COSTS AND BENEFITS: RETURN ON INVESTMENT

The most obvious reason to track and measure usage of any library resource is to assess whether its cost is justified. Knowing patterns of use can help guide future collection development decisions, ensure more benefit from expenditures from the materials budget, and, in the case of journals, help with individual renewal decisions.

DOCUMENTING CHANGES

Measurement of library services has long been considered important both within the profession and within the institutions housing libraries. Established units of measurement that continue to be used by libraries generally show fewer people coming to libraries, fewer books circulated, and fewer reference transactions. Traditional measures would indicate libraries in decline (and less deserving of financial support) unless we can show corresponding increases in other areas of activity, using other measures. Documenting the use of library Web pages, e-mail reference and chat activity, use of databases and use of articles from e-journals can round out the picture of library use, providing a much more accurate assessment of the value of library services.

Despite the shift in library activities in recent years, collecting statistics still focuses on print publications and the physical library (circulation, number of books added, gate count). To demonstrate the changes that have taken place in library operations and expenditures requires initiative on the part of the library staff so that they collect, analyze, and present the statistics that actually document the changes.

BENCHMARKING

"**Benchmark**: a measurement or standard that serves as a point of reference by which process performance is measured."

(Government Accountability Office [GAO])

In the process of better serving your remote users and shifting your journal collection from print-based to electronic format, it is useful to be able to measure your progress, in terms of where you started and the distance from your goals, and in terms of your peer libraries and "next-level" libraries. For example, Los Alamos National Laboratories (LANL) carried out a benchmarking study of the number of top-cited journals made available electronically to LANL users in 2002 compared with other research libraries and Department of Energy libraries (Varjabedian, 2003). Results of studies of electronic journal use and their impact can serve as benchmarks for later studies.

Benchmarking can help identify "best practices" in libraries in terms of reallocating resources and optimizing the transition from one format to another.

DEFINING MANAGEMENT INFORMATION NEEDS

Data about your electronic journals tells a story, but only after it is analyzed. It could actually tell several different stories, depending on the way it is analyzed, so it will help to know in advance the stories that need to be told. Different groups in your library will want different particulars.

INFORMING ADMINISTRATION

Consider first what your administrators will want to know about your electronic journals, and what they will want to be able to tell others. Summary information about your collection, reported periodically, may be adequate.

Collection Assessment

Typically, acquisitions staff would be expected to be able to supply data to answer the following questions:

- How many electronic journals are available to your users?
- How has the number of e-journals increased over a designated period of time?
- How does the growth of your electronic journal collection impact the library's budget?
- How many new journals are available to your users as a result of e-journal packages and full-text databases?
- How much duplication of content is there between your print and electronic journals?
- How many print subscriptions have been dropped in favor of electronic access?

However, it is not as easy at it might seem to answer questions about the number of e-journals in your collection and how much you are paying for them.

Having a clear and consistent definition of e-journals is very important for statistical reports. Do you want to count journals in aggregator databases in the same way that you count e-journals that are substituted for expensive print subscriptions? You will not want to count the same journal three times if it is available in three aggregator databases, though it is much easier to add together the total number of journals in each database than it is to de-dupe your list for statistical purposes.

Degener and Waite (2000, p. 8) suggest coding records for easy calculation of the number of journals in several categories:

- Free with print
- Extra cost above the print rate
- Free online journal
- Online version only (paid)
- Partial payment for electronic access (joint purchase)
- Electronic access via another library's efforts

Being able to report the amount of money that is spent on electronic journals is a difficult challenge. Coding order records can help, but even if you do, you will encounter some messiness, since even if individual serials records are coded as print or electronic, a print journal that includes free online access might be replaced with the online-only version of the journal after that option becomes available. Maintaining records in an ILS or e-journal database to reflect changes in a journal's pricing model for statistical reporting purposes is unrealistic in many libraries. The interplay between print and electronic subscriptions can be intricate and inextricably intertwined.

As is the case with other new and onerous tasks for libraries involving information technology, entrepreneurial intermediaries have developed services to assist you with tracking your electronic collections. Serials Solutions, for example, in addition to sending you up-to-date lists of journals in your aggregator databases, provides a service called "Overlap Analysis," which will tell you for each full-text database how many of the journals are unique and how many of them are found in your other databases (www.serialssolutions.com/overlap.asp). You can generate statistical reports based on your library's collection. Most electronic journal management services offer a similar kind of service, either incorporated in other services or as an add-on module.

The Impact of E-Journals

Usage statistics can provide granular or summary data. Although administrators will usually want general information about the impact of electronic journals, you may need to do some detailed analysis and collect data from other areas in the library in order to compile it. And you may need to work with granular data to obtain summary information. All of the following questions can be answered using usage statistics from your vendors and local data:

- How much use is your e-journal collection getting?
- Is there a significant difference in the amount of use of (1) the e-journals that were previously selected as print subscriptions and (2) e-journals that are newly available as part of online packages and full-text databases?
- How many users are browsing tables of contents and how many are downloading (or viewing) articles?
- How has the use of e-journals affected the use of your print journals?
- How has the expansion of your journal collection through e-journal acquisitions affected borrowing through interlibrary loan or the use of your document delivery service?
- What is the proportion of on-site and remote use of your e-journals?
- How much time can users save by using electronic journals rather than print journals?

The answers to these questions will be interesting, but the amount of work to obtain them can be daunting. Make sure in advance that the plans for using your analyses will justify your efforts, set realistic goals, and reserve your best efforts for compiling the statistics that will help with decision making.

Required Reporting

Few library administrators can escape mandates to report statistics to a government agency or library organization. In some cases, the reporting of "e-metrics," or the use of electronic resources is still optional, or at least not enforced, with the understanding that data is difficult to collect and results may not be reliable or comparable across institutions. Various groups are working to remedy that situation with standard definitions and parameters for reports from vendors and reports from libraries. See the "Standards and Guidelines" section below.

Any library that reports statistics about its collection will be wise to include information about the growth of electronic journal collections. The Association of Research Libraries (ARL) has been collecting this information from research libraries for its Supplementary Statistics, but gradually, questions about electronic resources are being moved to the ARL Annual Surveys. Public libraries are encouraged to record the following data elements alongside more traditional statistics (Boss, 2003):

- Expenditures for electronic products and services
- Value of electronic products and services available as the result of consortia or state-agency purchases, but not reflected in the library budget
- Number of accesses to electronic products and services
- Number of page views of electronic products and services
- Number of accesses through the gateway or portal to all external resources

COLLECTION MANAGEMENT AND ACCESS

Those responsible for selecting, renewing, and providing access to electronic journals will want detailed information about how they are being used and about the information-seeking behaviors of e-journal users. Careful analysis can indicate research trends, reveal subject areas that may need attention, and point out problems users might be having with navigation of electronic journals. Your answers to the following questions can help you provide better services and resources to your users:

- Which e-journals are used most heavily?

- Are some e-journals consistently not being used? Are there any patterns?
- If the library has a link resolver, is it being used?
- Are users being turned away from databases or journals that are licensed for a limited number of simultaneous users?
- Are subject lists of e-journals being used?
- Are alphabetical lists being used?
- Do your users prefer HTML or PDF formats when they have a choice?
- Which member libraries in your consortium are benefiting most from a consortial license for a package of e-journals? Should costs be shared differently?
- What kinds of terms are being entered into the e-journal search form?
- Are there any signs of a breach of a license agreement?

During license renewals, usage statistics are tools to help you negotiate prices and adjust the number of simultaneous users. The only way you will know whether a package deal is cost effective is to determine whether the "bonus" journals are, in fact, being used. Your analysis might prove that the à la carte option is better for your library.

PUBLICITY AND OUTREACH

Usage statistics can identify which disciplines are using your library's electronic journals and which are not, giving you an opportunity to target the promotion of your electronic resources to those who may be unaware of them. You may discover that some segments of your user community have technical obstacles, such as firewalls or the lack of desktop support, that might cause their use of e-journals to be disproportionately low. Armed with data, you can tackle large and small problems of your users.

ACQUIRING USAGE DATA

Basically, usage data comes from three main sources. Content providers can supply information about your institution's use of their content, your library can collect it from your own Web pages, or intermediaries can collect it for you as part of the services they provide. Each source has its strengths and its weaknesses.

Much to the disappointment of many librarians, problems with data collection and analysis frequently outweigh the promise that online resources will automatically generate accurate and usable usage data. However, librarians have found ways to use partial and imperfect data to answer some of the above questions, and the general situation is improving as standards are developed and implemented.

PUBLISHERS AND DATABASE VENDORS

In the rush to make their content available online, to develop user interfaces, and to solve access problems, many e-journal providers neglected in the beginning to develop functional systems for reporting usage. For the first two or three years, they provided what data they could, and for the most part librarians, in their rush to develop delivery systems for electronic resources and solve local access problems, were not overly concerned with the inconsistency in what types of information vendors were providing and the confusing formats of the reports the librarians received.

However, once things had settled down somewhat for publishers, vendors, and libraries, attention was turned to the need for usage measurements. E-journal providers developed a variety of systems for logging and reporting usage data, usually sending spreadsheets in electronic format by e-mail or in print format by mail, or posting reports on an administrative Web page made available to designated library staff. The main advantage of vendor-based data is that e-journal providers can accurately and thoroughly log the details of your users' interactions with their content on their servers.

Librarians did their best to collect and compile various forms of data from their many providers. It became immediately clear that the available usage statistics were "inadequate, inconsistent, and difficult to work with, unreliable" (Watson, 2003), and that standards were lacking. Such shortcomings undermine the validity of library usage analyses. These are some of the problems librarians have run into in working with data from e-journal providers:

- Some vendors do not supply any usage data.
- There is inconsistency among providers concerning what is counted—a lack of agreement on what constitutes a "session" or a "query."
- Some vendors retain usage data on their Web sites for only a limited period of time.
- System crashes can result in data loss.
- A vendor's upgraded system may be incompatible with an older system, resulting in the non-migration of data.

- Server caches designed to avoid repeated downloads (to conserve bandwidth and save time) will intercept and fill requests for pages before they reach the publisher's site—and those downloads won't be counted.
- One search in a segmented database can be overcounted as a search in each segment.
- A single session will be recorded as multiple sessions if users inadvertently close a session before finishing (a common occurrence, since some databases invoke multiple windows and others do not).
- The format of some vendors' reports will not allow for data integration.
- Double clicks can be counted twice in some systems.
- Variations in user behavior can result in overcounting (for example, an article download might be counted multiple times if a multitasking user clicks in and out of it more than once in a session).
- Some vendors supply too much unprocessed data, which are then difficult or impossible to analyze.
- Reporting periods vary—reports might be issued monthly, quarterly, annually, irregularly, or only on demand.
- Usage data that are aggregated on a consortium-wide basis for consortially licensed e-journals may be unavailable for individual participating institutions.
- Metasearching can result in inflated results, especially for "search" counts.
- Some vendors include "zero-hit" searches and others do not.
- A link from a database to an article at another site might be counted at both sites.
- Some Web logs will count each page of a PDF download as a separate document.
- In a full-text database, the citation page might include the entire article; the user may not look at the full text, but it will be counted as such.

Although this long list of problems might discourage those who would hope to be able to compile and compare usage statistics for all of their libraries' e-journals, publishers' statistics should not be considered useless. In preparing for renewal decisions, renegotiating a license, or justifying a large expenditure, it can be extremely valuable to analyze your library's use of an individual publisher's e-journals. For example, the Ontario Council of University Libraries (OCUL) carried out a cost-benefit analysis for *Annual Reviews Online* that calculated the amount of time saved by students and faculty in OCUL institutions by using the online rather than the print versions of *Annual Reviews*. When translated into monetary terms, the savings to institutions through subscribing to this one online resource was estimated to be over CA$500,000 (Scigliano, 2002).

LOCAL DATA COLLECTION

To simplify and standardize the collection of usage data, some libraries have devised methods for tracking the use of their e-journals from their own Web pages. By so doing, they can monitor the use of all their journals, not just those from vendors that provide adequate statistics. However, they can learn only the most basic facts about usage, which is the number of times a particular journal is visited from the library's Web site or catalog. Users who access e-journals from outside the library's Web pages or catalog (for example, through a bookmark) will not be counted.

An e-journal provider can tell you how many times tables of contents are browsed or abstracts or articles are viewed, and how many searches are conducted in their database no matter how the users arrived at their site, and the number of turnaways if limits are in place. Library-generated statistics can document the increase in usage over time, with the understanding that actual use will be even higher. Locally collected Web data can also help you enhance the ways that users find your e-journals.

Redirection

A system can be designed in such a way that if a user finds the journal on a title list, a subject list, the catalog, or a search of the library's site, the link will go to an intermediate page that can keep track of the hits (with the use of Web-log analysis tools). From that page, the users will be directed to the e-journal on the publisher's site, or in an aggregator database, or they might be given a choice of locations. From that point, the library has no way of tracking subsequent use.

Data captured from the redirection of links are useful primarily for learning the comparative popularity of e-journals accessed one way. In addition to the superficiality of the data that collected with this method, there are a few other drawbacks:

- The extra step on the way to full text might be an irritation to users.
- Funneling users through data-capturing pages may slow down the linking process, especially when traffic on the system is heavy.

- Users may get to licensed journals through other means than the library's Web pages and catalog—through bookmarks they have made, through links from a database or another article's references, or through the publisher's gateway or database interface.
- Unauthorized users may click through the intermediate page in an unsuccessful attempt to connect to the journal, but they would be counted as users nevertheless.
- Anyone turned away because of limits on the number of simultaneous users will still be counted as a user.
- The referring page for a journal could be cached on the proxy server of an Internet service provider (ISP), so that after the first use, subsequent access by those who use the proxy server will not be counted.

By logging data from their own pages, libraries can determine the patterns of e-journal use by date, days of the week, and the time of day; what kinds of browsers and ISPs are being used; and the IP addresses of users. Through close analysis, a library can correlate the location of users with the journals being used.

The University of Saskatchewan (Canada) has developed an interactive form for requesting and reporting e-journal statistics collected locally. See it at http://library.usask.ca/ejournals/stats.php.

Access-Management Systems

Depending on how users are authenticated at your library, you might be able to collect statistics at the point of authentication. If your ILS has an authentication component, you may be able to correlate the remote use of licensed resources with patron types. For example, the Innovative Interface Inc. (III) system can generate statistics both for the remote patron types and for the target resources from the Web Access Management (WAM) module that authenticates against the patron database. Most resources in the III WAM table will be publisher sites and databases rather than individual e-journals, but it can be useful to know the proportion of remote users who are undergraduate students, graduate students, faculty, and staff, and the relative popularity of your various publisher sites and databases among remote users.

Reader Logs

A library that is willing to invest a significant amount of effort to analyze the use of e-journals to discern research trends might want to consult an article in *D-Lib Magazine* (Bollen, Luce, Vemulapalli, and Xu, 2003) describing a project at Los Alamos National Laboratories that analyzed "reader logs" for individual researchers, captured with the aid of cookies. The privacy of users was protected through the use of "anonymization" by replacing IP addresses with randomized ID numbers.

The Los Alamos study identified relationships among journals and identified user communities according to journal use, based on downloaded articles. For an individual library or group of researchers, studies such as this can determine local journal impact factors that might be very different from ISI's international impact factors, resulting in very targeted collection development.

Personalization Systems

Requiring registration for a personalized interface or enhanced services can give you demographic profiles of your users that can be correlated with types of use (again, to use this type of data you will want to protect your users' privacy by stripping away information that would identify them). It can be useful to monitor incomplete registrations and to know where users typically stop in the registration process in order to simplify or otherwise improve the process. Knowing the log-in rate for registered users will enable you to justify the time spent maintaining the system— or support a decision to discontinue the system.

Link Resolvers

When usage statistics come from publishers or hosts of electronic journals, we can assume that they capture activity of your users who arrive from all quarters—directly, from library links, or through links from other sources, including external databases. However, if you collect and compile your own "link-out" statistics through your Web site, and if you use a link resolver that generates statistical reports, you can include database-to-journal traffic, whether your link resolver is housed on a local server or on a vendor's site. For example, SFX will produce a report on target resources accessed during a particular time period, as will the Serials Solutions (SS) link resolver on the SS site. In addition to measuring the use of the link resolver, you will be getting accurate information about the use of individual journals by those who have encountered them through your licensed databases.

Web-Server Logs

Most Web-analysis software gives you the opportunity to capture quite a bit of detail about the visits to each page, including the date and time of each visit; the IP address of the visitor; the country from which the visit originates; the type and version of browser used; the "referring site," or page from which the user arrived; and the length of time spent on the page. Knowing the navigational choices that users make can help you improve the navigation of your Web site. Knowing the geographical origins of your remote users can be interesting, and it can also uncover breaches in security (for example, an implausible number of users from a certain country might indicate that a user name and password for access to e-journals through a proxy server has been widely shared).

THIRD-PARTY SOURCES

Usage statistics can also be collected by intermediaries and service providers with whom your library does business. If you use a serials-management service that maintains a database through which your users access your e-journals, or if you subscribe to an off-site link resolver, you will generally be able to receive or access reports of the number of times your users access individual titles.

STANDARDS AND GUIDELINES

Statistics from vendors are potentially the most complete and reliable measure of the use of a library's e-journal collection, and the library community agrees that standards are necessary to ensure compatibility. Vendors also welcome standards that will curb some of the variation in what they are asked to provide to libraries. Organizations and agencies that collect and compare statistics from multiple libraries also seek to standardize the usage data that libraries report. Fortunately, several groups have created standards and guidelines for the collection and reporting of usage statistics for electronic resources, and the standards-producing groups are working together to ensure compatibility of their efforts. Asking vendors whether they comply with existing or emerging standards for usage statistics will encourage them to take these standards seriously.

ANSI/NISO Z39.7–2004

The (U.S.) National Information Standards Organization (NISO) has recently revised its Z39.7 standard, "Information Services and Use: Metrics and Statistics for Libraries and Information Providers—Data Dictionary," which governs the elements of library statistical data as reported at the national level. The standard has

Keeping up-to-date:

NISO

www.niso.org

ARL E-Metrics

www.arl.org/stats/newmeas/emetrics/

COUNTER

www.counter.org

been updated as NISO Z39.7–2004 and can be found at http://
www.niso.org/emetrics. The "E-Metrics" section in Appendix A
("Methods of Measurement") of this draft document identifies
four data sets to be collected for each service, and "summed for
all services" (www.niso.org/emetrics/current/appendixA.html):

- Number of sessions
- Number of searches (queries)
- Number of units or descriptive records examined (including downloads)
- Number of virtual visits

Additional data should be collected and reported "when possible
and appropriate":

- Number of rejected sessions (turnaways)
- Number of menu selections

Sessions, searches, and other terms are defined in the standard.
Section 4.10 of the standard defines the parameters of electronic
collections, including electronic serials, which are defined as "Serials published in electronic form only or in both electronic and
other format."

ARL E-METRICS PROJECT

ARL has long been active in collecting and disseminating statistics about U.S. academic and research libraries. In 2000, as part
of what was called the "New Measures" program, ARL sponsored the E-Metrics project to help standardize the reporting of
statistics relating to electronic resources. As a result, measures of
electronic resources and digital services are being added to the
ARL annual surveys, and staff at participating libraries are being
trained to collect new kinds of statistics. See www.arl.org/stats/
newmeas/emetrics/ for more information.

COUNTER—COUNTING ONLINE USAGE IN NETWORKED ELECTRONIC RESOURCES

Project COUNTER was initiated in the UK as an international cooperative effort among many publisher and library organizations (including ARL). Directed towards electronic journal providers,
compliance with the COUNTER Code of Practice can be specified
by libraries in their license agreements to ensure that usage statistics
will conform to standards (www.projectcounter.org). At the same
time, e-journal providers with COUNTER-compliant status should

FIGURE 9–1. Suggested Format for a COUNTER-Compliant Turnaway Report

Journal Report 1a: Number of Successful Full-text Request in html and PDF Formats
(Full Journal name, print ISSN and Online ISSN are listed)

| Journal Report 1a: |
| <Criteria> |
| Date run: Yyyy-mm-dd |

Journal Name	Publisher	Print ISSN	Online ISSN	Page Type	Jan-2001	Feb-2001	Mar-2001	Total
Total for all journals				Full-text PDF Requests	2876	3793	3329	26424
Total for all journals				Full-text html Requests	3201	4392	3982	27902
Journal of AA		1212-3131	3225-3123	Full-text PDF Requests	621	670	598	4657
Journal of AA		1212-3131	3225-3123	Full-text html Requests	322	420	543	4433

(Project COUNTER, 2004a)

have a competitive advantage in the marketplace. COUNTER reports

- must be provided either in CSV, Microsoft Excel file, or a format that can be easily exported to Microsoft Excel,
- should be made available on a password-controlled Web site (accompanied by an e-mail alert when data is updated),
- must be readily available,
- must be provided at least monthly,
- must include data that are updated within four weeks of the end of the reporting period, and
- must include all of the previous calendar year's data and the current calendar year's statistics to date.

There will be no question about a vendor's claim to be COUNTER-compliant, because their reports will be audited by a COUNTER-approved auditor. To be in compliance with the COUNTER code, vendors must provide the appropriate Level-1 Usage Reports for their products:

FIGURE 9–2. Suggested Format for COUNTER-Compliant Usage Report

Journal Report 2: Turnaways by Month and Journal
(Full Journal name, print ISSN and Online ISSN are listed)

Journal Report 2:
<Criteria>
Date run:
Yyyy-mm-dd

	Publisher	Print ISSN	Online ISSN	Page Type	Jan-2001	Feb-2001	Mar-2001	Total
Total Full-text Turnways for all Journals					453	233	318	4765
Journal of AA		1212-3131	3225-3123	Full-text Turnaways	23	40	12	342
Journal of BB		9821-3361	2312-8751	Full-text Turnaways	18	20	16	287

(Project COUNTER, 2004a)

- Journal Report 1: number of successful full-text article requests by month and journal
- Journal Report 2: turnaways by month and journal (for access models based on simultaneous usage)
- Database Report 1: total searches and sessions by month and database
- Database Report 2: turnaways by month and database
- Database Report 3: total searches and sessions by month and service

Figure 9–1 illustrates a sample COUNTER-compliant format for a usage report, and Figure 9–2 is a suggested report format for turnaway statistics.

The COUNTER Code is very specific about what to count and how to count it. COUNTER compliance with the following instructions will prevent many of the problems that have been outlined:

a   Only successful and valid requests should be counted. For webserver-logs successful requests are those with a specific return code. The standards for return codes are defined and maintained by NCSA (http://archive.ncsa.uiuc.edu/edu/trg/webstats/). In case key events are used their definition should match the NCSA standards.

b   Records generated by the server together with the requested page (e.g., images, gifs, style sheets (.css) should be ignored.

c   Internal usage should be filtered out.

d   All users' double-clicks on an http-link should be counted as only 1 request. The time window for occurrence of a double-click should be set at 10 seconds between the first and the second mouse-click. There are a number of options to make sure that a double-click comes from one and the same user:

   1.   Where only the IP address of a user is logged that IP should be taken as the field to trace double-clicks.

   2.   When a session-cookie is implemented and logged, the session-cookie should be used to trace the double-clicks.

   3.   When user-cookies are available and logged, the user-cookie should be used to trace double-clicks.

   4.   When the username of a registered user is logged, this username should be used to trace double-clicks.

The options 1 to 4 above have an increasing level of reliability for filtering out double-clicks: option 1 has the lowest level of precision (and may lead to underreporting from the vendor perspective) while with option 4 the result will be optimal.

e   The rendering of a PDF takes longer than the rendering of an HTML page. Therefore, requests by one and the same IP.username/session—or user cookie for one and the same pdf should be counted as a single request if these multiple requests occur within a 30 seconds time window. These multiple requests may also be triggered by pressing a refresh or back button on the desktop by the user.

(Project COUNTER, 2004b)

ICOLC

As mentioned in other chapters, library consortia have been instrumental in getting electronic journals into libraries. Collectively, through the International Coalition of Library Consortia (ICOLC), library consortia were instrumental in setting guidelines for licensing electronic resources, and also for providing usage statistics, the "Guidelines for Statistical Measures of Usage of Web-based Indexed, Abstracted, and Full Text Resources," issued in 1998 and updated in 2001. The ICOLC (2001) guidelines pay special attention to the statistical reporting needs of library consortia. These guidelines specify how to classify data:

> Each data element defined below should be delineated by the following subdivisions:
>
> • By each specific database of the provider
> • By each set of institutional IP addresses or other special data element (e.g., account number), using the institutional name as specified by the institution or consortium.
> • By overall consortium, aggregated at the consortium level

Furthermore,

> Consortium administrators must have access through a single access method to usage information for each institution covered by the consortium license. Usage data for all consortium member libraries should be available to all other member libraries, unless an individual member library requests that its usage data not be made available to the other members. In the latter case, all usage data must be reported in the consortium summaries

(see the complete document at www.library.yale.edu/consortia/2001webstats.htm).

ICOLC has endorsed COUNTER efforts. However, ICOLC leaders have also encouraged consortia to become COUNTER members and actively participate in the further development of COUNTER standards to bring them into compliance with ICOLC guidelines.

PRIVACY GUIDELINES

The collection of usage statistics should never compromise the privacy of individual users. Most members of ICOLC have endorsed the "Privacy Guidelines for Electronic Resources Vendors," which suggest that vendors include the following statement on their Web sites:

> PUBLISHER respects the privacy of the users of its products. Accordingly, PUBLISHER will not disclose information about any individual user of its products

Keeping up-to-date:

E-Metrics Instructional System

Information Institute, Florida State University

www.ii.fsu.edu/emis/

(hereinafter referred to as "personal information"), including information about the specific content of a user's searches, to a third party without the permission of that individual user, except as required by law (ICOLC, 2002).

PROCESSING AND ANALYZING USAGE DATA

Collecting usage data is of course only the first step. Processing and organizing that data so that it can be analyzed is the next step. Analysis discerns the meaning of the data in answering predetermined questions.

WHO WILL COLLECT AND PROCESS AND ANALYZE THE DATA?

As with other new tasks related to electronic journals, collecting, processing, and analyzing usage statistics may not be part of anyone's job description, though there are exceptions. For example, the University of Georgia Libraries has (or had) a "Database Performance and Assessment Librarian." In most libraries, e-journal assessment will probably have to be done by the Little Red Hen from the folktale ("Then I'll do it myself!"). If your library has a coordinator for electronic resources, that person could be considered responsible for providing e-journal usage reports. The work itself can be shared, however. Compiling usage statistics can be done by staff in any department during a lull in the routine.

If the collection and processing of statistics is handled by only one person, that person should cross-train a substitute or maintain very detailed instructions. Instructions for obtaining usage statistics from vendors or local systems should be maintained in such a way that they can be accessed by anyone who might be taking over if the usual person(s) cannot do it.

Some electronic resource management systems include a means for keeping track of administrative information, such as the URL, username and password for retrieving Web-based data, or the name and e-mail address of the vendor's representative with whom the library corresponds about statistics. Without such a system, a secure library intranet is a good place to keep such information together and accessible.

HOW OFTEN?

If a library subscribes to e-journals and databases from a number of providers, different vendors will make usage statistics available at different times. In some cases they are sent or posted to a Web site regularly (usually monthly), but in other cases they are sent only when requested. Having a routine will ensure active collection and timely processing of the statistics. Monthly updates to a spreadsheet or database, based on the most recently available data, will keep the task manageable, but each library will need to determine a routine that is appropriate and workable.

OVERVIEW OF THE PROCESS

Basically, you will be collecting, manipulating, organizing, and translating raw data into meaningful reports. How you do that will depend on the complexity of the raw data and the purpose of your reports. There are some general steps you will want to follow:

1. Decide on the elements to be analyzed, the audience, and the purpose.
2. Collect the data from local and/or remote sources.
3. Normalize the format of that data that comes from more than one source.
4. Transfer/import data into appropriate fields of your database or the columns and rows of your spreadsheet.
5. Sort the spreadsheet or design a report structure for optimal output that can be easily understood by interested parties.
6. Provide meaningful interpretations of the important data elements.

DATA COLLECTION, PROCESSING, AND ANALYSIS TOOLS

The software tools that you use will depend on your systems, local availability and expertise, and the type of data you are processing. Using existing e-metrics, or clearly defined measures that meet industry standards, will ensure that statistics will be comparable to those from other institutions and that they will be collected consistently in subsequent years.

Existing E-Metrics

E-metrics are measures of electronic resources and services. A great deal of effort has gone into creating a common understanding of terms and what is being measured (see the "Standards" section, above). The E-Metrics Instructional System (EMIS) of the Information Use Management Policy Institute at Florida State University, Tallahassee, funded by a grant from the U.S. Institute of Museum and Library Services (IMLS), includes a catalog "identifying known, standardized and field-tested e-metrics from various sources." This project focuses on e-metrics for public libraries, but the definitions can be useful for any library. Using this site can save libraries from having to spend time defining exactly what each measure means and deciding what to count. For example, if you are responding to a survey that asks for "Items Requested in Electronic Databases" by your users during a certain time period, the EMIS site will clarify that this means:

> Number of items requested in all of the library's licensed electronic resources. These resources may include journal articles, e-books, reference materials, and non-textual resources that are provided to the library's users through licensing and contractual agreements. The user requests may include viewing, downloading, emailing, and printing to the extent the activity can be recorded and controlled by the server rather than browser (see the e-metrics catalog at www.ii.fsu.edu/emis/Catalog.cfm).

The EMIS site also offers an "annual report template," which provides a context for e-metrics relating to your library (www.ii.fsu.edu/emis/annualReport.cfm).

Spreadsheets

A spreadsheet may be sufficient for compiling and presenting data. COUNTER-compliant statistics are already in a format that can be read by Microsoft Excel, Corel Quattro, and other spreadsheet programs, and even most vendors that do not comply with COUNTER will provide delimited files that are compatible with common spreadsheet programs. With basic knowledge of spreadsheets, you can sort, add, and average statistics, as well as calculate cost per use and percentages of increase. Most spreadsheet programs can be used to create graphs of various types to illustrate trends and relationships among statistics.

Databases

Statistics can also be downloaded or imported into commonly used database programs, such as Microsoft Access, Lotus Notes, and Corel Paradox. With a relational database, you will be able to correlate more elements and produce more complex reports.

Web-Log Analysis

Commercially available software is available to harvest and analyze data from local servers, producing canned or customized reports. To choose among several competing Web-traffic-analysis products, you will need to consider the amount of traffic your site generates, the server hosting your e-journal Web pages, your budget, and the parameters of your information needs. Some of the most popular Web-traffic analysis products are:

- ClickTracks (www.clicktracks.com)
- HitBox Professional (www.websidestory.com/products/professional/)
- Log Analyzer (www.netiq.com)
- NetTracker (www.sane.com)
- WebTrends (www.netiq.com)

There are many more products available. To find lists and reviews, do a Google search:

 | web traffic analysis | Search |

Collection Analysis

A product from Bowker, Ulrich's Serials Analysis System, generates customized reports on a library's journal collection using various criteria. Using *Ulrich's Directory* and other data such as ISI impact factors, this service can help you evaluate the quality of your electronic and/or print collection and identify gaps. See www.ulrichsweb.com/ulrichsweb/analysis/ for more information.

MAINTENANCE AND PRESERVATION OF DATA

Often in libraries, a flurry of activity will result in a report that is needed for a specific purpose—a strategic plan, an annual report, or a budget request. This kind of report is much easier to prepare when statistics are compiled and processed on an ongoing basis, but that is not always possible. Save any processed data and reports that have been compiled for comparison purposes and to save your having to go back to the raw data if those same statistics are needed in the future. Once you have set up a process for entering data in a spreadsheet or database, it is a good practice to input data as you receive it, or on a regular schedule, such as once a month.

Shared Files and Intranets

The easiest way to share a living repository of usage data is to make it available to your staff on an intranet or networked server. Questions about e-journals and their use come up in various parts of the library, and one type of report may not answer every question. Be sure to use controls so that data on the intranet can be updated by authorized staff but won't be destroyed or damaged by unwitting visitors.

Interactive Systems

With a little bit of Web programming or the use of certain types of database software, staff in larger libraries will be able to generate customized reports of usage data with or without intermediaries. A database at the Arizona State (Tempe) University Libraries produce spreadsheets that incorporate formulas that enable librarians "to creatively work the data" (Shim, Murphy, and Brunning, 2004, p. 39).

ANALYZING USAGE STATISTICS

Some librarians make the mistake of believing that collecting and organizing usage statistics and making them available is enough. However, someone will need to carry out an analysis, because without analysis, statistics have little value.

Answering Questions

Analyzing usage statistics means using them to answer questions. The key to successful analysis of usage statistics is to formulate questions that are important and can be answered with usage data. Each library will have its own questions, but most will fall into some general categories: costs/benefits, trends, and user preferences and behavior.

Rather than feeling overwhelmed by a perceived need for a large-scale analysis of e-journal use, carry out focused analyses to answer specific questions and enable informed decision making. For example, if your cost for licensing a full-text database is based on the number of simultaneous users, you will want to know how many times the maximum number of ports were in use, and how many users were turned away during a designated time period. That number by itself won't give you the information you need to make a decision about increasing the number of simultaneous users for that product. How much will it cost to upgrade? Are there any patterns to the turnaway statistics? If it will be expensive to add more simultaneous users, and the turnaways are clustered, for example, clues within the statistics may allow you

"At the most concrete level, usage statistics are nothing more than the artifacts of online transactions stored in web server logs; but at the most abstract level, they represent nothing less than an effort to understand changing patterns of scholarly behavior by tracing and analyzing scholars' interactions with online resources through time without invading their privacy."

—Bernard Rous (2004, Introduction, p. 2)

to prevent future turnaways by working with faculty to suggest alternative databases for class assignments. Or your turnaway patterns might confirm the need and justify the expense for an upgrade of the license.

Costs and Benefits

One common approach to using statistics to support collection decisions is to calculate the cost per some kind of standard activity. The Arizona State University database mentioned above (Shim, Murphy, and Brunning, 2004, p. 39) generates preformatted reports that show:

- Cost per search
- Cost per connect time
- Cost per turnaway
- Cost per full-text unit viewed or downloaded
- Searches per session
- Records viewed per search or session
- Full content units viewed or downloaded per session or search

Some caution is in order when using these kinds of ratios. A resource might be expensive and unique and supports a specialized group of researchers, and the cost per use might be high compared to the cost per use of an inexpensive general database. You would not necessarily think of canceling the specialized database. Cost-per-use data are often used in conjunction with other measures:

- If you are considering the cancellation of an expensive online journal, you might compare the cost per use to the cost of getting the same number of articles through a document-delivery service, or through subsidizing pay-per-view, if that is an option. You would need estimates of these other costs, and you would need to factor in the intangible tradeoffs such as immediacy and budgetary control.
- You might want to compare the use of print and electronic versions of a journal, in which case you would need to estimate the cost of processing and binding the print journal and the cost of the space it will occupy.

User Preferences and Behaviors

Most usage statistics won't tell you very much about your individual users, but they can help you understand your users collectively. The amount of time they spend in relation to their results can indicate a level of success or failure with different full-text resources. Their patterns of use throughout the day can indicate when real-time online help might be most useful. By combining statistics from different sources you can determine the remote versus on-site use of various resources.

Trends

Tracking the use of electronic resources over time can be an extremely valuable planning tool. The number of searches conducted over time or the growth or decline of usage in an individual database may or may not surprise you, but you definitely need this information for graphs that will help tell the story of how priorities are shifting for your users and your staff.

DESCRIBING, DISTILLING, AND PRESENTING DATA

One of the most challenging aspects of analyzing statistics is presenting your results in such a way that they will be easily understood and, therefore, used. Never present more information than your target audience is willing to spend the time to comprehend, or they may not comprehend any of it.

LAYERING DATA

Since it is not unusual to present a statistical report to multiple audiences, or to an audience that includes multiple individuals with different levels of interest, you will want to layer your information, with the most stripped-down, simplified version of your main conclusions at the forefront, and any additional, more complex information easily available, but not interfering with the communication of your main points.

The simplest method is to begin a report with summary information, preferably illustrated with a graph, followed by more detailed information for those who are interested. If your library is moving rapidly towards electronic delivery of journals, you might want to share a simple line graph such as the one in Figure 9–3, easily generated from an Excel spreadsheet. For certain audiences, a companion bar graph (for example, Figure 9–4) would illustrate the effect of the format shift on library staffing.

In these two examples, the actual numbers are important, and they should be included in your report, but the charts will make

FIGURE 9–3. Illustrating a Journal-Format Shift

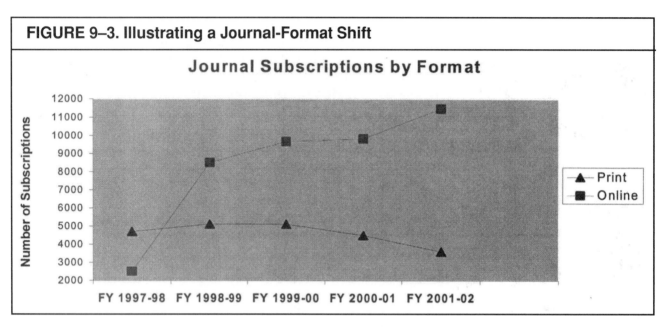

FIGURE 9–4. Illustrating a Shift in Staff Duties

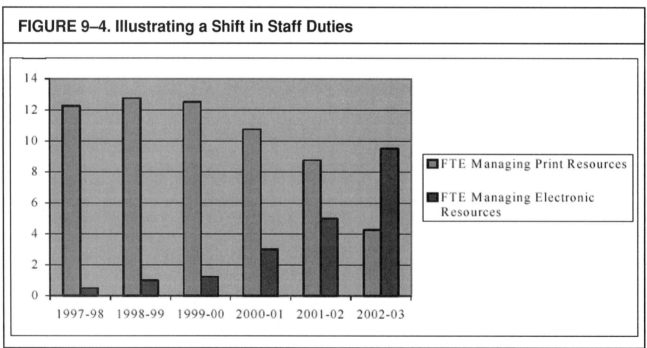

a more lasting impression. Unfortunately, not all types of information about electronic journals will be as easy to convey visually. Consider your material and your audience, and select the most appropriate format—a chart, a line graph, a list, or a combination of formats.

TIPS FOR USING EXCEL FOR PRESENTATION

Those who work with numbers in libraries know that Excel is quite versatile for processing and analyzing statistics. Experts who manipulate any kind of data can use it to de-dupe lists with filters and cross-tabulate with pivot tables and apply complex formulas. Beginners can sort and add numbers and calculate percentages. With a little practice, tables can turn into charts with a few clicks. However, Excel is only as good as its operator for conveying information effectively. These suggestions will help:

- Before sending a spreadsheet to someone else, particularly if it will be discussed at a meeting, try printing it, or at least use "print preview." It may look very different as a printed sheet from how it looks on your monitor. The gridlines won't print unless you activate them (Format/ Cells/Border/Outside and Inside, or select the Gridlines check box on the Sheet tab of the Page Setup dialog box, depending on your version).
- Use column heading names that are meaningful and understandable. Change the text orientation of your heading to vertical to save space.
- Try to size your columns to fit on one printed 8.5″ 11″ sheet. Use the Landscape orientation under File/Page Setup if necessary. Use the Legal-size paper setting only as a last resort after trying Scaling options under Page Setup (later versions) and readjusting your column widths and fonts.
- Use Bold and Italics sparingly to differentiate elements for better readability.
- If you use colors in your tables or charts, make sure that your meaning will survive if the document is printed in black and white. Even those who have color printers may do most of their printing in black-and-white.
- Remember that spreadsheets can't be sorted by colored text or colored cells. If you use colors or other formatting for differentiating items, be sure that other elements will allow columns to be sorted.
- If you use more than one sheet in a workbook, label the tabs and alert your audience to the presence of the other sheets in the document. Even when tabs are labeled, they might go unnoticed.
- Use advanced features only if you need them. Enable experienced Excel users to interact with your spreadsheet.
- Use pastel colors or light gray in alternating rows or columns to help with readability, particularly if you do not want to use gridlines in a spreadsheet.

- Use titles for your spreadsheets and graphs, and date them.
- If your report is a draft, label it as such.
- Keep in mind that your recipients may have an older version of Excel that is not able to take advantage of some of the features of your spreadsheet.
- Do not try to put too much information into one graph. Use multiple graphs to convey multiple concepts.
- Use traditional graph types that will be familiar to your readers. Choose the most appropriate type for the visualization of your data: Line graphs for trends, bar graphs for comparisons, pie charts for proportions, etc. Excel defines the purpose of each type of graph in the Chart Wizard. Use 3-D only when it clarifies data.
- Avoid large expanses of dark colors in graphs and charts; save your recipients' ink.
- Delete extraneous columns that may have been used for processing data or that were imported along with the data that you are using. (If the numbers in your meaningful column are the result of a formula, copy the meaningful column and use "paste special" and "values" to overwrite the same column. Then you will be able to delete the columns used in the calculations.)
- Avoid decimals in number representations. Precision is rarely as important as simplification. Round prices to the nearest dollar and percentages to the nearest whole number.

A CASE STUDY

There was quite a bit of interest at the University of Nevada, Reno, in how the individual journals in our Elsevier package were being used, since it was a major acquisition and we had gained online access to at least 900 journals that we did not subscribe to in print format. Several of our questions could be answered by the usage statistics that showed the browsing (number of table-of-contents pages viewed) and downloading (articles viewed) activities of our users. We wanted answers to the following questions:

- How much use are the journals getting altogether? Is it increasing? Was there a decrease after the novelty wore off?
- What is the relationship of browsing to the viewing of articles?
- Which new journals are being used? Are there any patterns?

- When there is a choice between print and electronic journals, are the e-journals used? Are there any differences between browsing and viewing for the journals we have subscribed to in the past and the ones that are new to our users?
- What are the most heavily used journals?
- Is it cost effective to retain the package?

We expected only light use of the new journals obtained through the package. Our interlibrary loan staff reported that prior to obtaining the package, articles had not been heavily requested from Elsevier journals we did not subscribe to. However, other libraries and consortia with this package had been reporting a surprising amount of use of new e-journals, indicating that it is difficult to anticipate and select the journals of interest to a particular community.

To answer some of the questions required some initial work, checking the usage reports against the library's catalog to determine existing print subscriptions. Also, during the first few years we received usage statistics, we got monthly reports we had to cumulate ourselves. Because the lists were not the same each month (only journals that were used by one of the libraries in the consortium during that month were listed) most of the merging was manual—until we learned how to use pivot tables in Excel.

Reports were sent to interested staff (and to administrators for their purposes, including the negotiation of the renewal of a three-year license). Figure 9–5 shows a typical report that summarizes the first three years of usage, answering most of the above questions. The Excel spreadsheet was attached to this e-mailed report for those who wanted more detail.

Various other reports were compiled and distributed based on the usage statistics for this package. The reports showed that it was cost effective to renew the license for the entire list, based on the projected cost of providing the same articles through other means.

Some of our users found their way to the ScienceDirect (SD) site regardless of the fact that our Web and catalog links directed them to our preferred provider, Science Server@LANL (SS). A significant number of articles were downloaded from SD and, therefore, were not represented in our reports until late 2002, when we began getting usage statistics from SD. The summary on the right side of Figure 9–6 illustrates the magnitude of users' access choices (see Figure 9–7 for visual representation), but it wasn't until we looked at individual titles that we found that almost all the articles downloaded from ScienceDirect were from medical

---

FIGURE 9–5. Usage Statistics in a Report Format

UNR usage of Elsevier online journals has risen dramatically.

> **Articles viewed:**
> FY 1999–2000—17,845
> FY 2000–2001—29,216 (64% increase)
> FY 2001–2002—48,317 (73% increase)
> **Journals browsed:**
> FY 1999–2000—50,674
> FY 2000–2001—59,886 (18% increase)
> FY 2001–2002—98,624 (65% increase)

All three years, about half the total articles viewed were from the **384 journals to which we subscribe(d)** in print:

> FY 1999–2000—48%
> FY 2000–2001—47%
> FY 2001–2002—51%

But because the other half are from the **974 online-only journals**, the number of articles viewed per journal is much higher from the journals to which we subscribe(d) in print:

> FY 1999–2000—22.2 articles per journal
> FY 2000–2001—35.4 articles per journal
> FY 2001–2002—64.5 articles per journal

compared to the proportion of articles viewed per online-only journal:

> FY 1999–2000—9.6 articles per online-only journal
> FY 2000–2001—16 articles per online-only journal
> FY 2001–2002—24.2 articles per online-only journal

The heaviest use is clearly from the journals we selected as print subscriptions. Of the 21 journals with over 500 articles viewed during the 3 years, we subscribe(d) to 17 in print format (11,685 articles from these, or 82.4% of the articles viewed). The 4 most heavily used journals we did not receive in print were:

- *Water Science and Technology* (784 articles downloaded)
- *Materials Science and Engineering. A, Structural Materials: Properties, Microstructure and Processing* (647 articles)
- *Journal of Membrane Science* (536 articles)
- *Trends in Plant Science* (533 articles)

Only 82 (6%) of the 1,358 journals did not have any articles viewed by UNR users during the 3 years.

FIGURE 9–5. *Continued*

38,936 of the articles downloaded from online-only Elsevier journals exceeded the 5-articles-per-journal-per-year limit. In other words, **if our users had requested these articles through interlibrary loan, we would have had to pay a copyright fee to the CCC for them**. Of course, many of them would not have been requested, as our pre-Elsevier-online-package ILL statistics show.

The relationship of browsing TOCs to viewing articles has changed from 4:1 the first year to 2:1 the third year.

---

journals. Further investigation indicated that an increasing number of faculty members in the growing medical school were linking to ScienceDirect through PubMed or by going directly to sciencedirect.com.

To visualize the data in terms of the overall patterns of our users' article use from Elsevier journals from both sites over time and how their use fluctuated during the school year, the spreadsheet was rearranged and a line chart was used (Figure 9–8). A chart like this is more useful with data from a longer period of time. But even this one raises interesting questions. Between semesters, during December 2002 and January 2003, the downloading activity was similar to what we see for summer months. But for those same two months the next year, the downloading activity was significantly higher, resembling the activity during the school year. One hypothesis is that during that period the university buildings were closed for two weeks the first year and one week the second year, and that faculty were more knowledgeable and prepared the second year to do research off campus.

REFORMATTING AND NORMALIZING STATISTICS

Some statistics in their native form do not lend themselves to visualization, and one more step in processing them can make them much more understandable. For example, the spreadsheet at the top of Figure 9–9 shows searches in some of a library's databases during one year, arranged by month. The education librarian wants to know if the usage pattern is different for education databases since there are summer programs for education students. The librarian can call up this information in graph format by

1. highlighting columns A–M of rows 1, 3, and 11 of the spreadsheet;
2. clicking on the graph icon (indicated by top arrow);

FIGURE 9–6. Comparing Access Channels for Articles Viewed

	A	B	C	D	E	F	G	H	I	J	K	L	M	N	O	P	Q
1	Elsevier Article Downloads														SS totals	SD totals	All downld
2												Nov 02	Dec 02		2002	2002	2002
3	Science Server											5,134	3,089		8,223	2,034	10,257
4	Science Direct											859	1,175		80%	20%	
5																	
6															SS totals	SD totals	total
7		Jan 03	Feb 03	Mar 03	Apr 03	May 03	Jun 03	Jul 03	Aug 03	Sep 03	Oct 03	Nov 03	Dec 03		2003	2003	2003
8	Science Server	3,363	4,451	4,950	5,305	3,466	2,897	2,957	2,174	3,902	4,746	4,089	5,474		47,774	26,789	74,563
9	Science Direct	2,006	2,037	2,206	2,486	1,432	1,661	1,541	2,071	2,504	3,057	2,630	3,158		64%	36%	
10																	
11															SS totals	SD totals	total
12		Jan 04	Feb 04	Mar 04	Apr 04										2004	2004	2004
13	Science Server	5,177	3,641	4,287	4,816										17,921	13,626	31,547
14	Science Direct	2,643	3,350	3,581	4,052										57%	43%	
15																	
16															SS totals	SD totals	grand total
17															73,918	42,449	116,367
18															64%	36%	

FIGURE 9–7. Visual Representation of Access Channels and Combined Downloads

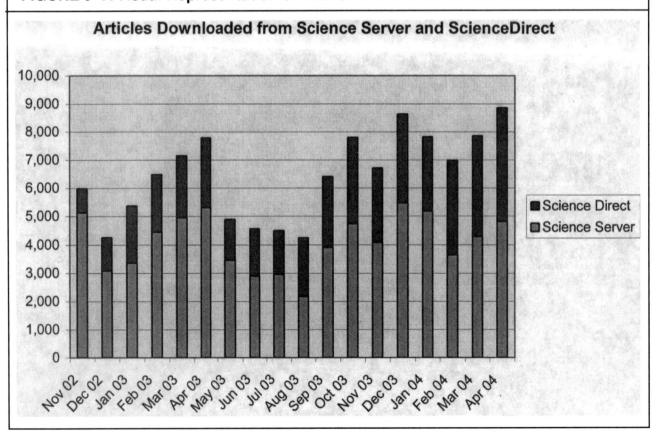

Articles Downloaded from Science Server and ScienceDirect

FIGURE 9–8. Visualization of School-Year Patterns

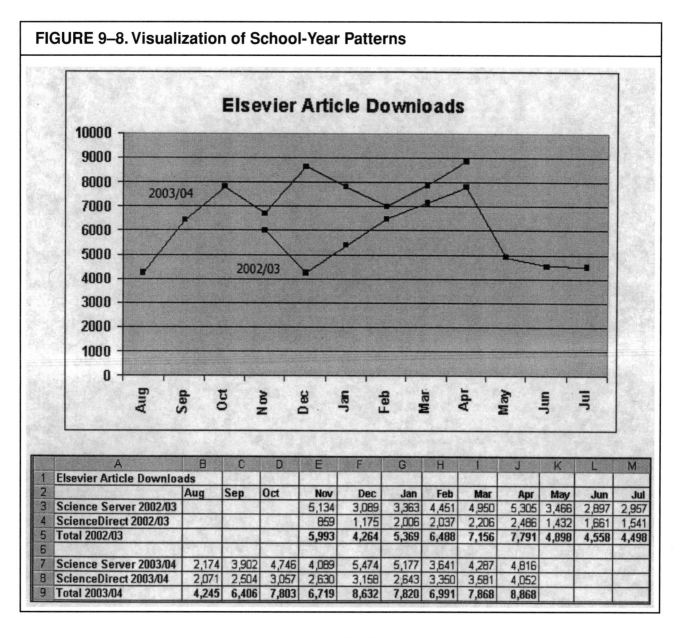

3. choosing the bar graph, which will show the education searches and other searches side by side for each month. The result is shown on the left below the spreadsheet.

Because there is a significantly larger number of searches in all the other types of databases, it is difficult to compare the education-usage patterns to general-usage patterns with this graph. To make the units comparable for the purpose of the study, the librarian can carry out an exercise that would hypothesize a situa-

FIGURE 9-9. Normalizing Statistics

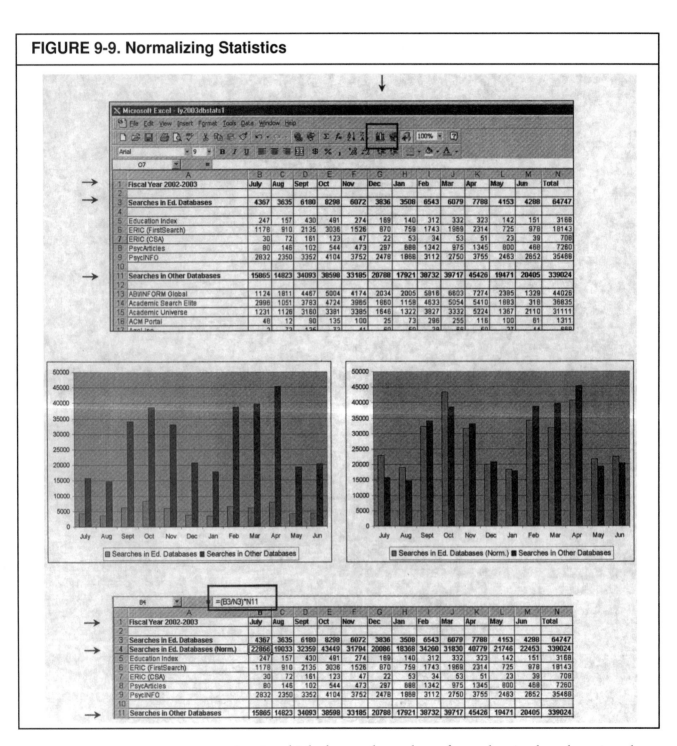

tion in which the total number of searches in the education databases were equal to the number of searches in all other databases. For each month, the percentage of hypothetical searches in the education databases will be the same as for the actual searches, and these percentages would be multiplied by the new total. To do this the librarian adds data to row 4 in the spreadsheet, as illustrated in the spreadsheet at the bottom of Figure 9–9:

- To get the percentages, the actual number of education searches for each month will be divided by the total number of education searches for the whole year to get the percentage, and then for normalization purposes, the percentage is multiplied by the hypothetical total number of searches (equal to the total searches in the other databases).
- The new numbers (as shown in row 4) are graphed alongside the searches for each month in the other databases (rows 1, 4, and 11 of the modified spreadsheet).

In the graph on the right, we can now easily compare the usage patterns for the education databases and the library's other databases. The graph shows that education-related databases are indeed searched at a relatively higher rate in the summer months. During the school year, users of the other databases are relatively more active, except during the month of October. While April appears to be the big month for database searching in general, in October something is going on in education. A curious librarian would investigate whether this pattern repeats itself every year.

SOME FINAL WORDS ABOUT PRESENTING DATA

In analyzing usage data (or any data), you will develop a close relationship to the subject of your analysis. You will come to appreciate its nuances and its importances. Patterns will excite you. Your target audience, on the other hand, will not share your perspective, so you will need to find ways to attract and hold their attention if you must present information that is complex. Whether you are designing a formal PowerPoint presentation for a group, a report for an administrator, or an e-mail description to colleagues, begin with a sentence or two that explains your reasons for analyzing the data. Present the most useful or meaningful conclusions first, in a simple and general way, followed by information that is increasingly more detailed. In a face-to-face situation, monitor your audience for signs of disinterest and be prepared to stop when they have had enough. Summarize by repeating the main points.

Color and graphics can be very important to the success of a visual presentation. Graphic design is beyond the scope of this book, but if you experiment with different color combinations and fonts, you will notice that some work better than others.

Finally, have someone else look at your tables and charts before you submit or present them. A disinterested set of eyes can spot potentially embarrassing errors and will detect areas of possible confusion. You, as the analyst, will have a hard time attaining enough distance to see your results with the eyes of someone who is unfamiliar with your material.

One last piece of advice is to save your calculations and the early versions of your analyses. If you find a glaring mistake in your final presentation, you will not want to have to start at the beginning in order to correct it.

REFERENCES

Bollen, Johan, Rick Luce, Soma Sekhara Vemulapalli, and Weining Xu. 2003. "Usage Analysis for the Identification of Research Trends in Digital Libraries." *D-Lib Magazine* 9, no. 5 (May). Retrieved Sept. 17, 2004, from www.dlib.org/dlib/may03/bollen/05bollen.html.

Boss, Richard W. 2003. "Rethinking Library Statistics in a Changing Environment." *Tech Notes* 9, no. 5. Public Library Association. Retrieved Sept. 17, 2004, from www.ala.org/ala/pla/plapubs/technotes/rethinkinglibrary.htm.

Degener, Christie T., and Marjory A. Waite. 2000. "Fools Rush in . . . Thoughts about, and a Model for, Measuring Electronic Journal Collections." *Serials Review* 26, no. 4 (October–December): 3–11.

International Coalition of Library Consortia (ICOLC). 2001. "Guidelines for Statistical Measures of Usage of Web-Based Information Resources" (December 2001 revision of original November 1998 Guidelines). Retrieved Sept. 19, 2004, from www.library.yale.edu/consortia/2001webstats.htm.

———. 2002, July. "Privacy Guidelines for Electronic Resources Vendors." Retrieved Sept. 20, 2004, from www.library.yale.edu/consortia/202privacyguidelines.html.

Peters, Thomas A. 2002. "What's the Use? The Value of E-Resource Usage Statistics." *New Library World* 103, no. 1: 39–47.

Project COUNTER. 2004a. "4.1 Usage Reports." *Release 2 of the COUNTER Code of Practice*. Retrieved Sept. 18, 2004, from www.projectcounter.org/cop2.html#start_r2.

———. 2004b. "5. Data Processing." *Release 2 of the COUNTER Code of Practice*. Retrieved Sept. 18, 2004, from www.projectcounter.org/cop2.html#start_r2.

Rous, Bernard, ed. 2004. *Online Usage: A Publisher's Guide*. New York: Association of American Publishers.

Scigliano, Marisa. 2002. "Consortium Purchases: Case Study for a Cost-Benefit Analysis." *Journal of Academic Librarianship* 28, no. 6 (November): 393–399.

Shim, Wonsik, Kurt Murphy, and Dennis Brunning. 2004. "Usage Statistics for Electronic Services and Resources: A Library Perspective." In *Online Usage Statistics: A Publisher's Guide*, ed. Bernard Rous, 34–46. New York: Association of American Publishers.

Watson, Paula. 2003. "E-Journals: Access and Management." *Library Technology Reports* 39, no. 2 (March/April): 44–69.

MORE INFORMATION SOURCES

Duy, Joanna, and Liwen Vaughan. 2003. "Usage Data for Electronic Resources: A Comparison between Locally Collected and Vendor-Provided Statistics." *Journal of Academic Librarianship* 29, no. 1 (January): 16–22.

Enssle, Halcyon R., and Michelle L. Wilde. 2002. "So You Have to Cancel Journals? Statistics That Help." *Library Collections, Acquisitions, and Technical Services* 26, no. 3 (Autumn): 259–281.

Ferguson, Anthony W. 2002–03. "Back Talk—Use Statistics: Are They Worth It?" *Against the Grain* 14, no. 6 (December/January): 93–94.

King, Donald W., Peter B. Boyce, Carol Hansen Montgomery, and Carol Tenopir. "Library Economic Metrics: Examples of the Comparison of Electronic and Print Journal Collections and Collection Services." 2003. *Library Trends* 51, no. 3 (Winter): 376–400.

McGinty, Jim. 2003. "Merging External Data with Serials Holdings . . . the Next Generation of Serials Management." *Serials* 16, no. 1 (March): 57–61.

Schonfeld, Roger C., Donald W. King, Ann Okerson, and Eileen Gifford Fenton. 2004. *The Nonsubscription Side of Periodicals: Changes in Library Operations and Costs between Print and Electronic Formats*. Research Report. Washington, D.C.: Council on Library and Information Resources.

Shim, Wonsik, and Charles R. McClure. 2002. "Data Needs and Use of Electronic Resources and Services at Academic Research Libraries." *Portal: Libraries and the Academy* 2, no. 2: 217–236.

Varjabedian, Kathy. 2003. "Journals Benchmarking: How Do We Stack Up?" *Research Library Newsletter, Los Alamos National Labs* (December). Retrieved Sept. 17, 2004, from http://lib-www.lanl.gov/libinfo/news/2003/200312.htm#jourbench.

Wilkie, Tom. 2003. "Tracking Users: Technology Designed for Tracking Readers Turns Over a New Leaf." *Research Information* (Summer). Retrieved Sept. 13, 2004, from www.researchinformation.info/risum03trackingusers.html.

APPENDIX A: E-JOURNAL COLLECTION POLICIES

Sample

ELECTRONIC JOURNAL COLLECTION POLICY FOR PAID SUBSCRIPTIONS

A. Cost
   1. The subscription should not represent an additional long-term investment. The library is willing to pay an initial (reasonable) surcharge for electronic access to individual titles during a transitional/evaluative period (maximum of 2 years), after which it is expected that the print subscription will be discontinued. The electronic-only subscription should cost the same as or less than the print subscription; preference will be given to packages that do not require the retention of print subscriptions
   2. Packages will be licensed for up to three years if the cost/benefit forecast is deemed acceptable by the Collection Development Team (CDT); consortial options should be investigated for a publisher's package.
   3. Title-level usage statistics (preferably COUNTER-compliant) must be supplied for packages and must be analyzed by the library before renewal is authorized.
   4. To select free electronic journals, refer to "Free-Access Electronic Journal Collection Policy."

B. Publisher/Reputation
   1. The library already subscribes to the print equivalent; or the journal meets one or more of the following criteria:
      • It is peer reviewed.
      • It is published by an academic institution.
      • It is published by a professional society.
      • It is published by a commercial enterprise with an established reputation.
      • It has an impact factor higher than 2.0.
      • It is listed in *Magazines for Libraries*.
      • It is on a standard list of core journals for the discipline.
   2. Exceptions will be made on a case-by-case basis.
   3. Preference will be given to journals that are indexed in at least one of the library's SFX-enabled bibliographic

databases and are configurable as targets through OpenURL or DOI protocols.

C. Accessibility
   1. Journals must be accessible by IP recognition; access should not require individual registration or user IDs or passwords. Rare exceptions will be allowed for a compelling reason (must be approved by CDT).
   2. Journals must be accessible to walk-in library users.
   3. Journals must be accessible to authorized remote users (exceptions approved by CDT).
   4. Articles must be easy to print and download.
   5. Articles must be readable on computer screens.
   6. Response time must be within acceptable limits.
   7. Access should not require a proprietary plug-in without a compelling reason (to be approved by CDT).

D. Content
   1. Journals must support the curriculum, research, or administrative needs of the university.
   2. Journals must be entirely full text.
   3. Preference will be given to journals requested by departmental faculty.

E. Format
   1. Journal sites must be navigable; i.e., past issues must be easy to find.
   2. Preference is given to hyperlinked formats.

F. Longevity/Currency
   1. Archives of past issues must be available and maintained.
   2. Issues must be made available within a reasonable period of time after the equivalent print issues are published.
   3. Preference will be given to journals that are available in electronic format before print issues are published.

G. Licensing
   1. Licenses should permit fair use of all information for noncommercial educational, instructional, and research purposes by authorized users, including electronic reserves and some form of interlibrary loan.
   2. Licenses must not put unreasonable restrictions or requirements on users or staff.

H. Consortial considerations
1. The library will support, whenever possible, Open Access initiatives and other cost-effective alternative publishing efforts by SPARC and other such groups.
2. A clause will be added to the license, whenever possible, stating that the license will be superseded by a license with named consortia.

Sample

FREE-ACCESS ELECTRONIC JOURNAL COLLECTION POLICY

A. When electronic access is free with the library's print subscription, it will be activated as long as the following conditions are met:
1. IP authentication is allowed.
2. Walk-in patrons can use it in the library.
3. Authorized remote users have access.

B. If the library does not subscribe to the print version and the electronic version is offered on a trial basis, it will be added to the Web lists but not cataloged if:
1. The trial appears to be longlasting and may never end.
2. It is likely or possible that the library will pay the subscription fee if there is a demand for it.

C. If the journal is free but the library does not have a print subscription, or if it is an electronic-only journal, it will be cataloged and added to the Web lists only if it meets **all** of the following criteria:
1. The content is complete for each issue (applies to journals with print equivalent).
2. It is a regular (or fairly regular) publication.
3. Past issues are available at the Web site.
4. There is at least one other issue (unless the journal is very new and expected to remain current).
5. Issues are enumerated and/or dated and it is clearly a serial publication.
6. Individual registration is not required.

D. In addition to the above conditions, the journal must meet **at least one** of the following criteria:
1. The content and tone are scholarly.
2. It clearly supports teaching, research, or administration at the university.
3. It has been requested by faculty.
4. It has a good reputation and would be used.
5. It has reference value.

E. To select journals with a subscription cost, use the "Electronic Journal Collection Policy for Paid Subscriptions" policy.

ONLINE JOURNAL EVALUATION FORM

Electronic Resources Team, NIH Library

Evaluator:
Journal titles:

A. **Licensing**
    Print out a copy of the license agreement and attach it to the evaluation form.
    1. What kinds of licenses are available? Institutional? Site? Unlimited access? Other?
    2. Does the license allow multi-user access from the user's desktop, outside the Library?
    3. How does the license define authorized sites? Does the license contain geographic site restrictions?
    4. How does the license define authorized users? (prefer authorized users defined as all employees)
    5. Does the license language accord with Principles for Licensing Electronic Resources? (http://www.arl.org/scomm/licensing/principles.html)

B. **Format and content**
    1. What format is used? PDF, HTML, etc.?
    2. Is text only available? Are all graphics in the print journal replicated in the online version?
    3. Does the e-version provide cover-to-cover access to the contents of the print counterpart (except for advertisements)?

C. **Web Access**
1. Does the journal require IP address validation; if yes, is IP address registration provided for?
2. Does the journal require domain name validation?
3. Does the journal require password access? (prefer no password access)
    a. Does the password access replace or supplement IP address validation?
    b. Does the journal require individual users to create their own passwords or will a single institution-wide password established by the Library suffice (prefer single if passworded access is required)
4. Do the individual articles have discrete URLs that can be accessed in a Web browser independently of the journal's site?
    Test: go to an article in the journal's site, copy the URL, exit the journal's site, paste the URL into your Web browser, and attempt to access.

D. **Currency of volumes** (are the most recent volumes/issues available?)

E. **Update frequency**
1. How frequently is the site updated?
2. How quickly are new issues available online in comparison to print counterparts?

F. **Price**
1. What is the price of a one-year subscription (include details)?
2. Does the price cover all available years, or are there separate fees for individual years?
3. If the library discontinues a subscription, does the library retain access to the years for which it paid?
4. Are there additional fees for more than one IP address?

G. **Print version** (priority is given to electronic versions of established print journals; does a print counterpart exist?)

H. **Use**
1. Does the library have multiple copies of the print version of the title?
2. What is the journal's ranking on the journal use report?
3. Does the publisher provide statistics on Web site use by NIH staff? Characterize the available statistics by for-

mat (.txt file, .csv file, fax), schedule (monthly, quarterly, biannually), type of count (hits, requests, visits), and breakdown (IP address).

4. Have NIH staff requested purchase? How many/how often?

I. **Subject coverage** (Please describe importance of subject coverage in terms of NIH research interests. Consult with collection development librarian for the subject area if needed.)

Reprinted from Serial Review 25(3), Publicker, Stephanie, and Kristen Stoklosa. "How the National Institues of Health Library Selects and Provides E-Journals via the World Wide Web. Pages 13-23, 1999, with permission from Elsevier.

APPENDIX B: STANDARDIZING TITLES FOR WEB LISTS

If you maintain your own database or spreadsheet for generating e-journal Web pages, you will have to standardize or normalize titles that might come to you in various formats for the same journal. For example, you might have acquired these representations for *The Lancet* from four different database source lists:

- Lancet
- The Lancet
- Lancet, The
- Lancet (The)

And even though *The Lancet* may be its official title, most users will know to look under "Lancet" instead of "The," and it's easy to globally remove all the formats of "The" in your database or spreadsheet (but be sure to use a case sensitive "search and replace" function to avoid removing "the" in the middle of a title). Other replacements you will need to make in normalizing your titles are

- "and" for "&" (or vice versa—though if you are replacing "and" with "&" be sure to include the space before and after the word "and," or you'll end up with the "New Engl& Journal of Medicine," "Sc&inavian Studies" and "Adweek Superbr&s");
- punctuation between titles and subtitles—replace semicolons with colons.

Do not worry about perfect synchronization of titles. One vendor might include a subtitle for a journal when another does not, and the only way to identify the two titles as the same journal would be through a de-duping process using the ISSN, which will require some manual procedures to change one of the titles.

Certain journals have "alternate titles" that are used interchangeably. For these journals, you should add additional entries in your database or spreadsheet. Some libraries that provide a search function for their e-journal pages check the "no hits" section of their Web logs for common errors in searching for titles and add those titles to their database, though it would not be a good idea to display these false cross references on lists. For example, UNCG added "News Week" to their Journal Finder database as an alternate title for *Newsweek*.

APPENDIX C: E-JOURNAL WEB LISTS BY SUBJECT

Chapter 7 discusses general options for determining subject categories and ways to present them. Categorizing e-journals by subject is one of the more challenging tasks in developing e-journal Web pages.

Within any one library there can be a sharp difference of opinion about whether a subject list should be exhaustive or selective, which can result in misleading inconsistencies among subject pages that are maintained by subject specialists. **If possible, develop a consensus in your library on whether subject pages will list core journals for a discipline or all possible journals, or develop a two-tier system.**

- Some subjects, such as biology, have such distinct subdisciplines (botany, biotechnology, microbiology, zoology, etc.) that one list of all biology journals, reflecting a large collection, might not be useful to anyone.
- For other subjects, such as philosophy, there may be specialties within the discipline, but to subclassify e-journals would be difficult and time consuming, and might not serve the needs of the target audience.

Interdisciplinary journals often fit on more than one subject list. Make sure your system can handle multiple subject categories. **For ease of managing journals with multiple subject codes, use a database rather than a spreadsheet to generate your lists.**

Some journals will come from more than one source—at different times. When subject categories are chosen, the selectors may not always be consistent. **You will probably need to regularize your lists periodically.**

Libraries that contract with Serials Solutions to provide lists of the journals from their aggregator databases and publisher packages can use the subject-display feature, which includes subdivisions of major subjects for their journals. According to the Serials Solutions Web site, "Patrons can find e-journals by browsing nearly 700 subject headings from *Ulrich's Periodicals Directory*." Browsing is made somewhat more manageable through the initial selection of one of 12 broad subject categories, such as "Business and Economics," "Fine Arts and Music," etc.

Libraries using the Ulrich's headings through Serials Solutions (or another vendor) can provide subject access with minimal local work, but they will need to decide whether Ulrich's subjects are meaningful for their own users. Some of Ulrich's headings would make sense in an academic library:

- Accounting
- Anthropology
- Chemistry
- Medical Sciences—Pediatrics
- Political Science
- Psychology
- Statistics

Other Ulrich's subjects would identify a group of journals that is of interest to a specific audience, but the subject headings use terminology that is not commonly understood or currently used:

- Handicapped
- Literary and Political Reviews
- Machinery
- Matrimony
- Metrology and Standardization
- Motion pictures

And some Ulrich's subjects would describe such a small number of journals as to add clutter to a subject menu:

- Beauty Culture—Perfumes and Cosmetics
- Beverages
- Communications—Postal Affairs
- Funerals
- Shoes and Boots
- Tobacco

If you are a Serials Solutions customer, you may need to massage their subject menu a bit, changing some terms for your users and even eliminating some categories.

Some libraries, presumably those that generate lists from their catalog, use Library of Congress Subject Headings on their e-journal menu page for subjects. Because these headings are so specific, most LC Subject headings would only lead to one or two e-journals, even in a large collection. Thus, the list of subject headings will be very long. One library's subject menu page, "Electronic Journals by Library of Congress Subject Heading" requires 18 "page downs" to get to the end of the letter "A" list. Most subject headings on the page, such as "Aquatic animals—Effect of water pollution on" lead to only one e-journal. A few of the broader headings (Accounting; African Americans; Agriculture; Anthropology) lead to several titles, but those tend to be only the most general titles in those subject areas. From a user's point of view, e-journals listed by LC Subject Heading have little value.

If you generate your Web subject lists from your catalog and you must use LC (or Dewey) headings, try assigning the broadest possible headings, and stick to a very basic controlled list.

EBSCO's A-to-Z service provides subject access to customers using Library of Congress subject headings; however, they are grouped in very broad categories and then further identified by fairly broad LCSH headings, 21 major headings/categories and 184 headings in all for the sample "large list" of e-journals at the A-to-Z site (www.ebsco.com/atoz/default.asp). To see this entire list of EBSCO's LCSH subject headings for the large list takes only four "page downs." LCSH is not an intuitive classification system for e-journals—EBSCO has pared it down to a useful size, but even some of the EBSCO terms still seem arcane for today's information seeker ("Auxiliary Sciences of History," "Diplomatics," "Juvenile Belles Lettres," "Indices," etc.).

Library of Congress Subject Headings for EBSCO's A-to-Z Service Demo List

Agriculture (183 Journals)
    Animal Culture (42 Journals)
    Aquaculture. Fisheries. Angling (22 Journals)
    Forestry (16 Journals)
    Hunting (8 Journals)
    Plant Culture (40 Journals)

Auxiliary Sciences of History (26 Journals)
    Archaeology (13 Journals)
    Biography (1 Journal)
    Diplomatics. Archives. Seals (5 Journals)
    History of Civilization (6 Journals)
    Numismatics (1 Journal)

Education (343 Journals)
    History of Education (19 Journals)
    Special Aspects of Education (64 Journals)
    Student Fraternities & Societies (United States) (3 Journals)
    Theory and Practice of Education (161 Journals)

APPENDIX D:
THE AGGREGATOR-
NEUTRAL RECORD

Some data in the aggregator-neutral record refers to the journal's history and characteristics as a physical item, but the new rules allow the cataloger to view the online version rather than the print version in creating the record. The publisher's site is the preferred source for descriptive information. The 500 field would have notes such as these:

- 500 Description based on: Vol. 7, no. 1 (Jan. 2000); title from caption of PDF (publisher's Web site, viewed February 6, 2004).
- 500 Title from title screen (publisher's Web site, viewed Mar. 22, 2003).
- 500 Description based on: Vol. 1, no. 1 (Jan. 1995); title from contents (EBSCO Electronic Journals Service, viewed March 3, 2004).
- 500 Title from caption (Kluwer PDF, viewed Oct. 17, 2003).

Basic MARC tags for the Aggregator Neutral Record:

022 $a	e-ISSN
022 $y	Print ISSN
130/240	Uniform title (Online)
246l1 $l	"Issues from some providers have title $a [variant title]"
260 $a $b	Place/publisher same as print, usually
260 $c	If 362l0 has a first/last issue, record date as found in that issue
310/321	Current and former frequency as found in the e-serial
362	"Print began with:" note [i.e., vol. 3, no. 1 (Jan. 1984)]
538	"Mode of access: Internet" [or World Wide Web]

For more detailed information on creating your own aggregator-neutral records, see the *CONSER Cataloging Manual*, Module 31, at www.loc.gov/acq/conser/agg-neutral-recs.html.

An example of an aggregator-neutral MARC record from the CONSER Manual (http://www.loc.gov/acq/conser/guidelines.pdf):

022 $y 0385-2342
130 0 Asian folklore studies (Online)
245 00 Asian folklore studies $h [electronic resource].
260 Tokyo : $b Society for Asian Folklore
310 Seminannual, $b 1964 -
321 Annual, $b 1963
362 1 Print began with vol. 22, no. 1 (1963).
500 Published: Tokyo : Society for Asian Folklore, 1963-1972; Nagoya : Asian Folklore Institute,
1973-1975; Nanzan Institute for Religion and Culture, 1976-1978; Nanzan University Institute of Anthropology, 1979-
500 Description based on: Vol. 50-1 (1991); title from t.p. (ATLASerials, viewed on May 6, 2003).
500 Latest issue consulted: Vol. 61-1 (2002); ATLASerials, viewed on May 6, 2003).
538 Mode of access: World Wide Web.
530 Online version of print and microfiche eds.
546 English, French, or German.
650 0 Folklore $z Asia $v Periodicals.
651 0 Asia $x Social life and customs $v Periodicals.
710s (4 fields)
776 1 $c Original $x 0385-2342 $w (DLC) 74647066 $w (OcoLC)1514433
776 1 $c Microfiche $d University Microfilms International $w (OcoLC)32283418
780 00 $t Folklore studies
856 40 $z Subscription required $u
http://purl.org/atlanonline/pls/eli/%5Fbd.volsuperTXT=n0385-2342

APPENDIX E: USING A SPREADSHEET TO CREATE WEB LISTS OF E-JOURNALS

Step 1—Create spreadsheet with titles, URLs, and subject codes, sorted by title

	A	*B*	*C*
1	http://ap.psychiatryonline.org/djfldkj.html	Academic Psychiatry	psy
2	http://pubs.acs.org/journals/ACR.html	Accounts of Chemical Reactions	che
3	http://ajr.newslink.org/menu/journals/AJR/	AJR: American Journalism Review	jou
4	http://www.asa.org/AJS/	American Journal of Sociology	soc
5	http://anthro.AnnualReview/	Annual Review of Anthropology	ant
6	http://ag.arizona.edu/OALS	Arid Lands Newsletter	agr

Step 2—Insert columns with HTML coding for alphabetical list with links to titles

	A	*B*	*C*	*D*	*E*
1	\<li>\<a href="	http://ap.psychiatryonl	">	Academic Psychiatry	\</a>
2	\<li>\<a href="	http://pubs.acs.org/jou	">	Accounts of Chemical Reactions	\</a>
3	\<li>\<a href="	http://ajr.newslink.org	">	AJR: American Journalism Review	\</a>
4	\<li>\<a href="	http://www.asa.org/A	">	American Journal of Sociology	\</a>
5	\<li>\<a href="	http://anthro.AnnualR	">	Annual Review of Anthropology	\</a>
6	\<li>\<a href="	http://ag.arizona.edu/	">	Arid Lands Newsletter	\</a>

Step 3—Save as formatted text (space delimited)

\<li>\<a href="http://ap.psychiatryonline.org/lkjlk.html">Academic Psychiatry\</a>
\<li>\<a href="http://pubs.acs.org/journals/ACR.html">Accounts of Chemical Reactions\</a>
\<li>\<a href="http://ajr.newslink.org/geriatrics.html">AJR: American Journalism Review\</a>
\<li>\<a href="http://www.asa.org/AJS/">American Journal of Sociology\</a>

<li><a href="http://anthro.AnnualReview/">Annual Review of Anthropology</a>
<li><a href="http://ag.arizona.edu/OALS">Arid Lands Newsletter</a>

Step 4—Using a Web editor, paste the above HTML code into a Web document.

- *Academic Psychiatry*
- *Accounts of Chemical Reactions*
- *AJR: American Journalism Review*
- *American Journal of Geriatrics*
- *Annual Review of Anthropology*
- *Arid Lands Newsletter*

To display the example text block as a bulleted list, you would precede it with the <ul> tag.
[Note: Text copied directly from a Word file will include unwelcome formatting codes. Close your word file and open it in Notepad to prevent that from happening.]

You can use the same process to create subject lists by using a subject code for each journal, then sorting the spreadsheet by journal code and then alphabetically.

INDEX

ABOUT THE AUTHORS

As Director of Research Services at the University of Nevada, Reno Libraries, Donnelyn Curtis has administrative responsibilities for three branch science libraries, Business and Government Information Center, Special Collections and Archives, DataWorks, Digital Projects, and the Basque Library. She co-authored *Developing and Managing Electronic Journal Collections* and edited *Attracting, Educating and Serving Remote Users through the Web*, both in the *How-To-Do-It Manuals for Librarians* series published by Neal-Schuman. She has written articles and book chapters on technical communication, reference chat, information-literacy training, and children's and young adult literature. She was formerly Head of Collection Services at the New Mexico State University Library.

Virginia Scheschy is enjoying her retirement in Reno after serving as Director of Technical Services at the University of Nevada, Reno for five years. Prior to that she was Assistant Director for Technical Services at Marquette University in Milwaukee, Wisconsin. She co-authored the Neal-Schuman book, *Developing and Managing Electronic Journal Collections*.